Toward a Cooperative Commonwealth

THE WORKING CLASS IN AMERICAN HISTORY

Editorial Advisors
James R. Barrett, Thavolia Glymph, Julie Greene,
William P. Jones, Alice Kessler-Harris, and Nelson Lichtenstein

A list of books in the series appears at the end of this book.

Toward a Cooperative Commonwealth

The Transplanted Roots of Farmer-Labor Radicalism in Texas

THOMAS ALTER II

UNIVERSITY OF ILLINOIS PRESS
Urbana, Chicago, and Springfield

© 2022 by the Board of Trustees
of the University of Illinois
All rights reserved
1 2 3 4 5 C P 5 4 3 2 1
♾ This book is printed on acid-free paper.

Portions of chapter 5 previously appeared in "From the Copper-Colored Sons of Montezuma to Comrade Pancho Villa," *Labor* 12, no. 4 (2015).

Names: Alter, Thomas, II, author.
Title: Toward a cooperative commonwealth : the transplanted roots of farmer-labor radicalism in Texas / Thomas Alter II.
Other titles: Working class in American history.
Description: Urbana : University of Illinois Press, [2022] | Series: The working class in American history | Includes bibliographical references and index.
Identifiers: LCCN 2021042871 (print) | LCCN 2021042872 (ebook) | ISBN 9780252044281 (cloth) | ISBN 9780252086366 (paperback) | ISBN 9780252053276 (ebook)
Subjects: LCSH: Populism—Texas—History. | Farmers—Political activity—Texas—History. | Working class—Political activity—Texas—History. | Land reform—Texas—History. | Radicalism—Texas—History. | Texas—Politics and government.
Classification: LCC JK2374.T4 A57 2022 (print) | LCC JK2374.T4 (ebook) | DDC 324.2764—dc23
LC record available at https://lccn.loc.gov/2021042871
LC ebook record available at https://lccn.loc.gov/2021042872

For those in the streets,
walking picket lines,
and on the barricades
around the world

Contents

Acknowledgments ix

Introduction 1

1 What Was Lost in Germany Might, in Texas, Be Won 13
2 Inheritors of the Revolution 45
3 Populist Revolt 75
4 The Battle for Socialism in Texas, 1900–1911 107
5 *Tierra y Libertad* 135
6 From the Cooperative Commonwealth to the Invisible Empire 171

Conclusion: Descent into New Deal Liberalism 205

Notes 219
Bibliography 251
Index 265

Acknowledgments

This project, though a work of history, has been continually informed by the present. The Arab Spring; the 2011 Wisconsin protests; Occupy Wall Street; the 2012 Chicago Teachers Union strike; the environmental justice movement; the continuing struggles for immigrant, women's, and LBGTQ rights; and the black liberation movement. They all inspired and gave me the motivation to make available to today's activists the example of struggle provided by the historic farmer-labor bloc and its vision of a Cooperative Commonwealth. Much like these movements, the writing of history is a collective effort and, as a result, I have many people to thank for their assistance in making this project possible. Gregg Andrews has been with this project since its origins and to the very end. He was the one who introduced me to the figure of E. O. Meitzen when this project began. When it came time to make the dreaded final cuts to the manuscript, Gregg volunteered to help and did the yeoman's work of getting this thing in shape. Gregg's help has never been limited to my scholarship. In so many ways, I would not be where I am today without him. When I left my slacker existence in Austin behind for Chicago, I was unsure of what challenges I might face. While the weather was undoubtedly colder, I found I had a new mentor with a warm and generous spirit, Robert Johnston. At the same time, Robert provided the challenge I needed. His critical yet supportive comments have enhanced this project immensely. When I thought I was losing my voice in speaking to the activists I wanted to reach, Robert helped this project maintain a fighting spirit. While one can be considered fortunate to have one great adviser, let alone two, I even had a third in Leon Fink. Leon allowed me to tap his vast knowledge of working-class history. We also participated in making working-class history by marching together in Madison and in the streets of Chicago during Occupy.

Acknowledgments

Through the many years of researching and writing, a great many people have helped me by reading chapters, directing me toward and locating sources, offering advice, or just listening to me vent over a beer—I thank them all. In particular, I thank: John Alter, Travis Andrews, Dawson Barrett, Vikki Bynum, Lorenzo Costaguta, Sarah Darling, Tom Dorrance, the editors of the Working Class in American History series, Rosemary Feurer, Julie Greene, Paul Hart, Jeff Helgeson, Nate Hensley, Sonia Hernández, Matthew Hild and the other, anonymous, reviewer of my manuscript, Suellen Hoy, Benjamin Johnson, Rox Ann Johnson, Will Jones, Walter Kamphoefner, Stetson Kennedy (rest in power), Michael Lansing, Mark Lause, Susan Levine, Matthew Levinger, James Mestaz, Rebecca Montgomery, Angie Murphy, Alejandra Navarrete, Walter Nugent, Dominic Pacyga, Josh Paddison, Mary Parks, Chad Pearson, David Ransel, John Riddell, Jason Rivas, Maria Rocha, Nancy Rosenstock, Ann Rothe, Margaret Schlankey, Molly Schwartz, Jon Shelton, Jeff Sklansky, the students of Robert Johnston's fall '17 and fall '20 graduate seminars, my Texas State collogues in Swinney Reading Group, Mike Taber, the Texas State and University of Illinois at Chicago interlibrary loan departments, Linda Van Puyenbroeck, Marynel Ryan Van Zee, Dwight Watson, Suzanne Weiss, Kyle Wilkinson, and Eddie Wolsch. I must thank the great team I worked with at the University of Illinois Press, my editors James Englehardt, who pushed me at the beginning, and Alison Syring Bassford, who got me to the end, as well as Geof Garvey, Ellie Hinton, and Tad Ringo. A special thank you goes to Walter Schmidt. When I entered the relatively unknown (to myself) territory of Silesian radicalism, I found that I was following a path charted by Walter. I was fortunate enough to spend an afternoon with him at his East Berlin apartment, where I learned not only of Silesia during the 1848 Revolution, but we also, through international working-class solidarity, broke down some of the lingering barriers of the Cold War.

During the course of this project, I have had the privilege of meeting with and communicating with members of today's Meitzen family and a descendant of a leader of the Renters' Union—Jo-Lou Gaupp, Peter Gaupp, Kathy Williams Bryson, John Meitzen, Ann Meitzen, William Meitzen, Jeffrey Williams, and Lotus Cirilo. Their memories and passed-down knowledge truly helped bring this project alive and provided the human moments that connect us all.

Just as familial bonds were important to the Meitzen family, they were essential to the completion of this project. My parents, Tom and Maryanne Alter, have always been there for me, their love and example have been constants. In the midst of working on this project, Jamilia and Nikolaus entered my life. Their joy and rambunctiousness gave me the urgency of learning from the past in order to fight for the present and the future. Throughout it all, Marianna was my travel companion, friend, and partner. Marianna, I could not have done this without you.

Toward a Cooperative Commonwealth

Introduction

"I was born in Fayette County [Texas], from German parents, and who fled from the reaction of the 1848 revolution. I think that I inherited some of my revolutionary qualifications. I am not responsible for them. I can not [sic] help it."[1] So testified E. O. Meitzen before the Commission on Industrial Relations in March 1915 about why he involved himself in the political struggles of working farmers. At the time, Meitzen was a veteran leader of the Texas Socialist Party. Nearly thirty years earlier, his inheritance led him to help organize and lead the Fayette County Farmers' Alliance. When the Farmers' Alliance failed to bring relief to farmers, Meitzen joined the Populist revolt, becoming a statewide leader of the People's Party. The Meitzen political legacy extended to E. O.'s children, in particular his son E. R., who was a leader successively in the Farmers' Union, the Socialist Party, the Nonpartisan League, and the Farm-Labor Union of America. For three generations, from the 1840s to 1940s, the Meitzens spearheaded movements and organizations that fought for the economic and political rights of laborers and working farmers.

The Meitzens actively sought to shape the political and economic contours of democracy at a time when war, industrialization, and immigration dramatically transformed the United States. The dictates of finance and industrial capitalism brought about war at home in order to ensure the dominance of free over slave labor, and then abroad to secure international markets and resources. Industrial capitalism replaced the independent artisan and yeoman with the factory worker and tenant farmer. As the tool of capital formation, government promoted the individual accumulation and concentration of wealth into the hands of a wealthy few. After the genocidal removal of many of the continent's indigenous people, the owners of capital encouraged the workers of the world to immigrate to the United States to fill the factories and fields. These mass migrations changed the racial and ethnic composition of the nation. These transformations, though, did not go uncontested, as workers and farmers organized collectively, in both forward-looking and reactionary ways, to resist the economic, political, and social demands of capitalism.

The presence of organizations and parties, from the 1870s through the 1920s, representing the interests of working farmers and laborers, demonstrates the existence of a decades-long farmer-labor bloc in US political culture. Though its origins go back further, the sustained farmer-labor bloc began with the Knights of Labor, Greenback Labor Party, and Grange of the 1870s. The farmer-labor bloc then progressed through the Farmers' Alliance, the Populist movement, the Socialist Party, the Nonpartisan League, and the Farmer-Labor conventions of the 1920s. The farmer-labor bloc was not something that flared up now and then, punctuated by periods of hibernation, as third parties and protest movements are often incorrectly viewed. The bloc was a regular feature of US political culture for more than five decades.

Failure to see the continuities and evolution of the farmer-labor bloc from the 1870s to the 1920s has influenced not only our historiography, but even our current political culture. Instead of seeing how third parties and protest movements that challenged the basic economic underpinnings of industrial and finance capitalism were a regular facet of US politics, today third parties are viewed as quixotic. This study also seeks to show that—besides the centrality of agrarian radicalism to working-class ideology and political action in the United States—land, as powerfully as wages, shaped working-class ideology and politics in the United States.

A shared producerist philosophy connected the organizations of the farmer-labor bloc. The belief that those who labor should control what they produce differed radically from the corporate practice of controlling and profiting from the labor of others. Though never achieving electoral success at a national level, and with only limited electoral victories at regional and local levels, the farmer-labor bloc nevertheless played a crucial role in the United States. Working independently of the Democratic and Republican parties, the bloc served as a bulwark against unrestrained capitalism. The continual organized agitation of the farmer-labor bloc moved the political spectrum of US political culture both substantively and ideologically to the left. Though enacted into law, in much watered-down versions, by Democrats and Republicans, many of the historic reforms of the Progressive and New Deal Eras originated and were tirelessly championed by individuals and organizations within the farmer-labor bloc. Indeed, without their efforts, a Progressive Era or New Deal likely never would have happened. I make such a statement as both a major historiographical intervention and, in many ways even more, as a political intervention—backed by history—that argues that working-class protest movements have more success achieving their demands when they politically organize themselves as a partisan party independent of the two-party system.

The Meitzens provide an excellent example of the flesh-and-blood continuity that constituted the farmer-labor bloc from the 1870s through the 1920s. There are three historical components of working-class movements—unions, political parties, and cooperatives. The Meitzens were active in all efforts of the bloc, first as rank-and-file members and then as leaders in all three components. Both E. O. Meitzen and his son, E. R., built unions, directed cooperatives, and also served as electoral candidates for government offices.

As rank-and-file leaders, the Meitzens did not have the cache or attract as much national attention as Tom Watson, Eugene Debs, or Robert La Follette. But they were more in tune than national leaders with how the national campaigns of the farmer-labor bloc influenced workers and farmers at the local level. Thus, while this study utilizes the form of a multigenerational biography, it is at heart a bottom-up community history of the farmer-labor bloc. Like many local working-class leaders, the archival sources of the Meitzens are not contained in a single collection of their own. Their story is found in archives stretching from Central Europe to Lubbock, Texas, and up to Grand Forks, North Dakota, with numerous stops between. The Meitzens' archival trail goes cold at times and as a result they are sometimes absent for lengthy periods in this written narrative. This does not mean the Meitzens were not historically present, and so the narrative moves to discuss the places, events, organizations, and people who shaped the Meitzens and their fellow farmer-labor radicals.

The three generations of Meitzens covered in this study spent most of their lives in Texas. Arguably, no state witnessed a more sustained and militant farmer-labor bloc than Texas; the Meitzens were part of the radical glue that held the coalition together. Yet much of the historiography of radical movements of the Gilded Age and Progressive Era focuses on northern, urban, and European immigrant experiences. This study adds southern, rural, and Mexican immigrant experiences to this heady mix. Moreover, the story here is truly a global one of cosmopolitan radicals. Through a political activism grounded in a German revolutionary heritage, the Meitzens and their descendants were decisively influenced by interactions with Mexican political refugees during the Mexican Revolution. They were also shaped by Irish radicals and adherents of the Bolshevik Revolution, illustrating the transnational nature of contemporary radicalism.

Otto and Jennie Meitzen arrived in Texas in January 1850. Otto was born in Breslau in 1811, the capital of what was then the Prussian province of Silesia—now a part of western Poland called Wrocław. Upon reaching adulthood, Otto moved to Liegnitz (modern Legnica), west of Breslau, to ply his trade. He made a modest living as a millwright, but because of his participation in the 1848 German Revolution, he and his family were forced to flee to America.

To understand that revolution's influence on agrarian radicalism in Texas, we require a reconceptualization of that explosive moment in the heart of Europe. The prevailing representation of the revolution presents the main revolutionary forces as coming from the middle classes in a nationalist uprising for a united Germany, founded on the liberal demands of freedom of the press and speech and representative democracy. Largely absent from these histories are the laboring classes and the region of Silesia.[2] Silesia has recently become a highly studied region, but historians of the region have focused primarily on issues of national identity and examined its status as a borderland.[3] Adding the actions of the revolutionary farmers and workers of the Meitzens' home province of Silesia dramatically changes our perceptions of the 1848 German Revolution (and, ultimately, some of the origins of US radicalism). Doing so ensures that the legacy of the revolution is not one of liberalism, but of working-class radicalism.

The omission of the Meitzens' home province of Silesia has had a detrimental effect not only on our overall understanding of the 1848 Revolution, but also on the agrarian working-class origins of Marxism—not to mention the history of agrarian radicalism across the Atlantic in the United States. Silesia, prior to the revolution, was one the most industrialized regions of Prussia. At the same time, the area had a large agricultural base. A unique convergence of farmer and labor economic demands emerged in Silesia before and during the revolution. For Marx, the 1844 Silesian Weaver's Revolt provided a materialist example of the working class in action, complementing, if not confirming, his theories of dialectics and class struggle. During the revolution, Silesians were among the most committed and radical of revolutionaries, and the province suffered some of the harshest repression in Prussia during the counterrevolution as a result.

The embodiment of conjoined farmer and labor radicalism in Silesia during the revolution was the Rustic Alliance. The Silesian Rustic Alliance was the only provincewide organization representing the interest of rural workers to emerge in Germany during the revolution. The organizational stimulus for the Rustic Alliance came out of the democratic movements in the urban centers of Breslau and Liegnitz. The Democratic Club of Liegnitz, of which Otto Meitzen was likely a member, aided the creation of the Rustic Alliance in order to encourage an alliance of peasants and laborers. The alliance shared a striking resemblance to the farmer-labor radicalism of the Farmers' Alliance and the Populist movement witnessed in Texas a few decades later.

After the failure of the revolution, a significant number of German 48ers, including the Meitzens and others from Silesia, fled the counterrevolution to make new beginnings in Texas and other parts of the United States. They carried with them their revolutionary experiences and radical politics. Nationally, as historian Mark Lause has shown, German 48ers helped speed the already occurring transition of US agrarian radicals from communitarian utopian socialism to political activism through the formation of parties as the main tactic to achieve labor reforms and the end of slavery.[4] German Texan 48ers were the first to introduce radical farmer-labor politics to Texas. The outbreak of the Civil War slowed the growth of 48er political influence in Texas, but in the North, 48ers threw themselves into the cause to preserve the Union and abolish slavery. Once the war ended, German Texan 48ers reasserted themselves on the political field in their state.

Initiated by German Texans, the 1873 People's Party provided much of the political and organizational foundation for the farmer-labor bloc that became a consistent force in Texas politics for the next five decades. During the same period in which this short-lived People's Party existed, the Grange also entered Texas. With the arrival of the Grange began the organizational continuity of the farmer-labor bloc in Texas that lasted until the mid-1920s.

Much of the working class viewed land ownership as the key to independence and self-sufficiency. Up until the beginnings of the twentieth century, many workers aspired to own land, clinging to popular republican notions that equated liberty and land ownership. From Tom Paine's *Agrarian Justice* and the Agrarian Party of Thomas Skidmore to the unfulfilled promise of forty acres and mule for freedmen to the promise of cheap land drawing wave upon wave of immigrants, land meant freedom.

Wage-labor status, in the minds of many workers, was only to be temporary—until they could earn enough money to obtain land. This condition, however, proved to be more permanent as the percentage of farmers in the labor force dwindled from 53 percent in 1870 to 27 percent in 1920, the same year the United States went from a majority rural to a majority urban nation. Still, many workers remained connected to the land in occupations such as the transportation of agricultural products and the manufacturing of farming implements. Despite the traditional notion of an inherent hostility between urban toilers and rural tillers of the soil, demands related to land ownership were a consistent part of working-class political platforms from the 1840s to 1920s.

For those who worked the land, especially in the South, they did so not as owners but as sharecroppers or tenant farmers. In many rural southern counties, tenants were the majority of farmers. The living and working conditions of tenant farmers was comparable to the worst of those faced by factories workers. Whether one toiled as a coal miner in West Virginia or a tenant farmer in a Texas cotton field, their economic, social, and political standing placed them both in the working class.

Historically, the factory or the field has not been the main division within the US working class. Instead, the primary fulcrum of conflict was, and remains, race. By studying the Meitzens, we learn much about race in the southern wing of the farmer-labor bloc. The Meitzens at times yielded to and at others challenged white supremacist rule. E. O. first encouraged African Americans to join the People's Party, yet, later in 1904, he and his supporters used the white man's primary to gain elected office. The Meitzens initially supported the whites-only policy of the Socialist Party–backed Renter's Union but then had their racial beliefs challenged by Mexican revolutionaries. Ultimately, E. R. walked a dangerous tightrope during the 1920s Jim Crow South in calling for political and economic equality for African Americans. He joined the successful campaign against the poll tax in Florida and was hounded by the Ku Klux Klan.

Political organizing efforts by working-class black Texans from Reconstruction to the 1920s ran parallel to and at times interconnected with that of working-class white Texans.[5] They faced similar economic difficulties. Barred from the Democratic Party, black Texans carved out a political space for themselves within the Republican Party. For black Texans, being in the Republican Party had real meaning and material benefits from the political patronage system during an era of Republican near-dominance of the White House. Blacks were hesitant to concede this space for an unequal alliance with white farmer-labor radicals, who, while largely not the vilest of racists, still held paternalistic white supremacist views of African Americans. Despite blacks' reluctance to join agrarian radicals outside the two-party system, the changing possibilities of a black and white interracial political alliance were never better demonstrated than during the Populist era of the 1890s. The Populist Revolt was and remains the largest challenge to the two-party system in US history. Working-class blacks and whites uniting around a shared set of economic grievances and demands played no small role in making the challenge real.

"Populist" has become a nebulous term. Political pundits use it to describe politicians from Bernie Sanders to Donald Trump—and even plenty in between. This study seeks to provide a historical context to populism to give that concept deeper meaning for the present. Populism, either as a movement or as a description, is characterized by anxiety caused by economic insecurity, resulting in a focused anger at a perceived establishment. The establishment can be giant corporations, the government, or both. Economics, not race, ethnicity, or nationalism, sits at the base of populism. As a movement, populists have demanded more democracy in the marketplace and governance. Demagogues have used populist sentiments to whip up racial hate and nationalism, but such invocations of white supremacy are outliers of populism—and not in themselves populism.

Economic and political elites responded to the interracial Populist challenge of the 1890s with election fraud, violent repression, and Jim Crow segregation. In the years to follow, many rural whites distanced themselves from their previous interracial alliance with blacks and put their own economic interests first. In some cases, they supported openly racist candidates who posed as reformers of the economic system. Those events reveal a historical precedent for rural whites who voted for Barack Obama in 2008 and 2012 and then played a large role in sending Donald Trump to the White House in 2016.

After the failure of Populism, the farmer-labor bloc progressed into the Socialist Party. The predominance of northern, urban, and European immigrants in the reform and radical movements of the Gilded Age and Progressive Era is especially apparent in the historiography of the Socialist Party. James Green's decades-old *Grass-Roots Socialism* remains the primary book on the Socialist Party in the Southwest. Green explores how self-educated farmers and workers fused nineteenth-century moralistic radicalism with scientific socialism to make the Southwest the Socialist Party's largest area of grass-roots support.[6] In the ensuing decades, however, social and political attitudes have changed, rightfully placing more focus on the Mexican American experience.

These new social-political concerns dramatically change our understanding of the early Socialist Party and political culture of the Progressive Era, especially in relation to the transnational effects of the Mexican Revolution on the Texas Socialist Party. In the years preceding the Mexican Revolution, organizational disputes between Texas Socialists (part of the party's national left faction) and the Right-dominated Socialist Party national office were a regular feature of internal party life. Interactions with Mexican revolutionaries furthered radicalized Texas Socialists and exacerbated the divide between and Left and Right Socialists, resulting in much of the agrarian wing of the Socialist Party leaving the party and joining the Nonpartisan League (NPL) in North Dakota. This split, even before differences over World War I and the Bolshevik Revolution, was the initial fracture of the Socialist Party—a fracture that reduced the national strength of the Socialist Party, leaving it much more vulnerable to government-backed repression. At the same time, collaboration with Mexican revolutionaries challenged the racist attitudes of many white Texas Socialists who no longer viewed Mexicans, Mexican Americans, and Tejanos as slavish peons but as comrades. In many ways, the desire of southwestern Socialists to emulate the land demands of Mexican revolutionaries did more to tear the Socialist Party asunder than northern immigrant Socialists' praise of Bolshevism.[7]

After the repression of the Texas Socialist Party in 1917, the Meitzens moved to Minnesota and North Dakota to assist the growing NPL. E. O. edited the German-language edition of the NPL's newspaper, and E. R. became one of five national organizers for the NPL. E. R. was a part of a large national network of political radicals across the United States that was connected by the radical press, national farm-labor conferences, and overlapping membership in numerous political organizations. During this time, he encountered radicals who would become early leaders of the communist movement.

This book reintroduces the NPL as part of the radical agrarian continuity of the farmer-labor bloc. Previous studies of the NPL have described it as a distinct, almost separatist, chapter of agrarian history. According to this distinct history, although the NPL adhered to a producerist ideology, it came from a commitment to middle-class ideals, capitalist markets, and ownership of property that was distinct from the US socialist tradition.[8] Yet the end goals of socialists, such as the Meitzens, and the NPL were not that dissimilar—a more democratic society, both politically and economically, run in the interests of producers. Former Socialist Party members founded the NPL. Many of its organizers were former Socialist Party members, including the Meitzens. The break of these socialists from the Socialist Party, and their subsequent joining of the NPL, was not a break from socialist ideology. Agrarian socialists departed a party controlled by right-wing socialists who, they felt, no longer represented the interests of working farmers. Rather than a break, the actions of agrarian socialists represented more of an informal fusion of much of the agrarian wing of the Socialist Party with the NPL, maintaining the continuity of the farmer-labor bloc within the NPL and well into the 1920s.

While E. R. Meitzen organized for the NPL in the upper Great Plains, farmer-labor activists in Texas sought ways to rejuvenate their movement after World War I. They hoped to do so by forming an alliance with impeached former Texas governor James Ferguson's rhetorically pro-worker-farmer, but socially conservative, American Party. Scholars of Texas history have often misunderstood and mischaracterized the American Party as a mere vehicle for Ferguson to keep himself before the Texas electorate in his ongoing attempts to regain state office at a time when he was barred from doing so.

In contrast, I contend the American Party was also a genuine vehicle for the farmer-labor bloc. Despite Ferguson's personal ambitions and designs, farmer-labor activists used the party to continue their fight for the Cooperative Commonwealth before Ferguson disbanded the party in 1922. The farmer-labor bloc's brief alliance with Ferguson, however, had drastic long-term consequences that changed the course of Texas politics in ways that point toward the fate of much of populism across the twentieth century (and beyond). Working-class politics shifted sharply away from leftwing critiques of monopoly capitalism and toward a conservative hatred of government. And Texas went from a hotbed of economic radicalism to a bastion of social conservatism.

The farmer-labor bloc's refusal to take a stand against the white primary law of 1923 stands as a main exemplar of the rightward shift in Texas politics. Before its partnership with Ferguson, the farmer-labor bloc often called for economic and political equality for African Americans, advocated woman suffrage, and even supported Margaret Sanger's campaign for birth control. Yet with the American Party, the Texas farmer-labor bloc shunned social issues and for the first time primarily focused purely on economics. This left the bloc ill prepared to combat the rise of the Ku Klux Klan, which was able to effectively focus on and mobilize around social and cultural issues.

In May 1923, the Texas Legislature passed a white primary statute. The law declared that all qualified members of the Democratic Party—the only effectual party in the state—were eligible to vote in the party's primary. The law, however, specifically stated that Negroes were not qualified for membership in the Democratic Party. As historian Darlene Clark Hine observed, "White Primary laws were among the most effective and blatantly discriminatory disenfranchisement schemes adopted in one-party southern states."[9] While Hine's 1979 *Black Victory* provides an excellent narrative of the legal battle to end Texas's white primary, it does not explain why the law was created at this specific moment when other Jim Crow measures were already in place. It leaves one to view the 1923 white primary statute as simply another example of predictable, stereotypical southern racism. However, an analysis of this period's working-class politics and the farmer-labor bloc in Texas once again reveals otherwise.

After the recall of North Dakota's NPL-backed governor in 1921, E. R. Meitzen returned to Texas to assist the Farm-Labor Union of America (FLUA), first out of Bonham and then Texarkana. Organizationally and politically, the FLUA followed in the tradition of the Farmers' Alliance. The new organization soon grew to 125,000 members in Texas and spread into Oklahoma, Arkansas, Louisiana, Alabama, Mississippi, and Florida. Unfortunately, the FLUA, like the American Party, has been an under-studied part of Texas labor history.

The early 1920s were busy years for E. R. Meitzen. He spent much of this time representing the FLUA in efforts to create a national Farmer-Labor Party. The efforts of Farmer-Labor Party activists came to a head when a broad array of progressive forces supported Robert La Follette's campaign for president in 1924. Though losing the election, La Follette received the only endorsement the American Federation of Labor (AFL) ever gave to a presidential candidate outside the two major parties, ultimately garnering the highest nationwide vote total ever for an independent candidate up to that time.

Regardless of the achievements of the La Follette campaign, La Follette insisted that he run as an independent, not as the candidate of a new party. With no new party to cohere around, the Farmer-Labor Party movement on a national level fell apart. More significant, La Follette's defeat, after so much effort had been put into his campaign, represented the collapse of the farmer-labor bloc in US politics. For moderate radicals within the farm-labor bloc, the Meitzens included, a large amount of frustration and exhaustion set in. More radical elements were drawn to the revolutionary example of the Soviet Union.

The FLUA simultaneously fell into decline in Texas. The FLUA's disregard of economic and political equality for African Americans and the creation of the whites-only primary prevented an interracial alliance of black and white working-class Texans that harked back to the days of Populism. The increased agitation of the farmer-labor bloc divided the white vote between FLUA supporters and traditional Democrats. At the same time, black Texans and their white allies in the Republican Party—the Black and Tans—were losing a factional fight against racist Lily White Republicans. With farmer-labor radicals on the move and blacks looking for a way to assert themselves outside the Republican Party, traditional Democrats (with Klan support) felt a dire need to create a whites-only primary to prevent black votes from being a decisive electoral bloc in Texas elections—thus answering "why 1923?" With Texas, for all practical purposes, being a one-party state, denying African Americans the right to vote in the Democratic primary barred them from the state's only meaningful election.

Before its demise, the FLUA attracted the attention of communists in the Workers Party. The Workers Party initially ignored the plight of working farmers in the United States but, after a directive from Vladimir I. Lenin, it created the United Farmers Educational League (UFEL), to reach farmers. E. R. Meitzen, having served on committees of the Farmer-Labor Party with communists such as James Cannon, agreed to serve on the national committee of the UFEL. This brought E. R. into the orbit of the international communist movement. Though E. R. never became a communist (at least openly—whether briefly in secret one can only speculate), Cannon also invited E. R. to serve on the national committee of the International Defense League (IDL). The IDL, organized and controlled by Cannon, besides campaigning for the defense of political prisoners around the world, became the main vehicle of the Left Opposition in the United States in the fight against Stalinism.

Eventually, both the FLUA and UFEL collapsed and E. R. was left with the realities of financially providing for a growing family during difficult economic times. He moved his family to northern Florida in 1927 after purchasing a small county newspaper in Live Oak. He later relocated to Lake City but moved back to Texas in 1940. He decided the best way to continue the fight for a Cooperative Commonwealth would be to work within the left wing of the Democratic Party. This tactic—adopted by many in the farmer-labor bloc—played a large role in the complete collapse of the historic farmer-labor bloc into New Deal liberalism. After the 1924 election, the political landscape was devoid of a political party rooted in the farmer-labor bloc.

Around a century has transpired since the collapse of the agrarian-based farmer-labor bloc. The general public has largely forgotten the people of the farmer-labor bloc and the parties and mass mobilizations they created. When historians discuss the farmer-labor bloc, they craft a characterization of misguided hayseeds, isolated in their local communities, who looked more to the past than to the future. Intellectuals have dismissed farmer-labor radicalism as wild-eyed messianic evangelism or a product of a business orientation or coming from undefined middle-class values.[10] Yet a deeper analysis shows that without the actions and organizations of these country bumpkins who contested the robber barons, we might never have left the Gilded Age and would be denied their example in fighting our own latter-day robber barons.

In the 1925 *American Labor Who's Who*, E. R. Meitzen described himself as "active since 21 of age in promoting dirt-farmer organizations and other political and indust[rial] mov[ements] toward [a] coop[erative] commonwealth."[11] By exploring the transnational history and lessons of the Texas farmer-labor bloc that three generations of the Meitzen family shaped, we can better understand the continuity of agrarian radicalism in the United States. We can also celebrate their legacy. The family's history and experiences made them dirt-farmer internationalists who played an important role in creating a dynamic alternative political movement for economic democracy in opposition to corporate capitalism.

1 What Was Lost in Germany Might, in Texas, Be Won

In January 1850 Otto Meitzen stood on the deck of the brig *Herschel* off the Texas coast near Galveston. With him was his wife of eleven years, Jennie, and their three young children. After sailing for nearly six weeks from the port of Bremen across the Atlantic Ocean and through the Gulf of Mexico, their destination was in sight. A blue norther, however, blew them back into the gulf and delayed their landing by a week.

Much more had to be on Otto's mind, though, than the cold. The Prussian king still ruled. Otto would have to achieve his dream of economic and political freedom in Texas, not in a united Germany. He had embraced the revolutionary tide that swept Europe in 1848 and actively participated in the attempts to forge a democratic republic in opposition to the despotism of Prussian king Friedrich Wilhelm IV. During the revolution, some of the more radical working-class demands emanated from the Meitzens' home province of Silesia. When the revolution failed and the counterrevolution ensued, the Meitzens, according to family lore, made "their escape to the sailing vessel one jump ahead of the emperor's bayonets." They were not alone; other Silesians also chose exile in Texas. These Silesian immigrants and their fellow *Achtundvierzieger*s influenced working-class Texas politics in the decades to follow.[1]

A powerful connection exists between the Silesian region of Central Europe and central Texas, ultimately linking the radical working-class demands of the Revolutions of 1848, Texas Populism, the Socialist Party of the early twentieth century, and attempts to create a labor party in the United States after World War I. During the Revolutions of 1848, Silesia was the only region in Europe that developed a provincewide organization, the Rustic Alliance, whose membership was composed of and fought for the demands of the agrarian working class. The Rustic Alliance's origins began in the Democratic Club of Liegnitz (present-day

Legnica), Silesia, when the club's members ventured into the countryside with the intent of linking the radical democratic and economic demands of workers with those of rural peasants. The Rustic Alliance and Democratic Clubs of Silesia served as politically left pulls on the overall course of the 1848 German Revolution.

The farmer-labor alliance in Silesia during the Revolutions of 1848 was remarkably similar to alliances seen in Texas Populist and socialist movements. The similarity was due in part to the significant number of Silesian and other 48er political exiles and their descendants who chose to continue the fight for their political beliefs in Texas, after fleeing the counterrevolution in Europe. The Texas sections of the People's and Socialist Parties were among the largest of their movements in the United States. Just as the Silesian radical farmer-labor movement acted as a left pull on the 1848 German Revolution, the Populist and socialist movements exerted left pressure on US politics. One bright red thread linking these momentous movements together is the German Texan Meitzen family.

Silesia, currently a part of southwestern Poland, sits at one of the not-altogether-unique convergence points of peoples and empires in Europe. The first state to control the area was Greater Moravia in the late ninth century, followed briefly by Bohemia. In the late tenth century, the Piast dynasty brought much of Silesia into the Polish state. After a series of conflicts, Poland surrendered rule of Silesia to the Kingdom of Bohemia in 1335. From Bohemia, the region passed into the realm of the Hapsburg Empire. As a result of eventual Hapsburg rule, Silesia had a strong Germanic presence to go along with its Bohemians and Poles. German power and influence ascended with the Prussian conquest of Silesia in 1741 and remained strong until the end of World War II. The ethnic cleansing terror during Nazi rule, cession of Silesia to Poland after the defeat of Nazi Germany, and the forced removal of millions of ethnic Germans from Silesia and nearby areas ended much of the region's centuries-long multicultural identity.[2]

While the horrors of the twentieth century waited in the future, Silesia, like much of Europe, was embroiled in political turmoil when Otto Meitzen was born in the provincial capital of Breslau on February 12, 1811. The American and French revolutions of the late eighteenth century inspired Europe's laboring masses and liberal intellectuals with the ideas of liberty, fraternity, and equality. The French Revolution also produced the Napoleonic armies that, though it destroyed the reactionary and obsolete Germanic Holy Roman Empire, brought war and foreign military occupation. After Napoleon's retreat from Moscow in 1812, Breslau became the center of German resistance against the French. The French defeat in 1813 at the Battle of Leipzig did not usher in a new era of liberty but instead the formation of the Austria-dominated German Confederation and the consolidation of a bureaucratic, aristocratic-minded government.[3]

Concurrent with the redrawing of Europe's political geography, the economic transition from feudalism to capitalism was underway as well. The process of German industrialization began in the Rhineland and Silesia toward the end of the eighteenth century. In Silesia, the center of the German textile industry, the number of looms went from 19,800 in 1748 to 28,700 in 1790. Most of the looms were not steam-powered modern looms, but the numbers demonstrate a transition from subsistence agriculture to modern industry and wage labor. Though undergoing industrialization, Silesia still had a large agricultural sector, which created a unique convergence of farm and labor demands in 1848.[4]

The Meitzen family was emblematic of the historical shifts of this period. The earliest known Meitzens were from Pomerania, a northeastern Prussian province. Most likely they were farmers. Well into the twentieth century, the family held significant political ties to farmers and the land. Otto Meitzen's father, Melchior, was born in Berlin in 1772 and later moved with his brother August to Breslau. We know little about his position in society other than that he married a noblewoman of the Kalckreuth family. The Kalckreuths were an old and wealthy Silesian family who traced their nobility back to the beginning of the thirteenth century.[5]

Nevertheless, a life within the Prussian aristocracy did not last long for the Meitzens. Melchior divorced the Kalckreuth noblewoman and married her maid. He had one child with the noblewoman, a son, August, who stayed connected to his mother. With his new wife, Melchior had three children—Otto, Marie born in 1816, and William in 1818. From Melchior's divorce and new marriage, the Meitzens slipped from feudal nobility back into the laboring classes at a time when a broader transition from feudalism to capitalism was underway.[6]

With a developing textile industry and most arable land controlled by the Junker class, Silesian peasants and laborers were subjected to the double yoke of feudalism and capitalist exploitation. Historically overshadowed by the radicalization of the French Revolution in 1792, Silesian peasants stood up that year against feudal exactions and revolted against their Junker landlords. The Prussian government declared martial law and used military force to halt the uprising. The revolt was only the beginnings of a decades-long Silesian peasant resistance to the old feudal order.

During this period of Silesian peasant revolts, improvements in agricultural techniques lessened farm labor demands and lowered food prices. Lack of farmwork resulted in the expulsion of many peasants from the land, forcing them into the nascent working class centered on the textile industry. The growing labor pool brought wages down and put workers into conflict with the budding capitalist order.

Following their fellow Silesians in the countryside, journeymen in Breslau revolted in 1793. Thirty-seven people were killed and seventy-eight injured before the revolt was put down. It would not take long for Silesian peasants and workers to link in resistance against their shared double yoke of economic oppression. On March 23, 1793, weavers in the town of Schömberg (present-day Chełmsko Śląskie), fifty-three miles southwest of Breslau, revolted for better working conditions. They were joined by peasants in the countryside in what became a general conflict to overthrow Prussian feudalism. In April, Prussian soldiers ruthlessly suppressed the revolt, which included approximately twenty thousand people. Revolts by weavers and peasants occurred again in Silesia in 1807 and 1811. Each time, they were brutally put down. Conjoined workers' and peasants' resistance to feudalism and capitalism culminated in the 1848 German Revolution.[7]

Silesian militancy represented the struggle of an embryonic working class against the aristocracy and the emerging capitalist class. In late-eighteenth and early-nineteenth-century Europe, however, class designations were rarely so sharply delineated. Between poor peasants and unskilled laborers on one side, and aristocrats on the other, a growing, fluid middle class was on the rise. Its origins derived from the beginnings of a profit-driven capitalist economy, early industrialization, and the professionalization of trades related to law, education, and economics.[8]

As the early careers of Otto and William indicate, the Meitzens were part of this middle class, even though their vocations were technical and skill-related and placed them closer to the ranks of the rapidly swelling working class. Educated as a mechanical engineer, Otto became a millwright in Liegnitz, west of Breslau. He probably ran a small shop where he worked alongside at least one known employee, a cousin from Pomerania. Millwrights at this time were carpenters who specialized in building machines used to process agricultural and lumber products. Otto's machinist skills could very well have been applied to the building of Silesia's first modern textile mills in the 1830s and 1840s.[9]

Mechanical engineering not only provided Otto Meitzen with a source of income but also likely led him to his future wife, Jennie Caroline Alpine Holmgren. Jennie was the daughter of Prussian government architect Jens Engelbrecht Holmgren, who in 1832 was sent to Liegnitz to oversee public works projects in the city. Jens Holmgren was born in Copenhagen in 1784. His Swedish-born father made six trading voyages to China working with the Danish Asiatic Company, amassing a small fortune in the process. On Jennie's maternal side, she descended from the Swiss knight Burghard von Wurden, who arrived in Germany in 800 AD in the retinue of the emperor Charlemagne.[10]

When Otto met Jennie, she was "a lady with gloves, servants, and a carriage." She fell in love, however, with the "quiet spoken" and studious millwright who had little money. Jennie's von Wurden family did not approve of her attraction to Otto. He lacked wealth and refused to be baptized. "Tiny fiery" Jennie stood up to her mother and married Otto on July 28, 1838. Otto's younger brother William followed a similar track. Through the guild system, which was becoming archaic, William become a master of mines and smelters in Breslau. In 1842 he married the Polish lady Antonia Tschikovsky.[11]

At the time when the Meitzen family came of age in the early 1840s, sweeping changes were overtaking Europe in the aftermath of the French Revolution. The old aristocratic social order of feudal Europe faced a threat from rising middle classes. Affairs of trade and industry were no longer exclusively the purview of monarchs and their royal retainers. Bourgeois elements increasingly demanded access to the sources of private profit. With the bourgeoisie came fundamental beliefs in liberalism and nationalism that were in conflict with the forces of conservatism, aristocratic privilege, and hereditary monarchy. Neither the aristocracy nor the bourgeoisie was strong enough to supplant the other as the dominant power. In fact, each needed the other as industrialization gave birth to a working class, a class whose interests were diametrically opposed to feudalism and capitalism.

Industrial expansion in Silesia did not follow clear patterns that separated aristocrat from capitalist, peasant from laborer, and the state from the entrepreneur. The lines were often blurred. Unlike England, where private hands guided industrialization to a greater extent, the monarchal Prussian state directly guided industrialization by providing grants, loans, and special privileges to industrialists. What was even more different from England, the Prussian state nationalized and operated manufacturing enterprises in multiple industries. In the 1840s, Silesia featured more state-run enterprises (18) than all other Prussian provinces combined (17).[12]

Some Silesian noble families financed manufacturing endeavors, and others actively engaged in capitalist industrialization by founding collieries, ironworks, and textile operations on their estates. In contrast to other Prussian areas where Junkers disdained industry, the Silesian nobility succumbed to embourgeoisement. "Industrial capitalism in Silesia evolved directly out of the former feudal economy," observed historian W. O. Henderson. "Feudal magnates became capitalist entrepreneurs and their serfs became miners and factory hands."[13]

For working-class Silesians, the double yoke of feudal and capitalist oppression often came from the same person. When one's lord switched from agriculture to industry, a peasant could lose his small land holding and became a coal miner or textile weaver. Former peasants turned textile workers, now subjected to capitalist labor exploitation in the form of low wages and long hours, still had to pay a weaver's tax (*Weberzin*) to their feudal lord. The squeeze led to the weaver's revolt of 1793.[14] Because peasant weavers in Silesia revolted against lords who controlled their labor options, these conflicts are commonly portrayed simply as antifeudal, but the failure to look below the feudal surface has caused some historians to ignore the formation of a working class in Silesia and its role in the 1848 Revolution.

In the years leading up to 1848, Silesia was the center of peasant and working-class protests against both the dying feudal and the burgeoning capitalist industrial order. In response to the lowering of wages below subsistence levels, weavers in the villages of Peterswaldau (present-day Pieszyce) and Langenbielau (present-day Bielawa) revolted on June 4, 1844. The weavers who worked at home marched to textile factories and destroyed the machines they saw as threats to their livelihood. They also protested in front of the homes of manufacturers and destroyed the merchant books that recorded their debts. The next day, in the face of gunfire from soldiers that killed eleven and injured twenty-four, weavers armed with clubs, axes, and stones forced the military to flee. Soldiers returned the following day with artillery and cavalry and smashed the rebellion.[15]

Conditions only worsened in the years to follow. Potato disease and the failure of the grain harvest caused famine in Silesia during 1847, contributing to around eighty thousand people contracting typhus, of which an estimated sixteen thousand died. In response to famine, food shortages, and starvation, village workers joined militant peasants in unauthorized incursions onto Junker-held lands to poach and gather firewood. At times they set fire to and looted manor houses and tax offices. Food shortages led to a hunger demonstration in Breslau on March 22, 1847, and food riots broke out across Germany in April and May. *Katzenmusiker* (cats' chorus), a kind of "flying picket," became a frequent sight in Breslau as protesters surrounded buildings, yelling and making catcalls to protest laws and state officials.[16]

Much as in the rest of Germany, Silesia's middle-class democratic clubs and student fraternities responded to the political ferment and demands for change. They formed discussion groups to debate the meaning and limits of democracy and nationalism, but a small group of Silesian democrats went further. They embedded themselves in the struggles of worker and peasants to address their concerns. They sought out solutions to *die soziale Frage* (the social question), a contemporary term given to the need to address the economic plight of workers and peasants faced with poverty and famine in a society transitioning to a new capitalist industrial order.[17]

In Otto Meitzen's hometown, the Breslau fraternity (*Die Breslauer Burschenschaft*) at the University of Breslau was an incubator of radical democratic politics. From the early 1820s, student fraternities across Germany discussed political questions to foster German national unity and liberal ideas. Facing government repression, they often operated in secret. To avoid further harassment, the Breslau fraternity in the late 1820s discouraged members from getting involved in politics.[18]

In early 1832, however, a small political core of members led by Wilhelm Wolff and Robert Julius Bartsch argued that the Breslau fraternity should be devoted to discussion of political issues. Wolff later became a prominent leader of working-class radicalism in Silesia and a seminal Marxist as a close confidant of Marx and Engels. The core included brothers Ludwig and Ewald Matthäi, who, like Wolff, had close connections with the Silesian countryside and its long history of peasant insurgency. Their father worked two jobs as an estate inspector and bailiff to escape tenancy and provide an education for his children. As the son of a hereditary serf, Wolff had performed statute labor for the local lord as a child.[19]

Working as a private tutor while attending the university, Wolff and the Matthäi brothers tackled the political questions of their day in the fraternity. They supported the Polish Revolution of 1830 and pushed for equal membership in the fraternity for Jews—an atypical stance for most fraternity members. Much of their focus was on the peasant struggle in their home province. Wolff developed into a leading writer on the subject.[20]

Their activities soon led to arrest and imprisonment. In June 1834 Prussian authorities arrested Wolff, who received an eight-year prison sentence. A commutation released him after four years. Authorities also arrested the Matthäi brothers in December 1837 and sentenced them to six years in jail. Ludwig served a year before being released, and Ewald, eighteen months.[21]

Upon his release from prison in 1838, Wolff, despite constant harassment from government censors, took to the pen to expose oppression. Robbed of a university degree because of imprisonment, he worked as a private tutor in Breslau. He penned oppositional articles criticizing the political and economic conditions in Prussia and Silesia, in particular. These articles would have a major impact on how the working class in Germany was conceptualized, in turn influencing radical politics in the coming revolution and the future course of socialist thought and action.[22]

On November 18, 1843, an article by Wolff in the *Breslauer Zeitung* exposed the miserable conditions of Breslau's homeless people, who huddled in a decrepit, overcrowded former prison. According to his biographer, Walter Schmidt, the article had "a tremendous impact and literally hit like a bomb." It gained Wolff notoriety across Europe because of his concrete description of Silesia's working class. Prior to Wolff's article, discussions of the German working class tended to be more theoretical in nature, with many even doubting the existence of a working class in Germany—the prevailing thought being the conditions that created working classes in England and France were not yet present in Germany, conditions some believed might never occur in Germany. Wolff exploded that argument by laying out the conditions of the Silesian working class. As a result of Wolff's article, the existence of a German working class now became a widely recognized fact. It would not be long before he showed the working class in action.[23]

Demonstrating the existence of a German working class was not simply an academic matter to Wolff. In 1843 Wolff helped found the Association for the Education of Helpless Proletarian Children in Breslau. Wolff would conclude that charity work was not enough and that a revolutionary change in economic systems was needed. In 1844, he cofounded the Silesian Socialists Circle. This same year, directly after the Silesian Weavers' Revolt, Wolff published "*Das Elend und der Aufruhr in Schlesien*" (*The Misery and Turmoil in Silesia*). His study described a working-class movement with revolutionary potential and gained him a wide readership across the continent. He soon wrote for the Parisian *Vörwärts!*, a German-language newspaper of radical political émigrés influenced heavily by Marx and Engels.[24]

Wolff's writings and activism put him in unremitting conflict with Prussian authorities. In the fall of 1845, they charged Wolff with "offences against the press laws" and in early 1846 sentenced him to three months' imprisonment. To avoid arrest, Wolff fled to London where he joined the German Communist Workers' Educational Society. Soon Wolff moved to Brussels, where he sought out Marx and Engels.[25]

Once Wolff connected with these revolutionary titans, through his endearing personality and direct experiences with Silesia's working class, he rose to leadership positions within a communist movement then very much in its infancy. When Engels first met Wolff in April 1846, he described Wolff as "the figure of an East German peasant." This "East German peasant"—by bringing the experiences of Silesia's workers and peasants to his relationship with Marx and Engels—had a profound impact on the early development of what would become Marxism. He sat on the executive committee of the Communist League and was one of the six signers, along with Marx and Engels, of the *Demands of the Communist Party in Germany*. First printed in March 1848, these demands would influence radical democrats during the Revolutions of 1848. When Marx and Engels refer to "the German working-class risings" in the *Communist Manifesto*, it is in main an allusion to the Silesian Weavers' Revolt.[26] Throughout the revolution, Wolff worked tirelessly to advance the social question of workers and peasants and the creation of a democratic republic over the constitutional monarchy advocated by the liberal bourgeoisie.

The *Communist Manifesto*, one of the most influential political documents in world history, is imbued with its authors' desire to reach peasants and unite them with workers in a revolutionary struggle against capitalism. The very first measure listed in the *Manifesto* addresses land, demanding "abolition of property in land and application of all rents of land to public purposes," which refers to the abolition of bourgeois property. The *Manifesto* specifically asks the rhetorical question on what type of property communists seek to abolish. "Do you mean the property of the petty artisan and of the small peasant, a form of property that preceded the bourgeois form?" To which the *Manifesto* answers, "there is no need to abolish that." Through the abolition of bourgeois property, landlords would no longer be able to own land to collect rent and increase their individual wealth from the labor of their tenants. Instead, with the profit motivation eliminated and land controlled by the community and used by those working it, rent would be lowered and expended for the public good. The second measure in the *Manifesto* calls for "a heavy progressive or graduated income tax."[27] In reading these demands, one could think they had struck upon an early draft of the 1892 Populist platform with its focus on land and taxes. Marx and Engels used these as transitional demands designed to bring about a democratic workers' state, while the Populists saw them as ways to reform capitalism. It would take going through the experience and failure of the multiclass People's Party for working-class radicals such as Eugene Debs and E. O. Meitzen to come to the same conclusions as Marx and Engels and see the need for workers and farmers to have their own revolutionary party. As a result in large part of the ceaseless efforts of farmer-labor activists in the United States, a federal income tax would be enacted during the Progressive Era through the ratification of the Sixteenth Amendment in 1913.

Two of the key components of Marxism are dialectical materialism and the concept of class conflict, with the working class being the only revolutionary class capable of establishing a democratic socialist society. Marx developed dialectical materialism as a young student of philosophy. During Marx's early years, most socialists were utopians who believed socialism would come about without class conflict through a gradual evolution to a voluntary planned society. Wolff's writings on Breslau's working class and the Silesian Weaver's Revolt of 1844 provided Marx the material he needed to demonstrate the inevitability of class conflict and the revolutionary potential of the working class.

Once Wolff joined Marx and Engels in exile, he often acted as Marx's point man. He served as a delegate to numerous heated communist meetings arguing for proletarian revolution against utopian socialism. During the 1848 Revolution, Wolff carried out most of the "on the ground" work within workers' organizations, as a Left delegate in parliament and editor of revolutionary newspapers. His efforts, both during and after the revolution, in addition to those of Engels, freed Marx to devote his time to his theoretical masterworks. In many ways, Wolff's Silesia is the soul of Marxism. When *Das Kapital* was first published in 1867, Marx dedicated it "To my unforgettable friend Wilhelm Wolff. Intrepid, faithful, noble protagonist of the proletariat."[28]

Rudolph Matthäi, younger brother of Ludwig and Ewald Matthäi, was another exponent of Silesian radicalism. A frequent contributor to one of Germany's leading socialist journals, the *Schlesische Chronik*, he was a member of Wolff's Silesian Socialist Circle formed in 1845. From July 1845 to June 1846, Matthäi served as editor of the Liegnitz-based *Boteausdem Katzenbachthale*, the first socialist periodical in Silesia. Matthäi also popularized Engels's *Condition of the Working Class in England* (1845), which particularly resonated in Breslau.[29]

Inspired by Parisians who took to the streets on February 22, 1848, to force the abdication of French monarch Louis-Philippe and the declaration of the Second Republic, the German middle classes joined peasants and workers in a revolutionary struggle to end aristocratic rule and create a unified German republic. The German middle classes, according to Engels, were no longer willing to be held back by "the pressure of a half-feudal, half-bureaucratic Monarchism."[30] They helped popularize and generalize the discontent across Germany through their already established democratic associations, student clubs, journals, and newspapers. With its long history of peasant revolts, an increasing number of workers' strikes, and an emerging socialist movement, Silesia was particularly ripe for revolution.

Silesians were the first to act directly for their nationalist and economic demands. On March 17, 1848, barricades went up in Otto Meitzen's hometown of Breslau, a day before they did in Berlin. The mayor and police chief fled two days later with armed workers in control of the streets. Militants destroyed the railroad line to Berlin and barricaded the city to defend themselves from government troops. The cross-class Breslau insurgents created a citizens militia, which by fall occupied all municipal buildings and halted tax payments to Berlin. Rural Silesians responded to the urban uprising and joined the revolt.[31]

The exact details of Otto Meitzen's participation in the 1848 Revolution are unknown. He lived and worked in Liegnitz, had family in Breslau where he was born, and according to his son, E. O., was involved in revolutionary activities in Berlin. Otto's actions were enough that, when the counterrevolution began, he had to flee with his family, which included a month-old infant. Even his wealthy and aristocratic in-laws could not, or would not, save them.[32] No matter what his direct involvement in the revolutionary events of 1848 and 1849 were, Meitzen must have witnessed actions, which later gave substance to his family's radical legacy. One can, however, paint a portrait of revolutionary actions in Silesia whose brushstrokes would leave an impression on agrarian radicalism in Texas in the decades to come.

During the revolution, Silesia demonstrated characteristics differentiating it from other regions. Silesia's regular agrarian protests and growing working class made the province particularly volatile. More than other regions, the *soziale Frage* was a central issue for many radicalizing Silesians. In Silesia, democratic organization arose provincewide, which was different from other areas, where organization was primarily limited to a town or a trade. What made Silesia

Revolutionaries defending a barricade in Breslau on May 7, 1849. Contemporary lithograph. Neuruppiner Bilderbogen no. 1457. Neuruppin, Heimatmuseum. AKG-Images.

further stand out was that it was the only region where the agricultural population formed their own political organization.[33] These conditions and the actions of revolutionary Silesians were the incubator of Otto Meitzen's radical beliefs.

Responding to the barricade fighting in the streets of Breslau and Berlin, rural Silesians joined the revolt. By March 21, the mountain areas of western Silesia and the rural district around Liegnitz were filled with unrest. In groups as large as five hundred, peasants and villagers confronted Junker landlords and forced them to sign documents surrendering their feudal privileges.[34]

In Breslau, a citywide democratic club (*Breslauer Demokratische Verein*) formed on April 7. Four days earlier, the city's workers met "to form an association to convey the spiritual and physical well-being of all workers." The meeting led to the creation of the Breslau Workers Club on April 14.[35]

After the democrats of Breslau organized themselves and rural peasants put the Junkers in check, the thrust of political activity in Silesia was the election of representatives to the constitutional assemblies in Frankfurt-am-Main and Berlin. The Frankfurt National Assembly was, at minimum, tasked with uniting the numerous German lands into a single Germany and creating a constitution that would enact liberal reforms such as the rights of freedom of speech, press, and assembly. The form of government that would preserve these rights—either a democratic republic or constitutional monarchy—and whether a united Germany would include Austria and other German-speaking lands of the Hapsburg Empire, became points of contention ultimately paralyzing the Frankfurt Assembly. Meanwhile, the Prussian or Berlin Assembly deviated from its mandate to create a constitutional monarchy and evolved into a parliament in which fractions representing the crown, the bourgeoisie, and radicals contested matters of state.[36]

The national election results in the Frankfurt Assembly reflected the initial bourgeois character of the March Revolution. The deputies elected were overwhelmingly middle class, 370 members being professionals such as judges, lawyers, and civil servants; another 140 were businessmen; and only four master artisans, one peasant (from Silesia), and no workers served in the assembly. Many of the Left deputies were from Silesia and neighboring Saxony and were led by Robert Blum, a radical journalist and bookseller from Leipzig. Wolff was elected as a substitute member from Breslau; after the election, he moved to Cologne to work as an editor of the *Neue Rheinische Zeitung*. Its first issue appeared on June 1, 1848.[37]

The Prussian Assembly was only slightly more representative of the population, containing twenty-eight artisan deputies among the 398 members. Middle-class professionals were again the largest group of deputies in this assembly. Silesia's history of rural resistance was reflected more in the Prussian than in the Frankfurt Assembly. Out of the 97 Left deputies, 44 were from Silesia. Overall, Right deputies outnumbered the Left 146 to 97, with 155 sitting in the middle.[38] This balance of representation, tilted in favor of bourgeois liberalism, would determine the future course of the revolution to the detriment of Germany's working class and the revolution's ultimate failure.

Whatever hope workers and peasants might have had in the Frankfurt and Prussian assemblies to enact reforms to alleviate their economic condition were quickly dashed. When the Frankfurt Assembly convened, its proposals reflected the class composition of the assembly, favoring merchants and industrialists and a laissez-faire approach to the general economy. Seeing that they would gain no help from the Frankfurt Assembly, workers across Germany turned to their own self-organization. Beginning in the spring of 1848 and until the triumph of the counterrevolution in 1849, a significant number of strikes and workers' conferences and assemblies were held across Germany, organized variously by trade, locally, regionally, and nationally. The Breslau Workers Club was one of the more radical workers' organizations, explicitly shunning the liberal label and embracing socialism. The working class, however, proved to be deeply divided. One of the chief points of contention was the perennial conflict between master artisans and journeymen. Master artisans sought to preserve and strengthen the guild system, while many journeymen and workers viewed the hierarchical guild as a hindrance to their own improvement and broader working-class unity. The emergence of industrial workers further confounded attempts to achieve anything resembling a united labor movement.[39]

Silesian peasants, too, found no remedies forthcoming from the Prussian Assembly to address their specific concerns. Through their own militant actions in the early days of the revolution, they abolished feudal privileges. They now wanted the end of feudalism codified in law. This was not to be. In June 1848 the Prussian Assembly discussed a proposal on regulating the abolition of feudalism in the countryside. The plan would establish mortgage banks that would compensate Junkers eighteen times the value of the annual obligations of the peasants. The peasants would then have to pay the banks the amount the banks had compensated the Junkers. In effect, peasants would still be paying dues, though now to a bank instead of a lord. Peasants across Prussia were enraged by the proposals being discussed in Berlin that would only transition them from feudal to capitalist oppression.[40] With the assemblies in Frankfurt and Berlin virtually negating the gains of workers and peasants during the March revolution, the conditions were ripe for a farmer-labor political alliance. Such an alliance would emanate from Liegnitz.

In Liegnitz, where Otto Meitzen lived and worked, the radical Liegnitz Democratic Club instigated a worker-peasant, urban-rural alliance that was unique in the Revolutions of 1848. Two of the club's founding members were Otto Wüstrich, a farmer and journalist, and Carl Otto Cunerth, a teacher who later married Meitzen's sister Marie. In July the club put out a newspaper, *Der Demokrat*, that appeared weekly until October. Cunerth and Rudolph Matthäi were the paper's editors. By early August, the club had six hundred members. Otto Meitzen was likely among them.[41]

The Liegnitz Democratic Club, in crafting its founding manifesto, took directly from *Demands of the Communist Party in Germany*, which specifically addressed peasants and small tenant farmers. The club's *Manifesto* called for the elimination of all feudal obligations without compensation and condemned the nobility as a "medieval institution" that is "worthless in the eyes of the rational."

The first issue of *Der Demokrat* invited "brothers of the country" to join the Liegnitz Democratic Club and attend its weekly Friday People's Assembly.[42]

Around the time *Der Demokrat* appeared, the first Democratic Congress of Silesia met in Breslau on July 16, 1848. This was the first provincial congress held in Germany during the revolution. A second Silesian congress met in October. More than sixty delegates from twenty-one locations across Silesia attended the first Silesian Democratic Congress. The opening debate was over what type of government the congress should advocate for a unified Germany. A proposal called for a democratic republic, but Cunerth went further, proposing a socialist ("social-demokratische") republic. After a long debate, the congress adopted an ambiguous proposal that "the congress should recognize that the pure and undivided sovereignty of the people is the only moral basis of a state constitution." Simultaneously, though no specific proposals were adopted, the congress declared "that the solution of the social question was the first and last task of democracy."[43]

The democratic aspirations of revolutionary Silesians did not hinge solely on congresses. The local democratic club served as the base of the democratic movement in Silesia. The democratic clubs of Liegnitz and Schweidnitz sent members into the countryside to address the political and economic demands of the rural population. Twenty-six rural communities created branch clubs associated with a nearby town's democratic club. This organization drive led to the formation of the Silesian *Rustikalverein* (Rustic Alliance), the only such grassroots peasant organization in Germany during the revolution. By advocating the elimination of feudal privileges without compensation to the Junkers, the Rustic Alliance attracted around two hundred thousand members by the end of October. In September a Rustic Congress met in Breslau to unite the local Rustic Alliances into a provincewide organization.[44]

The activities of the Rustic Alliance in Silesia contradict the view of many historians that the 1848 German Revolution was primarily a revolution of middle-class intellectuals, punctuated by only sporadic working-class protests. The overall absence of Silesia in the dominant histories of the 1848 Revolution is the equivalent of excluding Massachusetts from histories of the American Revolution. The farmer-labor alliance embodied in the Rustic Alliance also challenges the notion that workers and farmers had little in common. Despite obvious differences, Silesian peasants and urban workers shared a common oppression from the dying feudal order and the ascending market economy. They shared a vision of a more equitable society.

While the growth of the Rustic Alliance and Democratic Clubs in Silesia seemed to indicate a bright future for the revolution, elsewhere the storm clouds of reaction were gathering. The barricade fighting and peasant protests of March 1848 led to the creation of the National Assembly in Frankfurt. Instead of asserting the power given to it by the revolution to enact revolutionary demands, the Frankfurt Assembly was an indecisive body that continually sought the favor of the Prussian monarchy and ignored the economic demands of the working classes. A crisis of faith in the Frankfurt Assembly was brewing among Germany's democratic masses.

Emboldened by the weakness of the Frankfurt Assembly, nobles in Bavaria, Saxony, and Silesia attempted to collect the taxes and levies that were ripped from them in March. Amid a renewed wave of rural protests, *Der Demokrat* encouraged Silesia's rural communities to refuse to pay their feudal obligations, "since everyone knows that the era of oppression is over" and even though "the aristocracy does have the means, the people have the power.... It is high time to act together... for the oppressed people!" Again, the Crown deployed troops to stifle the protests and conducted mass arrests of democratic and revolutionary leaders.[45]

The revolution had come to an impasse. Bourgeois elements who favored a constitutional monarch were too weak to put an end to the aristocratic order that provided the props for the absolute monarchy. Many clung to the hope that Friedrich Wilhelm IV might be receptive to a crown bestowed on him by a constitution rather than "divine right." To overthrow the monarchy would require unleashing workers and peasants in further revolutionary struggle, but bourgeois radicals feared the violence of working-class "mobs." In the end, they found unpalatable the notion of sharing political power with the unwashed masses, fearing a possible deepening of the revolution.

Prussian government ministers and others loyal to the Crown saw an opening. The stage was now set for counterrevolution. The Hapsburg dynasty struck and decisively crushed the revolutionary forces in Vienna in October 1848. The retaking of Vienna was a major defeat for German nationalism and the revolution. Seizing on the victory of the Hapsburg crown, Friedrich Wilhelm IV went on the offensive. He viewed himself as an absolute monarch and was through trifling with the Prussian Assembly over a constitutional monarchy. In the beginning of November 1848, the king without warning moved fifty thousand troops into Berlin, catching democrats off guard. The city fell without resistance. The counterrevolution had openly begun.[46]

The Crown deployed Prussian troops in strategic locations throughout Silesia, especially Liegnitz, home of the Meitzens. The Committees of Public Safety in Silesia could do little more than organize a few protests. Since the middle of October, Prussian authorities had increased surveillance and harassment of democrats. Amid the crackdown, the last issue of *Der Demokrat* appeared, and leaders of the Rustic Alliance fled to avoid arrest.[47]

The democratic movement in Silesia continued, but it was now on the defensive. When the upper chamber of the Prussian Parliament met on February

26, 1849, it proposed a pro-Junker bill on feudal dues. The bill acknowledged that the system of feudal dues was on its way out, but specified that the dues would resume until the system is abolished. "The worthy lords are in a hurry. They wish to squeeze enough out of the rural population before closing time," wrote Wolff in a bitter response. "Silesia, particularly, hitherto the golden land of feudal and industrial barons, is to be thoroughly rifled once again in order that the splendor of its land-owning knights may shine on, enhanced and fortified." Silesian Junkers challenged the contracts forced on them by peasants in the first weeks of the Revolution. In criminal courts of law, the contracts served as evidence used to prosecute peasants for belonging to rebellious mobs. If judicial prosecutions did not suffice, the government employed military units to force peasants to perform their feudal obligations.[48]

The Rustic Alliance launched a campaign to block the restoration of feudal dues, but in the end, peasants were powerless in the face of counterrevolution. The Frankfort Assembly grew increasingly servile to the Prussian Crown and, in the spring of 1849, Prussian authorities arrested radical democrats across Silesia. As state repression increased, the democratic movement further fractured from internal differences between liberals and socialists.[49]

Armed units composed mainly of workers in Dresden, Breslau, Baden, Elberfeld, and the Palatinate were soon overwhelmed by troops, who crushed the resistance. On May 14 the Prussian Crown ordered Prussian delegates in the ineffectual Frankfurt Assembly to return home. The final issue of the *Neue Rheinische Zeitung* appeared five days later. The forces of reaction had triumphed.[50]

Military terror spread across Germany, stamping out all pockets of resistance. "After bloody struggles and military executions, particularly in Silesia, feudalism was restored," wrote Engels in the *New York Daily Tribune*. Simultaneous with the military terror, the police and judiciary system arrested and imprisoned revolutionaries. Some participants in the revolution managed to avoid execution or imprisonment but, even in their cases, finding employment might be incredibly difficult after the full restoration of the aristocracy and monarchy. Faced with dire conditions, many German revolutionaries chose emigration and exile. This was the decision Otto Meitzen and his family made in leaving Silesia for Texas.[51]

During the counterrevolution and in its aftermath, thousands fled Germany. Some emigrated to Switzerland and France, but most left for North America. In 1850 nearly seventy-nine thousand Germans arrived in the United States. By 1854, the number reached 215,009. Between 1840 and 1860, around one and a half million Germans emigrated to the United States. With more arriving in the decades to follow, by the end of the nineteenth century Germans were the largest immigrant group in the nation. Many Germans settled in the urban areas of New York City, Chicago, Milwaukee, Saint Louis, Cincinnati, and other cities. Some gave farming a try in northwest Ohio and Illinois. A small but significant minority settled in Texas. In 1850 more than thirty thousand Germans were in Texas, constituting 20 percent of the total white population.[52]

Many German immigrants held a romanticized image of the United States as a land of political and religious freedoms. During the Frankfurt Assembly, some delegates put forward the US Constitution as a model for a German political charter. During democratic meetings in Germany, the US flag, at times, appeared alongside the French and revolutionary red flags. Disregarding the contradiction of a slaveowner writing on freedom and democracy, the works of Thomas Jefferson and his ambiguous visions of a nation in which independent artisans and yeoman farmers formed the backbone of democracy were popular among many German revolutionaries.[53]

German revolutionaries seeking to evoke the American Revolution's more egalitarian and radical heritage drew inspiration from the writings of Thomas Paine. Paine's *Common Sense* was printed in German in 1777. But it was Paine's specific measures to create a just society contained in his later works that truly animated radical German 48ers. First appearing in German in 1794, and reprinted numerous times, Paine's *The Age of Reason* was especially popular for its deist thought and attacks on institutionalized religion. It is in Paine's *Rights of Man* and *Agrarian Justice* where he outlines his plans for an estate tax to fund an old-age and disability pension, a guaranteed living wage for all men and women, child welfare programs, public housing, massive public-works programs, earned-income tax credits, graduated income taxes, public education, the end of slavery, and government provision of land for all its residents. As historian Catherine Hall explained, "Paineite Radicalism was central to the political discourses of working people . . . with its stress on Radical egalitarianism, its rejection of the traditions of the past, its convention that the future could be different, its belief in natural rights and the power of reason, its questioning of established institutions and its firm commitment to the view that government must represent the people, it gave a cutting thrust to radical demands." From 1847 to 1852, numerous new editions of Paine's work appeared in German.[54]

Paineite radicalism took a political form in the United States in 1829 with the Workingmen's Party led by Thomas Skidmore in New York City. In this most urban of areas, a citywide mass meeting adopted Skidmore's "Agrarian Resolves." Skidmore saw society as divided between a monopolistic landowning class and landless laborers caught in economic slavery. Skidmore called for a redistribution of land to laborers to bring about a more democratic and egalitarian society. The party had a good showing in the fall elections, but infighting quickly followed, and the largest section of the movement was led into the Democratic

Party and neutered. Skidmore formed an Agrarian Party in 1830, though it never gained much traction and he died of cholera in 1832.[55]

While the political movement centered on Skidmore's "Agrarian Resolves" declined, the cause of agrarianism began to slowly politicize the socialist movement. Socialist thought and action at this time in the United States was dominated by communitarians, whom Marx and Engels labeled utopian socialists. The goal of communitarians was not to win political power but to establish model communities, based on equality, that would serve as an example for other communities to emulate. Robert Owen's New Harmony, Indiana, colony was the most noteworthy of the intentional communities. After New Harmony failed in 1827, Owen's son Robert Dale Owen and fellow communitarian socialist Frances Wright, whose own utopian community in Tennessee failed in 1829, came to New York to politically support the Workingmen's Party. After the defeat of the Workingmen's Party, Robert Dale Owen would return to Indiana and win election as a Democrat to the Indiana House of Representatives (1835–39, 1851–53) and the US House of Representative (1843–47), where he successfully pushed for education reforms and legal rights for women. Though Robert Dale Owen had turned to the political, the communitarianism of his father and the French utopian socialist, Charles Fourier, continued to guide most socialists.[56]

Not only did socialists eschew the political, but so did abolitionists, though this began to change by the mid-1840s. Many early abolitionists led by William Lloyd Garrison argued that they should not enter politics because they considered the US Constitution a proslavery document. Instead, abolitionists should use moral suasion and passive resistance to achieve emancipation. Meanwhile, the expansion of the United States through the violent removal of Native Americans and war with Mexico opened vast territories of land for settlement, agricultural development, and mineral extraction. At the same time, the growth of a capitalist economy based on wage labor and slavery had significantly increased the numbers of both wage laborers and slaves. Neither moral suasion nor relying on philanthropists like Owen or Wright to establish utopian colonies could solve the political question of whether these new territories would be settled by free or slave labor. The land question was the dominate issue of the time.

A small core of working-class printers in New York City led by George Henry Evans had kept the agrarianism of Paine and Skidmore alive. According to Lause, "Evans looked at his society through the eyes of the working people he hoped to reach and recognized the potential of land reform to radicalize American civilization." In March 1844 Evans and a few other workers founded the National Reform Association (NRA). Through mass political action centered on agrarianism and labor reform, the NRA would influence the socialist and abolitionist movements and direct them toward seeking political power. This was the state of social and economic reform movements when exiled German 48ers began arriving in the United States.[57]

In the *Communist Manifesto*, Marx and Engels state, "communists do not form a separate party opposed to other working-class parties."[58] In a later section, they specifically cite "the Chartists in England and the Agrarian Reformers in America" as parties for communists to work with. What they meant by "the Agrarian Reformers" was the NRA. The NRA did not last long as a solid continuous organization, though its agrarian adherents would move through and help form and lead the Liberty, Free Soil, and Republican parties.[59]

US agrarian reformers and German 48er made ready allies. The Americans knew the political traditions and political landscape of their native home, while German 48ers were battle-hardened revolutionaries who had contested for state power. Together they sped the transition of US socialists and reform movements toward seeking political power to abolish slavery, dignify labor, and truly make the United States a land with liberty and justice for all.

Conditions in Texas seemed ideally suited for German 48ers seeking to bring to realization their own radical agrarian ideals as a seemingly open space waiting for possibilities. Before 1830 German immigration to Texas hardly existed, but in 1831 Friedrich Ernst of Oldenburg, Germany, acquired a land grant from the Mexican government, in what is now Austin County, and began farming. Ernst found success and wrote a letter to a friend in Germany, in which he exuberantly described conditions in Texas. An Oldenburg newspaper published the letter, and so did other newspapers and a travel book on Texas. Thenceforth, a small trickle of German immigrants settled in present-day Austin, Colorado, and Fayette Counties.[60]

From 1830 to 1860, the founding period of German settlement in Texas, publishers in Germany printed more immigration accounts of Texas than of any other region in North America. These accounts portrayed Texas as a land of milk and honey with plenty of cheap, fertile land available. What really stirred the imagination of politically minded emigrants were the tales of the Texas Revolution of 1835–36, in which settlers formed their own short-lived republic after defeating a military dictatorship that did not allow separation of church and state. This romantic view of Texas skirted the issue of slavery. Idealistic German settlers figured the comparative isolation and unsettled nature of Texas would allow them to form communities that could preserve their German language and culture apart from the slaveholding southern United States.[61]

Though published accounts of Texas in Germany did bring about a fair share of immigrants, the main stimulus to German settlement came from the *Verein zum Schutze deutscher Einwanderer in Texas* (Society for the Protection of German Immigrants in Texas), know more commonly as the *Adelsverein* (noble's society). A group of wealthy, aristocratic Germans formed the *Adelsverein* near Mainz on April 20, 1842. The twenty founding members concluded that overpopulation had caused Germany's desperate social and economic conditions. They settled on the creation of an emigration society to help ease Germany's supposed overpopulation and to turn a profit for its founders through land sales and markets created for German exports. The *Adelsverein* established the communities of New Braunfels and Fredericksburg in what was then the western frontier of Texas in the Comancheria borderlands. The *Adelsverein* secured a treaty with the Comanche, one of the few honored treaties between European settlers and Native Americans, easing the way for peaceful German settlement. Between 1844 and 1846, the *Adelsverein* brought 7,380 German immigrants to Texas.[62]

In addition to assisting Germans looking for better economic opportunities, the *Adelsverein* actively recruited to its Texas colonies intellectuals looking to rid themselves of German absolutism. Among those who arrived in Texas via the *Adelsverein* was Edgar von Westphalen (Karl Marx's brother-in-law and a communist himself), as well as the *Darmstädter* group—a group of roughly forty individuals who set out to establish a communistic colony in Texas. The name comes from the fact that many of the group of forty were part of the student fraternity at the industrial academy in Darmstadt in the Grand Duchy of Hesse-Darmstadt. The Group of Forty, as they were often called, was inspired by the ideas of French communitarians Étienne Cabet and Charles Fourier. The *Darmstädter* group's colony attempts failed because of internal disputes, and the *Adelsverein* itself went bankrupt in 1847 from mismanagement. Members of the former colony would go on to make individual civic, cultural, and political contributions to Texas society, but not as organized communitarians.[63]

Germans were not the only ones to attempt utopian socialist communities in Texas. Other followers of Cabet, mainly French immigrants, would attempt a colony in Denton County that lasted only seven months in 1848. Hacking a settlement out of the wilderness proved to be more work than many colonists anticipated. In 1855 French utopian socialist Victor Prosper Considerant, the leader of an international movement based on the ideas of Fourier, led a group of around two hundred French immigrants and established a colony, La Réunion, near present-day Dallas. The colony peaked at roughly 350 members in the fall of 1856. Colonists came to farm, but they were artists and skilled craftsmen, none of them farmers. Even if some had learned farming, the area soil was not conducive to agriculture. In January 1857 the colony was dissolved. Half the colonists either returned to Europe or settled in New Orleans, and the rest moved to other communities in Texas.[64] Communitarianism never took hold in Texas, and with the arrival of 48ers, the seeking of political power became the dominant form of efforts to reform society rather than creating doomed from the beginning model communities.

What Was Lost in Germany Might, in Texas, Be Won

Map of Texas with select cities and counties (in all caps). Map by Bill Nelson.

Although the *Adelsverein* went bankrupt, waves of German immigrants, including the Meitzens, kept arriving in central Texas throughout the nineteenth century. William Meitzen with his wife and three children, along with his sister Marie and her then husband, Edward Gentner, reached Galveston on the ship *Franziska* on December 2, 1849. His older brother Otto and his family arrived later the next month. The Meitzens traveled by rail to Houston. There they hired a freight and passenger ox wagon to carry their children, a few pieces of furniture, and feather bed coverings while the adults walked. The Meitzen's money came from the quick sale of their home in Liegnitz.[65]

The Meitzens planned to push on toward the areas settled by the German *Adelsverein* immigrants around New Braunfels and Fredericksburg, but along the way they learned that New Braunfels was recovering from a cholera outbreak that claimed more than forty lives. Hesitant to continue and weary from traveling in a torrential rain that turned the roads to mud and made it nearly impossible to build a fire, they met Joseph Biegel. In 1832 Biegel received a land grant from the Mexican government in what would become Fayette County. Beginning in 1839, he sold parcels of land to German immigrants, transforming the area into one of German settlement. Biegel convinced the Meitzen brothers to settle in Fayette County and sold Otto Meitzen 32.5 acres for $40.50. On his land, Otto built a story-and-a-half log cabin and began farming. By 1852, Otto had increased his holdings to 60 acres, with a livestock of three horses and five head of cattle.[66]

Though not farmers by trade, Otto and Jennie Meitzen's family eked out a living from the land without slaves. Otto and his brother William's mechanical and engineering skills contributed to the growth of Fayette County. The Meitzen brothers built the county's grist mill, cotton gin, and sawmill. In 1859 they went into business together operating their own mule-powered gin and mill in Fayetteville. In 1860 they switched to steam power. Jennie put her husband's skills to use by directing him to build a still that she operated, from which she sold whiskey. She also taught school and made cigars and candles. The early years in Texas were especially hard for Otto and Jennie, and their three children that arrived with them from Germany died between 1851 and 1857. These were years of constant birth and death for the couple. From 1851 to 1863 Jennie gave birth to thirteen more children, of whom just five survived to adulthood—Herman (1851–1927), Edward Otto (1855–1935), Ernest August (1857–1892), Julia (1859–1947), and Ida (1863–1918).[67]

The Meitzens were part of a chain migration from Silesia to Texas. Many Silesian immigrants settled in Fayette County and the neighboring counties of Washington, Colorado, and Lavaca. German immigrants in Fayette County demonstrated their political revolutionary heritage by naming one of their settlements "Blum Hill" in honor of martyred German revolutionary Robert Blum. The Silesian immigrants reflected the multiethnic character of Silesia and included Bohemians, Moravians, and Poles. The Silesian Poles who settled in Texas founded the first Polish colonies in the United States.[68]

In recounting the motivations for German and Silesian immigration to Texas after the Revolutions of 1848, one should be careful not to exaggerate political factors. Many immigrants left their homelands to flee grim economic conditions at home and perceived opportunities in the United States. Some Silesians, however, like the Meitzens and Josef Georg Wagner of Breslau, had participated in the Revolutions of 1848 and working-class politics in Silesia. Wagner was a shoemaker who "took an active part in politics and was a founder of many labor organizations" before leaving for Texas in 1853. He settled in Round Top, Fayette County, where he became a farmer. Another German Silesian 48er, Ernst Gustav Maetze, settled in Austin County. During the revolution, he served as a Left delegate in the Prussian Assembly. In Texas, he became an influential educator and served two terms in the Texas Senate. Also from Silesia, though she did not arrive in Galveston until 1872, was Maria Wolf Boeer, who began her new life in Colorado County but later moved to west Texas. She played a leading role in establishing the Socialist Party in Texas. Among the Polish Silesian immigrants, too, was Stanisław Kiołbassa, who settled in Karnes County. He had served as a Left-Center delegate to the Prussian Assembly. His son Peter Kiołbassa moved to Chicago after the Civil War, where he became a successful businessman and helped found the first Polish-Catholic church in the city.[69]

The most prominent Silesian 48er who settled in Fayette County with a direct connection to the Meitzens was Carl Otto Cunerth. In Germany, Cunerth had been editor of *Der Demokrat* and a leader of the Liegnitz Democratic Club that helped created the Rustic Alliance. He immigrated to Texas in 1850. On December 6, 1856, he married Marie Meitzen Gentner in La Grange, Fayette County. Her first husband, Edward Gentner, had died earlier in the year. Cunerth farmed in Fayette County until 1862. Nothing is known of his political activities in Texas before the war, but his shared experiences as an organizer and proponent of a farmer-labor alliance in the 1848 German Revolution left a lasting political impression on his nephew, Edward Otto (E. O.) Meitzen.[70]

When the Meitzens first arrived in Fayette County, the local economy was primarily based on subsistence farming, with only a few plantations and farmers who in total held in bondage 820 slaves. By the end of the 1850s, however, the county had a flourishing market economy based on corn, tobacco, wool, and cotton. In 1859 Fayette County produced 320,580 bushels of corn and 12,683 bales of cotton, making it one of the state's leaders in both categories. Much of this increased production was based on the exploitation of slave labor. Fayette County's slaves now totaled 3,786. Overall, the county's population skyrocketed from 3,756 in 1850 to 11,604 (including slaves) in 1860, an indication of its importance as one of the most developed counties in Texas.[71]

Though late to appear in central Texas, the empire of cotton had conquered another region. Whatever illusions German immigrants to Texas may have had about life as enlightened farmers in a producers' republic, or whatever hopes they entertained that slavery might peacefully fade away, were quickly dashed. No longer was the question how to fulfill their yeomen dreams, but instead how to survive a brewing civil war over the institution of slavery.

After a few years of settlement and adjustment, many German Texans were confronted with the political and economic realities of their new home. They had crossed the Atlantic in hopes of living in a democratic and equalitarian society. As whites, German Texans possessed more legal rights than they had in Germany. But these rights were not for all. The presence of enslaved African Americans directly confronted their notions of liberty and justice for all.

Slavery was not the only issue troubling German political émigrés. Modern capitalism was transforming the United States and threatening the Jeffersonian ideal of a republic of independent artisans and self-sufficient farmers that many immigrants held as the promise of America. Industrialization increasingly threatened to reduce artisans to wage laborers, and land speculation and the beginnings of large-scale commercial agriculture tied to national and international markets threatened to squeeze out small self-sufficient farmers. Especially troubling to German immigrants was a growing nativist and moral reform movement that blamed them for the country's economic problems and targeted their drinking habits and refusal to abide by Sabbath day practices.[72]

Already tempered in the flames of revolution, German 48ers in Texas formed political organizations in the mid-1850s. In New Braunfels, they stood up to the moral attacks against them by holding a meeting in January 1854 "at which a very *spirited* resolution was passed, maintaining their Republican right to drink as much schnops [sic] as they pleased." The next month, a *Handwerker-Bund* (Workingmen's Club) was founded in New Braunfels to create a workers' illness fund and provide educational activities. The organization that had wide-ranging ramifications in the years to come, however, was created a few months earlier, northwest of New Braunfels, in the town of Sisterdale.[73]

Founded in 1847, Sisterdale arguably contained the highest concentration of 48ers in Texas. It was also where many participants in the *Darmstädter* group settled after the collapse of their colony, many of whom were now followers of Wilhelm Weitling. Weitling started as a tailor in Magdeburg, Germany, before being radicalized by the socialist writings of Cabet, Fourier, and Robert Owen. In 1847 he joined the Communist League led by Marx and Engels. Fleeing the counterrevolution, Weitling settled in New York City, where in January 1850 he started a newspaper and then an organization, the Arbeiterbund (worker's union), to spread communist ideas and advocate for agrarian land reform along NRA lines. From its large number of educated inhabitants, Sisterdale was known as the "Latin Settlement." Residents of the colony included Ernst Kapp, who fled the threat of prison in Germany from his liberal writings, and Julius Froebel, a delegate to the Frankfurt Assembly who was sentenced to death along with Robert Blum in Vienna but received a pardon before the sentence was carried out. Also settling in Sisterdale were Adolf Douai, a teacher and revolutionary writer, as well as educator August Siemering and Edgar von Westphalen.[74]

In the autumn of 1853, residents of Sisterdale created *Der Freie Verein* (Free Society) "for the purpose of striving for and promoting the greatest possible freedom of mind in all directions." Its members were freethinkers and socialists who held antislavery views. *Der Freie Verein* was associated with the national *Bund Freier Maenner* (League of Free Men), which was organized earlier that year in Louisville, Kentucky. The *Bund Freier Maenner* sought to coordinate the political activities of German-Americans nationally and called for state conventions to be held in states with large German populations. From December

1853 to September 1854, state conventions were held in Milwaukee, Louisville, Cincinnati, Indianapolis, and Wheeling, West Virginia. Of these conventions, the Louisville meeting was the most significant.[75]

"'Liberty, prosperity, and education for all!' This is the great principle of the revolution which all free Germans . . . brought with them from the old country" began the series of resolutions adopted by the convention of Germans in Louisville in February 1854. The Louisville platform was a broad defense of democratic rights and attacked special privilege, the "despotism" of religion, and the "moral cancer" of slavery. Though deeming slavery a cancer, the convention concluded "its sudden abolition neither possible or advisable." Instead, it adopted the free-soil position of opposing the expansion of slavery into the territories and the "gradual extermination of slavery."[76]

Other demands of the Louisville Platform were "the free cession of Public Land to actual settlers," an easy path to citizenship for immigrants, "the radical reform of the judicial system . . . the law being at present a mystery for the people and a means to deceive them." The platform further called for direct elections, internal improvements financed by the federal government, an interventionist foreign policy "against despotism," equal rights for women, and repeal of the odious Fugitive Slave Law. Included was a declaration that "in free States the color of skin cannot justify a difference of legal rights." The Louisville Platform concluded that "the welfare of a nation cannot be generally and permanently assured unless its laboring classes be made independent of the oppression of the capitalist."[77]

The demands of the Louisville Platform were not new for their time and reflected a blending of 48er political demands and American agrarianism. The platform was similar to Free Soil platforms adopted in Buffalo in 1848 and Pittsburgh in 1852. All three platforms condemned slavery as evil, supported democratic rights, and called for federally funded internal improvements and free land grants to settlers. Unique to the Louisville Platform was the call for equal rights for women, which was not included in the Free Soil platforms or the 1856 Republican Party platform.[78]

The inclusion of equal rights for women in the Louisville Platform did not happen without controversy. German-American socialists opposed its inclusion. They viewed their struggle against capitalism through a purely class-based lens. As social and political equality had not liberated working-class men, they argued that a campaign for women's rights would distract from the class struggle. Only through the influence of German freethinkers and their connections to US reform movements did equal rights for women make it into the Louisville Platform.[79]

The Louisville Platform played an important role in promoting antislavery, prolabor, and settler land rights, especially among Germans. The Louisville

Platform was reprinted in at least thirty German-language newspapers. The proliferation of the Louisville Platform alerted conservatives to the radical immigrants in their midst, fueling the growing nativist movement. Adolf Douai, having moved from Sisterdale to San Antonio, promulgated the Louisville Platform in Texas by printing the complete platform in his newspaper the *San Antonio Zeitung*, on March 25, 1854. Douai made the socialist viewpoint of the paper clear in its masthead, which, translated from German to English, read, "a social-democratic newspaper for the Germans in West Texas."[80]

Taking advantage of the second annual *Sängerfest* (singer festival) in San Antonio on May 14 and 15, 1854, the Sisterdale *Freier Verein* called for a political state convention of Germans to take place during the festival. The task of the convention, as put forth by Siemering, was to act in unison on important political events, the most important being the upcoming 1856 presidential election, and to adopt a platform as had been done in Louisville. Germans from across the state attended the San Antonio convention.[81]

Although based on the Louisville Platform, the platform adopted in San Antonio was more detailed and specific in its demands. It contained fewer rhetorical flourishes about democracy and liberty and was more in line with German socialist thought. "We are convinced that the people of the United States do not enjoy the liberties guaranteed to them by the constitution," began the San Antonio Platform, "we are satisfied that the existing parties have neither the will nor the power to improve the political, social, and religious relations of the country." The preamble ended by making clear that the intention of the convention was not to form a "German party."[82]

Like the Louisville Platform, the San Antonio Platform expressed the agrarian ideals of German Texans dating back to the influence of Paine. "The soil should not be an article of speculation," declared the San Antonio document. Everyone—citizens and noncitizens alike—under the "protection of the government," should be granted free land. Calling further for "equality of labor and capital in all laws relating to them," the convention adopted planks demanding the elimination of debtor prisons, greater protection of immigrants, progressive income and inheritance taxes, and the "abolition of banks in their present establishment." Judicial reforms included abolition of the grand jury system and a simplification of the legal system in order to eliminate the need for lawyers. Moreover, the platform contended that "it is the duty of the State to provide for the education of the youth." Convention delegates demanded free schools and the "establishment of universities with admission to all." The education planks intersected with the platform's religious reforms by calling for the "total exclusion of religious training, as well as of religious books, from schools." They demanded that "no preacher may be a teacher." The platform ended by asserting that "religion is a private matter. The United States are political states and have no right to interfere in matters of religion, either favoring or restricting."[83]

Notably absent from the San Antonio Platform was a commitment to women's rights. Its omission was due in large part to the influence of German socialists. As leader of the convention, Douai adhered more to the socialist position on women's rights than to that of the freethinkers. At that time, German socialists believed in separate spheres for men and women. Men were to provide for the needs of the home with their faithful *Hausfrauen* as guardians of the proletarian family. As Douai later wrote in 1878, "one of the most beautiful aims" of socialism was to restore the family unit, which capitalism had destroyed. "Thus," as historian Mari Jo Buhle explains, "Socialists transmuted 'scientific' principles into a reaffirmation of woman's traditional role."[84]

Though the San Antonio Platform echoed much of the Louisville Platform and its predecessors, this was the first time such demands emanated from a political gathering in Texas. The San Antonio Platform reached beyond a German-language audience. The *Western Texan* printed the platform in English on June 1, 1854. The political demands laid out by German Texans in San Antonio would reverberate in Texas in the decades to come. They foreshadowed debates during Reconstruction and anticipated ideals laid out by reformers in the Greenback Labor Party of the 1870s and 1880s and the Populist movement of the 1890s.[85]

Although the San Antonio Platform encompassed a wide range of economic and social issues, it was the plank on slavery that produced a firestorm. "Slavery is an evil, the abolition of which is a requirement of democratic principles," the plank declared, "but, as it affects only single states we desire: That the federal government abstain from all interference in the question of slavery, but that, if a state resolves upon the abolition of the evil, such state may claim the assistance of the general government for the purpose of carrying out such resolve."[86]

Proslavery and other conservative advocates immediately questioned the loyalty of German Texans, wondering aloud whether they were abolitionists or even revolutionary socialists. "If a portion of our German population have come among us with a view of engrafting upon the organization of civil society, the abominable heresies of . . . infidel socialism . . . they will very soon find that they have very widely mistaken the latitude in which either they, or their disorganizing doctrines can find a respectable foot-hold," announced the editor of the *Texas Monument* in La Grange, Fayette County. The editor added that "American republicanism is not free enough for their licentious notions of political equality." The Austin-based newspaper, the *Texas State Gazette*, warned, "We hope that the charges are unfounded . . . for let any portion of our population undertake a crusade . . . against slavery, our laws, religion and its ministers in Texas, and they will raise a storm of indignation from which they will be glad to escape by any means within their power." Conservative and moderate Germans hurriedly organized meetings and wrote letters to newspaper editors to denounce the San Antonio convention, especially its slavery plank, in order to avoid being painted as abolitionists. Some German Texans feared that the antislavery stance might prompt slaveholders and nativists to deny German immigrants their rights.[87]

The rancor over the convention and accusations of abolitionism hurled against German Texans might have died down if not for the continued agitation of Douai. Undaunted and emboldened by the controversy, Douai's *San Antonio Zeitung* became an openly abolitionist newspaper. With financial assistance from Frederick Law Olmsted, Douai also created a Spanish-language Free Soil newspaper to enlist Tejanos and Mexican immigrants in the cause.[88]

Douai was unable to hold on for long in San Antonio. Conservative Germans canceled their subscriptions and organized a boycott of the *San Antonio Zeitung*. Money from northern abolitionists helped Douai keep the paper running, though he was incapable of weathering the increasingly violent attacks from supporters of slavery and nativists alike. In the middle of 1855, a band of twelve slavery supporters rode into San Antonio, vowing to lynch Douai if residents of the town did not do so themselves. Upon hearing this, members of the local German *Turnverein* took to the streets armed and defended Douai and his press until the threat abated. By the end of 1855, Douai had had enough. He sold the paper and moved to Boston, where he was active in the abolitionist movement. In the North, Douai also participated in the efforts of fellow exiled 48ers and German immigrants in building the Republican Party and pushing the party to adopt land reform and antislavery positions. While in Boston, he opened the nation's first kindergarten in 1859. By the 1860s, Douai had become an advocate of Marxist socialism, working closely with Friedrich Sorge, who in 1869 established Section One of the International Workingmen's Association (First International) in the United States, and in the 1870s the two of them assisted in the creation of the Socialist Labor Party.[89]

The actions of many German Texans in opposition to the San Antonio Platform and the antislavery politics of the *San Antonio Zeitung* show that German Texans were not united against slavery. A small number even owned slaves, mainly in the eastern settlements. Between 1840 and 1865, approximately sixty Germans owned slaves in the counties of Austin, Fayette, and Colorado. German Texans made up less than 5 percent of the area's slaveowners, however. Most opposed slavery, as evidenced by their votes against secession, the formation of Union Loyal Leagues in heavily German areas, and their less-than-enthusiastic service in the Confederate military.[90]

The 1854 San Antonio Platform and the antislavery positions of the *San Antonio Zeitung* directly fueled the fledgling nativist Know Nothing movement in

Texas. In the heavily German-populated cities of San Antonio and Galveston, native-born white support of Know Nothing candidates resulted in nativists carrying the San Antonio municipal elections of December 1854 and the mayor's office of Galveston in March 1855. Texas Know Nothings elected twelve state legislators, the state land commissioner, and one representative to the US Congress. US Senator Sam Houston put his support behind the Know Nothings for its stance on preserving the federal Union in opposition to the sectionalism of leading Democrats.[91]

As supporters of the federal Union, German Texans faced conflicting, contradictory political options. The Democratic Party, though opposed to nativism, fanned the sectional crisis in its unyielding defense of slavery. The Know Nothings defended the Union but opposed the very existence of Germans in Texas. In the end, though, internal differences at the national level led to the demise of Know Nothings in Texas. The party's influence in Texas waned after efforts to include a proslavery plank in the national platform failed. The Whig Party was never a force in Texas politics and disappeared from the Texas political scene after its abysmal showing in the 1852 elections. As a result, Fayette County Germans relied on their own self-organizing. On June 9, 1855, a meeting of area Germans in LaGrange "Resolved, that a committee be appointed to draw preliminary articles of a constitution for a Society, to be called 'Social Democratic Society,' which has in view to unite the German population as a body, encourage and assist the more ignorant and indifferent of their countrymen to become citizens of the United States, and use all means as a political body, to defend and uphold Democratic principles." More than likely, Otto Cunerth belonged to this society, for he had called for a social democratic republic in Germany.[92]

In the presidential election year of 1856, slavery was the all-consuming issue. Southern slaveholders saw a direct threat to their power in the candidacy of Republican nominee John Frémont, who opposed extending slavery into the territories. Slaves, on the other hand, saw hope, which added to the fear in slaveholders. On December 11, 1856, the *New York Herald* captured the fears of southern slaveholders: "The idea, no doubt was that with Fremont's election all the negroes of the South would be instantly emancipated or supported from the North in a bloody revolt."[93]

In Columbus, Texas, Colorado County slaveowners' Vigilance Committee discovered an alleged plot in September 1856 for a large slave uprising involving more than two hundred slaves. The slaves reportedly possessed a large number of pistols, bowie knives, guns, and ammunition. Upon killing all whites in the area, they planned to fight their way to freedom in Mexico. In a preemptive strike by slave owners, two slaves were whipped to death and three hanged to serve as examples. Because of the slaves' intention to make it to Mexico, all Mexicans were ordered out of Colorado County and warned never to return on penalty of death.[94]

A month later, a similar uprising was uncovered in Lavaca County that reportedly involved arms and plans to escape to Mexico. Three white men were implicated in the plot, one of whom, an abolitionist named Davidson from Ohio, was captured. After receiving one hundred lashes, Davidson was ordered out of the county. In November, more rumored insurrectionary plots were uncovered in Lavaca, DeWitt, and Victoria Counties. There were no reports of punishment of slaves, but several white men implicated in the plots were "severely horsewhipped" and banished.[95]

By 1859, the extremist fire-eaters firmly controlled the Democratic Party in Texas. They advocated reopening the foreign slave trade and even secession to defend slavery. The 1859 campaign for governor, however, did provide an opening for pro-Union German Texans to play a meaningful role. With the Democratic Party under the control of extremists, a coalition of pro-Union Democrats, former Whigs, and Germans—known collectively in Texas as the Opposition—formed the Union Democrat party. At a mass meeting in Austin in May 1859, Union Democrats put forth Sam Houston as their candidate for governor and invited "all who are opposed to the re-opening of the African Slave Trade, Secession and other disunion issues . . . to unite with us."[96]

Houston, brushing aside his former Know Nothing support, paved the way for German support of the Union Democrats. A group of German Democrats issued what became known as the German Platform. The platform, which insisted that the Texas Democratic convention was not representative of Democrats in the state, declared its support for the Compromise of 1850 and the Kansas-Nebraska Act. These moderate positions were still too radical for fire-eaters, who in a reference to the antislavery paper that was forced to close three years earlier, complained that the "'German Platform' . . . seems to be an extract taken from a late number of the *San Antonio Zeitung*." Yet again, conservative German Texans came out to distance themselves from the German Platform and reiterated their support for the regular Democratic Party.[97] That both progressive and conservative Germans came out with statements on the Texas Democratic Party shows that some German Texans had gained at least political toeholds within the Democratic Party and its competing factions.

Houston won the August election with 59 percent of the popular vote. Two factors helped to carry the day for Houston. First was the inability of the regular Democrats to defend the western frontier against attacks from Comanches and Kiowas. Second was what many Texans felt was the unnecessary insertion of sectional slavery issues into state politics. Houston campaigned against his opponents' extreme proslavery positions, which he worried might lead to secession and civil war. Support for Houston, though, was not tantamount to a vote against slavery. The South's ruling elite overwhelmingly approved a state's right to maintain slavery. The *Colorado Citizen* newspaper of Columbus, Texas, voiced a representative sample of reasons to back Houston: "We have advocated the re-opening of the African slave trade, and we are still in favor of it, if it can be done without destroying the Union; but we think it impracticable at the moment. We would not destroy the Union for the advantages of the slave trade. We are willing in the spirit of compromise and peace to give up something for the sake of the Union. Therefore we will support the Union Ticket. . . . For our part, we are not tired of the Union and are content to live a while longer under the stars and stripes." The hope in Houston's election was that cooler heads would prevail.[98]

Two months after Houston's election, John Brown's raid on Harpers Ferry prompted many Texans to cast aside whatever misgivings they had about proslavery extremists. What once was deemed an obsessive fantasy of proslavery fanatics that northern abolitionists might invade the South and incite a slave revolt no longer seemed far-fetched. The next year, panic over possible slave revolts spread in Texas, with Fayette County, home of the Meitzens, at its center.[99]

In August 1860, in lower Fayette County, authorities reportedly uncovered yet another attempted plan by insurrectionary slaves to fight their way to Mexico. In response, more than twenty-five whites and fifty blacks were hanged in Fayette County from July to September. In a study of slave insurrections in Texas, Wendell Addington wrote, "Frequent white support to slave revolts in Texas seems to have come from local farmers and artisans—the poor whites who were also oppressed by the slavocracy. Special mention should be made of the Germans in Texas, almost none of whom held slaves and who were themselves refugees from Prussian tyranny."[100] This was the beginnings of an often-strained, on-again-off-again, political collaboration between radical German and black Texans that would last until the end of the century.

By the end of September, the panic over slave revolts had subsided, only to be replaced by anxiety over the coming presidential elections. Secessionist stump speakers spread across Texas, warning people of the dangers of "Black Republicanism." The Union Democrats of the 1859 election, who joined the national Constitutional Union party, were the main opposition to the secessionist movement in the state. The electoral coalition of 1859 that pushed Houston into the governor's office did not materialize again in 1860. Many Germans who supported the Union Democrats did not support the Constitutional Union party because of its presidential candidate John Bell's ties to the Know Nothings. John Brown's raid and the summer's slave revolt panic turned others against Unionism. What Walt Whitman called the Year of Meteors was at hand.[101]

2   Inheritors of the Revolution

"During the war I was brought up, jerked up," reminisced E. O. Meitzen on his childhood during the US Civil War. In leaving Prussia and settling in Texas, the Meitzens had only left one political conflict and entered another. The issues of secession and slavery had Fayette County and the surrounding area deeply divided in the years preceding and during the Civil War.[1] Amid this period, working-class German Texans, as well as other Texans, had to abandon their yeoman dreams to the realities of a now-dominant market-based capitalist economy. Also, German immigrant hopes that slavery would gradually fade away or that at least they could exist separate from it, proved to be increasingly ill founded as the planter class showed its willingness for war to defend their peculiar institution. Faced with these political and economic conditions, German Texans adapted their 48er radicalism to conditions more specific to their present situation in Texas. Their radicalism tempered once again in the flames of revolution in the form of civil war and Reconstruction, aging 48ers would pass on their revolutionary zeal to a second generation of German Texans. These German Texans would not be alone as they joined forces with like-minded Texans, of multiple races and ethnicities, to quell the growth of unrestrained capitalism laying the foundation for the Populist movement. First they would have to survive the war.

Once Abraham Lincoln won the White House, the movement for secession proved unstoppable. A referendum on secession in Texas was organized for February 23, 1861. The two months leading up to the referendum were full of violence and intimidation against anyone who dared oppose secession. When the votes were totaled, the results were 46,153 for and 14,747 against, with only 18 counties out of 122 casting majorities against secession. Texas became one of the original seven Confederate states. "It Is Finished," enthusiastically declared La Grange's *States Rights Democrat*. "The deed has been done. We breathe deeper and freer for it. The Union is dead; and with it all the hopes and all the fears which divided and agitated our people. It was a glorious fabric, but its timbers had rotted at the heart."[2]

The two counties with the highest percentage against secession were the western German frontier counties of Gillespie and Mason, with 96 percent against. San Antonio, the Texas city with the largest German population, voted against secession, but the totals from the surrounding county put Bexar County barely into the secessionist column. Elsewhere in Texas, many German-dominated communities voted against secession but were outvoted in the county totals. Much of the antisecession vote also came from the frontier counties of Uvalde and Medina, several counties along Texas's northern border, and a few central counties, including Travis County, where Austin is located.[3]

In Fayette County, the vote for secession was defeated by a count of 580 for and 628 against. The county's newly arrived German, Czech, and other immigrants, numbering 2,027 out of a free population of 7,818, proved to be a deciding factor. The *States Rights Democrat* blamed the antisecession vote in Fayette County on "sauerkraut dirt-eaters" and wondered whether the influence of the 1854 San Antonio Convention still pervaded the county.[4]

Germans were less than enthusiastic when it came to service in the Confederate military. Very few German Texans voluntarily joined the Confederate cause in the first year of the war. Not until the Confederate draft was instituted in April 1862 did Germans in significant numbers appear on Confederate rolls. The initial draft was for men aged 18–35, and in September 1862 the Confederate government expanded the draft to the age of forty-five. To flee the draft often meant leaving loved ones behind to a dubious fate, or it meant abandoning farms and other property earned through years of hard work. When Germans did enlist in the Confederate Army, most did so when service seemed unavoidable. They joined to serve in the company of people they knew—not out of fidelity to the Confederacy.[5]

This was apparently the case with Otto Cunerth, former leader of the radical Democratic Club of Liegnitz, Silesia, who advocated a socialist republic for a unified Germany in the 1848 Revolution. When the Civil War broke out, he was farming 180 acres of land in Fayette County owned by his wife Marie (Meitzen), which she probably obtained upon the death of her first husband. Cunerth was a teacher who, like many German immigrants, attempted to become a yeoman farmer. He did not enlist when the war started. At the age of forty-four, he was past draft age when it began in April 1862. Five months later, officials raised the age limit to forty-five.[6]

Otto Cunerth (1817–?), circa 1860. Photo courtesy of Fayette Heritage Museum and Archives.

Unwilling to be subjected to the randomness of the draft, Cunerth enlisted. On March 18, 1862, he joined the Twenty-fourth Texas Cavalry, which, along with the Sixth Texas Infantry, contained the largest number of Silesians, many of whom were ethnic Poles. During the fall and winter, both units were sent to Fort Hindman, an earthen fort along the Arkansas River near Arkansas Post, Arkansas. The fort served as a base for Confederates to disrupt Union shipping on the Mississippi River. It stood at the rear of the Union's impending attack on Vicksburg.[7]

The soldiers' time at Fort Hindman passed rather uneventfully until January 9, 1863, when Union gunboats neared the fort. The next morning, the gunboats began their bombardment. At a range of only four hundred yards, Union ships fired shells weighing between 30 and 105 pounds at the earthen fort walls while their troops disembarked for a ground assault. Confederate soldiers repelled the initial Union ground invasion, but in the process the fort's walls crumbled and its guns were disabled. The Union Army prepared a massive advance, but white flags appeared in the Confederate trenches. The white flags came from Cunerth's

Twenty-fourth Texas Cavalry. Though ordered to hold the fort, the soldiers of the Twenty-fourth Texas acted on their own and surrendered, while other Confederate units continued the fight. Because of the confusion in Confederate ranks, Union forces captured the fort and won the battle. The exact details have been lost in the clouds of war, but on the surface, we have unenthusiastic Confederate Silesians, who enlisted only so they could serve together, surrendering to Union forces at their first opportunity, resulting in the capture of 4,700 Confederate soldiers, the largest Confederate loss west of the Mississippi until the end of the war.[8]

Cunerth and his captured comrades were sent to the POW camp at Fort Butler near Springfield, Illinois. Shortly after they arrived at Fort Butler in early February 1863, the Union commander discovered that many of the captured Confederates, particularly the "foreigners, Germans, Polanders, &c," had been pressed into service and now desired to join the Union forces. Thirty-eight men from the Twenty-fourth Texas Cavalry and 152 from the Sixth Texas—mostly Germans and Poles—swore an oath of allegiance to the United States and joined the Union Army. Cunerth was not among them, perhaps fearing retribution to his wife and farm back in Fayette County. He was part of a group of 508 Confederate prisoners sent to Virginia in April, where they were paroled in a prisoner exchange with Union forces. The remnants of the Twenty-fourth Texas were assigned to the Confederate Army of Tennessee. While stationed in Tennessee, the soldiers of the Twenty-fourth Texas were harassed for their surrender at Arkansas Post, and most officers did not want them under their command because of their reputation. They participated in one major battle, that of Chickamauga in September 1863, before being consolidated into Granbury's Texas Brigade. While in Granbury's Brigade, they were in near endless combat, participating in the battles of Missionary Ridge, Resaca, New Hope Church, Kennesaw Mountain, Peachtree Creek, Atlanta, Jonesboro, Franklin, and Nashville before the few remaining soldiers surrendered at Greensboro in April 1865. Out of the approximately 9,800 Texans from various regiments who served in Granbury's Brigade, only 401 survived to Greensboro. When he was not in combat, Cunerth's personal military experience was worsened by two bouts of suffering from "diarrhoea chronica" at military hospitals in Georgia and Alabama."[9]

In many ways, the home front was more harrowing for German Texans and other Unionists than the front lines. Germans referred to the war period as *der Henkerzeit*, or hanging times, because of the acts of violence carried out against them. Many German Texans organized to defend themselves. In June 1861 German immigrants in the Hill Country organized a Union Loyal League. Similar groups formed in Bexar, Austin, and Travis Counties. To combat the Union Loyal League, the state government declared martial law in Gillespie County and parts of bordering counties, arrested several residents, and hanged two German "troublemakers." In response, a group of an estimated sixty-one German men decided on August 1 to arm themselves and flee to Mexico. In the very early hours of August 10, 1862, a band of Confederate soldiers and irregulars attacked the Germans while they slept near the Nueces River. In the ensuing firefight, nineteen Unionists were killed and nine wounded. On the Confederate side, two were killed and eighteen wounded. After the battle, the nine captured wounded Unionists were executed. Of those Unionists who fled, eight more were killed on October 18 when they tried to cross into Mexico. Whether viewed as a battle or massacre, the event sparked a bushwhacker war in the Hill Country for the duration of the war.[10]

After the Nueces Massacre, eastern German settlements in Texas held meetings to discuss how to resist the draft. The communities came together for a two-day convention at Roeder's Mill that began on December 31, 1862. The convention drew between four hundred and six hundred participants from Fayette, Washington, Austin, and Colorado Counties. According to witnesses, the Germans, well armed, used the gathering to drill and skirmish in addition to engaging in political discussions. In response, Confederate authorities placed Austin, Fayette, and Colorado Counties under martial law. Others chose individual ways to avoid the draft, such as cutting off one's fingers. A Houston newspaper called attention to a case in which a German in Brenham even "blew his brains out."[11]

The dismal economic conditions faced by just about everyone in Texas and the South exacerbated the dire political situation of German Texans during the war. With brother and business partner William in the Confederate Army, Otto Meitzen ran the gristmill and gin on his own during the war. The Union naval blockade of the Gulf Coast cut off area farmers from their previous markets. Business at the mill came to a standstill. As Otto's granddaughter, Frieda Meitzen Williams, later recounted, he "sat reading many hours with his rawhide bottom chair tipped back and his head against the wall."[12]

Jennie Meitzen's multifaceted activities in those years of war, struggle, and deprivation illustrate the vital importance of women in sustaining and holding families together on the home front. When the mill struggled and failed, she pursued other economic options to provide for the family. She sold cigars she made from tobacco that she grew herself. She also taught at a school for German-language children, riding miles on horseback to do so. In addition, she cooked three meals a day, cleaned, and made clothing, soap, candles, and wurst. The family also made corn whiskey, which they sold to local general stores. Mostly, they lived off fish and wild game. Roasted acorns substituted for coffee, and sorghum replaced sugar as a delicacy. "Corn bread and cowpeas, a diet a German detested but forced to become accustomed to, were staples," Williams recalled.[13]

Otto Meitzen (1811–82) and Jennie Meitzen (1818–77), date unknown. Public domain.

The Meitzen brothers' mill operations went bust, but when William returned to Fayetteville, he began farming and opened another mill of his own. Otto, financially ruined by the war, was forced to sell his home and enter tenant farming. Cunerth after the war returned to his wife, Marie, in Fayette County and started farming again. After Marie died in February 1868, he gave up the land and moved to La Grange, where he took up his old profession of teaching. He also took on the responsibility of teaching his nephews English. In his nephew E. O.'s reminiscences of his uncle are no glorified accounts of his service in the Confederate Army. His lost cause was the 1848 Revolution, not the Confederacy.[14]

A prewar vote against secession did not automatically translate into support for the Republican Party in Texas after the war. Unlike much of the former Confederacy, the postwar political struggle in Texas did not fall into clearly delineated lines of blacks and working-class white Unionists in the Republican Party versus the old planter class in the Democratic Party. Political and economic elites were present in each party, who used them to advance their own interests. Local factors often determined which party Germans and other advocates of working-class-based politics joined. In areas with German majorities, German Texans mainly supported the Republican Party. San Antonio, with its large population of Germans and Tejanos, elected Edward Degener, a 48er and Republican who lost two sons in the Nueces Massacre, to Congress with the state's first congressional delegation during Reconstruction.[15]

In Colorado and Washington Counties, where Germans were only a sizable minority, they formed a political alliance with blacks to create a Republican political majority. In Colorado County, blacks, Germans, and Czechs together made up 55 percent of the population, while in Washington they were nearly 61 percent. Through this alliance, in the face of racially motivated violence, both counties would remain Republican beyond Reconstruction into the 1880s. Washington County, in the first Reconstruction Texas legislature, sent a black to the Senate and a German immigrant to the House. It took violence and stolen ballot boxes to return these counties to Democratic control by 1890.[16]

In adjacent Fayette County, blacks, Germans, and Czechs made up only 49 percent of the population, but it elected Republicans to office during Reconstruction. Without a clear majority, shows of force were required to maintain black-German Republican political power in the county. On election day in February 1868, blacks organized an armed company and marched into La Grange to vote. Federal troops were also stationed in the county to protect Germans and blacks targeted by "rowdy gangs." Otto Meitzen was among those who supported the Republican Party. He continued to back it for the rest of his life.[17]

In that political regard, Otto broke ranks with his brother William and brother-in-law Cunerth. On October 16, 1869, Cunerth was appointed to the Central Executive Committee of the Fayette County Democratic Party. Not much is known about William's political views, but he joined Cunerth on the party's auxiliary committee. On the surface, Cunerth's acceptance of a leadership position in the Democratic Party contradicts his earlier socialist and radical farmer-labor political views in Silesia, an especially surprising decision when one considers that Victor Thompson, an ardent secessionist, was chairman of the county Democratic Party.[18]

Thompson, editor of La Grange's *States Rights Democrat*, vehemently opposed the "Radical party," the label Democrats hung on Republicans. He was an archracist who attacked "Radicals" for their support of "negro equality." He viewed opposition to the Republican Party as "the only hope and safety of the white race in Texas." During the secession crisis, the *States Rights Democrat* was the official paper of the Knights of the Golden Circle—a proslavery paramilitary group that terrorized Unionists. After the war, Thompson supported the Ku Klux Klan in his paper.[19]

Local considerations may have influenced Cunerth's decision to join the Democratic Party's Central Executive Committee in Fayette County. The Republican Party, which increasingly became the political instrument of northern big business, was not a clear pole of attraction for all radical-minded German Texans. Before the war, Fayette County had an active nativist movement. It was the Democratic Party that opposed nativism and attracted immigrants. After the war, many nativists were prominent Republicans, thus alienating a number of Germans from the party. Some Germans who found a small place in the

Union Democrat wing of the Democratic Party before the war did not want to relinquish their voice in county and state politics in the postwar period. Some Republican leaders in Texas favored disenfranchising even reluctant Confederates like Cunerth.[20]

After the 1868 state constitutional convention, the Texas Republican Party basically split into two wings—conservative and radical. The conservatives, overwhelmingly white in composition and led by Governor Elisha Pease, controlled patronage and the party's statewide machinery. They opposed the Reconstruction policies of Radical Republicans nationally and prevented a civil-rights section from being added to the Texas state constitution. The top-down party apparatus depended on patronage doled out by federal military forces stationed in Texas. White Republicans in the state opposed a vigorous commitment to rights of freedmen. More often than not, they manipulated black voters through the party's machinery to advance the political and economic objectives of white party elites.[21]

George T. Ruby, an African American born in New York City in 1841 who arrived in Texas in 1866 as a representative of the Freedman's Bureau, led the radical wing of the Republican Party. In June 1868 he was elected the first state president of the Loyal Union League. Ruby's power base came from Galveston's black dockworkers, and he organized the Colored National Labor Convention to represent nonagricultural black laborers in 1869. He was twice elected to the Texas Legislature from Galveston (1870–1873) and was the chief spokesperson for Radical Republicans in the statehouse. His main allies in the party were west Texans.[22]

Whatever Cunerth's motivations, concerns, or prejudices, he opted for the Jeffersonian agrarian-based ideals of the Democratic Party, which also opposed temperance and nativism. Evidence suggests that a radical-agrarian faction existed within the Democratic Party based in Fayette and neighboring Bastrop County that fought for the economic interests of working farmers. They decided to work within the Democratic Party even if doing so meant being in the same party as old Confederate plantation elites seeking to regain control of the levers of power in the southern Democratic Party. This was only the beginning of many times that white Texan agrarian radicals chose to fight for economic issues over social issues such as black equality, contributing much to the detriment, and eventual collapse, of farmer-labor radicalism in Texas in the early twentieth century.

Bastrop and Fayette Counties belonged to the Fourth US Congressional District. Joining Cunerth in a leadership position in the Fayette County Democratic Party was fellow German radical Louis Franke, who fled Germany in 1847 because of his opposition to the Prussian monarchy. In Bastrop County, they found an ally in Julius Noeggerath, a German elected to the State House as a Democrat and future member of the Greenback Labor Party.[23]

If Cunerth, by this time, was still holding true to his 48er beliefs, he must have been a part of the faction within the Democratic Party of Fayette and Bastrop Counties with Noeggerath, and others who fought for the economic interests of working farmers. Agrarian radicals such as Noeggerath first fought within the Democratic Party. When that failed, they broke from the narrow restraints of the two-party system and set out on the course of independent political action. This began a six-decade pattern of farmer-labor radicals in Texas first attempting to work within the Democratic Party and forging their own independent political party when working with the Democrats failed. Former Confederate planters did regain control of the Democratic Party. They went on the offensive, utilizing racism and terrorism to keep blacks and poor whites subordinate as Northern politicians proved more and more unwilling to enforce black equality with the use of federal troops. The developments led agrarian radicals in Texas to take independent political action.[24]

Cunerth, though, would not be around for this new stage of independent working-class political action in Texas. In March 1871 Cunerth traveled to Washington, DC, applied for a passport, and returned to Germany. During the previous twenty-three years, Cunerth had lived through revolution, counterrevolution, immigration and exile, civil war, a prisoner of war camp, more war, the death of his wife, and political struggles against the old planter class.[25]

Cunerth returned to a united Germany, something he had fought for during the 1848 Revolution. Though instead of the socialist republic he had advocated, Germany was united under the authoritarian rule of Otto von Bismarck. Cunerth resettled in Görlitz, where he was born in 1817. There he worked as a language teacher at a girls' school for a year, then taught at a local high school (*Gymnasium*), where he was until 1882, when he accepted the head teaching position at a trade school in Gleiwitz (present-day Gliwice). In 1883 Cunerth left for an Easter vacation and vanished without a trace. German scholars believe Cunerth either emigrated back to the United States, though there are no records of this happening, or committed suicide.[26]

Young E. O. Meitzen must have been saddened by the departure of his Uncle Otto back to Germany. He lost not just an uncle, but a teacher and mentor. In 1870, at the age of fifteen, E. O. Meitzen left the poverty of his family's tenant farm and become an apprentice blacksmith. If any truth can be gleaned from E. O.'s daughter Frieda's fictionalized account of her father's life in her novel, *New Breslau (Oil Town, Later)*, E. O. apprenticed for a Bohemian man who, besides blacksmithing, taught E. O. to speak the Bohemian language. Around this time, E. O. befriended a doctor who lent him books to further his self-education.[27]

E. O. Meitzen set out on his own in tumultuous times, both economically and politically. For him and other working-class southerners, still struggling to recover from the war, the depression of 1873 hit especially hard. Speculation and overvaluation of railroad bonds caused a financial panic, forcing the stock market to close temporarily. An ensuing six-year depression closed thousands of businesses and cost millions of people their jobs.

The expansion of railroads brought farmers into the modern world of finance capitalism and connected them to the world market. As historian Robert McMath Jr. put it, southern yeomen began "the historic shift from self-sufficiency to cotton speculation."[28] While hoping for a higher standard of living, farmers instead were now more vulnerable to world market fluctuations. Before 1875, cotton prices varied from 12 to 18 cents per pound, but in 1875 they fell to 11 cents. Cotton generally cost farmers between 5 and 8 cents per pound to produce. Cotton prices did not rise above the 1875 equivalent levels for the rest of the century.[29]

After the fall of world cotton prices, many farmers, after harvest, were left without the monetary means to purchase the materials necessary to plant the next season's crop. Numerous farmers fell into debt, losing their land and independence. In an area of the country that historically lacked banks, the collapse of the southern economy after the Civil War left many areas without a bank from which farmers might procure financing. Into the void stepped furnishing merchants, who furnished a farmer the necessary supplies in exchange for a lien on the crop. More often than not, the crop did not yield enough to pay off the lien, which then extended from year to year until the farmer was forced to pay the lien by turning over his land to the merchant. As a result, the merchant in many cases became the landlord and the farmer a sharecropper or tenant farmer.[30]

In the same period, workers began to see that industrial wage work, whether in a factory, mine, or elsewhere, was not a temporary step toward becoming an independent artisan but something more permanent—even "wage slavery." More and more Americans toiled as wage laborers their entire working lives. Subsequently, the faith that US democracy would lead to economic independence proved a fantasy.[31]

In the aftermath of the Civil War, a highly politicized electorate of workers and farmers faced a rising corporate elite, each side with rapidly diverging views on the future of democracy. Many nineteenth-century workers and farmers saw themselves as producers. Their concept of citizenship and democracy expressed itself through producerism, which is based on the labor theory of value holding that the producer deserves the fruits of his or her work. In Gilded Age America, however, the worker-farmer vision of a producerist society was being crushed by the juggernaut of corporate capitalism. As McMath explains, "profits were accruing not to the person who produced the crop, but to the one with capital or credit enough to hold it for speculation."[32]

In addition to losing their economic independence, working-class Texans, like their counterparts across the country by the 1870s, were losing their political voice in the two-party system. After the war, Texans joined across class lines the party they felt best represented their interests, often based on region or race. On March 30, 1870, Texas was readmitted to the Union. With the Thirteenth and Fourteenth Amendments upon them, economic elites moved to maximize their profits from the state's agricultural resources, of which cotton was king, and to devise ways to control the labor that grew and harvested the state's wealth. At the same time, working-class Texans in each party struggled to maintain their political and economic independence.

By 1870, the issues of railroad construction and farm tenancy no longer divided Texans by party, but by class. Despite heated and frequently violent conflicts between Democrats and Republicans during Reconstruction, economic elites of each party backed government support to private railroad corporations. In 1865 Texas had only around 341 miles of railroads in operation. From 1870 to 1873 railroad mileage increased to nearly 1,600 miles. This substantial increase was the result of bipartisan legislation that provided railroad companies with government subsidies, government-backed bonds, and land grants to finance railroad construction.[33]

The expansion of railroads provided easier access to markets for agricultural products. Before and even after the 1873 collapse in cotton prices, most Texans believed cotton was the main crop to earn them money. As railroads expanded, so did cotton cultivation into the state's interior and frontiers.[34] The central question was over who would control the cotton wealth. Whoever controlled labor would control the wealth.

Early in 1873, the Landlord and Tenant Bill was introduced into the Texas legislature. After the 1872 elections, Democrats regained control of the Texas House. Republicans maintained a slim majority in the Senate only because of staggered terms. The Landlord and Tenant Bill was a clear piece of class-based legislation designed to control the state's agricultural workforce and codify into law the crop lien system to the benefit of agricultural elites. For all persons renting or leasing land, the bill proposed putting a lien not only on the tenant's crop but on his personal property as well. If a tenant could not pay rent, the bill empowered the landlord with the help of the local sheriff to seize the crop and personal property. The bill, which provided tenants with no legal recourse, also stipulated that tenants must obtain the landlord's permission before selling their crop. Radical Republican governor Edmund Davis vetoed the bill, but the veto was overridden with bipartisan support. One of those who voted against the bill was Fayette County Democrat Julius Noeggerath.[35]

Immediate dissent developed in the ranks of working farmers as state Democratic leaders supported the oppressive Landlord and Tenant Bill, land grants, and bonds to finance railroad corporations. "The leading organs of the Democracy are allied with the bond holding human oppressors of the land.... [T]he honest farmer has no choice between a spurious Democracy and fraudulent Republicanism," wrote the *Victoria Advocate* in July 1873. The paper previously supported the Democratic Party but now raised the question of the need to create a farmers' party. "The Democratic Party, we suppose, has always had a few such crazy asses in it," replied the Democratic Party's statewide organ, the *Weekly Democratic Statesman* in Austin.[36]

At this divisive political moment, a group of leading German Texans from both parties organized a convention to take place in Austin on August 7, 1873, "for the purpose of a free discussion of the present political situation of the country; an expression of our wishes as American citizens; a definition of our position toward the different parties, and uniting on the platform on which we intend to work, pending the next election." On the surface, it appeared that German Texans were coming together across party lines, but the leaders attended the convention for the purpose of attracting German votes to their respective parties. These partisan leaders included August Siemering, a leader of the Republican Party in San Antonio. On the first day of the convention, delegates adopted a few innocuous resolutions calling for "a more liberal system of public schools" and "sufficient protection of the life and property of all citizens." When the issue of railroad subsidies was broached, political divisions surfaced and the issue was dropped from further consideration. On the second day, the convention condemned temperance and Sunday laws as an "attempt to deprive the citizen of his personal rights." A bit of the 48er spirit materialized above the partisan divide with the adoption of a resolution: "We declare ourselves against any law which may aim at the oppression of any class of citizen of the State on account of race and color or previous condition."[37]

Although German Democrats and Republicans participated in the Austin convention to rally Germans to their parties, the bringing together of disgruntled members from the two parties had unintended consequences for the convention organizers. After failing to change the Democratic Party from within, renegade German Democrats, together with like-minded German Republicans, held a German Convention in La Grange in early October. The end result of the La Grange German Convention was the formation of the independent working-class "People's Party" in Texas.[38] In the preamble of the convention, delegates expressed their deep level of dissatisfaction with the two-party system:

> We are perfectly satisfied and aware that both present political parties have outlived themselves, and their sole object is to keep up their organization in order to keep the power in the hands of the successful party, and for the sake of office seekers and holders.

Therefore, we deem it necessary to cut ourselves loose from all party organizations, to bring the politic body in a healthy condition again, which we think can only be done by a new party organization, which must be built up gradually and is bound to cut itself of all old party organizations, and be it *Resolved*, That from now on we will act independent of the Republican and Democratic party.[39]

Resolutions adopted at the convention expressed "opposition to monied capitalists, who form powerful corporations and who form coalitions by an undue influence on the Legislature at the expense of the mass of the people." The convention called for free public education and "a reform of the elective franchise to enable minorities in proportion to their number and intelligence to take part in the government."[40]

Germans in Bastrop County also held a convention of their own. In attendance was Democratic state representative Julius Noeggerath. Because of a dearth of sources, the details of the platform are unclear. The *Bastrop Advertiser*, an organ of the Democratic Party that denounced all independent candidates as "radicals"—Republicans in disguise—mockingly claimed that the convention "adopted the radical [Republican Party] Dallas platform."[41]

Fayette and Bastrop County Germans were not alone in their bid for political independence from Democrats and Republicans alike. They were joined by area Anglos as well. Foremost among the Anglos who joined the independent movement was Captain Jesse Billingsley, a highly respected veteran of the Texas Revolution. He fought in the Battle of San Jacinto, the decisive Texas victory over Mexican forces led by Antonio López de Santa Anna that won Texas independence. Folklorist J. Frank Dobie credited Billingsley as the first who cried at San Jacinto, "Remember the Alamo! Remember Goliad!"[42]

In early August 1873, prior to the La Grange Convention, Billingsley announced that he was leaving the Democratic Party to run as an independent candidate representing Bastrop and Fayette Counties in the Texas House. He broke with the Democratic Party because of his opposition to the Landlord and Tenant Bill and government subsidies to railroad corporations, as well as his support of free public education. Democrats were abashed that this once "firm and unshaken Democrat" was now standing against them. For his defection, the once lionized hero was berated as "an old hypocrite," "Benedict Arnold," and "tool" of the radicals.[43]

With the independent movement growing and gaining momentum, a "people's convention" was organized in Fayette County in late October 1873. Both Billingsley and Noeggerath sought nomination as one of the district's three representatives to the state house. The convention chose Billingsley, and two men associated with the Republican Party—Jack Walker, a farmer from La Grange, and R. F. Campbell from Bastrop—as their nominees. For state senate, the convention nominated Hamilton Ledbetter, a Round Top farmer who, before Emancipation, owned a plantation with a large number of slaves. The Democratic nominee who ran against Ledbetter was his own son, attorney William Hamilton Ledbetter. The *Democratic Statesman*, which blasted the People's Party as "a mongrel Radical Farmer's Party," proclaimed, "This is one of the cases in which the son ought to beat his daddy, and that too, soundly."[44]

The Republican Party of Fayette and Bastrop Counties was controlled by Germans and blacks who supported the radical wing of their party. After coming together with disaffected radical Democrats at the Austin and La Grange German conventions, area Republicans helped to lead the people's convention. The district Republican Party decided not to field any candidates, instead joining the People's Party, which gave a few Republicans spots on the ticket. This initiated a decades-long practice in which radical farmer-labor Republicans forwent their own ticket to support working-class parties such as the Greenback Labor Party in the early 1880s and the People's Party in the 1890s. State and national Republican leaders even supported the practice at times as a way to weaken if not defeat the Democratic Party.[45]

Fayette and Bastrop Counties were not the only Texas areas where individuals broke from the two major parties to form independent clubs and support independent candidates in the 1873 election. On October 7 a group of African Americans in San Antonio dissatisfied with the Republican Party met to organize an independent club. Several white Republicans showed up at the meeting, however, and persuaded many in attendance to return home. Thirty men stayed and organized a club, of which little else is known. In Caldwell and Hays Counties, a full farmers' ticket was fielded for the state House and Senate races.[46]

An additional factor contributing to the changing political landscape in Texas was the arrival of the Grange. On July 5, 1873, R. A. Baird, a national deputy of the Grange, organized the first subordinate Grange of Texas in Salado, Bell County. Formally known as the Patrons of Husbandry, the Grange was founded in 1867 by government clerks at the Agricultural Bureau in Washington, DC, to assist farmers by educating them in new scientific methods of farming. By 1873, the Grange had hundreds of thousands of members. Its leaders expressly forbade the organization from taking political stances. In their view, the Grange was a fraternal organization with a purely educational and business function, but when government railroad subsidies and land policies hurt farmers, many rank-and-file members saw it as a vehicle to organize politically.[47]

Farmers were not the only ones to see the political class-based potential of the Grange. So did the *Democratic Statesman*, which of course supported subsidies for railroad corporations and the Landlord and Tenant Bill, which favored elites. "We have no objection to the farmers of the country looking out sharply for their own interests . . . but we are opposed to getting up anything like a political farmer's party," warned a front-page article in the newspaper in the very week the Grange appeared in Texas. The newspaper fiercely criticized the organization, complaining that it divided people along class lines.[48]

Despite assurances by a Texas promoter that the Grange did not allow discussions of a political nature, the *Democratic Statesman* warned of the dangers of sowing class discontent. The paper acknowledged the good intentions of its founders in that regard but reminded its readers that "the devil got into Paradise. ... This is the old story, we suppose, in regard to all good works: 'No sooner doth the Lord erect a house of prayer, Than Satan surely comes and builds a chapel there.'"[49] Citing reports from the La Grange *New Era*, the *Democratic Statesman* emphasized that radical-minded farmers viewed the Grange as a political tool and warned that "the poison is working in Fayette county, where under color of the Granges, they are already calling for meetings of a 'people's party.'"[50] The reactions are evidence that, from the beginning, radical-minded farmers viewed the Grange with more of a political than a business purpose, despite the intentions of national Grange leaders.

With the white electorate growing more and more divided over the issues of railroads and farm tenancy, the Democratic Party relied on white supremacy to keep white men in its column. Democratic editors in Texas portrayed a vote against the Democratic Party as a vote against the white race and in favor of "mongrelization."[51] "The negro and the white man can never become homogeneous," asserted the *Democratic Statesman*. "Nature has forbidden homogeneity between them, and it is useless to strive against nature."[52] According to the paper, nothing less than white womanhood was at stake: "On the very day Governor Davis was in Waco, declaiming loudly for negro equality, a white woman of that city was united in the holy bonds of matrimony with a full-blooded negro, described as one of 'the biggest, blackest and strongest of his race.' ... Is our noble white blood to be contaminated with this shameless miscegenation?"[53]

The December election of 1873 was a near total victory for Democrats; they won all statewide offices and now controlled both houses of Congress. Texas was redeemed. There were, however, minor working-class victories in Fayette and Bastrop Counties. Walker, one of the three candidates for state representative backed by the People's Convention, was elected to the House as one of only ten Republicans (six of them black). Campbell, also backed by the People's Convention, lost by only twenty-five votes. The convention's candidate for state senate, Hamilton Ledbetter, won his race over his son. He was the only independent to win election, but it was a hollow victory. When not frequently absent from the Senate, he often voted with Democrats, including most notoriously for the Landlord and Tenant Bill, which Democrats now passed into law.[54]

The election results did nothing to hamper the growth of the Grange. Some Democratic papers such as the *Waxahachie Democrat* argued that the *Democratic*

Statesman misunderstood the organization. A Democratic politician at a campaign rally in November 1873 observed, "The Granges are composed of our best farmers" and are the "firmest friends" of the Democrats' winning candidate for governor, Richard Coke.[55]

The Grange became so palatable to Texas Democrats, in fact, that nearly half the newly elected legislators joined it. In many ways, the Grange became an auxiliary of the Democratic Party. "No politics" meant no politics outside the Democratic Party.[56]

As a mutual aid organization and social outlet for rural people, the Grange grew rapidly. By April 1874, there were 360 locals in Texas, including Bastrop and Fayette Counties. Membership peaked in 1877 at around forty-five thousand members, including six thousand women. As the economic crisis of the 1870s deepened, the Grange created a system of cash-only cooperative stores to aid farmers. The Grange stores sought to become an alternative to furnishing merchants, but for cash-starved farmers already trapped in the crop-lien system, the stores provided little relief.[57]

Despite the Grange's avowed nonpolitical stance, many members understood the political potential of farmers acting collectively. Abusive railroad practices more than any other issue motivated many Grangers to push their organization into politics. The expansion of railroads connecting farmers to national and international markets enticed many to transition from subsistence farming to a reliance on cash crops such as cotton and wheat. Doing so, in turn, made farmers heavily reliant on railroads for transporting their crops to market. With monopolies in many areas, railroad corporations charged what many farmers felt were exorbitant freight rates. Pressure from members in 1875 against the "fearful rate of freights" caused the leader or Worthy Master of the Texas Grange, William W. Lang, to blast railroads as "public tyrannies."[58]

Demands for railroad regulation became so great that the public forced the state Constitutional Convention, then in session, to act. Article X of the new constitution gave the legislature the power to regulate railroad schedules and fees and to halt the merging of competing lines to prevent monopolies. Worthy Master Lang even broke the Grange's sacred no-politics pledge and won election to the legislature as a Democratic representative from the district of Falls, Milam, and Bell Counties in 1876.[59]

Though now vested with power to regulate railroad practices, the legislature refused to act in defense of farmers. Lang continued to speak out against unfair railroad practices, both in the legislature and in speeches across the country. His activism led many supporters of the Grange to consider him as a candidate for governor in 1878. In a reference to Lang, a writer in the *San Antonio Express* asserted, "The people desire a change. The people begin to distrust even the Democratic party in the hands of men who have exhibited no disposition to make the promised reforms.... I think it the most opportune time for the farmers to make a rush for control of our state government.... A man capable, worthy and well known to the state, subject to a Democratic nomination for governor ... would be a rallying point for the farmers."[60]

Before the 1878 state Democratic Convention, Lang declared he was a loyal Democrat who would abide by the decisions of the convention. Delegates, however, did not look favorably on his candidacy and instead nominated the chief justice of the Texas Supreme Court, Oran Roberts. Roberts was president of Secession Convention in 1861 that led Texas into the Confederacy. During the early days of Reconstruction, the state legislature elected him US senator; Radical Republicans, however, voted to refuse to seat him, along with other former Confederates, using a constitutional provision on elections. Some urged Lang to run as an independent candidate, but he refused. For his loyalty, the Grover Cleveland administration appointed him consul in Hamburg, Germany, in 1885.[61]

Grange membership peaked during the height of its organizational activism in 1877–78 but rapidly plummeted after Lang refused to run an independent campaign for governor. At the Grange's 1879 state meeting, its membership was down to around ninety-five hundred, a nearly 79 percent drop since 1877.[62] Regardless of the avowed business orientation of the Grange, there was a clear correlation between political activism in the organization and its membership numbers. Political activism, not its business orientation, drove up enrollment and motivated its members.

Other factors further hampered Grange membership. The Southwest experienced successive financial panics in 1878 and 1879, that left currency scarce and Grangers unable to pay their dues. Once the panics ended, membership did not return to prepanic levels. The Grange also faced competition from a rival farmer organization established during this time that grew into the largest political revolt since the Civil War.

In September 1877 a group of farmers pressed hard by economic difficulties gathered in Lampasas County, Texas, to discuss what could be done to alleviate their plight. The meeting signified the beginning of the Farmers' Alliance. Many attendees believed that governmental policies on land, transportation, and currency caused their troubles, and they desired independent political action. Democrats in the organization sharply disagreed, insisting on the need to reform the Democratic Party. Still others argued the Alliance should stay out of politics altogether and focus on education and economic cooperative endeavors. When an officer of the Lampasas Alliance suggested they convert their organization into a local Grange, A. P. Hungate, a local farmer and one of the Alliance founders, opposed the suggestion and criticized the self-help business approach of the Grange. The Grange, Hungate felt, "might discover secrets of nature as would enable them to grow one hundred ears of corn where they now harvest fifty nubbins. But what benefit would that be if while engaged in that achievement, their negligence as citizens had allowed laws to find place upon our statute books that would render the fine ears worth less than the nubbins.... We have undertaken the erection of a more commodious structure." All agreed, though, that something had to be done and, in the summer of 1878, plans were made to launch a statewide "Grand State Farmers' Alliance."[63]

With no unifying ideology, the Farmers' Alliance grew slowly. Even with some members wanting the Alliance to move into politics, the Grange at this point was at the height of its brief openly political period, leaving little differentiation between the two organizations. While farmers in both organizations debated how to achieve their political ends, a new party arrived in Texas—the Greenback Party.

Greenbackers organized nationally in a series of conventions from 1874 to 1876. In Greenbacker ideology, the country's economic woes were caused by a shortage of government-issued paper money because an act of Congress in 1875 required paper currency to be backed by specie. The shortage, they believed, deflated prices and raised interest rates. Greenbackers advocated the issuing of more currency and the remonetization of silver to back up an expanded currency.[64]

Running primarily on currency issues, the Greenback Party had limited appeal to the nation's workers and farmers. In the midst of the Great Railroad Strike of 1877, however, many workers saw the need for independent political action and looked to the Greenback Party. During the strike, workers, farmers, and small businessmen aided the strikers because of their shared hatred of the railroad trusts. The three groups came together politically through a series of mergers beginning in August 1877 in Pennsylvania, with the fusion of the Greenback Party with the United Labor Party. In states and cities across the country, Greenbackers merged with state-based labor party formations in a manner similar to that conducted in Pennsylvania. Events in Texas actually preceded this development. In the spring of 1877, the Greenback Party began organizing in Texas. They established a newspaper in Austin, the *Texas Capital*, and promoted a fusion with the Austin Workingmen's Club. Seeing that many workers were joining the Greenback Party, Adolph Douai urged socialists to join as well and go through the experience with them. The Socialist Labor Party crafted a coalition with the Greenbackers and, with support from the Knights of Labor, formed the Greenback Labor Party (GLP) in 1878.[65]

The 1877 Railroad Strike influenced growth of the GLP in Texas. As part of the national strike wave sparked by West Virginia railroad workers, Galveston's all-black dockworker force of the Morgan steamship line went on strike after their wages were cut from forty to thirty cents an hour on Friday morning, July 27. Joining them in solidarity on the docks were white members of the longshoremen's union. After an hour, management restored their wages. Buoyed by the result, workers—primarily black—held meetings over the weekend to discuss a general strike to begin on Monday, demanding $2 a day in pay. Work hours on the docks were frequently irregular, based on when ships docked or not. A $2 a day wage would give dockworkers a more reliable pay. At 6:30 a.m. Monday morning, black construction workers, "organizing themselves into a sort of vanguard to the general revolt that was desired by the laboring classes against the prevailing rates of wages," began urging nearby laborers "to cease work and join the strike," according to the *Galveston Daily News*.[66]

Forming a body of around fifty men, and first marching down the Strand, the city's business district, the strikers convinced additional workers to join them. The strikers, now in the hundreds, marched to worksites around town. At each site, their numbers grew. When they arrived at the Galveston Flour Mill, they decided that these workers should not be induced to strike because bread prices were already too high. In response to why they were striking, "the men asserted that they could not pay house rent, which in no case had been reduced, buy clothing, food, and medicines for themselves and families, at the rates they were receiving for their labor," reported the *Galveston Daily News*. After marching through town, strikers numbered more than eight hundred by the afternoon. They then marched to the courthouse and adopted a series of resolutions asserting their right to protest peacefully. They insisted that $2 per day become the fixed rate of labor for the city. At the courthouse, white labor leaders joined them and pledged that "the white laborers of the city would never back out of the movement" for the $2 day. After electing a leadership committee, the strikers adjourned and planned to meet the next morning.[67]

At the next meeting, the strikers decided their elected leadership committee should visit each struck worksite to demand a $2 day and report back on the meetings at the courthouse in the early evening. During the adjournment, a fight broke out on the docks between a white man and a black man. According to the *Galveston Daily News*, after the city police arrested the white man, a large group of black strikers attempted to storm the jailhouse to lynch the white assaulter. The black strikers asserted they were merely peacefully protesting. To disperse the crowd, police fired into the strikers, wounding a man in the leg, and arrested three others. When strikers gathered at the courthouse, they found that city employers agreed to raise their wages, either immediately or soon, to $2 a day. Seizing on this sea change, black washerwomen then went on strike and quickly won themselves a raise to $1.50 a day.[68]

Although victorious in their wage demands, the strikers were incensed about the police brutality they suffered. Many now wanted to turn their movement into one against police brutality. At this point, Norris Wright Cuney, a local black businessman and statewide leader of the Republican Party, addressed the crowd. Cuney felt the shooting incident was the result of strikers parading in the streets and stirring up bad blood. He urged them to return home and let the law determine what should be done with the officers who shot at the strikers. Then, in what many strikers must have taken as a threat transmitted from white authorities, Cuney said that if they continued protesting, "There were over 700 armed men—trained soldiers—in the city, who could annihilate them all in an hour; and if they could not, he said that in the city of Houston there were 1000 men under arms, who could be brought to this city in two hours to accomplish the bloody work."[69]

Cuney's remarks did not go over well with most of those gathered, and for many working-class blacks put the Republican Party in a foul light and opened them to the new GLP. At the same time, many working-class whites had grown tired of the Democratic Party's empty promises to reform oppressive railroad practices and the inability of the Grange to break from the Democratic Party. The GLP was positioned to gain support from dissatisfied workers and farmers, both black and white.

Among those deciding to support the Greenback movement was E. O. Meitzen. In 1875, after five years of apprentice blacksmithing, he opened a blacksmith shop of his own in Cistern, Fayette County. Blacksmithing was profitable enough that he and his siblings bought back their parent's old home and farm. The purchase lifted his father, Otto Meitzen, out of tenancy, and no other Meitzen would ever be in tenancy again. Their experience with tenancy, though, never left them. Many of Otto's children and grandchildren devoted their political careers to standing up for the rights of tenant farmers. Unfortunately, the elder Meitzens did not have much time together back on their old homestead. Jennie Meitzen passed away on March 17, 1877, in Biegel at the age of fifty-eight.[70]

Happier times returned for the Meitzens when E. O. married Johanna Kettner on October 21, 1877. Johanna was born on January 9, 1858, in the German city of Coswig, Saxony-Anhalt. Her father was a cabinetmaker, and her family settled in southeast Texas in 1871. Within two years of their marriage, E. O. and Johanna would have two children, Jennie, born August 17, 1878, who sadly died five days later, and Edward J., born August 7, 1879.[71]

After ten years of blacksmithing in 1880, E. O. received a spinal injury while "shoeing an unruly horse," forcing him to quit the trade. While recovering, he engaged in reading and study oft denied him as a young boy. He was known since childhood to have an avid desire for knowledge. He read whatever books, pamphlets, and newspapers he could obtain, but he was denied a regular formal education because of the disorganization and disruption of the area school system during the years of war and Reconstruction that marked his childhood. After his spinal injury, and in need of a lighter form of work, he studied to become a teacher.[72]

After passing his teacher's examination, Meitzen took a position to teach second grade at Novohrad in Lavaca County. As he later recalled about his examination, "In those days it was a very easy matter. It took me fifteen minutes to be examined. I was examined by a lawyer who did not care whether I taught school or not, or whether I knew anything or not." As Meitzen put it, this is when his own schooling began, and he "had a race keeping ahead of the boys who were right behind me." During this period, he and Johanna had two more boys, Ernest Richard, born May 3, 1881, and Arnold Charles, born December 30, 1882. Both Ernest and Arnold later joined their father as leaders of the Texas Socialist Party in the 1910s.[73]

As a new generation of Meitzens entered the world, the old was passing away. Otto lived most of his remaining days at his home in Biegel, until ill health forced him to live out his last months at E. O.'s home near Novohrad. Otto died at age seventy-one on April 22, 1882.[74] Otto had lived long enough to see that his 48er political radicalism had been passed on to E. O., whose support of the GLP began his own political evolution.

By November 1877, around fifty-nine Greenback clubs had appeared in Texas. In April 1878, the number of clubs reached 250, including some racially segregated black clubs. The first state convention of the Texas GLP met in Waco on August 8, 1878. Two hundred seventeen delegates from 482 Greenback clubs, including seventy affiliated black clubs, attended. When a white delegate refused to sit next to black delegates, he was expelled from the convention (but later readmitted). The Texas GLP marked the beginnings of an interracial workers' and farmers' coalition in Texas outside the Republican Party. The platform included calls for an increase in paper currency, the cessation of government bonds, abolition of the national bank, halting Asian immigration, ending convict labor, preventing state governments from giving land and special privileges to railroad companies, fighting government bureaucracy, establishing free public schools, and a graduated income tax. The platform demanded "cheap capital and well paid labor in place of dear capital and cheap labor." Among the candidates nominated for office was German Texan Jacob Kuechler for land commissioner. Kuechler, who immigrated to Texas in 1847 as part of the communistic Darmstadt colony, survived the Nueces Massacre and spent the rest of the Civil War in Mexico. He once held the position of land commissioner as a Republican during Reconstruction.[75]

The GLP appealed to and won support from the Republican Party. Former Radical Republican governor Edmund Davis gave his support to the GLP ticket, the regular Republican Party made no nominations of its own, and radicals in the party put their full support behind the GLP. A small conservative faction of the Republican Party, made up of bankers and holders of federal patronage positions, including Cuney, opposed the GLP and held a small convention to nominate a straight Republican ticket. At a meeting of a Galveston black workingmen's club, Cuney called for "colored people" to "support the grand old party against democrats, greenbackers and everybody else."[76]

Cuney's pleas did not have their intended effect. Black Greenbackers were active in areas from Waco to northeast Texas. Black support proved especially decisive in the Fifth US Congressional District, which included Galveston. In that district, the former Democratic leader of Bastrop County, George Washington Jones, ran a vigorous Greenback campaign among white and black voters alike. It was quite an evolution, or perhaps opportunism, on Jones's part. In 1868 he led a crowd at a Bastrop polling place to harass black voters. Jones barely lost an 1876 congressional run as an independent after breaking with Democrats over the party's failure to enact railroad reforms. As a Greenbacker, he defeated his Democratic challenger. Overall, the Democrats still dominated statewide elections, but Greenbackers elected two state senators and ten representatives from central and east Texas and won several local offices. A delegate to the 1879 national Union Greenback Labor Party convention reported that Texas had 658 clubs, third behind only Missouri and Illinois.[77]

The 1880 Texas GLP platform added planks in favor of "a radical change in our cumbersome and expensive judiciary system" and against a poll tax.[78] Included among the 140 delegates at the 1880 convention were twenty African Americans. The Texas Republican Party did field a ticket of its own, but radicals in the party continued to support the GLP. The GLP failed to win support from the state Grange, though a few east Texas Granges merged with Greenback clubs, furthering the Grange's rapid decline. As in 1878, the statewide election results brought defeats. The GLP's state house representation dropped from ten to three, and the senate seats went from two to one, from Caldwell County. Jones once again won, but only by approximately two hundred votes. Dallas, though, elected a Greenback mayor.[79]

Though in decline, the 1882 Texas GLP's platform distinguished itself from previous platforms by directly addressing the demands of the state's agrarian working class. The platform condemned the state government's practice of granting land to railroad companies and exempting them from taxes. In a reference to a move by the state government to give a Chicago firm a large section of the Texas Panhandle in return for constructing a new capital building, the platform accused the state government of establishing "gigantic land monopolies in our midst by granting to four Chicago capitalists 3,000,000 acres of public domain to build a state house." The platform further complained that the state government "has inaugurated a system of class legislation in favor of the rich by refusing to sell the public domain in tracts less than 640 acres, thus depriving her men of the opportunity to acquire homes in our State."[80]

The GLP convention supported Jones for governor, and he ran on an Independent-Greenback ticket. With support from the Chester Arthur administration, Texas Republicans once again formally threw support behind independent and Greenback campaigns, giving Jones the undivided support of black Republican leaders and many black Texans. Robert Zapp, a German Fayette County Republican, ran for Jones's old congressional seat on the Greenback ticket. The Democrats, to counter the growing popularity of GLP positions, ran former state supreme court justice John Ireland for governor. Ireland supported public schools, land sales only to actual settlers, state regulation of railroads, and the founding Greenback position of expanding the national currency. Though Jones made a much better showing than previous GLP gubernatorial races, the Democrats' appropriation of the GLP platform worked. Ireland won, and GLP candidates lost all other statewide offices.[81]

Although the Texas GLP continued to run candidates through 1884, none won election and the party quickly dissipated. Several factors contributed to its demise. First, outside forces such as the antimonopoly movement drew conservative elements out of the party by focusing on regulating business behavior. Second, the more radical working-class elements called for more direct trade-union action and opposed the GLP's anticommunism. Finally, by the early 1880s, there were free-silver wings in both the Democratic and the Republican parties. Silverites in the GLP now found it easier to return to the fold of the two major parties.[82]

Although some were discouraged by the demise of the GLP, many others, such as E. O. Meitzen, gained their first taste of independent political action and looked toward continued protest. In 1885 he joined the Grange at Colony, Fayette County, six miles from his home in Cistern. A change in occupation induced E. O.'s membership in the Grange. In 1883, after three years of teaching, he used some of the money he had saved while blacksmithing to buy land in Cistern to give farming a try. He was now learning firsthand the economic realities confronting farmers. The Farmers' Alliance had not yet reached Fayette County, so only the stagnant Grange offered area farmers an organization that stood for improving their economic conditions.[83]

Detached from romantic notions, farming is hard work. A general day on the farm in the late nineteenth century began before sunrise feeding stock and tending to horses. The day was occupied until after sunset with plowing, sowing, mowing, and harvesting, in addition to any repairs or building maintenance. Mild Texas winters meant the growing season never really ended: there was always another rotation of crops suited to the season.

Meitzen was not exempt from the economic crisis facing farmers, and nature did not make things easier. The 1884 planting season was particularly difficult;

in fact, the first planting did not take. After a second planting, a storm damaged the crop. While farming, Meitzen kept his teaching credentials up-to-date when the state enforced more stringent standards. He passed the new teaching examination and secured a teaching certificate for first grade. In September 1884, he took a job teaching first grade in Cistern to supplement the family income while farming. Hard work and two jobs were not enough to improve the economic plight of the Meitzens. The monetary investments required to keep the farm operational brought the family closer to debt. With an economic system clearly stacked against them, farmers like Meitzen continued to seek ways to address economic and political grievances.[84]

For many farmers who came to see collective political action as an essential strategy to obtain better economic conditions, the Grange's alleged nonpolitical stance became an obstacle. As A. J. Rose, master of the Texas State Grange, insisted in a message to Grangers across Texas, "The grange has not nor never will take a political stance, as a body." Many Grange leaders, however, belonged to the Democratic Party and encouraged their members to vote as such. Many farmers, though still not breaking from the Democratic "Party of Our Fathers," believed their voice should be heard collectively.[85]

For an example of collective action in 1885, Texas farmers needed to look no further than the Knights of Labor (KOL), which took on railroad tycoon Jay Gould's southwestern railroad network, including the Texas and Pacific line that crossed the entire state. The strike against Gould's southwestern system began in March when rail workers in Missouri struck over wage cuts and the firing of longtime employees. With solid community backing in Missouri, the strike rapidly spread into Texas. The KOL in Texas and the previously dormant Farmers' Alliance organized joint rallies, picnics, and mass meetings to support striking workers. When Gould backed down and strikers won, national membership in the KOL soared from one hundred thousand to seven hundred thousand the next year. In Texas, membership peaked at around twenty thousand members in 238 KOL local assemblies. A few of the locals in rural areas consisted primarily of farmers. In part because of its support of the KOL strike, farmers flocked to the revitalized Farmers' Alliance. Some held memberships in both organizations—including E. O. Meitzen.[86]

Before 1885, the cooperative marketing and purchasing plans of the Grange and the Alliance were nearly identical. Both promoted cooperative stores, but what differentiated the Alliance from the Grange in the years ahead was the Alliance's development of a movement ideology. This ideology was best expressed by S. O. Daws, hired by the state Alliance in late 1883 to fill the newly created position of traveling lecturer. Daws, thirty-six years old, was empowered to appoint suborganizers in every county. As a Mississippi farmer trapped in the crop-lien system before he moved to Texas, Daws developed a more radical ideology. In the spring of 1884, he traveled throughout Texas with a political-economic message denouncing furnishing merchants, railroads, trusts, and capitalists. At the end of each lecture, he implored farmers to join the Alliance.[87]

Deteriorating economic conditions helped to transform agrarian unrest into an organized protest movement. In 1886 cotton prices hit a new low at 8.1 cents per pound. Many farmers now were growing cotton at a loss. Corn prices were equally depressed. Radicalizing farmers no longer viewed the economic crisis as temporary but as more permanent unless something were done politically. To join a protest organization became a risk more were willing to take. Through traveling lecturers, Alliance newspapers, and the cooperative store plan, farmers increasingly saw the commonality of their plight. As historian Lawrence Goodwyn argued, they developed "a mass expression of a new political vision . . . a movement culture."[88]

The movement culture of the Farmers' Alliance in many ways grew out of the support shown by its members for striking railroad workers against Gould's system again in 1886. Although the Great Southwest Railroad Strike of 1886 divided the Alliance, it nudged more militant farmers in the direction of independent political action. In February 1886, Gould, still bitter over the defeat he had suffered at the hands of organized labor on the southwest railroad lines the year before, provoked a conflict by firing a union leader in Marshall, Texas. Gould incited the strike in order to defeat the KOL. In preparation, he had replacement workers ready and backing from the governor of Texas.

The firing of the union leader had the intended result. The KOL called a strike on March 1 that spread from Texas into Arkansas, Missouri, Kansas, and Illinois and involved two hundred thousand strikers. Members of the Farmers' Alliance again came to the aid of striking KOL members and organized rallies and boycotts of Gould lines. When strikers blocked rail traffic and occupied switch junctures, Gould used scabs to replace strikers and hired Pinkerton detectives to attack them violently. Democratic Texas governor Ireland aided Gould by using the state militia and Texas Rangers to suppress the strike and ensure its defeat. On May 4, 1886, Grand Master Workman of the national KOL, Terence Powderly, called off the strike.[89]

The defeat of the Southwest Strike of 1886 did not end farmer-labor coalitions in the South or the burgeoning movement culture. Brought together by the strike, Alliance members and KOL solidified the incipient farmer-labor alliance of the previous decades. While the strike was still underway, an Alliance-KOL coalition elected H. S. Broiles, a member of both organizations, as an independent mayor of Fort Worth in April 1886. KOL locals and individual Alliance members in Texas formed independent political coalitions. In July the Farmers' Alliance and KOL held a joint convention in Tarrant County that endorsed Dallas lawyer Jerome Kearby for the US House. Kearby, who had run unsuccessfully for Congress on the GLP ticket in 1880 and 1882, gained the support of the convention by providing legal defense to strikers in the 1886 Southwest Strike.[90]

In September 1886 delegates from twenty-eight Texas counties (mainly northern) formed the Antimonopoly Party, which focused on congressional and local elections. Though none of its candidates won, a few made respectable showings, including Kearby. A successful farmer-labor coalition did take shape in Comanche County, where the Human Party elected a full slate of county officials.[91] Though organized outside the Alliance, these coalitions were made up largely of Alliance members and were led by them, who gained valuable political experience. The question was no longer whether the Alliance would enter politics, but rather a matter of when and how.

The positions that individual Alliance members and local sub-Alliances took toward the Great Southwest Railroad Strike generated a political split in the Texas Farmers' Alliance. The Jeffersonian vision of Alliance farmers coalesced with the producerist philosophy of the KOL in a shared antimonopoly ideology. Like many Alliance members, Martin Irons, a leader of the Southwest Railroad Strike, belonged to the Grange because of its opposition to monopolies. In the view of antimonopolists, the single-minded drive for wealth by industrial magnates caused economic misery and gave elites a dangerous amount of political influence and control that threatened a democratic republic. The question of how to stop the growing economic and political monopoly of robber barons became a central point of division within the Alliance.[92]

Until now, the Alliance in Texas under the leadership of state president Andrew Dunlap put its efforts into the establishment of Alliance-run cooperative stores. The Alliance believed that cooperative stores might help to break the monopolistic control of large economic concerns without explicit class conflict. Dunlap and other leaders who pushed cooperative stores sought to avoid the violence that occurred in the 1886 Southwest Strike. They believed that cooperative stores with the help of additional reforms pushed through the Democratic Party would halt the growing conflict between labor and capital that portended a tearing asunder of the country.

Radical-minded Alliance members from their experiences in the 1886 Southwest Strike came to different conclusions about how to confront the rising unchecked power of monopoly capitalists. Rather than distance themselves from the KOL, they favored a deeper alliance with the KOL and other labor organizations for independent working-class political action. They viewed the use of the state militia and Texas Rangers by Democratic governor Ireland, as well as Pinkerton agents and the courts to suppress the strike, as evidence that the government was already in the hands of corporate interests. Radical Alliance members concluded that they could not redress their grievances through the Democratic Party.

William Lamb, the person with the most direct knowledge of the cooperative plan, helped lead the radical Alliance faction toward a partnership with labor and the KOL. As the state purchasing agent for the Alliance's cooperative stores, he witnessed firsthand the limited effect of cooperative stores. Like E. O. Meitzen, he joined the KOL as part of a political network of radical KOL and Alliance members that dated back to their previous memberships in the GLP and the Grange. Through the strike, Lamb and other Alliance radicals began to see their struggle as one between economic classes. Lamb spoke out against manufacturers who have "organized against us." He favored a national farmer-labor political coalition to transform the US political landscape. He and other farmer-labor radicals in Texas saw that farmers were no longer independent yeomen, but part of the working class instead.[93]

The Dunlap-Lamb conflict revealed a deep conflict between the liberalism of the Alliance's top officials and the more radical outlook of much of the rank and file. Dunlap feared that a coalition between the Alliance and KOL might invite attacks from the probusiness press and large farm owners and violate the nonpartisan image of the Alliance. Lamb, on the other hand, considered a farmer-labor political alliance vital to the vision of a cooperative commonwealth. Many rank-and-file Alliance members agreed with Lamb. They saw that the same corporate interests allied against them were allied against the KOL too. Because of this internal split, the newly revitalized Farmers' Alliance stood on the verge of collapse.[94]

In August 1886, when delegates gathered in Cleburne for the state Alliance's first official convention after the Southwest Railroad Strike, the movement stood deeply divided. Liberals led by Dunlap opposed Alliance involvement in independent politics, while the more radical elements led by Daws and Lamb represented the continuity of the Greenback critique of capital and the vision of a farmer-labor coalition. With elections approaching in the fall, radicals composed a platform that demanded "such legislation as shall secure to our people freedom from the onerous and shameful abuses that the industrial classes are now suffering at the hands of the arrogant and powerful corporations."[95]

The Cleburne demands, as the platform became known, incorporated much of the KOL's Reading platform of 1878. They called for the recognition of trade unions and cooperative stores, equal taxation of land, a ban on foreign ownership of land, ending convict labor, and wage protection for laborers. Not included in the Reading platform, but included at Cleburne were demands to create an Interstate Commerce Commission to regulate railroads, outlaw trading in futures of agricultural commodities, remove illegal fences, increase the money supply through coinage of both gold and silver, and to convene a national conference "to discuss such measures as may be of interest to all laboring classes." The platform was adopted by a vote of 92 to 75 after much debate and opposition from the Alliance's liberal elements.[96]

Although the Cleburne demands did not mention women's rights or suffrage, thousands of women joined women's auxiliaries of the Texas Alliance and in some locations made up as much as half the membership. One of the Alliance's ablest, most popular leaders was Bettie Munn Gay. Born in Alabama in 1836, she was very young when her family moved to Texas, eventually settling in Fayette County. She married Rufus King Gay in 1851, and they prospered on a large farm in Colorado County. After Rufus died in 1880, she successfully ran the farm herself. She advocated woman suffrage, a position not held by most Alliance members, male or female. Most men held patriarchal views on the proper role for women, and many Alliance women felt they should stay out of the dirty business of politics. Instead, they were attracted to the economic message of the Alliance. They felt an improvement in their economic conditions would free them from the drudgery and isolation of farmwork. Gay and other Alliance suffragists felt in her words that "the Alliance had come to redeem woman from her enslaved condition." Gay's long view of struggle placed her on the side of Alliance radicals. She later became a Populist and then a socialist.[97]

Into the schism between the Dunlap officialdom and Alliance radicals stepped Charles Macune, a thirty-five-year-old farmer, physician, Methodist preacher, newspaper editor, and lawyer. He impressed convention delegates with his oratorical skills and grasp of economic matters. He brokered a truce between the factions in which Dunlap remained president of the Alliance. To satisfy radicals, Macune advocated expansion of the Alliance by merging with progressive farm organizations in other states. When Dunlap resigned from the Alliance shortly after the Cleburne convention, Macune stepped into the organization's state presidency. The state Alliance switched its official newspaper from the more conservative Jacksboro *Rural Citizen* to the state's leading antimonopoly paper, the *Mercury* (soon to be called the *Southern Mercury*), in Dallas. Despite defections by Dunlap and other business-oriented elements, the positive response by farmers to the Cleburne demands resulted in spectacular growth. By year's end, the Alliance numbered more than two hundred thousand members.[98]

For Grange leaders who sought to maintain the relevance of their organization, the political activism of farmers in the KOL and Alliance was disconcerting. In July 1886 A. J. Rose traveled to La Grange to address the Fayette County Grangers' picnic. At the picnic, Rose warned "that neither politics nor religion could be tolerated in the order; that its membership embraced men of all political parties and religious denominations."[99]

The message did not sit well with E. O. Meitzen and other politically minded farmers and allies. Shortly afterward, Meitzen became a charter member of the local Farmers' Alliance in Cistern. As the Farmers' Alliance took root, seeking political as well as economic solutions to the plight of farmers, it drew farmers who left the Grange en masse. By 1887, the number of Grange members had fallen to five thousand. The organization was no longer a factor in Texas politics. In late October 1886, a Farmers' Alliance chapter was organized in Fayette County, and members elected Meitzen as secretary of the county chapter.[100]

Industrialization and the rise of finance capitalism rapidly transformed the US political and economic landscape. The agrarian crusaders of Meitzen's type were not the reactionary farmers searching for a "lost agrarian Eden."[101] They did not fear the new technological advances in communication and transportation. Instead, they believed such advances should be used to benefit the common good. They called for the nationalization of the railroad and telegraph industries. What Meitzen and other farmer-labor radicals were reacting to was no less than the crisis of US democracy in which a million dollars held more power than a million voters. By creating an agrarian protest movement to address their grievances, agrarian radicals were heirs to a tradition of protest dating back to the American Revolution.

In Texas, the influx of radical German 48ers greatly strengthened this tradition. From the 1854 San Antonio Convention to the Fayette and Bastrop County German conventions of 1873, German Texans laid much of the political and organizational foundations of agrarian-based farmer-labor radicalism in the state. Their opposition to slavery and political collaboration with black Texans during Reconstruction provided a precedent for interracial political cooperation that surfaced again in the Populist Revolt of the 1890s. When E. O. Meitzen was elected secretary of the Fayette County Farmers' Alliance, he assumed a position of leadership in the agrarian protest movement that derived directly from the political ideology of his 48er inheritance.

3   Populist Revolt

The Texas Farmers' Alliance brought farmers and their allies into a single large organization to address their economic grievances against monopolies, abusive railroad practices, high tariffs, and land speculation. Members of the Alliance were far from unified on what approach they should take to achieve their desired reforms. Many advocated working within the power structure of the Democratic Party, but others sought an independent farmer-labor movement and the creation of a new party to represent their interests. These political differences eventually tore the Alliance apart and resulted in the formation of the People's Party in the early 1890s. E. O. Meitzen, as a leader of the Alliance, was directly engaged in this struggle, evolving from an active member of the Democratic Party into a Populist insurgent.

When the Alliance met in convention in Waco in January 1887, members still carried with them the divisions of the previous convention. To bring together contending fractions, Charles Macune proposed a statewide Alliance Exchange to unite the Alliance around a problem most farmers faced, that of obtaining credit. It was hoped that the Exchange, by serving as the main purchasing and marketing agent of Alliance members' cotton crops, and by offering savings on farm equipment through buying in bulk, might free members from the crop-lien system. Macune saw the need to unite the entire Cotton Belt to confront the economic monopolies that controlled southern agriculture. The Texas Farmers' Alliance merged with the Louisiana Farmers Union and became the National Farmers Alliance and Cooperative Union. The merger appeased the radical-minded Alliance members who desired a national organization.[1]

Imbued with the spirit of Macune's cooperative vision, Meitzen and members of the Fayette County Alliance met in April 1887. At that time, the county had 750 Alliance members and 26 suballiances. The main educational tool of Alliance members was the cooperative that included the statewide Exchange, but also cooperative stores, warehouses, mills, and gins.² As secretary, Meitzen helped pass the Fayette County Alliance resolution, arguing that "the erection of factories at home, on the cooperative plan, to include the money and influence of every laboring white man, seems to us a sore necessity to relieve the southern cotton farmer from that financial pressure, with which he is struggling more and more every year."³

The cooperative plan gave the struggling white farmers of Fayette County concrete objectives to fight for. In the end, it also became the vehicle for Meitzen and others to learn the limits of cooperatives under capitalism. Unlike the Grange, however, which also called for cooperative enterprises, the Alliance did not shy from politics. At a July meeting, the Fayette County Alliance declared, "we believe that the only security the people have for their future welfare is the ballot box. We suggest that the ballot box be guarded by electing men to make our laws, whose interests is [sic] identical with ours."⁴

Armed with the ideas of cooperative producerism, Alliance lecturers spread across the South in 1887. By the fall, there were state Alliances in Louisiana, Missouri, Mississippi, Alabama, Georgia, the Indian Territory, and North Carolina. In December 1888, the National Agricultural Wheel of Arkansas and the Southern Farmers' Alliance began the process of consolidation, which resulted in the Farmers' and Laborer's Union of America.⁵

Not included in the expansion were African American farmers. Bowing to the racial power dynamics of the era, the original Cleburne convention determined that Alliance membership was open only to "a white person and over the age of sixteen." The Dallas convention in August 1888 reaffirmed the racial restriction. Barred from the white Alliance, African Americans founded their own Colored Farmers' National Alliance in Houston County, Texas, in 1886, after the Cleburne convention. As African Americans embraced the vision of a cooperative commonwealth, the Colored Alliance grew to perhaps one million members across the South by 1890.⁶

While the Farmers' Alliance spread across the South, E. O. and Johanna Meitzen made a move of their own. At a meeting of the Fayette County Alliance on October 7, 1887, E. O. handed in his resignation as secretary. He and Johanna had accepted teaching positions at Witting in neighboring Lavaca County. Though Meitzen later described his farming experiences as "wonderful," financial pressures had forced him out of farming the previous year. He found that he could make a better living solely from teaching. Johanna taught German, and E. O. taught general studies. After his resignation, the Fayette County Alliance elected his younger brother, Ernest August (E. A.), as the county's

Meitzen family, circa 1904. Top row (left to right): Benjamin Franklin (1884–1929), Edward J. (1879–1931), Ernest Richard (1881–1948), Arnold Charles (1882–1969). Bottom row: Richard Waldemar (1897–1963), Edward Otto (1855–1935), Frieda (1892–1975), Johanna (1858–1923), Martin Luther (1895–1972). Photo courtesy of Jo-Lou and Peter Gaupp.

new Alliance secretary. E. O. then joined the Alliance in Lavaca County, which became the base for his future Populist and socialist campaigns.[7]

This period of E. O.'s Alliance activism was a time of continual family growth, but the Meitzens' sixth child, Nora Johanna, "a beautiful, chubby little child . . . the idol of her mother and father," died of congestion at eighteen months in January 1889. Their seventh, Gerda, did not survive the day she was born on September 19, 1890. Their only daughter to make it into adulthood was Frieda Johanna, born on December 16, 1892. Like her older brothers, E. R. and Arnold, Frieda also engaged in socialist activism, though only briefly. After Frieda came Martin Luther Meitzen, born January 19, 1895. The name reflected the Meitzens' nominal Lutheran religious beliefs. (The Lutheran Church provided a sense of community for many German Texans.) The birth of their final and tenth child, Richard Waldemar, on June 3, 1897, was a trying experience for E. O., and a torturous one for Johanna. E. O. helped to deliver the baby feet first.[8]

When E. O. first moved to Lavaca County, he continued his reform-oriented activism within the Democratic Party while more radical elements of the Alliance served as traveling lecturers to establish Alliances across the South and plant the seeds of independent political action. In May 1888, E. O. was elected as a Lavaca County delegate to the Democratic State Convention in Fort Worth. While the Democrats met in Fort Worth, a separate nonpartisan convention of Laborers, Farmers, and Stockraisers convened in Waco with around 280 delegates from sixty-one counties "for the purpose of considering what steps, if any, should be taken in the approaching campaign." Alliance members were the majority at the convention, and Knights of Labor (KOL) members controlled much of the convention's proceedings. The convention adopted a platform with many recognizable Greenback demands, but it recessed without selecting candidates.[9]

Alliance members not only made up the majority of delegates at the Waco convention, but they also had a sizable showing at the Democratic convention in Fort Worth. In fact, non-Alliance Democrats feared an Alliance takeover of the party.[10] In part to placate the large number of Alliance members and to hold the loyalty of farmers, the Democratic convention passed a resolution emphasizing "that we condemn the pools and trust combinations of financial power which are now organized and on a gigantic scale threaten with ruin every legitimate industry involved by them, and we commend the efforts being made in congress to expose and correct them."[11]

With sections of the Farmers' Alliance engaged in separate political activity, the Alliance faced the larger problem of a faltering state Exchange. The Exchange was to be funded by a $2 assessment fee from each of the Alliance's two hundred thousand members in Texas. By April 1888, however, the Exchange had ordered goods totaling $108,371 yet had collected only $20,215 in fees. Unable to secure loans from banks hostile to the Alliance, the Exchange stood on the verge of collapse as bills came due in May for the goods ordered. To address the problem, the state Alliance Executive Committee issued a call for courthouse rallies to gather support and funds for the Exchange on June 9. Rallies numbered in size from a few hundred to a thousand. Both Fayette and Lavaca counties had well-attended and successful rallies.[12]

Though the courthouse rallies gave the Alliance another powerful dose of "movement culture," the Exchange could not be saved. Many poor farmers, trapped in the crop-lien system, simply could not afford the $2 assessment. Others, who might have contributed at one time, were tapped dry by previous contributions to the Alliance's numerous other cooperative ventures. Once again, a cooperative venture within a corporate capitalist system failed to alleviate the dire plight of southern farmers.[13]

The failure of the state Exchange exacerbated political divisions in the Alliance. A second convention of Laborers, Farmers, and Stockraisers met in Fort Worth on July 3, 1888, a few days before the Texas Union Labor Party (ULP) met in the same city. Former Greenbackers, along with members of the KOL and Farmers' Alliance, founded the ULP at a convention in Cincinnati in February 1887 to bring together farmers and industrial workers, both black and white, for their political and economic rights. The Laborers, Farmers, and Stockraisers convention, chaired by William Lamb, adopted a platform similar to their May platform but this time nominated candidates for office. Texas Farmers' Alliance president, Evan Jones, received but turned down the nomination for governor. Although he was an advocate of independent political action, he feared that his candidacy would further fracture the Alliance. The ULP adopted the candidates nominated by the Laborers, Farmers, and Stockraisers, which included Prohibition Party candidate for governor, Marion Martin, who supported railroad regulation. The Texas ULP endorsed the national ULP ticket and platform, except for the woman-suffrage plank. The Texas Republican Party also put its support behind the Texas ULP.[14]

With third-party advocates campaigning for the ULP, Meitzen and many Alliance members sustained their attempts to reform the Democratic Party. Meitzen continued his rise through the ranks of the Alliance and the Democratic Party in Lavaca County. At a meeting of the Lavaca County Alliance attended by a thousand people in July 1888, he was elected secretary, the same position he once held in the Fayette County Alliance. Meitzen also served as the Democratic Party's precinct chairman in Witting and as delegate to the party's senatorial convention in Gonzales.[15]

The faltering of the state Exchange on the eve of the Farmers' Alliance's state convention in Dallas in August 1888 brought into question the viability of the cooperative economic enterprises fostered by Macune. With the Alliance's official newspaper, the *Southern Mercury,* leading the criticism of the Exchange, local alliances reported significant losses in membership. Some even questioned the future existence of the Alliance. Convention delegates, however, proved loyal to Macune and pledged to continue their commitment to the cooperative vision. Meitzen, elected to the board of directors of the Alliance store in the Lavaca county seat of Hallettsville shortly before he left for the convention,[16] insisted to delegates, "The few weak-kneed brothers and outsiders who imagined the Alliance is about 'ausgespielt' were never worse mistaken in their lives."[17]

As Lavaca's white farmers reaffirmed their commitment to cooperative principles, its black farmers mobilized. On August 4, 1888, African Americans organized the Lavaca County Colored Alliance in Hallettsville, joining the struggle for the same economic goals as their white Alliance neighbors. At times, the two alliances acted together and at others separately. The formation of the Colored Alliance held out hope of biracial political cooperation but invited repression from those committed to maintaining white supremacy. The November 1888 election returns in Lavaca County and across the state produced sweeping victories for the Democratic Party. Nevertheless, Martin, the insurgent ULP candidate for governor, received more than 28 percent of the statewide vote. Though not achieving electoral success, the respectable ULP vote showed Democrats that going forward they would need to field candidates that at least gave lip-service to working-class–based reforms.[18]

The problems plaguing cooperatives in 1888 taught Texas Alliance members valuable lessons and raised their political consciousness. Radical greenback doctrines, which had shaped the dominant ideology of the agrarian movement, now mixed with the crusade for cooperatives. If cooperatives were to survive, farmers needed control over the federal government to change the monetary system.[19] The question now stood whether Alliance members would take the reform path of Macune or the third-party path of Lamb.

Though the Hallettsville cooperative Alliance store was reportedly doing well, other nearby Alliance stores were not. By March 1889, the stores at La Grange and Schulenburg failed. The Alliance encouraged members to buy stock in the Hallettsville store to keep it afloat, but as one Alliance member noted, "One of the greatest hindrances to the Alliance is the individual indebtedness of the membership." Poor, debt-ridden farmers simply could not afford to buy stock in the Alliance's various financial schemes. In 1890 Meitzen moved his family to Hallettsville to run the Alliance store as a full-time job.[20]

As the Alliance's financial conditions worsened, its overall membership numbers declined. The economic plight of poor farmers had improved little, and the agrarian revolt led by the Alliance lost momentum through the winter and into the spring of 1889. Cash-poor, debt-ridden farmers trapped in the crop-lien system could not compete with the financial power of merchants, bankers, and the robber barons of corporate America. Recognizing the failure of its economic strategies, the Alliance entered electoral politics.

Heading into its St. Louis convention in December 1889, the Alliance sought greater numerical growth in order to expand its reach into politics. At the convention, activists sought a merger with the northern Alliance, KOL, and Farmers' Mutual Benefit Association—an organization akin to the Alliance in Illinois and neighboring states. Although a national merger of all participating organizations did not result from this convention, the stout Kansas and North and South Dakota Alliances joined the southern Alliance to form the National Farmers' Alliance and Industrial Union (NFA&IU). The Alliance chose as president former Confederate officer Leonidas L. Polk, of North Carolina, a leading advocate of sectional reconciliation.[21]

The most significant development coming out of the St. Louis convention was a broad agreement on the need to engage in politics. The convention adopted a seven-point platform containing many familiar Greenback demands dating back to the 1870s. Two new demands called for the nationalization of railroads and enactment of Macune's subtreasury plan. The subtreasury plan called for the federal government to establish a system of warehouses in agricultural areas of the country. The warehouses, or subtreasuries, would allow farmers to store their nonperishable crops until market conditions became favorable to sell. In the meantime, the federal government would provide low-interest loans with the crops as collateral to help farmers get by until the crops sold. Alliance members, particularly in the South, responded to the plan with great enthusiasm as a way to democratize the marketplace.[22]

The campaign to enact the subtreasury plan mobilized the Alliance into politics, first through the Democratic Party and then by creating a new party.[23] Before the subtreasury plan, serious efforts were already underway to establish a new party. What the subtreasury plan and the failed efforts to achieve its enactment did was to educate farmers on the ineffectiveness of working within the two-party system to improve their economic conditions. The educational experience of the subtreasury campaign created the critical mass necessary for a new party to emerge as a viable alternative to the twin parties of big capital.

The campaign to get reform Democrats behind the St. Louis platform politicized the Farmers' Alliance and demonstrated that Texas farmers were an important political force. The "Alliance yardstick" of how many Alliance planks a candidate supported served as the determining factor in whether Democratic candidates measured up to receive support in the 1890 election. By fall 1889, Alliance Democrats began to promote Texas attorney general James Stephen Hogg as a candidate for governor. The *Southern Mercury* proclaimed, "The people have long regarded him [Hogg] as a friend and fearless advocate of their rights."[24]

Hogg earned his reputation by advocating antimonopoly policies in Texas, particularly against railroads. Hogg's antimonopoly politics were not entirely, however, based on progressive reform, but also financial self-interest. After the discovery of oil at Spindletop in 1901, the antimonopoly legislation pushed by Hogg allowed his Hogg-Swayne Syndicate and other Texas oil interests to challenge Standard Oil's monopoly through the creation of the Texas Company (Texaco) in 1902. The directors of the Texas Company included much of the state's economic and political elite, including Hogg, Colonel Edward House, three former Texas governors, and lumber baron John Henry Kirby, among others. William Jennings Bryan participated in the company's land speculation in the Rio Grande Valley. The discovery of large oil fields made Texas an emerging economic and political powerhouse with interests stretching from New York to Mexico.[25]

Hogg received Alliance support, despite his clear opposition to the subtreasury plan. Alliance leaders reconciled themselves to Hogg by touting Hogg's support for a state commission that would regulate railroad corporations in Texas.

Though Alliance leaders abandoned the yardstick principle, many rank-and-file Alliance members did not, demanding at least that their candidates support the subtreasury plan. While the subtreasury held the possibility of economic improvement for tenant and small landowning farmers, it threatened powerful bankers, agricultural commodity speculators, and profiteers of the crop-lien system of finance.[26]

As a result of these struggles, Meitzen underwent a transformation from a local Democratic Party leader to a statewide leader of the emerging Populist movement. He was elected as a delegate from Lavaca County to the Democratic convention in San Antonio in August 1890. He and other Alliance Democrats meant to make their presence felt at the convention. Regular Democrats, however, viewed them as extremists and prevented the subtreasury plan from being included in the party's platform. Meitzen, "disgusted with the drunken antics of the Donk [Democratic Party]" at the convention, headed back to Lavaca County as a disgruntled Democrat and die-hard advocate of the subtreasury plan.[27] The *Mercury*, though, campaigned hard for Hogg, using the railroad commission issue as "a symbol of the struggle of the people to control the increasingly powerful corporations." Hogg easily won the governorship.[28]

Immediately after the Texas Democratic Party rejected the subtreasury plan, Alliance leader and long-time third-party advocate Lamb began an extensive campaign to educate Texas farmers on the subtreasury plan. For Lamb, the subtreasury issue became a tool to make a clear distinction between the Democrats and a prospective new party that would advance programs to help farmers. Through the subtreasury educational campaign, Lamb and other radicals sought to transform the NFA&IU into a new party.[29]

In December 1890, when the national Alliance met in Ocala, Florida, representatives of the Colored Alliance and KOL also attended. Both these organizations, as well as western Alliance members, were now firmly behind the push for independent political action and creation of a new political party. The battle for a new party would be fought in the South, however, where Alliance members remained hesitant to launch a national people's party. Macune put forth a compromise from the southern Alliance by proposing a conference of industrial farmer and labor organizations to meet in February 1892 to revisit the issue of whether to create a new party. The Ocala convention adopted a platform similar to previous conventions and endorsed the subtreasury plan, which had become a third-party issue. The question now was clear. Would southern Alliance members remain true to the subtreasury plan or to the party of their fathers?[30]

The subtreasury plan was more than a mere economic plan. It represented something greater in the minds of Texas farmers. For farmers in a rapidly industrializing country increasingly controlled by corporations, the subtreasury plan held out hope for a more democratic economy. The cooperative crusade allowed farmers to envision a future free from the chains of the crop-lien system and of furnishing merchants. The Democratic Party, the self-styled "party of the people," was proving to many farmers to be the party of big business.[31]

In Texas Hogg angered many Alliance members by making members of the railroad commission appointed rather than elected. He further alienated them when he refused to appoint an Alliance member to the commission, but a couple of his actions kept many farmers in the Democratic camp. The railroad commission did lower shipping rates within the state for grain, meal, flour, and cotton, and Hogg approved an antialien land bill to prohibit foreign nationals from acquiring land titles in Texas. He also made a promise to bar land corporations in Texas in the future.[32]

For Meitzen and other Alliance members, Hogg's actions were not enough. They demanded complete adherence to the Alliance platforms adopted at St. Louis and Ocala. To win converts to the subtreasury plan, the Alliance continued its extensive educational campaign across the state. Alliance lecturers spoke at encampment meetings that resembled religious revivals and numbered into the thousands at times. The encampments became a hallmark of the insurgent agrarian movement in Texas that continued through its Populist and later socialist phases.[33]

In 1891 the Texas Alliance split into pro- and anti-Hogg factions. The split led to formation of the People's Party in Texas in August 1891. From this factional struggle, Meitzen, who distinguished himself as a capable defender of the subtreasury plan, rose from the ranks to become a statewide subtreasury leader. In April Meitzen engaged in an extensive debate in the *Hallettsville Herald* over the principles of the subtreasury plan. By September his defense of the plan appeared in the *Galveston Daily News*, a major statewide daily of the time.[34]

The split within the Alliance took a dramatic turn on March 4, 1891, when Alliance friends of Governor Hogg issued the Austin Manifesto. The manifesto denounced the Alliance's legislative committee, complaining that it was taking the Alliance into politics and toward a union with the growing third-party movement. From this point forward, the Alliance's two wings were in open antagonism, neither side willing to compromise.[35] At the April meeting of the Lavaca County Alliance, resolutions were passed denouncing the Austin Manifesto and endorsing the Ocala platform. Though denouncing the Austin Manifesto, the county Alliance had yet to take the third-party path. After the county meeting, the *Hallettsville Herald* interviewed "a number of well-informed" Alliance members and reported that "The *Herald* has not found a general third party sentiment in this section. The opinion rather obtains that the best policy is to effect their purposes by influencing the present political organizations. But the order is essentially political."[36]

Although Lavaca County Alliance members thought it best to work within the Democratic Party, the party's actions caused them to rethink their loyalty.

For example, Hogg proposed that surplus money from public land sales be lent to railroad corporations rather than placed in a public school fund. Former US president Grover Cleveland, the party's likely candidate for president again in 1892, came out against the subtreasury plan and free coinage of silver. These actions led a Lavaca County Alliance member to ask, "What is the Democratic party that we are required to sacrifice everything on its altar? ... We feel our hearts going out to our brethren of the north, and the hold the Democratic party had upon us begins to slip."[37]

The Ocala conference had compromised on the question of a third party by deciding to hold a conference on the issue in February 1892. Third-party activists, though, acted on their own and called for all reform organizations to meet in Cincinnati in May 1891 to form a new national party. The Cincinnati conference adopted a familiar Alliance platform, elected a national executive committee, and adopted "People's Party" as the name of the new party. The Cincinnati conference received prominent coverage in newspapers across Texas, including Hallettsville.[38]

Animated by Texas workers' and farmers' enthusiastic response to the creation of the People's Party in Cincinnati, Lamb called for a founding convention in Texas to take place in Dallas on August 17, 1891. Lamb, elected to the National Executive Committee of the party in Cincinnati, issued the convention call in person at a meeting of the Texas State Federation of Labor in July. That Lamb made such a call at a meeting of the Texas State Federation of Labor shows the continued alliance of workers and farmers after the Southwest Strike of 1886. The People's Party convention met as planned, elected a state executive committee of seventeen (including two African Americans), and selected a platform committee.[39]

The subtreasury schism in the Democratic Party soon reached cataclysmic proportions. The split propelled subtreasury Democrats such as Meitzen into the People's Party. In late October, N. W. Finley, chairman of the Texas Democratic Party, issued a letter in which he argued that because the state convention of 1890 rejected the subtreasury plan, Alliance Democrats should be barred from Democratic primaries. Finley's ukase enraged Alliance members, who now faced an ultimatum: either resign from the Alliance or quit the Democratic Party. In response, prominent Alliance members met in secret in Dallas on November 14, 1891. Meitzen, now a recognized subtreasury leader, attended, along with state Alliance president Jones and other state leaders.[40] Upon returning to Hallettsville, Meitzen denounced Finley's threat: "We do not propose to be read out of the Democratic party by the dictum of one man. We are Democrats and Mr. Finley's letter cannot change the fact."[41]

On November 24, the Alliance leaders who met in Dallas issued the Subtreasury Manifesto, which asserted their rights as "freemen having full possession of and control over [their] own conscience." Calling themselves "true and loyal democrats," they proclaimed,

> We believe in common with the great mass of laborers and producers, that during the past thirty years, if not ever since its formation, our federal government has been administered in the interest of capital, to the prejudice of labor. The tillers of the soil, the producers and property owners generally, and all other values, have submitted for many years to systematic robbery by the government, for the enrichment of capitalistic classes. . . . [T]o the details of the subtreasury plan we are not wedded . . . but upon the principles of the subtreasury plan we remain inflexible . . . without taking the advice of some 'boss.'[42]

As the People's Party of Texas organized for its coming convention in February 1892, Meitzen and Subtreasury Democrats held a conference on February 10 in Dallas. The two hundred delegates in attendance, who constituted themselves as Jeffersonian Democrats, elected an executive committee that included Meitzen and adopted a set of principles. The principles embraced the Ocala platform and included the by-now characteristic demands about land, transportation, and finance. The conference ended by calling for the creation of Democratic clubs to carry out the demands. Asked to comment on the Dallas conference, Lamb, as chairman of the People's Party of Texas, retorted, "I expect no reform under neither of the old parties."[43]

During the year since the Ocala conference called for a national labor conference to discuss a third party, the NFA&IU expanded into thirty-six states with well over a million members. When the third-party conference convened on February 23 in St. Louis, Alliance members far outnumbered representatives of other organizations, including the KOL and the Colored Alliance. After a rowdy gathering, during which opponents of a new party failed to derail the movement, the conference urged citizens who supported a new party to organize public meetings to ratify demands and elect delegates to a national People's Party nominating convention in Omaha on July 4.[44]

After the St. Louis conference, the *Hallettsville Herald* reported, "Mr. Meitzen while he questioned the wisdom of the action taken at St. Louis, yet said very emphatically that a decision meant a third party in Texas, and that in due time county and minor organizations would be formed wherever the Alliance had a membership sufficient to justify it."[45] Meitzen was reluctant to abandon the Democratic Party, but the Alliance came first. If furthering the work of the Alliance now meant leaving the Democratic Party, he was ready to take that step. On March 11, 1892, he and eleven other Alliance members in Lavaca County issued a call "To every lover of our country residing in Lavaca county irrespective of former political affiliation" to join them at a meeting in Hallettsville to organize the People's Party in the county. Their appeal drew on the heritage of the American Revolution: "Bear in mind the noble ancestry from whom we descend. Follow the example set you by the patriots of 1776."[46]

With five hundred fellow residents, most of them farmers, gathered before him, Meitzen ascended a platform in front of the Hallettsville courthouse on March 26, 1892. Gripped in his hand was a copy of the St. Louis platform. Loosening the paper in his hand, Meitzen, full of determination, read aloud the platform denouncing monopolies, calling for direct democracy, land reform, the abolition of the national bank system, and the nationalization of transportation. After finishing, Meitzen read the platform again, this time in German. Then someone else read the platform in Bohemian. Upon completion, a show of hands was called for to approve the platform. The assembled crowd, as the *Hallettsville Herald* observed, "crossed the dead line that separated them from the party of their fathers and of their youth and manhood without regret, and with the enthusiasm of new converts some even administered a parting kick at its intangible corpus." In this manner, the People's Party of Lavaca County was formed. The mass meeting elected Meitzen as chairman. Meitzen accepted the honor and acknowledged that it would be "no soft job." Recognizing the large number of African Americans present, Meitzen suggested they choose chairmen of their own to represent the county's black population. The meeting approved Meitzen's proposal, and African American sections of the People's Party were organized in eight communities of Lavaca County. The meeting then selected the remaining officers and an executive committee to represent communities in the county. Elected to represent the town of Shiner was E. O.'s younger brother, Ernst August. The eldest Meitzen brother, Herman John, became a leader of the People's Party in Fayette County.[47]

The final act in leading Subtreasury Democrats into the People's Party came on April 11, 1892, in Dallas. There, in the Farmers' Alliance building, as the *Dallas Morning News* related, was "found a new infant, perhaps a giant at that. The child is the result of the marriage of the people's party and Jeffersonian democracy." Seven representatives each from the People's Party and the Jeffersonian Democrats met and merged their organizations into the People's Party to present "a solid front in the name of the farmers and laborers of the state." A convention on June 24 was called for in Dallas to create a permanent state organization and choose candidates for state offices.[48] The Farmers' Alliance, though it maintained independence as a separate organization, became an appendage of the People's Party.

Meitzen set about the task of organizing the People's Party in a series of speaking tours across the region that did not let up until the November election. The Hallettsville People's Party sent fourteen whites and seven African Americans to the upcoming Lavaca County convention. The new party spread into neighboring Gonzales, Colorado, and Fayette Counties and nearby Brazoria County.[49]

The Democratic Party, initially caught off guard by the emergence of the People's Party, quickly regrouped and went on the attack. The area point man for Lavaca County Democrats was state representative J. W. Kirk. After the call for the first People's Party convention in Lavaca County, Kirk called for Democratic unity, emphasizing that nine-tenths of the Alliance men were opposed to a third party. He vowed that Democrats would take on Standard Oil and other trusts. Meitzen responded in the *Hallettsville Herald* by noting the Democratic Party's failure to respond to the repeated reform demands of labor organizations. He pointed out its culpability in the rise of trusts and monopolies. "Therefore," Meitzen wrote, "I say cut loose from both old parties, drop our prejudice, let's come to the conclusion at last that the war is over, and let all who favor a government of, for and by the people, and not by and for political bosses and wirepullers, unite in one common cause." Meitzen further noted that if, as Kirk claimed, true Alliance men were opposed to a third party, then Kirk must be the only true Alliance man in the county.[50]

One of the main Democratic tactics was to attack Populists' loyalty to the South. The Democratic Party in the South was firmly associated with the "bloody shirt" of the Confederacy. Some felt it intolerable to those who came home maimed from the Civil War that Meitzen, "with his never tiring lungs," routinely called Democrats "bushwhackers," "grand rascals," and their party "a rotten old party."[51] Meitzen responded by pointing out that at the national People's Party convention, "200 old rebel soldier delegates and the 200 Yankee delegates met and shook hands across the bloody chasm and by a strong resolution buried that dirty old rag, 'the bloody shirt,' together with the hate and prejudice engendered during the war."[52]

After three months of relentless organizing in Texas, the People's Party state convention convened in Dallas on June 23, 1892. Lavaca County sent Meitzen and four other delegates, including Ben Bailey—an African American from Hallettsville. At the convention, the nearly eight hundred delegates approved the St. Louis platform and an additional state platform. The Texas People's Party platform was the synthesis of nearly four decades of farmer-labor insurgency in the state. The platform made the usual demands about land ownership and government ownership of railroads. To reach out to the state's laborers, the platform included demands for the eight-hour day, establishment of a state bureau of labor, and the end of convict labor. The platform included demands for an effective system of public schools, free textbooks in the public schools, and use of the Australian (or secret) ballot in elections. After adopting what the *Dallas Morning News* called "anti-corporation ideas," the convention nominated Thomas L. Nugent, a Christian socialist district judge from Stephenville, for governor and Marion Martin for lieutenant governor.[53]

Almost two weeks later, the national People's Party convention met from July 2 to July 4 in Omaha. The convention adopted a platform similar to the one approved in Texas, with a few notable additions. At the top of the platform was a demand for free and unlimited coinage of silver and gold at the ratio of 16 to 1 and for an increase in the amount of circulating currency. The rationale behind these demands was that an increase in money supply would result in higher prices for agricultural products, thus benefiting farmers. The platform also called for a graduated income tax and nationalization of the telegraph and telephone industries. Bowing to pressure from southern Populists, woman suffrage, though supported by many western and northern Populists, was not included.[54]

In choosing national candidates, the fledgling People's Party faced a more difficult challenge. NFA&IU president, Polk, the consensus choice as the party's presidential candidate before the convention, had died on June 11. Lacking a clear candidate, the party nominated the old Greenback warhorse and Union general from Iowa, James Weaver, for president. The party nominated ex-Confederate general James Field, of Virginia, for vice president to balance the ticket. The selection of a former Union general for president led to more bloody shirt waving across the South, even though a Confederate general was his running mate.[55]

While the national convention met, Meitzen continued his vigorous speaking tour around central and east Texas promoting the People's Party. By the end of July, he had spread the word of Populism across the counties of Colorado, Austin, Fort Bend, Wharton, and Brazoria. An account of the Colorado County People's Party convention described Meitzen as "perhaps the best political economist in the state." In August he was nominated as the party's candidate for US Congress in the tenth district stretching from Hallettsville to Galveston.[56]

The new party attracted a limited number of African Americans, as indicated by their presence at the local founding meeting in Lavaca County and at the state convention in Dallas. At the largely symbolic People's Party primary election on August 27 in Hallettsville, one-half of the one hundred votes cast came from African Americans. Populism at this stage did not, however, attract enough African Americans to constitute a wholesale break from the Republican Party. For example, a report indicated that after much effort in Wharton County to win African Americans over to the third party, Populists failed to make much progress. Many African Americans still held a deeply rooted loyalty to the party of Abraham Lincoln. Also, some African Americans supported Hogg because of statements he made condemning lynching. This in effect split the African American vote three ways in the 1892 election.[57]

Tejanos and Mexican Americans, centered in San Antonio and the southern borderlands, proved more problematic for Populists. Tejano elites and large ranch owners in the Democratic Party wielded enormous power and influence over their Mexican American employees at the ballot box. At times in the past, the Democratic party in south Texas brought thousands of Mexicans across the border to cast fraudulent votes in the United States. These votes often proved decisive for Democrats in defeating insurgent third-party campaigns at the state level. The Greenback Labor Party, KOL, and Farmers' Alliance gained little support near the border. An all-Mexican Populist club formed in Yoakum, a town that straddles the border of Lavaca and DeWitt Counties, and Populists carried many counties southeast of San Antonio in 1892 and 1894 after a few Tejano leaders in the area joined the Populist movement.[58]

Populists also put considerable time into recruiting wage laborers. Meitzen traveled specifically to Galveston to court the labor vote. As the major port along the Texas coast, a large number of rail and dockworkers worked in Galveston.[59] On September 4, 1892, the *Galveston Daily News* reported, "Meitzen is known throughout the Tenth as the 'learned blacksmith.'" Meitzen, describing his campaign, noted:

> I . . . have spoken wherever I could find a crowd to listen, and have talked with whomever [*sic*] would argue with me. . . . If I drove by a store and saw five or six or more men there I would jump out and talk with them and explain the People's party teachings. Then I would leave them a lot of circulars and would drive away, having made several converts. This I did on every occasion. If I met a man in a crowd of Democrats who wanted to discuss the political problems with me I always discussed with him—on the corner or anywhere else—and so I made converts among the listeners if I did not convert my opponent. . . . We are making a good fight, and we are the only party representing organized labor.[60]

Meitzen's Galveston campaign trip coincided with the state's second Labor Day celebration. He rode in a Farmers' Alliance–sponsored carriage behind a contingent of KOL organized bakers. After the parade, Meitzen and Nugent and area labor leaders addressed a crowd of three thousand made up of labor organizations and area Alliance members.[61]

By September 1892 the Texas People's Party had 113,000 members and 2,800 clubs.[62] The Populist campaign in Lavaca County concluded with a three-day encampment in Weimar's Pleasure Park at the end of October. Speakers included Nugent, "Cyclone" Davis, Meitzen, Ben Terrell, Bettie Munn Gay, and "Stump" Ashby. The encampment also included refreshments, music, and balls each night with "dancing to entertain those that are fond of the 'light fantastic.'"[63]

Although the encampment appears to have been a success, the local *Hallettsville Herald* gave the event little coverage. As long as the local Alliance was firmly rooted in the Democratic Party, the *Herald* gave prominent coverage to Alliance happenings. Once the Alliance went further down the third-party route, however, the pro-Hogg bias of the *Herald* tainted its reporting on the party. A lack of newspaper coverage was not the only handicap faced by the Populists. In Comanche, a mob of Hogg supporters destroyed the printing office of Populist newspaper editor Thomas Gaines. The mob then moved to his home. After they tried but failed to burn it, they smashed the windows with his family inside. Meitzen experienced the wrath of Hogg supporters on another trip to Galveston in November before the election. As Meitzen attempted a street-corner speech, a group of Hogg men surrounded him and prevented him from speaking.[64]

The People's Party faced a difficult task in challenging the Hogg machine. Hogg realized the large role Alliance support played in propelling him to the governorship in 1890. As a result, his 1892 platform was designed to win possible third-party converts. The platform included Populist demands of free silver, a graduated income tax, abolition of the national banking system, and maintaining the railroad commission. But the platform specifically denounced the subtreasury plan and government ownership of communication and transportation.

For some old-guard Democrats, the Hogg platform conceded too much to reform demands and stood in direct conflict with the national platform, particularly on free silver. In opposition to Hogg, a Democratic faction split from the state convention and nominated George Clark for governor. The Republican Party, not wanting to enter an already crowded race, endorsed Clark.[65]

The November election registered impressive gains for the new party but not enough to stop Meitzen from being soundly defeated in a three-way race for Congress with the old parties. In the nine-county district, Meitzen received 4,297 votes, Democratic railroad executive Walter Gresham 13,017, and Republican A. J. Rosenthal 9,453. However, Meitzen did win a plurality in Gonzales County, which had a high farm tenancy rate of more than 41 percent. He finished second in his own Lavaca County but did poorly in the remaining counties, including Galveston. Rosenthal won Colorado County with its strong black Republican vote that dated back to Reconstruction.[66]

Hogg won the gubernatorial race with 43.7 percent of the statewide vote. Clark finished second with 30.6 percent, and Nugent came in third with 24.9 percent, representing 108,483 votes. Many workers and farmers remained loyal to the party of their fathers, fearing the consequences of an openly procorporate Clark victory. The urban areas with larger concentrations of wage laborers all went with Hogg. Texas workers and farmers gave Hogg another chance to back his Populist-sounding rhetoric with action. The Populists did elect a member to the state senate and 8 of the state house's 128 representatives.[67]

The Texas People's Party executive committee met at the end of November with an air of optimism. They took heart that one of every four voters in Texas went Populist—a good number for a party in its first election. The committee made accusations of voter fraud by claiming "that every sinister and corrupt expedient known to practical politics was resorted to to break our ranks and the fidelity of our people, and that in certain localities many of our votes were not counted." They also pointed to the specter of the force bill that loomed over the election. The bill, pushed by northern Republicans calling for federal marshals to enforce black voting rights, may have helped to keep many voters in the Democratic camp by conjuring up images of federal troops returning to the South.[68]

After the election, Meitzen accepted an appointment as assistant state lecturer for the Alliance. The Lavaca County Alliance, realizing the large amount of time he would spend as a state lecturer, closed the county Mercantile Co-op that he managed for the past two years. Meitzen spent much of 1893 on the road, lecturing in German and English on the topic of hard times and the way out.[69]

Education stood at the center of Populist campaigning. At the start of the new year, the Texas People's Party made an effort to establish statewide party organs to educate the public on the party's platform before the next election. In 1894 the *Southern Mercury*, the main organ of the state Farmers' Alliance, became the official organ of the People's Party, a more-than-symbolic example of how the Alliance rapidly lost itself in the new party.

Taking their cue from state leaders, the Lavaca County People's Party met in August, 1893, and established an official county organ. The funding came from inducing stockholders of the defunct Alliance cooperative store to reinvest in a Populist paper. In November Meitzen and four other Populists purchased the *Hallettsville New Era*. Meitzen, who was named editor, vowed, "The basis of my editorial views will at all times be the principles of the present platform of the People's party." Meitzen, a former teacher of children, now "became an educator of the grown-up people" or, as local historian Paul Boethel put it, he became a plague on "the Establishment." From 1892 to 1895, the number of Texas reform papers grew from twenty-one to eighty-five.[70]

As the People's Party set upon an ambitious educational campaign in 1893, the nation was hit with its worst economic depression to date. Cotton sales dropped by 25 percent. During the year, fifteen thousand US businesses failed, causing widespread unemployment and financial hardship. Among industrial workers, unemployment reached 20 percent.[71] With the country in a full-blown depression, the Populist message struck home to the nation's workers and farmers.

Just as the Southwest Strike of 1886 had galvanized the Texas Farmers' Alliance, a railroad strike in 1894 did the same for the People's Party nationally. In May more than three thousand workers struck the Pullman railcar company outside Chicago over wages, high rent in the company town, and union rights. The strike, backed by Eugene Debs of Indiana and the American Railway Union, soon spread, paralyzing rail service out of Chicago. Utilizing the strike-busting weapons of the court injunction and the National Guard, rail bosses and their allies in the government fought back. Debs and other union leaders were arrested, and President Cleveland sent in two thousand federal troops to crush the strike. Twenty-five workers were killed. After months of struggle, the strike went down to defeat in August. To many workers and farmers raised on the ideals of the American Revolution, it seemed that something was fundamentally wrong with a government that operated as a tool of big business. As the *Texas Advance* put it, "The colossal power of the United States government is now being used to place the necks of all American laborers completely and permanently under the grinding heel of organized corporate greed, and for the avowed purpose of crushing the last spark of patriotism, independence and manhood out of every American who eats his bread in the sweat of his face."[72]

Populist support for the Pullman strike convinced many labor organizations to join and support the Populist movement. With the backing of unions, the People's Party was virtually a labor party in the Midwest. This was especially so in Ohio, where United Mine Workers president John McBride rallied organized labor to the Populist cause in the 1894 elections. McBride rode a wave of Populist labor support to unseat Samuel Gompers as president of the American Federation of Labor (AFL) in 1894.[73] Debs expressed Populism's growing appeal to labor: "I am a populist, and am in favor of wiping both the old parties out so they will never come into power again. I have been a democrat all my life and am ashamed to admit it. I want every one of you to go to the polls and vote the populist ticket."[74]

Texas Populists continued to seek labor's support at their convention in Waco in June 1894. The convention adopted planks calling for the eight-hour day, abolition of convict labor, a state bureau of labor, the creation of a state board of arbitration to settle disputes between workers and corporations, and government ownership of railroads and telegraph service. A mass meeting of Dallas labor organizations in August endorsed the Populist ticket.[75]

In the nomination speeches of Nugent for governor and Martin for lieutenant governor, the *Dallas Morning News* reported, "Negro and white man, ex-slave and ex-master, from the same chairs gave thanks that the barriers of race prejudice have been smashed and that hereafter at least in Texas all men of whatever political conviction can vote according to their judgment and not according to color, race or previous condition of servitude."[76] The color line was seemingly shattered. The hopes of a biracial alliance of workers and farmers, and its ramifications for society at-large, were now tied to the People's Party.

Meitzen, now recognized as a state leader because of the strong campaign he ran for Congress against "the greatest aristocrat in Texas, Walter Gresham," was nominated for the office of state comptroller. The issue of prohibition played a large role in Meitzen's nomination for statewide office. German voters strongly opposed prohibition, seeing Sunday beer as a right of hard work. Many feared that the People's Party favored prohibition because of the influence of prohibition leaders in the party. Martin, for example, was a Populist from the Prohibition Party. To ease antiprohibition fears, the convention adopted a plank in favor of local self-government, allowing communities to decide for themselves issues such as prohibition. German-language Democratic newspapers came out hard against Meitzen, whose nomination they attributed to pandering to German voters. The *Texas Vorwärts* called him a "German worm dangling from the political fishhook of the Populists to attract German bites."[77]

Rank-and-file Populists pushed the labor planks of their platform, but the silver issue began to draw more attention. The free-silver issue achieved national prominence after President Cleveland called Congress into a special session in August 1893 to repeal the Sherman Silver Purchase Act of 1890. After months of public debate, Congress repealed the law, which had required the government to purchase silver every month. Many farmers and debtors viewed the government's repeal of the purchasing clause of the Sherman Act as a major cause of the financial depression.[78] The Texas Populist platform condemned "persistent efforts of the favored classes to force the legal enactment of the gold standard, efforts which leave no doubt of the existence of a wider conspiracy in England and Europe to dominate the finances of the world."[79]

Within the Populist movement, free silver originated as one of the many reforms advocated by the People's Party. The issue soon overshadowed much of what the Populists represented in the next few years, however. The narrowing of Populist agitation to primarily free silver provoked radical opposition that engendered socialist ideology within the ranks of Populism. Free silver created a conflict within the Populist movement that brought about the effectual end of the People's Party. The rise of the silver issue, to the detriment of other Populist demands, did not happen on its own.

With the rapid growth of the People's Party, the Populist movement incorporated individuals accustomed to a brand of politics different from the more insurgent-minded Texans. Herman Taubeneck, national chairman and others of his kind, including James Weaver, came from a political experience in which they represented small pressure groups rather than a mass movement. They took a brokerage approach to politics that sought to achieve goals through accommodation with the two major parties. The silver issue allowed them to put into practice their brand of politics. Sizable silver wings existed in both the Democratic and Republican parties.[80]

In 1889–90, North Dakota, South Dakota, Montana, Washington, Idaho, and Wyoming were granted statehood, thus adding twelve senators who bolstered the power of western silver-mine owners who backed free-silver candidates.

In the West, Populists had achieved electoral success in many states by fusing with either free-silver Republicans or free-silver Democrats. On a national level, Taubeneck used free silver to fuse all the reform forces into the People's Party. His manipulations had disastrous consequences.[81]

With financial backing of silver-mine owners, free-silver became the most talked-about issue of the day. Silver interests backed the publication of William Harvey's pro-silver *Coin's Financial School*, which became a national bestseller. Democrats who sought to distance themselves from the disastrous deflationary "goldbug policies" of Cleveland became silverites. William Jennings Bryan, editor of the *Omaha World-Herald*, which was owned by silver interests, began actively campaigning for silver. Taubeneck, wanting a part of the spoils, sought campaign contributions from silver-mining interests, setting the stage for the Populist fusion convention of 1896.[82]

In the 1894 election, the Texas People's Party, running on its full platform, increased its vote total from that of 1892. The impressive voter turnout prompted state Populist chairman Ashby to declare on the day after the election that People's party candidate Thomas Nugent had won, but the official count gave Democrat Charles Culberson 49 percent of the vote, followed by Nugent with 36 percent. The result did, however, show a 25 percent decline for the Democrats from 1892 and an 11 percent increase for the Populists. Populists won twenty-two seats in the state house and two in the state senate. Aside from Nugent, Meitzen received more votes than any other statewide Populist candidate, but not enough to overcome his Democratic opponent. The "German worm" did not attract as many "German bites" as he had hoped. Lavaca was the only county with a large German population that went Populist and for Meitzen. Lavaca County voters also favored Nugent over Culberson and elected a Populist-backed county judge, James Ballard.[83]

Despite the gains of the 1894 election, Populists believed they were again victims of widespread voter fraud. On November 20, Meitzen attended an emergency meeting of the party's state executive committee in Waco. The committee claimed that "There has [sic] been frauds, intimidation, miscounts and open violations of the election laws." Populists contended that county commissioner courts, controlled by local Democrats, were responsible for widespread ballot miscounts. Democrats also used the White Man's Union in many African American strongholds to maintain white supremacy and Democratic rule through harassment and buying of black votes. Populist efforts to prove voter fraud went for naught. To keep postelection momentum, Texas Populist leaders decided to begin the 1896 election campaign right away, using education as the main vehicle to convince voters, both black and white, of the need to vote Populist.[84]

Nationally, Taubeneck tried to use the Populist electoral gains to make the People's Party the party of free silver. The few Populist-backed candidates elected to the US Congress had done so through fusion, or joining with another party, on the issue of free silver. Taubeneck called a conference of Populist leaders to meet in St. Louis on December 28, 1894. The purpose of the conference was well known, as Taubeneck made clear to the press he intended the People's Party to stand on the silver plank alone, thus eliminating the rest of the Omaha platform. If Taubeneck thought most Populists would approve of his course, he found out otherwise in St. Louis. As the *Southern Mercury* reported, "The effort of a few would be leaders of the people's party at the St. Louis conference to commit the party to silver to the shelving of the balance of the Omaha platform utterly failed."[85]

In St. Louis, a coalition of Texas radicals and Chicago socialists headed by reform editor Henry Demarest Lloyd beat back the silver plans of Taubeneck. This coalition began a working relationship in defense of the Omaha platform that climaxed at the 1896 national convention of the People's Party. The collaboration between the two groups over the next two years led to the transformation of many Texas radicals from Populists to socialists, among them E. O. Meitzen.

The debate over free silver revealed fundamental differences in how various reformers viewed the increasingly severe economic crises of capitalism. For Taubeneck and free-silver advocates in the Democratic and Republican parties, free silver was a way to reform the capitalist system and ease the conflict between labor and capital. They feared the more radical critique put forth by Meitzen and many Texas Populists. Hans Teichmueller, a Texas judge from La Grange, warned of the more dangerous road he felt Texas Populists were embarked on. "The people's party," he cautioned, "recognizes the menacing conflict of labor and capital as an inseparable incident of our industrial progress, and tracing existing wrongs to all organized capital.... This party, not yet in name, but in its tendencies and principles, unmistakably develops as the socialistic party of the future."[86]

With Taubeneck's plans derailed in St. Louis, the struggle between fusionists and the middle-of-the-roaders (as the antifusionists called themselves) intensified.[87] The *National Watchman*, a Taubeneck-backed Populist journal that worked with the Democratic silver lobby, complained that "the wicked and foolish surrender to the Chicago socialists by the St. Louis meeting has cost the populist party too much already."[88] Milton Park, editor of the *Southern Mercury* and recently elected national president of the National Reform Press Association, called such talk "nonsense," insisting that if they were socialists so were the framers of the US Constitution. "These plutocrats and socialistic howlers do not know what these constitution framers really did say[:] ... 'insure domestic tranquility, provide for the common defense, promote the general welfare' (surely this is socialism),'" Park retorted.[89]

The executive committee of the Texas People's Party expressed the political mindset of many Populists in its address to the state reform press meeting. The address, cowritten by Meitzen and eight other Populist leaders, shows an evolving class consciousness and antagonism toward finance capital: "The doctrines of vested rights and the sanctity of private property, so dear to the Anglo-Saxon heart, have been perverted to build bulwarks of defense around the unjust acquisitions of the rich and to break down the barriers once erected around the possessions of the poor. Thus the wealth produced by labor has been taken to fill the overflowing coffers of the indolent rich, while the agencies of the most powerful government on the globe have been employed to put shackles upon the laboring man."[90]

The address blasted the corporate takeover of government, a recent US Supreme Court decision against the income tax, and the denial of habeas corpus in the jailing of Debs for asserting the rights of workingmen. Criticizing the growth of rampant militarism as the United States prepared to intervene in the Cuban struggle for independence from Spain, Meitzen and coauthors of the address warned, "Thus does plutocracy in times of peace prepare to repress the rising spirit of freedom among the masses and provide itself with the means of perpetuating those unjust advantages which have enabled it to absorb so much of the county's wealth." In response to the divide-and-conquer attempts of the procorporate press that claimed that the predominantly Protestant People's Party supported the anti-Catholic American Protective Association (APA), the Texas executive committee declared that "no populist should champion the cause within the party lines of the A.P.A. order." For them, the duty of Populists was to focus on the principles of land, transportation, and financial reform.[91]

To reach German-speaking Texans more effectively, Meitzen advocated a German-language Populist paper. The Reform Press Association agreed to start one in San Antonio, but the paper never got off the ground. Meitzen then took on himself the responsibility of publishing a German Populist newspaper. On January 31, 1896, *Der Deutsche Anzeiger*, run by Meitzen in Hallettsville, made its appearance as the first such paper in Texas.[92]

In early 1896 Meitzen printed in the *New Era* a letter from John B. Rayner to the African Americans of Lavaca County. Rayner, the state's leading black Populist orator, urged the county's black citizens to "not make promises or pledges to any democrat." He stressed that the Democratic party was an enemy to all blacks in the South. The Democratic *Hallettsville Herald* responded by printing a letter from a local African American, W. J. Stevens. Stevens, in the same vein of Booker T. Washington's "Atlanta Compromise," delivered three months earlier, replied by chiding Rayner to mind his own affairs. Stevens emphasized that blacks in the county had always lived under a democratic administration, "and we have nothing very serious (all things considered) to complain of." Stevens urged Rayner to limit his views to black journals and recommended that blacks tend to their own business and be thankful for what they have.[93]

As reform editors campaigned to educate farmers and laborers on the principles of the Omaha platform, Taubeneck increased his fusion efforts. He, Weaver, and their lieutenants traveled to numerous states to promote fusion plans and supporters as delegates to the coming national convention. They made sure the date of the Populist national convention played into their fusion plans. Middle-of-the-roaders favored an early convention to stake their claim as the party of true reform. Taubeneck argued that neither the Democratic nor Republican Party would likely nominate a prosilver candidate, but, if they did, Populists should then join in a united campaign for free silver. He insisted that a later convention date after the Democratic and Republican conventions, would best serve the interests of the People's Party. The Taubeneck-controlled national committee chose to hold the Populist convention in St. Louis on July 22, 1896, two weeks after the Democratic convention. To further facilitate a fusion of silver forces, the free-silver American Bimetallic League, which politically and financially backed Taubeneck's efforts, created the National Silver Party and decided to hold its convention at the same date and place chosen by the Populists.[94]

Rank-and-file Populists saw Taubeneck's convention plans as a trap. The *Southern Mercury* ran the article "Is There Danger Ahead?—The Plans Are Already Laid to Capture the Populist Convention." Particularly disturbing were the plans to hold the convention at the same time and location as the silver convention, as well as Taubeneck's own statement that "A great deal will depend on the action of the bimetallic league." Die-hard insurgents feared their party would suffer the fate of fusion, just as it seemed they stood on the verge of a national electoral breakthrough.[95]

Articles and letters attacking fusion became a regular feature of the reform press in the months leading up to July. "I am fully convinced that there is something rotten in our national committee," Meitzen wrote to the *Mercury*. "They are sending out free silver literature to many of the reform papers. Don't be deceived brethren: the plot will unfold in due time. The fight will come off July 22 at St. Louis. Stand to your guns, and we have nothing to fear." Further anti-fusionist militancy, typical of letters printed in the *Mercury*, was expressed by William Whiteside of Voca, Texas: "I am 75 years old and near the end of my journey of life, but I can use a gun yet. If it is necessary to get our rights under the constitution, I am ready to do all I can physically or otherwise to drive our enemies from power. If we permit our enemies to win in 1896, we may never have an opportunity to assert ourselves."[96]

Joining the side of antifusion was the recently established newspaper in Girard, Kansas, *The Appeal to Reason*. According to historian James Green, the *Appeal*, started by Julius A. Wayland in August 1895, "became the most successful venture in the history of American left-wing journalism and the principle catalyst for the early Socialist movement in the Southwest."[97] Though a socialist, Wayland campaigned for Populism in 1892, despite criticism from the Socialist Labor Party's (SLP) Daniel DeLeon. Wayland realized the recruiting ground Populism provided for socialism, with its legions of small farmers driven by the anticorporate vision of a Cooperative Commonwealth. Many Texas Populists later cited the *Appeal* in their conversion to socialism.[98]

While the *Appeal* advocated socialism within the Populist movement, the *Mercury* reflected continual collaboration between Texas radicals and Chicago socialists. The *Mercury* routinely ran articles from Illinois Populists, as well as speeches from Henry Demarest Lloyd, and covered Debs's battle with the courts over his role in the Pullman strike.[99] Seeing the need for labor's support to secure a Populist electoral victory, the *Appeal* openly championed Debs as the People's Party's presidential candidate: "If the populists want the laboring people to vote for them, they should nominate a laboring man. Lawyers and played-out old party politicians will not create any enthusiasm. There are men whose hands are on intimate acquaintance with manual labor who have better heads and hearts than those who, while seeing the wrongs, have always succeeded in living on the sweat of other men's faces. There is not a clearer head or warmer heart in the nation than E. V. Debs."[100] The *Mercury*, too, endorsed Debs.[101]

These efforts against fusion and a single silver plank brought about Taubeneck's charges of a socialist takeover. Tom Watson, national Populist from Georgia, echoed such charges. Watson, a firm middle-of-the roader, complained that socialism was in conflict with American individualism. "Tom Watson appears to be greatly troubled by the socialistic ghost," wrote the *Mercury*. "Watson will please explain how a government of the people can be formed without the socialistic ingredient. Much congressional contest has made Tom Watson flighty."[102]

The debate over socialist influences revealed a growing rift between contending class forces within the Populist movement. Dating back to the Grange, the agrarian revolt had brought together both small farmers and large landowners to address the economic plight of all agriculturalists. As C. Vann Woodward observed, "It is undoubtedly true that the Populist ideology was dominantly that of the landowning farmer, who was, in many cases, the exploiter of landless tenant labor. . . . Obviously the Populist attack did not strike at the whole system of capitalist exploitation, as did socialism, but in its time and section the Populist party formed the vanguard against the advancing capitalist plutocracy, and its fate was of vital consequence to the future." Watson, one of the largest landowners in Georgia, had more tenants on his land than his grandfather had slaves.[103]

With the economic crisis deepening, more and more small farmers who slipped into the ranks of tenancy made up the majority of Populists. As the landowning class of farmers focused on currency reform to improve their economic plight, tenant farmers embraced calls for land reform and government ownership of transportation and communication. Meitzen, calling attention to reports that the US government planned to own and operate a canal through Nicaragua, insisted, "Then why should it not operate our railroads for the benefit of the people?"[104]

At the time, the class divisions within Populism were not as apparent to all those involved. After all, Watson without compromise had fought the battles of Populism since the days of the Farmers' Alliance, earning him the devotion of Populists across the nation "as extreme a mid-road Populist as ever breathed or wrote."[105] Yet, although some Populist farmers had difficulty in realizing the class differences within their movement, many laborers did not. The *Texas State Labor Journal* declared, "If the populist party expects to maintain its reputation and standing as the representative and exponent of the workingmen, it should at once eliminate the landlord element so strong in its party councils."[106]

Meitzen was chosen as one of one hundred and three delegates from Texas to the Populist national convention in St. Louis. The *Mercury* offered the following words to the Texas delegation as they prepared to leave for St. Louis: "Don't sacrifice one solitary principle of the party creed.... The *Mercury* would especially warn the delegates against the seductive blandishments of the fusionists who will be in St. Louis in great force. Remember the fate of other reform parties that entered into entangling alliances. Stick to the Omaha platform as the guiding star to success. It is the voice of the people."[107]

The cause of the middle-of-roaders in St. Louis became especially perilous after the actions of the Democratic national convention in Chicago, where the gold bugs lost and the Democrats nominated for president silverite William Jennings Bryan. Bryan's nomination played into the hands of Taubeneck's fusion plans. As the *Appeal* observed, "The [democratic] convention's act was a bid for the people's party endorsement. If this occurs the people's party is a thing of the past. In four years the two old parties will have the field to themselves and will do as they please and if the reformers find themselves left with[out] organization to assist, they can lay the blame where it belongs—fusion and death."[108]

Upon arriving at the convention, Meitzen and the Texas delegation immediately faced a challenge from fusionists. Two rival delegations from Chicago were vying to be seated as the official delegation for Cook County. One consisted of Taubeneck supporters while the other, led by Lloyd, was composed of socialists and Debs supporters from the American Railway Union. With the convention stacked against them, the Texas delegation needed their allies from Illinois if they stood any chance of beating back Taubeneck's fusion plans. Throwing to the wind the possibility of being labeled socialists, middle-of-the-roaders campaigned to include the "Debs delegates" and won by the slim margin of 665 to 642.[109]

After the seating of delegates, middle-of-the-roaders learned the fusionist efforts had come to such a point that convention organizers proposed that the People's Party endorse the Democratic ticket of Bryan for president and Arthur Sewall, of Maine, for vice president. This proposal did not sit well with those who favored a straight Populist ticket. A delegate from Houston voiced the concerns of the Texas delegation: "As far as I know the delegates from Texas are warm in opposition to an endorsement of Bryan. They are well acquainted with the fact that the Democrats have had a chance to remonetize silver thirteen times in the last nine years and failed to do it. That is the reason we don't believe that if Bryan is elected, with both branches Democratic, we will be any nearer remonetization than we are now."[110] The Texas delegation was deluged with telegrams from home urging them to stay middle-of-the-road and not to fuse. Five hundred people rallied in Dallas, sending their support: "Never surrender. Bryan means death." Besides Bryan, the nomination of Sewall, a conservative banker, was especially galling.[111]

In response, the Texas delegation organized a middle-of-the-road meeting attended by delegates from twenty-three states who resolved that a straight Populist ticket must be nominated and that no fusion should be entertained before the Electoral College convened. Fusion would be a matter of last resort, if a combination of Democratic and Populist electors was necessary to defeat Republican presidential candidate William McKinley. Upon fusing, the Populists and Democrats would split their tickets. The party gaining the most votes would assume the presidency and the other's presidential candidate, the vice presidency.[112]

Seeing Sewall as the weak link of the fusion ticket, the middle-of-the-roaders successfully maneuvered to have the vice president nominated first. Sewall, the antithesis of Populism, was soundly defeated in favor of Tom Watson for the post. Further heartening the middle-of-the-roaders was their successful defense of the Omaha platform for the 1896 campaign. Believing that Bryan would not accept Watson or the Populist platform, and therefore would decline the Populist nomination, the middle-of-the-roaders held out the hope for a straight ticket.[113]

When the convention reconvened on the final day to nominate a presidential candidate, St. Louis papers reported that Bryan refused to accept Watson and would not accept the Populist presidential nomination. The fusionists, however, proceeded with their plan, claiming they had received no official word from Bryan. Weaver then delivered the nominating speech for Bryan. Unfortunately for the middle-of-the-roaders, they lacked a big-name candidate to counter Bryan. Debs, the favorite of many middle-of-the-roaders before the convention, sent a telegraph to Lloyd: "Please, do not permit use of my name for nomination." The middle-of-the-roaders selected the less-than-inspiring reform editor from Chicago, S. F. Norton, as their nominee for president. Refusing to give up, the Texas delegation repeatedly interrupted the nominating roll call to inquire whether a formal communication had been received from Bryan. The middle-of-the-roaders put up the cry of "No Watson, No Bryan." In truth, word had been received from Bryan, who refused to accept Watson, but the fusion-controlled chairman of the convention kept this vital information from the delegates. When balloting ended, Bryan beat Norton by a vote of 1,047 to 331.[114]

The fusionist victory in St. Louis demoralized the insurgent-minded rank and file of the Populist movement, especially in states where insurgent radical Populism was still in its incipient stage. For example, in Indiana only one hundred of the nine hundred expected delegates showed up at the state's Populist convention after the St. Louis convention nominated Bryan. Lacking participation from the antifusion rank-and-file, the Indiana People's Party fused with the Democrats. A similar pattern occurred in other states. Though the People's Party lingered into the next century, the fusion victory at St. Louis all but ended the party's existence as a national mass party.[115]

Reeling from defeat at the national convention, Texas Populists gathered at their state convention in Galveston on August 5, 1896. "The immortal 103" had stood firm in St. Louis against fusion with Democrats. Many Texas Populists refused to accept Bryan, a close friend and political ally of their archenemy, Hogg, as their presidential candidate. Before the convention there had been discussion of a proposed fusion in Texas between Populists and Republicans. Republican leaders proposed that Populists support McKinley for president in exchange for Republican support of Populist congressional and state candidates. John Rayner was one of the architects of the proposal. White Populists generally rejected the Republican offer, but African American Populists entertained it because of their previous ties to the Republican Party.[116]

Meitzen worked to unite Texas Populists. The *Galveston Daily News* observed that he opposed fusion at the convention and "thought if the populists could give the democrats rope enough they would hang themselves." Early on, it appeared that the convention might declare for Norton as president. In the end, though, harmony prevailed, and unity in the ranks was preserved. The convention endorsed neither Norton nor Bryan. Lacking a true champion for their cause, most Texas Populists resigned themselves to the less evil option. As a farmer from Burleson County stated, "I believe the democrats should indorse Watson, but if they don't I am inclined to vote for Bryan anyway, believing that a half loaf is better than no loaf at all."[117]

Although middle-of-the-roaders in Texas did not adopt the cry of "No Watson, No Bryan," as some proposed, they expressed themselves in the selection of their state ticket and platform. They nominated Jerome Kearby, the radical lawyer who defended KOL leaders in the Great Southwest Railroad Strike of 1886, for governor. An old Alliance radical and long-time third-party man, Stump Ashby, received the nod for lieutenant governor. S. O. Daws, responsible for much of the Farmers' Alliance's original growth, won the nomination for treasurer. With a "whoop," Meitzen was nominated by acclamation for the office of comptroller once again. The convention adopted a straight Populist platform with no fusionist compromises.[118]

The 1896 state Populist convention was the largest Populist convention in Texas. Seven hundred people attended, including one hundred and fifty African Americans, thirty-one of whom acted as delegates. African American delegates called for a plank in the Texas Populist platform to address racism. The plank, introduced by Frank W. Thomas of Navarro County, insisted that African Americans receive full equality and justice under the law. Thomas deemed the plank necessary on grounds that African Americans, while held accountable to the law, were prohibited from jury duty and had been practically disenfranchised at the ballot box. Thomas pointed to Mississippi, where a Jim Crow Constitution in 1890 severely restricted African Americans' right to vote. The Galveston convention did not approve Thomas's proposal, adopting instead a resolution stating "We are in favor of equal justice and protection under the law to all citizens without reference to race, color, or nationality."[119]

While the convention as a whole remained silent on Republican fusion, African American delegates did not. Meeting as a separate caucus, African American delegates voted 18 to 13 to vote for McKinley electors in exchange for Republican votes for Populist state candidates. Although only African American Populists openly declared for fusion, the state chairman of the Republican Party directed Republicans to campaign for Populist candidates and Republicans fielded no statewide candidates of their own. The fusion plan fell apart, however, when William "Gooseneck Bill" McDonald, a leading black Republican, disregarded it and campaigned for Democrats among black Texans. Populists claimed that McDonald agreed to move black votes into the Democratic column in exchange for the position of superintendent of the state Negro insane asylum. The charge was never proven, but McDonald's effectiveness in garnering black votes was widely acknowledged as a factor in the Populist defeat at the polls. McDonald remained a leader of black Republicans into the 1920s and became one of the richest African Americans in the United States through his business and political dealings.[120]

On election day, Populist candidates in Texas received their largest vote totals to that date. Labor support helped Kearby win the Dallas and Austin vote.

Nevertheless, the total proved insufficient to defeat incumbent Democratic governor Culberson, who won with around sixty thousand more votes than Kearby. Populist representation in the state house declined from twenty-two to six, and the number in the senate remained at two. Meitzen received more votes than he did in 1894, but he lost once again. Judge Ballard also lost his reelection bid to a Democrat by 287 votes. In the Texas vote, Bryan soundly defeated McKinley, though a solid northern vote put McKinley in the White House.[121]

Anger over fusion contributed to the Populists' defeat, but the vote itself revealed numerous irregularities. The *Dallas Morning News* emphasized that "in several instances there is manifest inaccuracy due to carelessness. In some cases this carelessness is so gross and inexcusable as to appear willful." The paper estimated that ten thousand votes for Daws were counted as "scattering" or few because returning officers reported votes for Davis, a misspelling, instead of Daws. More prevalent than misspelling of names, according to Populist charges, was manipulation of black voters. According to Kearby, "The negro vote in many sections was manipulated by fraud, intimidation and open bribery; the ignorant were preyed upon by slander and falsehood; the vicious and purchasable were hired by campaign funds raised to debauch the elector." Populists claimed Hogg conducted a trip to the US northeast to collect money from the Sewall campaign fund to "save Texas by replacing the white trash vote with colored votes to be bought." Ballot stuffing in predominantly African American counties produced vote totals that outnumbered in some cases the number of voters. In Fort Bend County, the ballot was designed so that, when illiterate voters thought they were voting Populist, they voted Democratic. Populists believed once again that an election was taken from them, this time through fusion and fraud.[122]

The People's Party fusion with Democrats did not transform the Democratic Party into a vehicle of progressive reform. Instead, the Democratic Party crushed the Populist movement and became the party of Jim Crow. In response to the biracial Populist revolt, Jim Crow legislation swept the South in the years to follow, ushering in an era of terrorism against African Americans. The beginnings of political unity between poor black and white farmers forged by Populists was now shattered.

After the election, Meitzen raised the question "of a state meeting of the middle-of-the road anti-fusion boys at an early date in '97 for the purpose of renewing the fight on the 'Omaha' platform." He concluded with "let us hear from the workers," showing his stance that Populism must expand from its base among farmers and into wage workers.[123] He was not the only Populist calling for a reorganization of the party. Representing the stance of many Texas Populists, a certain W. L. Franklin of Weesatche wrote to the *Southern Mercury*, "Let us reorganize with a national meeting in Dallas and elect a national chairman after the manner of Milton Park, Eugene Debs, or Paul Vandervoot [president of the

National Reform Press Association]. Then we will move onward and upward and gain glorious victory in 1900."[124]

Debs campaigned for Bryan, hoping to keep the Populist movement united as the "only mass-based alternative to the values of industrial capitalism." After the election, however, Debs's study of Marxism while in jail led him to the conclude that labor must create its own party free from the control of corporations. He openly declared for socialism in January 1897: "The issue is Socialism versus Capitalism. I am for Socialism because I am for humanity. We have been cursed with the reign of gold long enough. Money constitutes no proper basis of civilization. The time has come to regenerate society—we are on the eve of universal change."[125] The Populists would have to reorganize without Debs.

In February 1897 the Texas Reform Press Association met in Dallas with Meitzen in attendance. The association elected delegates to the upcoming national convention of the association in Memphis that included Meitzen, Milton Park, Cyclone Davis, and several other reform editors. At the first unofficial national gathering of Populists since the St. Louis convention, Texas delegates meant to make their displeasure with fusion known. As the *Dallas Morning News* observed, "Every delegate selected at [the] meeting is a middle-of-the-road populist, bitterly opposed to fusion in the future with silver democrats." As one delegate put it, "They had us grabbed at St. Louis when they forced Bryan's nomination. We are prepared for them now and it is a cinch. At Memphis we will teach the fusionists a lesson."[126]

Vandervoot called the Memphis gathering "the beginning of a new era in the life of the People's party."[127] The meeting served as an unofficial conference of Populist leaders. In his opening remarks, Vandervoot denounced the leadership of Marion Butler and other fusion leaders. Illustrating left-wing Populists' break from the old greenback critique of capitalism and a move toward socialism, many at the convention no longer viewed free silver as a cure-all. They focused their demands on government ownership of the transportation and communication industries, as well as universal employment through government-backed public-works projects. In order to prevent fusion in the future, Vandervoot proposed two resolutions. The first recommended that proxies no longer be recognized in conventions and conferences of the People's Party, and the second reaffirmed the resolution of the Omaha convention that no officeholders shall be eligible as convention delegates. These resolutions acknowledged the role played by proxy voting and office-holding fusionist delegates in nominating Bryan in St. Louis. Meitzen spoke in favor of the resolutions. Jumping on party disorganizers, he complained that "If the Omaha convention had been followed at St. Louis, the life would not have been fused out of our party." After he spoke,

Cyclone Davis moved against the resolutions, arguing that officeholders "were usually men of discretion and wisdom." The majority of the conference disagreed with Davis and adopted the resolutions.[128]

Despite the optimism of antifusionists, the Populist base further eroded from lynchings, voter repression, and the controversy over fusion. Davis, a founder of the Populist movement, now began a path back into the Democratic Party and the Ku Klux Klan. In 1916 he won a seat in the US Congress as a Democrat. On July 24, 1897, J. B. Daniel, a labor leader and Populist editor, was assassinated at his home in Waco. As the Populist movement dwindled, the reform press in Texas went from eighty-five journals in 1895 to thirty-six journals in 1901.[129]

Any hope Populists held that the divisions within their movement would heal faded as they entered the election year of 1898. Continued quarreling over fusion tore the People's Party apart nationally and in Texas. Texas Populists fielded a straight Populist ticket headed by Barney Gibbs, a former Democratic lieutenant governor. Gibbs had provided free legal services to rail workers during the Great Southwest Railroad Strike. With a less-than-enthusiastic campaign, Gibbs received only 21 percent of the vote, although the Populists did elect eight members to the Texas legislature, including Ed Tarkington of Lavaca County. In 1900 the gubernatorial candidate of the Texas People's Party, Theodore McMinn, gained only 7 percent of the vote. As the Populist candidate for Lavaca County tax collector, Meitzen lost soundly. Nationally, the middle-of-the-road Populist presidential ticket of Wharton Barker and Ignatius Donnelly received only 50,989 votes, with 20,981 coming from Texas, now the last holdout of middle-of-the-road Populism.[130]

While the Populist movement fell apart, the economic conditions that spawned it persisted. The 1890s were particularly devastating for farmers in Texas. Soaring land values and plummeting crop prices caused many to lose their land and become tenant farmers. Contributing was a rise in absentee land ownership and speculation that inflated land values beyond the reach of tenant farmers who wanted to own their own farms. The number of tenant farmers and sharecroppers in Texas increased from 95,510 in 1890 to 174,991 in 1900. Farm tenancy in Texas rose from 37.6 percent in 1880 to over 52 percent in 1910. Populism did little to address the growing trend toward tenancy, instead calling for the unity of all farmers, whether landed or landless, against plutocracy. The boll weevil, which had plagued Mexican farmers for years, appeared in Corpus Christi in 1894 and rapidly spread across the state's cotton fields. In 1904 roughly seven hundred thousand bales of cotton, worth $42 million, were lost to the boll weevil. Meitzen and other agrarian radicals looked for a new strategy to achieve economic justice for working farmers.[131]

Attempts to maintain the Populist movement after 1896 proved to be a death rattle but did produce the birthing pains of a socialist movement. Two years before his run for governor, McMinn projected the future of agrarian radicalism: "The 'Proletariat' is increasing at a frightful rate, and so-called conservative people hold their hands up in holy horror at the mention of 'Socialism.' But Socialism is growing fast, and the time is rushing us on to a decision for or against it. . . . [B]ut in the absence of Populism, Socialism is at hand."[132]

4 The Battle for Socialism in Texas, 1900–1911

In the first decade of the twentieth century, E. O. Meitzen, joined by two of his sons, E. R. and Arnold, and fellow farmer labor radicals such as Thomas A. Hickey, set out to build an independent working-class party from the bottom up. They began by working within the preexisting network of farmer-labor activists that dated back to the Alliance–Knights of Labor (KOL) partnership and what remained of the Populist movement. They intended to transform the old network into one that pushed for socialism. The Meitzens also worked within the Farmers Union, a mass farmer's organization, to promote support for socialist ideas and recruit key leaders. All the while, they focused on building a strong base in their home of Hallettsville, a bastion of left-wing socialism in Texas.

Although the Populist revolt had petered out, the conditions that produced it were far from resolved. The pattern of economic decline for farmers continued. The tenancy rate in 1910 for white Texas farmers was 49 percent, but for black farmers it was even higher, at 70 percent. Poor white and black farmers had come together politically in the People's Party. After the repression of the Populist revolt, farmer-labor radicals not only had a severely weakened political party but now had to contend with Jim Crow laws designed by economic and political elites to prevent future interracial alliances. In the opening decade of the twentieth century, the Meitzens and other white farmer-labor radicals built political organizations that represented their class interests as working farmers. In so doing, they struggled to navigate the newly codified racial dynamic, often by bowing to the dictates of white supremacy.

Farmer-labor radicals still looked to electoral politics as their main instrument to bring about the Cooperative Commonwealth. How to do so became a point of contention. Should reformers work within the established Democratic and Republican parties or create a party that exclusively represented the working class? After the People's Party fusion with William Jennings Bryan in 1896, many workers and farmers continued to favor the Democratic Party as the best option to achieve progressive economic reforms. They hoped they could either capture the party or nudge Bryan toward reforms that the Democratic Party promised but seldom carried out.

Many rank-and-file farmer-labor militants opposed a relationship with the Democratic Party. The People's Party had brought the two-party system to the brink of collapse, but its multiclass composition produced a national leadership that dropped the party's working-class economic and political demands in exchange for the supposed cure-all of free silver and fusion. Bryan did not inspire confidence among farmer-labor radicals. E. O. Meitzen called him "the counterfeit champion of the common people" who preached "Back to the People" but practiced "Back to the Corporation."[1]

Having evolved beyond the reform-oriented Greenback critique of capitalism, numerous agrarian militants schooled in Populism joined the emerging socialist movement. The growing frequency and severity of economic crises and the use of courts and state violence on behalf of economic elites convinced farmer-labor radicals that they were living in a period of cataclysmic changes. They believed that the economic system and the two-party system that represented it must be replaced, not reformed. As the nationally distributed *Appeal to Reason* argued, "Socialism is all of Populism plus more that is wholesome and good."[2]

On the national level, the socialist movement was going through a period of reorganization and sectarian splits that revolved around the Socialist Labor Party (SLP). The SLP, which had a few chapters in Houston and San Antonio, held its first state convention in late 1898, but it appealed very little to Texas farmers. The party made no serious inroads in the state, focusing almost entirely on industrial unionism.[3]

Much of what became the Texas Socialist Party (SP) derived from the old Alliance-KOL political network and what remained of the Populist movement. In 1898 William Farmer, a former Greenbacker and KOL member, quit the People's Party and formed an independent socialist party in Bonham. Eugene Debs, while on an organizing tour in Texas the following year, convinced Farmer to join the Social Democratic Party. Shortly afterward, the party hired Martin Irons, the railroad worker who helped lead the Southwest Strike of 1886, to organize in the southwest. Milton Park, now sole editor of the *Southern Mercury*, promoted the "sewer socialism" of Samuel "Golden Rule" Jones, mayor of Toledo, Ohio, who advocated public ownership of municipal utilities. Two of the most vital Populist converts to socialism were the brothers Lee and Jacob Rhodes of Van Zandt County in northeastern Texas. Lee Rhodes was a former Populist state representative. He and Jacob made Van Zandt County a stronghold of socialism. In west Texas, Maria Boeer held together a band of socialist farmers. These individuals, along with E. O. Meitzen, laid the foundation for the spread of socialism in Texas.[4]

E. O. Meitzen's transition from populism to socialism at the turn of the century appears to have been greatly influenced by the *Appeal to Reason*. By using the language of Populism, the *Appeal*'s brand of homegrown socialism germinated across the South. Articles from the *Appeal* frequently appeared in Meitzen's *New Era*. As early as March 1899, Meitzen printed a front-page column, "What Socialism Is." The column consisted of dictionary and encyclopedia entries defining socialism as a cooperative system that promotes equality and identifies with Christian ethics.[5]

Beyond Meitzen's formulaic answers, what did socialism mean to turn-of-the-century agrarian radicals? One possible insight came from Christian socialist George Herron, whose articles ran in the influential *Southern Mercury* and later in the Texas socialist newspaper the *Rebel*. Herron viewed socialism as the collectivization of production and distribution for the benefit of everyone. He contrasted the system to capitalism, where production and distribution are governed by competitive private industry. Agrarian radicals drawn to socialism saw in capitalism an illogical, morally corrupt system that was neither equal nor just. They understood that control of labor was the key to capitalists' success, and they condemned the idleness and aristocratic pursuits of the upper class, which had gained much of its wealth through inheritance dating back generations.[6] They rejected a system that, according to E. R. Meitzen, promoted "the man who lives and thrives off the labor of others rather than by the sweat of his own face."[7]

Agrarian radicals argued that those who perform labor should be the ones to profit from it. They also believed that whoever worked the land should own it. They called for nationalization of basic industries so that the betterment of all humankind—not private profit—would be the driving force of society. Farmer-labor radicals often referred to the future socialist society as the Cooperative Commonwealth. Taking from Edward Bellamy's bestselling utopian socialist novel, *Looking Backward: 2000–1887* (1888), they viewed the Cooperative Commonwealth as "a social order at once so simple and logical that it seems but the triumph of common sense."[8]

Because many agrarian radicals were fans of Bellamy's utopian novels and often utilized the language of Protestant evangelism, contemporary critics and scholars often have portrayed their brand of socialism as utopian moralism rather than Marxism. To be sure, there were plenty of utopians and moralists within the socialist movement. Nevertheless, the dominant ideological strain in the socialist movement, even its agrarian wing, was Marxist. For the Meitzens and many others, Marx's analysis of capitalism and the need for revolutionary change described the world they saw and offered a way forward.

For many rural Texans, their deeply held Christian beliefs influenced their path to socialism.[9] For them, economics and morality were intertwined. Socialist stump speakers recognized their principles and utilized evangelical Protestant language and imagery to attack what they viewed as the immorality of capitalism. Texas Socialists courted Christians by drawing connections between Christ's mission of service and mercy and the overall contours of a future Cooperative Commonwealth. Their approach stands in stark contrast to socialists since, who often belittle the various religious beliefs of working-class people as not sufficiently based on scientific materialism. Instead of religious spaces in the United States being contested political spaces as some once were, the overall retreat of socialists from the terrain, and their message of social regeneration for the benefit of the majority, has left the field to conservatives and their corporate-dominated message of individual regeneration.

Two of the Texas SP's most effective stump speakers, Stanley Clark and M. A. Smith, were former Methodist preachers. In describing Smith's speaking style, Dallas socialist George Clifton Edwards Sr. related, "He was . . . well read in the Bible and hymns and was quite skillful as a versifier. He often used some of his poems and songs in the style of Methodist hymns with great effect with country audiences."[10] Smith used a vocabulary and style that plain folk deeply understood. In rural communities, the church was often the most important social institution. Though drawing on evangelical language, Smith's "sermons" were Marxist at their core. He denounced capitalism and preached class conflict. "The blessed day is near at hand, when rich men will not own the land; when all who toiled will have a home, and be no longer forced to roam," extolled Smith as he advocated for the collective ownership of the land.[11]

Many rank-and-file socialists echoed Smith's sermons. In the "Why I Am a Socialist" section of the *Rebel*, created in 1911, readers shared the foundations of their beliefs. "My own reasons for being a Socialist are based on the Bible," wrote a reader from Memphis, Texas. He felt that both socialism and Jesus teach brotherly love.[12] In an expression of a Christian producerist-socialist philosophy, George Benson, of Lampasas, observed, "Among the early and true Christians everyone had according to their needs and then received of the products of labor according to their deeds. This is Socialism and it is Christianity."[13] The *Rebel*, while often using the language of evangelical Protestantism, frequently cited Marx and referred to the *Communist Manifesto*. Texas Socialists may have been down on the farm, but they were very much a part of the international revolutionary Marxist socialist movement. When E. R. Meitzen died in 1948, among his belongings that his daughter and son-in-law found was a very used copy of Marx's *Capital*.[14]

Though E. O. Meitzen and others like him had begun their transition to socialism, they hoped to use the national network of reformers and radicals created by the Populist movement to craft a new party. In April 1902, a convention in Louisville gathered all those "opposed to the centralization of capital." Among those organizations and individuals attending were Populists, single taxers, liberal socialists, the Independent Labor Party, the Public Ownership Party, and representatives of the SP, which formed in July 1901 under the leadership of Debs and Victor Berger. The convention adopted a platform reaffirming Populist demands, which resulted in the merging of the People's Party, the Public Ownership Party, and the Independent Labor Party into a single Allied People's Party.[15] In commenting on the Allied People's Party, the *Philadelphia Times* observed, "Under the name Socialist we might count their heads. They are Socialists and they should be plainly designated so that they may be reckoned with as Socialists."[16] As Jo. A. Parker, chairman of the Allied People's Party, noted to fellow Populist James Baird, "Everything seems to be turning to socialism. Everybody is talking about socialism, and I fear that we will be engulfed by the tide. . . . [The] Socialist movement has taken our place in the public mind."[17]

Populism had almost run its course. Its final fate in Texas would not be determined by socialism, but by infighting within the state Democratic Party. Progressive Democrats utilized white supremacy to bring many Populists back into the Democratic Party. In 1890, before the creation of the People's Party, the Farmers' Alliance forged a coalition with reform Democrats who shared their hostility toward northern capitalists and railroad trusts. In Texas this coalition resulted in the election of Democrat James Hogg as governor. Once elected, Hogg did little to assist hard-pressed farmers, thus encouraging them to create a party of their own.

Hogg served four years as governor, but by 1900, conservative Democrats regained control of the party, in part a result of the exodus of reformers to the People's Party. Hogg, a Progressive, reentered the political ring in 1900 to aid the reelection campaign of longtime friend US Senator Horace Chilton. Hogg sought to revive the coalition with Populists that won him the governorship in 1890 to assist reform Democrats in regaining control of the party. To do so, Hogg proposed in 1900 to add three antirailroad corporation amendments to the state constitution. As historian Robert Worth Miller argued, "The proposals constituted an open invitation for white Populists to return to the party of their fathers." The *Southern Mercury* endorsed Hogg's amendments as a way to rekindle Populist sentiments.[18]

To facilitate the return of Populists into the Democratic fold, changes in election laws were needed. With the rise of the Populist movement, Democrats in Texas sought to maintain monopolistic control by requiring loyalty oaths and by stipulating that in most cases voters must have previously voted in at least the last two Democratic primaries in order to qualify as a Democrat. The measures kept anyone who had voted Populist in either of the last two primaries from voting in the Democratic primary. With Populists no longer a threat, the Democratic primary was more meaningful than the general election. Hogg successfully pushed for changes to the Democratic primary process. Nearly every county agreed to conform to a uniform primary law and throw out restrictive party tests. Hogg's changes cleared the path for reform Democrats who had voted Populist to participate again in the Democratic primary. The Hogg strategy paid off in 1906, when the reform Democrat, Thomas Campbell, won the governor's office.[19]

The new primary, however, was still not open to all. Democrats learned their lessons from the interracial black-white unity that propelled Populists to the brink of power. In 1903 Democrats crafted a primary for whites only. They justified the exclusion of African Americans as necessary to purify the vote. Many Populists, still stinging from what they saw as a manipulation of black votes to halt their success at the ballot box, acquiesced to the cruel logic of a purified vote.

The new White Man's Primary effectively disenfranchised African Americans from the political process in Texas. In Lavaca County, it meant that the county's 4,890 black citizens, or 17.4 percent of the population, were all but removed from meaningful political participation. The primary restrictions came a year after a poll tax was enacted in 1902. With the average wageworker in Texas making little more $425 a year and farmers perpetually in debt, a poll tax of between $1.50 and $1.75 made voting prohibitive for not only blacks, but for nearly all workers and farmers.[20]

When chairman Meitzen and Lavaca County's Populists met in April 1902, they concluded that because of "the recent radical changes in the democratic primaries, which virtually changed the same to a white man's primary, regardless of past or present party affiliation," they opted "not to encourage independent candidates for county office." Embracing the changes, they "urged that the good work of purifying county politics should be encouraged."[21]

The White Man's Primary not only ended Populism but also brought about the practical end of another long-term political alliance, that of black and German Texans. Since their arrival in Texas, Germans were marked as outsiders in the dominant Anglo Texas world. From German immigrants' assistance to slave revolts in the 1850s through Reconstruction and into the late nineteenth century, many black and German Texans after the Civil War formed a political alliance centered on the Republican Party.

Some German Texans who had prospered economically and grown more conservative than their 48er brethren saw in the new primary a chance for Germans to enter the white mainstream. The new election oath specified that "the term white includes all races except negroes."[22] William Trenckmann, prominent publisher and editor of the influential German-language weekly *Das Wochenblatt*, urged German Texans to participate in the new White Man's Primary. He saw the new primary as a way for German Texans to separate themselves from their alliance with African Americans and to gain influence in the Democratic Party. "I saw in the new law a possibility for accomplishing reform," recalled Trenckmann.[23] As historians Walter Buenger and Walter Kamphoefner note, for German Texans, "sacrificing greater African American equality was the price for membership in the reform Democratic coalition."[24]

Trenckmann urging German Texan participation in the White Man's Primary harked back to the Democratic Party's manipulation of white racist fears of negro domination during Reconstruction. He claimed in his home of Austin County that "although it constituted only one-fourth of the population, the colored element had been making decisions in filling the county offices."[25] Trenckmann recalled "how frightened I was as a small child by a husky twelve-year-old Negro boy whom my father had hired from his parents." With his own racial fears running wild, he wrote, "Although there were not many Negroes, there were enough of them for me to realize that in their hearts, particularly in those of the most intelligent, hatred for the whites was fermenting."[26] On the basis of his exaggerated personal fears, Trenckmann felt justified disenfranchising African Americans and encouraging German Texans to adopt white supremacy.

Although the White Man's Primary yielded promising statewide results for Hogg Democrats, it produced unexpected results in Lavaca County. Meitzen won the 1904 primary for county judge with the support of white Populists and Central European immigrants. The *Houston Post* blasted Meitzen's immigrant support: "No regard was had for the . . . election law, and people who could not speak the English language were voted like Mexicans on the border in times gone by." This a reference to the practice of political elites along the border paying Mexican citizens to fraudulently vote in Texas elections. As Meitzen later explained, "I was elected county judge by accident—slipped up on the blind side of politicians in a local fight regarding better conditions."[27]

Meitzen succeeded by targeting the graft and corruption of the residing county commissioners and judge. He exposed a scheme in which each member of the county commission received $300 a year for road supervision. Texas law did not allow commissioners to receive more than $120 a year for road supervision, but Lavaca's Democratic state senator, David Augustus Paulus, secured an exemption for the county. To return the favor, the commissioner's court gave Paulus a $250 gift from bond-sale money.[28]

Meitzen's campaigns for county judge demonstrates how he used his political standing as a former Alliance and Populist leader to build a base for socialism in Lavaca County. Without a preexisting socialist base, he ran as an independent. Though not openly declaring himself a socialist, he used his campaign and elected position to educate Lavaca County's working class on the basic principles of socialism. But in contrast with the time Meitzen helped found the People's Party in Lavaca County in March 1892, this time he failed to publicly encourage African Americans to join the new movement. Instead of challenging the harsh realities of Jim Crow, Meitzen bowed to them—a decision in the early stages of codified racial segregation that held important implications for the course of working-class radicalism in Texas.

Shortly before the 1904 election, Meitzen and his sons, E. R. and Arnold, joined the fledgling SP and helped organize a local in Hallettsville. By December, the local had seventeen dues-paying members, held weekly membership meetings, and held a public meeting at the courthouse. Upon his election to county judge, Meitzen resigned his membership in the SP to present an air of nonpartisanship while serving as an elected official. Still, after the buoying results of the 1904 elections, his newspaper, the *New Era*, became a firebrand of socialism. The paper followed with interest the struggles of the Western Federation of Miners, led by William "Big Bill" Haywood and Charles Moyer against Colorado mineowners.[29] After a column announcing that socialist Gary Miller, president of the Telluride Miners Union in Colorado, would soon be speaking in Huntsville, Texas, the newspaper boldly asserted, "The Socialist Party will soon be a power in national politics, and whether you are for it, against it, or indifferent, you should come out and learn something about it and be entertained at the same time."[30]

Meitzen's primary form of protest and agitational organizing still came from his attachment to the plight of farmers. In 1902 a new farmer's organization formed in Rains County, Texas, that followed in the tradition of the old Farmer's Alliance—the Farmer's Educational and Cooperative Union of America, known as the Farmers Union (FU). Meitzen and his sons used the FU to recruit angry farmers to socialism. Newt Gresham was the individual most responsible for founding the FU. He had been an organizer of the Alliance in Texas as well as in Alabama, Tennessee, and Mississippi. Like many Alliance members, Gresham became a Populist but returned to the Democratic fold through fusion. In the years since the end of the Alliance, Gresham had eked out a living running rural newspapers. He held fast to the position that farmers should organize politically. By 1900, about half the farmers of Rains County were tenant farmers, while non-tenant farmers faced losing their farms from the high interest rates charged by the county's banks. In the spirit of the old Alliance, ten Rains County residents came together and chartered the FU. Of these original ten members, three were Populists, one a socialist, one an independent, and five Democrats.[31] The political differences would strain the unity of the FU throughout its brief existence.

In 1904 the FU became a statewide organization with a reported hundred twenty thousand members by early 1905. Demonstrating the institutional continuity of the Alliance and Populist movement to the FU, the *Southern Mercury* in May 1905 merged with the FU's newspaper, the *Farmers Union Password*. Because conditions of farmers had worsened since the days of the old Alliance, farmers flocked to the FU not only in Texas but across the country. The FU became a national organization in 1906 with nearly a million members by 1907.[32]

At local and national levels, farmer-labor radicals used the FU to advance their interests. Lavaca County farmers and supporters formed a countywide FU branch in July 1905. With a state organizer speaking in English and Meitzen in German, locals were quickly organized in every farm community in the county. Meitzen was elected as the FU's county president, and his son E. R., who was now coming into his political own, was elected as delegate for Lavaca County to the state FU meeting in Waco. Nationally, the FU reached out to the AFL, expressed solidarity with labor struggles, and encouraged the purchase of items marked with union labels. The FU also identified with the reform wing of the Democratic Party, which further facilitated the return of Populists into the Democratic Party.[33]

Officially the FU took a nonpartisan political stance. The adoption of this position came during the FU's third Texas state convention in February 1905. At the convention, Lee Rhodes, a national FU lecturer, gave a speech using socialistic language that angered FU Democrats. They succeeded in changing the FU's constitution so that members were forbidden, under penalty of expulsion, from discussing partisan politics at FU meetings.[34] In this era, FU and AFL leaders such as Samuel Gompers invoked nonpartisanship as a code that meant support only for the Democratic Party or, as simplified by historian Julie Greene, "nonpartisan in theory though pro-Democrat in fact."[35] Later in the summer it became apparent that the FU's nonpartisan rule applied only to non-Democrats. Former Democratic US senator from Texas Joseph Bailey spoke at an FU meeting in Gordon in which he attacked several political parties and praised Democrats, thus violating the supposedly nonpartisan principles of the FU. The still-Populist *Abilene Farmers Journal* denounced the appearance of Bailey, who especially galled Left FU members because of his close ties to Standard Oil.[36]

Nationally and statewide, the FU mixed with Democrats, but under the leadership of the Meitzens in Lavaca County, the mixing was with socialists. Members of the Hallettsville SP also held memberships in the FU. On March 24, 1906, for example, A. Haynes Sr. spoke on FU topics in the town of Seclusion, but the very next night he lectured on the doctrines of socialism in the same town. Socialism and the FU went hand in hand in Lavaca County.[37]

The efforts of socialists within the FU paid off in 1908 when they recruited the influential editor of the *Farmers Journal* to their cause—Joshua L. Hicks. Hicks was born on December 23, 1857, in Clarke County, Alabama, and moved to Texas in December 1875. He began his political journey as a deeply religious prohibitionist. Seeing no difference between the Democrats and Republicans on prohibition led Hicks down the path of independent political action. The cause of prohibition also led Hicks to take a stand for black political rights. He believed that both whites and blacks faced a common danger in alcohol and should not be divided at the ballot box. In 1891, Hicks and his brother, W. P., were won over to the labor reform movement and became Populists after listening to a speech by William Farmer. In a letter to the *Vindicator* in June 1891, W. P. Hicks wrote, "We want equal rights to all and special privileges to none.... There is bound to be something wrong in a government when a few men can get to be millionaires so quickly while there are thousands of people on starvation. ... They are throwing many things in the way of this labor movement, but still they march right on toward the tables of the money changers."[38]

Joshua Hicks farmed before starting the *Farmers Journal* as a Populist paper in the 1890s. He stuck to the cause of working farmers and remained a Populist when he joined the FU. Hicks's interactions with Populists-turned-socialists in the FU played a role in his conversion to socialism in early 1908. As the socialist newspaper the *National Rip-Saw* reported, "'The Farmer's Journal,' one of the biggest little journals in all America ... which has been purely a farmer's journal for many years, in its issue of January 13th, last, DELIBERATELY, CANDIDLY and UNHESITATINGLY laid aside all of its Populistic ideas, which do not harmonize with the doctrines of Socialism, and like a man, that its editor is, boldly declared for Socialism."[39]

In Lavaca County, E. O. Meitzen, besides promoting the FU and socialism, carried on as an activist judge. He pushed for reforms in how the county government operated. He made sure unclaimed monies collected by county officials were put into the County Road and Bridge Fund instead of into the pockets of county officials. He also started requiring competitive bids for county projects from outside contractors. In the past, contracts had usually gone to patrons of county officials at inflated costs to taxpayers.[40]

In early 1906 Meitzen stepped down as head of the Lavaca County FU. He did so in support of a resolution requiring that only actual farmers could hold office in the FU. This resolution came in the context of protests by Texas FU locals against the appointment of two nonfarmers by the national FU to the offices of national president and national organizer. This led to a split between the Texas and the national FU, which continued to appoint nonfarmers to leadership positions, while the Texas FU allowed only farmers to hold such posts. Despite Meitzen's resignation as head of the county FU, he and other agrarian radicals of Lavaca County continued organizing FU locals. They also busied themselves with spreading socialism and supporting Meitzen's reelection campaign for county judge.[41]

Throughout the partisan bickering, racism prevailed on both sides of the electoral divide. The *Gazette* and *Herald* insisted that the recently enacted poll tax and a Democratic primary under partisan control would keep many African Americans from voting. In the same vein, the *New Era* argued that Lavaca County's 4,000 legal voters included 400 to 500 black voters "who constitute a dangerous balance of power that can often defeat good men and elect rascals that scruple not to buy their way into office. This has been done and can be done again." The white farmers who once embraced interracial unity only to have it used against them now bowed to the white supremacist attitudes of the time.[42]

Supporters of the White Man's Union, created to promote the white primary, held a mass meeting at the Hallettsville courthouse on March 10. Speakers in English, German, and Bohemian discussed what type of primary to conduct. At the meeting chaired by Meitzen, the White Man's Union and the Democratic Party decided to hold two separate primaries. Nominees of the White Man's Primary would be placed on the Democratic primary ballot. The White Man's Primary, though, did not receive official sanctioning from the state Democratic Party as it had in 1904. The Lavaca County White Man's Primary would be run only as a show of public support from those whom primary officials deemed to be worthy white people.[43]

Meitzen ran unopposed and won the White Man's Primary. By the time the Democratic primary was held nearly two months later, however, the Democrats went back on their word to place all nominees of the White Man's Primary on their primary ballot. The Democrats also reinstated their loyalty oath. Meitzen, refusing to take the oath, decided to run as an independent. The Democrats, in their partisan primary, nominated Democratic county chair W. R. McCutchan to run against him.[44]

Meitzen and McCutchan began a series of debates from late June till the election. McCutchan attacked Meitzen for his socialist beliefs. Meitzen countered that socialism was not the real issue, emphasizing how he had exposed graft and was the only one on the commissioners' court to vote to raise the county railroad assessment on railroad corporations. The increased assessment would have brought an additional six hundred twenty thousand dollars into the county coffers. The Democratic press were relentless in its efforts to make socialism the main issue of the race.[45]

Though Meitzen claimed socialism was not at issue, Socialists were extremely active in the area at this time. Meetings were held with growing frequency, often featuring national speakers. The SP in Lavaca County put forward candidates of its own for the first time. Albert Haynes Sr. ran for state representative and James Bates Gay for US representative. Gay was a former Populist and son of Alliance leader and women's rights advocate Bettie Gay. The *Hallettsville Herald* criticized E. O. Meitzen for running as an independent while his cohorts showed their true colors and ran as socialists.[46]

The Democrats continued their attacks on Meitzen. Efforts were made in July to prevent his campaign literature from going through the US mail, but the area postmaster refused to ban the literature. Democrats stirred up religious prejudices against Meitzen, claiming at a large Catholic festival that Meitzen opposed religion and marriage. Meitzen replied that religion had nothing to do with county affairs.[47] The campaign got personal when rumors circulated that Meitzen "had been 'running around' with other women," a charge Meitzen denied. When confronted by E. O.'s sons, E. R. and Arnold, about the accusation, the purveyor of the rumor pulled a knife on Arnold, prompting E. R. to strike down the slanderer with his fists.[48]

During the campaign, the US Congress passed a new naturalization act on June 29, 1906, that affected Meitzen's core immigrant contingency. The new act switched the power to grant citizenship from local to federal courts beginning on September 27, 1906. The naturalization process would become costlier and more difficult. Meitzen, who as judge liberally granted citizenship, hastened the process in the days leading up to the federal takeover of naturalization. Whereas the previous county judge naturalized 16 individuals during his two-year term, Meitzen granted citizenship to 147 people, including 21 in a four-day special session before the new law went into effect. Meitzen's efforts gained him the endorsement of the Hallettsville Czech language newspaper *Obzor*.[49]

In an election with low voter turnout, McCutchan defeated Meitzen by 137 votes. Factoring into the low turnout was the poll tax, which affected Meitzen's constituency of poor farmers. Meitzen carried the rural German and Czech communities of Breslau, Witting, Moravia, Baursville, and Vienna. He also carried Sublime and Ezzell, which had a strong FU presence. Ezzell was also a socialist stronghold, the only community that voted in the majority for socialists Gay and Haynes. The towns of Hallettsville and Shiner went to McCutchan. The *Hallettsville Herald*, celebrating McCutchan's victory, ran the headline "Democracy Triumphs over Socialism."[50]

The *New Era* blamed Meitzen's defeat on the opposition's ability to convince voters that "Socialism stood for all sorts of terrible things such as anarchy, 'dividing up,' taking away farms, Negro equality, abolishment of religion and marriage." Meitzen's campaign, which assured voters months before the election that he was not against religion, now sought to clarify its position on "Negro equality."[51] The SP, since its formal organization in Lavaca County, abided by Jim Crow norms at its public meetings, announcing that "arrangements will be made for the separate seating of whites and blacks."[52] A week after the election, the *New Era* printed a column written by an anonymous "Country Hayseed" from Ezzell in response to the Democratic *Hallettsville Herald*'s query: "Does

Socialism preach equal rights for the negro, the white man, and yellow man?" The Country Hayseed replied, "Socialism preaches equal rights only to the extent that each have the full value of what he produces—be he white, black or yellow. Because a negro perhaps would produce more than a white man does not signify that he should be permitted to eat at the same table with a white man or ride in the same car with him etc."[53]

Lavaca County Socialists had fallen for "all the senseless agitation in capitalist society . . . in respect to 'social equality'" that Debs argued against in his stand for racial equality. Their racial stance must have been particularly vexing to him. Three years earlier, Debs used an experience at a Lavaca County depot in Yoakum in an article, "The Negro in the Class Struggle," to call for Socialists to stand against racial prejudices and welcome blacks into the SP on equal terms. Debs recounted that, while carrying his own bags at the Yoakum depot, three white men told him "a nigger" would carry them because that is what God had put them here to do. "Here was a savory bouquet of white supremacy," Debs wrote. "They [the three white men] were ignorant, lazy, unclean, totally void of ambition, themselves the foul product of the capitalist system and held in lowest contempt by the master class, yet esteeming themselves immeasurably above the cleanest, most intelligent and self-respecting negro, having absorbed the 'nigger' hatred of their masters."[54]

Crying "forsooth!" Debs argued that capitalists use the "shrill cry" of social equality to distract the working class from the real issue of economic freedom. "As a socialist party we receive the negro and all other races upon absolutely equal terms," he wrote. "We are the party of the working class, the whole working class, and we will not suffer ourselves to be divided by any specious appeal to race prejudice."[55] His words never completely took among most white Texan Socialists. The Texas SP failed to demonstrate the level of interracial political unity that occurred during the Populist era. One can arguably cite this failure as a reason socialism failed to achieve the electoral success of its radical agrarian predecessor. A socialist black vote might have prevented Meitzen's close election defeat in 1906. The racial violence of the Jim Crow era, though, made socialist outreach to blacks a dangerous proposition—one that white Texan socialists often avoided.

Though Socialists were defeated in the election, the *New Era* pointed out the Socialist vote in the county had increased from 45 to 100 since the previous election. The newspaper also proclaimed Meitzen would now be "'foot-loose' to spread the doctrines to which he has so consistently adhered." Meitzen, upon leaving office, officially rejoined the SP.[56]

Socialist tallies in votes and members were on the rise, but their overall numbers were still small. In 1906 the Texas SP could claim only around 350 dues-paying members in roughly twenty locals, and its candidate for governor garnered just 2,958 votes or 1.61 percent of the total statewide vote.[57] Before the Texas SP could become a real force in Texas politics, it faced an internal party fight and a reorientation from the town to the countryside.

Socialists formally organized the Texas SP at the statewide level in the fall of 1904. Before then, SP locals existed in Dallas and Houston and in rural areas such as Van Zandt County. There were individual members scattered around the state, but they were not organized under a state leadership committee. Texas Socialists ran W. W. Freeman of Val Verde County on the Texas-Mexico border for governor in 1902. Freeman's vote total was under 1 percent and recorded, like the Texas SP's membership, as "scattering."[58]

In 1904 the Texas SP received its first injection of the old Populist movement culture when it held its first summer encampment at Grand Saline, Van Zandt County. Lee Rhodes organized the weeklong camp meeting on the old Populist model. The Grand Saline encampment featured food, music, dancing, fair rides, and a good dose of political speeches by Rhodes, M. A. Smith, regional SP organizer Frank O'Hare, and others. Described by historian James Green as "a cross between an American revival and a European political carnival," the event drew four thousand people. In 1906 the Grand Saline encampment drew even more people and had Mother Jones as the featured speaker. Besides the Grand Saline encampment, which became an annual event for more than a decade, the SP organized encampments across the state. Some drew tens of thousands and featured Debs, Bill Haywood, Kate Richards O'Hare, the Meitzens, and Tom Hickey, among others.[59]

Because of the organizational efforts of the Rhodes brothers and the success of the original Grand Saline encampment, the early Texas SP located its headquarters in Grand Saline. For the 1904 election, the SP ran popular stump and encampment speakers Lee Rhodes for lieutenant governor and M. A. Smith for attorney general. SP national committee member Word H. Mills of Dallas was the party's choice for governor. The platform adopted by convention at the end of the Grand Saline encampment lacked individual planks addressing the specific needs of workers and farmers. Instead, the platform reads more as an ideological tract borrowing heavily from the *Communist Manifesto*. Without land or labor planks, other than calling for the collective ownership of land and machinery, the SP election results were no better than they were in 1902.[60]

By the next election cycle in 1906, the Texas SP had yet to address the land issue, but their platform did contain a new formulation: "In the wage earners of our towns and cities and the farmer, we recognize the types of the producing elements of the country.... [B]oth are exploited for the benefit of the capitalist class."[61] This recognition that farmers were part of the producing or working class stood in contrast with workerist-oriented socialists who viewed farmers as part of the petite bourgeoisie or middle class. These distinctions are important.

Farmers, if part of the petite bourgeoisie, had interests separate from the working class, and if not allies were potentially reactionary foes. As part of the working class, farmers, especially tenants and sharecroppers, held the same anticapitalist revolutionary potential as wage workers and should be organized within the SP on equal terms. It was this later view that guided members of the Texas SP and served them in the coming years as they sought to shape the SP's national policy on farmers and land.

Though lacking a clear land policy, the Texas SP's 1906 platform did contain more specific demands. The convention in Dallas called for shorter workdays and higher wages, health and unemployment insurance, old age pensions, public education, "public ownership of all means of transportation, communication, and exchange," "equal suffrage for men and women," and the repeal of the poll tax. Again Rhodes was nominated for lieutenant governor and Smith for attorney general. E. R. Meitzen entered the state leadership ranks as the nominee for railroad commissioner.[62]

The Socialist candidate for governor was twenty-nine-year-old George Clifton Edwards of Dallas, a Harvard-educated night school teacher of illiterate adults. His father was a local justice of the peace and his brother was a Dallas alderman—both Democrats who disapproved of George's socialist beliefs. In 1904 Edwards bought the *Dallas Labor Journal*, changed its name to the *Laborer*, and succeeded in having it recognized as the official organ of the Dallas Labor Council. "I knew little about Marx and European Socialism and was distinctly a Utopian rather than a 'scientific' Socialist," Edwards later admitted. He pictured Bellamy's *Looking Backward* as the future socialist society. With the top of their ticket aimed more at the town than the country, the SP received only 2,958 votes, or 1.6 percent of the total.[63]

Progressive Democrat Thomas Campbell won the 1906 governor's race. Hogg's strategy to bring former Populists back into the Democratic Party through changes in the electoral system worked. With many former Populists now in tow, progressive Democrats recaptured their party from its conservative wing. Though not addressing the land issue or supporting woman suffrage, the 1906 Democratic platform declared that "trusts, monopolies, and combinations . . . are the most insidious agencies used to oppress the people and destroy the freedom of the citizens" and pledged "the full power of the Democratic party to utterly destroy them." Democrats called for the removal of occupation taxes, good public roads, and the prohibition by law of lobbying and contributions from corporations to political campaigns. The platform won them the endorsement of the large FU and the small but influential Texas State Federation of Labor.[64]

Disregarding the appeal of a progressive Democratic Party that paid lip service to the anti-big-business concerns of the working class, Texas SP state secretary

W. J. Bell blamed his party's poor showing on the lack of organization between its state and local levels. The Texas SP elected Bell state secretary in 1905 and relocated state headquarters to Tyler, where Bell resided. The party needed a full-time secretary, and Bell received a salary of just under $400 a year, which he supplemented by tuning pianos on the side to support his family. Bell disapproved of the practice of sending Socialist stump speakers to an area, inspiring residents with a rousing speech, organizing a local, but then leaving it to wither with no organizational guidance. Bell sought to rein in freewheeling state organizers and provide more state-level assistance to locals.[65]

In a state dominated by agriculture, landownership was the vital issue for working farmers. None of the political parties confronted the land issue. The FU remained the main organization promoting the interests of farmers. Since the SP lacked a land policy, the Meitzens devoted much of their energy to building the FU and infusing it with socialist principles. E. R. Meitzen's work for the FU brought him to a position of leadership as a member of the state constitutional committee.[66]

In 1906–7 the FU reached its organizational and membership height but then went into rapid decline. The FU's August 1907 convention reported that the FU had 4,472 locals in Texas with approximately one hundred thousand members. Early in the year, the FU successfully petitioned the Texas state legislature to pass anti-bucket-shop legislation. A bucket shop is an establishment that deals in stock futures and margins and allows individuals to bet on the rise or fall of stocks and commodities without the expectation of delivery—in other words, speculative gambling. The FU's greatest accomplishment was that it built more than three hundred warehouses in Texas and established a central sales agency in Houston. Now, with the FU's own warehouses and sales agency, its members were in a position to hold their cotton and sell it on the most favorable terms. Beginning in mid-October 1907, however, yet another financial crisis shook the nation.[67]

The Panic of 1907 could not have hit the Texas FU at a more inopportune time. Shortly before the crisis, the FU central sales agency in Houston was in the process of aiding members by storing their cotton and negotiating financial arrangements with banks until cotton prices increased. Anticipating a good return on their stored cotton, many farmers borrowed money from banks to get by in the meantime. Just as it seemed that the FU's cotton holding plan would come to fruition, the panic struck. Banks called in the loans. To repay its loans, the FU central agency had to sell its member's cotton at a lower than anticipated price. This led many desperate regional FU locals to sell their warehouses to creditors.[68]

The warehouse system that stood to be the FU's crowning achievement was now in ruins. The FU had attempted to better the conditions of working farmers within the capitalist system by setting up their own parallel system of marketing and selling. In the end, though, the warehouse scheme was subjugated to the endemic boom-and-bust cycle of capitalism. With the FU in rapid decline, the Meitzens, along with Hicks and other allies, sought to transform the Texas SP into a party that spoke for the interests of farmers. To do so, however, required the Texas SP to revamp, both organizationally and politically.

Socialists at their May 1908 national convention debated "the farmer question." Throughout the debate, it was apparent that there were multiple understandings, or misunderstandings, of farmers and their place in capitalist society. Most took the preconceived view that farmers owned their land. "These [farmers] are called capitalists by a number of men now in the socialist movement," stated a delegate from Illinois. "The average farmer is not a proletarian," insisted Victor Berger of Milwaukee, a leader of the SP's right-wing. He regarded farmers as part of a separate "farming class." On the other hand, most of the Texas delegation and other radicals with connections to the land viewed farmers as part of the working class. "The farmer comes into the socialist movement as a class-conscious workingman," expressed South Dakota delegate E. Francis Atwood. "Today our western farmer has nothing. He is skinned by the capitalist class, and staggers under the same burdens as the other workingmen." Jacob Rhodes provided a slightly more nuanced take: "We have two classes of farmers—one class that farms the soil and another class that farms him. Their interests, of course, are opposed."[69]

Rhodes's comments were the closest anyone came to differentiating between land-owning and tenant farmers. Otherwise, delegates mentioned the issue of land tenancy without directly addressing it. While some farmers owned their land and had more control of their livelihood, tenant farmers were subjugated to the directives of their landlords, much like laborers and their bosses. Without this important illumination, delegates struggled to come to a consensus on "the farmer question."

The majority report of the farmers' committee, submitted by Carl Thompson of Wisconsin, sought to reassure land-owning farmers. The report argued that improving the "condition of the wage working class, raising their standard of living and thereby increasing their power, will render more stable the market for farm products. . . . And as for the ownership of the land by the small farmers, it is not essential to the Socialist program that any farmer shall be dispossessed of the land which he himself occupies and tills." A minority report declared, "any attempt to pledge to the farmer anything but a complete socialization of the industries of the nation to be unsocialistic."[70]

Texas delegates not only supported the minority report but also called for the collectivization of land. "If the Socialist movement stands for anything it stands for the working class, the proletariat," reminded Laura Payne, a delegate from

Fort Worth. "The condition of the farmer today is exactly the same as that of the wage worker ... We stand for the collective ownership of capital ... and I want to know if this convention ... is going to go down in history as catering to a small middle class of land owners, or are you going to stand for the great proletarian farming class?" In the absence of a plank that spoke to tenant farmers, the SP national convention adopted the minority report by a vote of 99 to 51, and approved the demand for the collectivization of land.[71]

Prior to 1908, the SP nationally failed to address the specific needs of working-class women. At the local level, female party members acted on their own and established women's branches of the party, mainly in urban areas. In the summer of 1907, Josephine Conger, with the help of her husband and leading Japanese socialist Kiichi Kaneko, released a new newspaper *Socialist Woman*. Also, acting at the initiative of Clara Zetkin, of the German Social-Democratic Party, the 1907 Stuttgart International Socialist Congress adopted the position that "the Socialist Parties of all countries are duty-bound to fight energetically for the implementation of universal women's suffrage."[72]

In response, the SP's National Executive Committee (NEC) in January 1908 appointed a national lecturer to agitate among women, and prepared to address the status of women in the movement for the first time at its upcoming national convention in May. The SP created a five-member National Women's Committee, which included Laura Payne, to manage organizational work among women. The committee, tasked with drafting a position on women and socialism at the 1908 convention, issued a majority report that urged the party to get more involved in the campaign for woman suffrage. It also proposed that the party devote more resources to "stimulating the growing interests in Socialism among women."[73]

The majority report of the women's committee at the convention endorsed woman suffrage, but Payne offered a dissenter's voice. She found herself nearly alone in her opposition. "The Socialist movement is the political expression of the working class regardless of sex," began her minority report. "The same blow necessary to strike the chains from the hands of the working man will also strike them from the hands of the working woman." She continued, "It is contended by some that women because of their disfranchisement and because of their economic dependence on men, bear a different relationship to the Socialist movement from that of men. That is not so. The economic dependence of our men, women, and children ... can be traced to the same cause which Socialism will alone remove."[74]

Payne, a teacher born in 1865, was an early member of the Texas SP who distinguished herself as an eloquent, forceful stump speaker for socialism in the Dallas-Fort Worth area. In 1906, she became the first southern woman to run for the US House of Representatives when the SP chose her as its candidate for the Twelfth Congressional District in north Texas. In her opening campaign speech in 1906, she spoke on "The Relation of Socialism to Woman." After detailing the historic oppression of women from primeval times to the present, Payne argued that with the coming of socialism, women would be made economically independent. That she mentioned only economic independence is significant. Although a tireless advocate for women's participation in the socialist movement, she feared that the suffrage movement, which she dismissed as bourgeois, would distract the party from its main economic objectives.[75]

To give women the vote "would do very little good under capitalism," Payne emphasized from the floor of the 1908 convention. Socialists would be better served, she stressed, by focusing on the economic demands of working-class women. She pointed out that working-class men were wage slaves even though they had the right to vote. The bourgeois nature of the suffrage movement in the Dallas area led at the time by upper-middle-class women who organized by holding parlor meetings disgusted her. "I believe in going among the ranks of the women workers anywhere and everywhere," she continued from the floor, but "sometimes when I go to the cities to discuss Socialism, I find the women gathering around in parlors having these little pink teas."[76]

Payne's position held back the Texas SP's organizing efforts among women. After the SP national convention adopted the women's committee's majority report, state parties were to appoint female correspondences to the Women's National Committee (WNC), but it appears that Texas did not. While most state parties dove into the work of building the suffrage movement along socialist principles and enthusiastically reported their progress in *Socialist Woman*, reports from Texas were notably absent. This stands in contrast to the Oklahoma SP, which mirrored the Texas SP in many ways in terms of demographics and the importance of land issues. The Oklahoma SP developed a strong presence in the suffrage movement and carried out the work of the WNC.[77]

After the national convention, Texas Socialists set themselves to the task of the 1908 election campaign. At their state convention, they reaffirmed the 1906 platform, again without a land plank. This time around Jacob Rhodes was nominated for governor, and Smith once again for attorney general. E. R. Meitzen was the nominee for railroad commissioner, and Alice McFadden, a wealthy Williamson County cattle rancher and recent delegate to the national convention, received the nomination for superintendent of public instruction. With the top of the ticket tied closer to the land than in 1906, Rhodes received 8,100 votes or 1.6 percent of the total. The percentage was identical to 1906, but the SP vote nearly tripled—perhaps because of the higher turnout during a presidential election year. In Texas, SP presidential candidate Debs received fewer votes than Rhodes at 7,870 but a higher percentage of the total, at 2.6 percent.[78]

Even if the SP had adopted a land plank in 1908 that appealed to Texas tenant farmers, turmoil within the Texas SP would have prevented them from successfully communicating it to the masses. By this year, a political and organizational conflict originating in Dallas developed in the party. The outcome of the conflict would determine whether the Texas SP would be a middle-class reform organization or a working-class-based revolutionary socialist party.

The Dallas SP local was one of the earliest, largest, and most influential locals in the state. Its leaders—lawyers, teachers, and an ex-preacher—had ties to the reform-based AFL. With few connections to the state's agrarian working class, the Dallas local in this period functioned more as an urban reform organization than a revolutionary socialist party. With right-wing factions in control, the local SP diluted its message in hopes of appealing to a broader base. A left-wing group led by Bell favored a more vigorous public commitment to socialism that would include educating the working class on its tenets. Bell briefly revoked the Dallas local's charter but, when he restored it, the internal bickering continued.[79]

Similar battles plagued the state SP, which in summer 1909 split into two rival organizations with separate headquarters and competing encampments. Leaders of the national party's right wing saw an opportunity to advance their position as a result of the schism. Left Texas Socialists were a thorn in the side of the SP's NEC controlled by Berger and other Right Socialists. The NEC favored a centralized form of administration. In opposition, many Texas Socialists favored more state autonomy and majority rule democracy. They supported such amendments to change the SP's national constitution. As one of the fastest-growing state organizations, the left-leaning Texas SP posed a threat to the continued boss rule of Berger. In response to the Texas split, the NEC intervened on the side of the right wing of the state party. It sent a party professional to Texas on a speaking tour and recognized a dubious election that replaced Bell as state secretary with a leader of the Right faction. The NEC had earlier deployed this tactic successfully in Ohio, Nebraska, and Washington to help the SP's right wing gain greater control of its state branches.[80]

Into the fray to help end the Texas SP's factional fight came Thomas A. Hickey. He was no novice when it came to socialist infighting. Born in Ireland in 1868, Hickey arrived in the United States in 1892, the year of the great Homestead strike, which drew him to the US labor movement. While working in a pump works, he read the works of Marx extensively, became a socialist, and joined the SLP. In 1895 he helped found the Socialist Trade and Labor Alliance, a revolutionary socialist trade union tied to the SLP. For the next five years, Hickey worked as a national organizer for the SLP and became one of the top lieutenants of party leader Daniel De Leon.[81]

In 1901, however, Hickey was expelled from the SLP for opposing the doctrinaire and authoritarian control of DeLeon. No longer a paid organizer, Hickey headed west and eventually found work as a lumberjack in Washington, where he joined the SP. After a brief time in Washington, he moved to Butte, Montana, considered then one of the most Irish towns of America, finding employment as a miner. Using his brief experiences as a miner, Hickey toured the country in 1904, detailing the horrible conditions faced by miners under the economic grip of the mining barons. His speaking tours also doubled as organizing for the SP. Hickey became the state organizer of the Arizona SP in late 1906.[82]

Based first in Globe, Arizona, and then Phoenix, Hickey's tours frequently took him to Texas, where he became a popular stump speaker. As a regular on the Texas Socialist speaking circuit, he became acquainted with those involved on each side of the factional fights. Having opposed the strict rule of DeLeon in the SLP, Hickey came to the aid of Bell in his struggle against the Dallas group and their right-wing allies in the national leadership of the SP. Bell and Hickey, together with E. R. Meitzen, drafted what they called the Texas Program for organizing the SP at both the state and national levels.[83]

The differences between the right and left factions of the SP got to the heart of what the SP's vision of a future socialist society would be. Left Socialists, including most members of the Texas party, envisioned a decentralized, bottom-up party from which rank-and-file members would guide and set party policy, positions, and strategy. They were critical of top-down Right Socialists who left decisions to career-minded party professionals. The left believed that socialism could be achieved only through direct action—protests, strikes, and revolution (be it through the ballot box or violence if the capitalist government forced it). The right clung to the notion that socialism would come about by step-at-a-time reforms through the electoral process.[84]

Hickey, Meitzen, and Bell put forth the Texas Program to counter the degenerative effects of bureaucratic centralism on the party. The program called for a decentralized form of party organization. Its central thrust was to strengthen the authority of the county organization. Under the program, state and county secretaries without interference by numerous committees were the only executive officers. They were answerable directly to the rank-and-file membership. The Texas Program also stipulated that all candidates for political office must be nominated by a referendum and that all state party officials be required to step down at the end of two one-year terms.[85]

To heal the breach in the state party, Bell called an election to choose a new state secretary. Four days after the election won by E. R. Meitzen, the Texas SP, with overwhelming approval by its rank-and-file, adopted the Texas Program as its party constitution. The impact was immediate. Stagnant members and locals, previously discouraged by factional fights, became active again. Membership in the Texas SP doubled, and the number of county organizations reached fifty. "One of the chief benefits has been the increased activity of the rank and file. The work is brought home to them and they take more interest in party affairs," wrote Texas Socialist Nat Hardy.[86]

With a new form of organization and a leadership now directly responsive to the party's rank and file, the political orientation of the Texas SP turned to the land issue. The previous leadership under Rhodes, Smith, and Clark advocated the collectivization of farmland, which they viewed as consistent with the socialist call for government ownership of factories to end the exploitation of wageworkers. The Meitzens, though, remained sympathetic to the landownership aspirations of tenant farmers and sharecroppers. In their view, small family-owned, family-run farms were not exploitative and therefore were not capitalist in orientation. Their view coincided with that of Marx, who put forth that private property "which rests on the labor of the producer" is different from private property gained "on the exploitation of the labor of others."[87] (Some socialists countered, though, that male farmers exploited the labor of their wives and children.) Until 1910, the land collectivization position of the SP remained an obstacle to recruiting Texas farmers to socialism. The failure of the 1910 national convention to adopt a farm program, because of heated disagreements, cleared the way for state parties to draft their own land platforms.[88]

The Texas SP's 1910 platform registered the party's shift to an agrarian-based, rank-and-file party designed to place the working-class majority into political power. The August convention in Corpus Christi approved the most detailed and extensive platform to that date. The platform's preamble reaffirmed the Texas SP's "allegiance to the principles of international Socialism." It praised the "wonderful" advances in technology made by modern manufacturing and agricultural machinery but pointed out that "because of this evolution of machinery . . . the members of society have been separated into classes—the owners or nonworkers, and the nonowners or workers." The platform also called for the democratic reforms of the initiative, referendum, and recall of elected officials, as well as full suffrage for women and abolition of the poll tax. It included traditional socialist planks such as the eight-hour work day, abolition of child labor, and state "accident and sick insurance" with all physicians and surgeons being employees of the state. Their plan for health insurance provided for erecting three state sanitariums and state-run drug dispensaries in every county.[89]

The heart of the Texas SP's platform offered solutions to the dire conditions that farmers faced. By 1910, the problem of landownership had reached epic proportions. Most Texas farmers did not own land. They had lost their land and slipped into sharecropping and tenancy for numerous reasons, including land and commodity speculation that artificially drove up land prices, high transportation costs, periodic crop failures, and lack of access to credit. Sharecroppers and tenant farmers found themselves in debt to their landlord and local merchants with little control over the crops they planted and few guarantees that they would be invited to farm the same land next season. Tenant farmers took the financial risks while landlords reaped most of the profit. To address these conditions, the main planks of the SP's platform called for the state to halt the sale of public land and purchase land held by nonresidents. The platform endorsed a graduated land tax on all land held for speculation and put forth a proposal that once tenants paid in rent a sum equal to half the value of the land they occupied, the land would be theirs to own.[90]

The Texas SP chose someone close to the cultural and social backgrounds of many Texans to stand at the top of their 1910 electoral ticket. As reported by E. O. Meitzen in the *New Era*, "The nominee of the Socialist party of Texas for Governor, Reddin Andrews, is well known in this part of the state: in fact, spent his boyhood in Lavaca County: was a Texas cowboy in his younger days, is a Confederate veteran, and has been one of the ablest and best known preachers in the State, being of the Missionary Baptist denomination." Besides spending his boyhood in Lavaca County, Andrews, like E. O. Meitzen, was born in Fayette County in January 1848. At the age of fifteen, Andrews enlisted in the Confederate army as a scout. The experience made him a pacifist. After the war, he joined a Baptist church and in 1871 graduated from Baylor University as valedictorian and an ordained minister. In 1885 Andrews briefly served as president of Baylor. His numerous ministries in rural disadvantaged communities deepened his religious faith in Christ's mission to aid the poor. Putting faith into action, Andrews became an organizer for the People's Party in 1892. After the collapse of the Populist movement, believing that Christianity and socialism represented the same moral beliefs, he proclaimed, "I am a class conscious Socialist."[91]

Andrews's socialism was by no means a watered-down version of Marxism. In front of nearly fifteen hundred people at a 1909 Socialist meeting in Taylor, Andrews exhorted, "General education is making possible and inevitable a world-wide revolution, which finds its parallel only in spiritual doctrines of life. The oppressed millions see the way of deliverance from the abnormal conditions of poverty and slavery. Socialism derives its life and nourishment from truth, justice, and humanity. It advocates, not reform, but revolution; the substitution of a good in place of bad thing: the displacement of a competitive, capitalistic government by a co-operative commonwealth."[92] Spiritual revolutionary speeches like these made Andrews popular with the rural poor and earned him the Socialist nomination for governor.

The 1910 Socialist campaign benefited immensely from the efforts of Hickey, who became a full-time SP organizer in Texas. Hickey's Irish roots made him particularly compassionate and attuned to the land issue. He often compared Texas's land problem to that of Ireland's: "The 245 counties of Texas are becoming turned into 245 Irelands with their accompanying evils of landlordism. . . . [I]n 1870 there was 5 per cent of the land tilled by renters, now 70 per cent of the population is renters, homeless and hopeless under Democratic party rule."[93]

The response to the new land program registered in the SP's increasing electoral strength. Andrews received 5.3 percent of the 1910 total vote. Progressive Democrat Oscar Colquitt won the governor's race in a landslide with 80 percent of the vote. For a new party, the Socialist vote in Texas had grown substantially since 1902. During the following two years, Socialists campaigned hard on the landownership problems of poor farmers. In 1912, with Andrews running again, Socialist votes more than doubled to 25,258 and 8.4 percent of the total. It was the highest number of votes the Texas SP ever received and it passed the Republican Party as the second-largest party in the state.

To aid the SP's rising electoral popularity, the Meitzens founded a new weekly newspaper, the *Rebel*, which was printed in their New Era print shop in Hallettsville. The print shop employed eleven people, including Arnold Meitzen. In June 1911 Hicks ended the seven-year run of the *Farmers Journal* to back the new socialist newspaper. The *Rebel* retained Hicks as an associate editor, but Hickey took over as managing editor. As business manager, E. R. Meitzen remained largely behind the scenes, focusing on his responsibilities as SP state secretary. The name of the newspaper did not derive from Confederate origins, as might be assumed for a southern newspaper. "Rebel" referred to Socialists in America who opposed the centralized rule of Berger. Hickey and the Meitzens embraced the name in their rebellion against Berger to promote Left over Right socialism.[94]

The first issue of the *Rebel* appeared on July 1, 1911. "*The Rebel* is here because of an insistent demand for a clean-cut paper that will fight the battles of the socialist party in Texas and the South," wrote Hickey in the first issue. Making clear the paper's revolutionary ideology, he expanded: "we will continue to appear weekly until the conflict between classes that brought the Socialist party into being has ended. With the complete overthrow of the present anarchistic, war breeding, cannibalistic, woman killing, cradle robbing system of capitalism, civilization will be developed and humanity shall step to a higher plane." The masthead of the *Rebel* was the motto of the Irish Socialist Republican Party led by James Connolly: "The great appear great to us only because we are on our knees—LET US ARISE."[95]

Because of the efforts of rank-and-file rebels, the *Rebel* had a circulation of more than eighteen thousand within six months. The circulation, which grew to twenty-six thousand with one hundred thousand copies printed for special editions, made the newspaper one of the largest socialist publications in the nation. To finance the paper, the Meitzens created the Socialist Printing Company. The Meitzens owned half the company and the Boeer family of Stonewall County owned the other half.[96]

The Boeers served as a linchpin of the SP in Texas. The matriarch of the family was Maria Wolf Boeer. Born in Silesia on April 12, 1844, she immigrated to

Texas in 1872. In March 1875, she married Wilhelm Boeer in Colorado County. Wilhelm, born in Prussia in 1833, first appeared in US census records in Fayette County in 1860. He opposed Prussian absolutism and militarism and often said, "I rather be dead than be a soldier and kill others." Together Wilhelm and Maria farmed in Colorado County into the 1880s and had at least six children. Wilhelm died sometime around the turn of the century, shortly after the family moved to west Texas to start anew.[97]

As a widow, Maria kept the farm running, raised her children, and was an active socialist. German remained Maria's primary language, and she maintained an extensive correspondence with writers and activists in Germany. While in Texas, she worked to get *Habt Acht*, the German-language socialist newspaper published by the Meitzens, and other socialist literature into the hands of fellow German Texans.[98] Her political work with the Meitzens represented one of the last threads of German-language radicalism in Texas dating back to its peak from the 1850s through the 1870s. Assimilation and a steep decline in German immigration by 1900 lessened the influence of the German element in Texas politics.

During the tumultuous period of the factional fights of 1909, west Texas was the only area of the state where the SP was not in decline or stagnant. The organizing efforts of the Boeers, Hicks, and others made west Texas an area

Brandenburg Socialist Brass Band at Brazos River Campground, Stonewall County, circa 1911. Photo courtesy of Eddie Wolsch.

Stammtisch (regular friendly get-together) of socialists at Boeer home in Brandenburg, Texas, circa 1910–12. Maria Boeer (1844–1936) is in the center of the bottom row in white with sunglasses. Photo courtesy of Eddie Wolsch.

of growth for the party. Maria Boeer's daughters—Louise (born 1877), Alma (1880), and Clara (1884)—joined their mother in the socialist movement. Louise married Karl Wolf, a radical thinker born in Germany in 1877 who immigrated with his parents to Texas in 1891. Wolf joined the SP and helped build it in west Texas with the Boeers. The annual picnic for west Texas Socialists was held on Wolf's farm. A 1910 newspaper reported that the picnic was attended by "all German farmers . . . and some of their American neighbors." Hickey aided the Boeer-Wolf family's organizing. He spoke at the Wolf farm socialist picnic in 1910, and he and Wolf became close political confidants. More than politics motivated Hickey's frequent trips to west Texas. He and Clara Boeer fell in love and were married on March 1, 1912.[99]

Being the only party in Texas with a land plank helped the SP's growth among farmers, but land was not the only issue differentiating the party from its political rivals. The Texas SP was the only party that supported woman suffrage in the state. After the departure of Laura Payne from Texas, the Texas SP fell in line with the SP nationally by being more forthright in its support for woman suffrage. The second plank of the state platform of 1910 called for "the extension of the full right of franchise to women."[100] So did every subsequent platform of the party throughout its existence. The *Rebel* touted itself as "the Southern organ for the women's suffragists."[101] In contrast, the Texas Democratic Party in its 1916 main platform remained silent on this issue with a minority report stating, "We declare our unalterable opposition to female suffrage through an amendment to the Federal Constitution."[102]

In October 1910 E. R. Meitzen attempted to correct the Texas SP's previous nonparticipation in the SP's WNC. He wrote Caroline Lowe, general coordinator of the SP's WNC, about appointments to the party's state women's committee and let her know that "there are quite a number of active women comrades in the movement here." As laborers and farmers themselves, working-class women were attracted to the SP's labor and land planks. Meitzen appointed Alma Boeer the Texas SP's state correspondent to the committee. Later, his mother, Johanna, also served as a correspondent to the WNC, but neither Alma nor Johanna seems to have actively participated. Neither the *Rebel* nor *Socialist Woman* reports on their work. The work for socialism and suffrage in the Texas SP came from the rank and file and from women socialist leaders such as Kate Richards O'Hare, of Missouri, doing work in Texas.[103]

When it came to women's rights, the Texas SP did not stop at suffrage. "The women of the south are beginning to cry out more or less in revolt against the continuous child-bearing that is forced on them by Bourbon tradition," wrote Hickey in a 1916 letter on birth control.[104] The *Rebel* frequently championed Margaret Sanger and her fight for women's access to birth control, calling her "one of the noblest women in the world."[105]

The economic realities of the rural South pressured women into having large families. When a renter sought to work a piece of land, the two questions the landlord regularly asked were "How many mules do you have" and "how many children do you have?" The landlord rented to the largest family applying. Early marriage often became the rule in order to maximize the number of children available for labor, putting an extra burden on female reproductive labor. Rural women often became brides at the age of thirteen or fourteen.[106]

The *Rebel* suggested "that every tenant in Texas who is encouraged by his priests, landlords and bankers to raise a large family regardless of the effect on the health of his wife and her children, should write to Mrs. Margaret Sanger." Although the *Rebel* was addressing male readers, the response was massive. The office handling demands for Sanger's pamphlets was overwhelmed with requests from the South.[107] "Dear Comrades Hickey and Meitzen," wrote Sanger:

> I have often wanted to write to you Rebel friends down there to tell you that I heard from hundreds and hundreds of women in the South asking for pamphlets. They mention The Rebel or friends who had read it. I am always so glad to send literature down there where women have less opportunity to get in touch with the

movement like in the cities. The farm women especially, I am anxious to reach. I never realized how much good and what a powerful factor the small radical paper has been in America until this work came up.[108]

According to Sanger's secretary, Texas ranked third, behind New York and Pennsylvania, in states requesting birth-control information from Sanger. Hickey boasted that "Mrs. Sanger credits The Rebel with this excellent showing."[109]

The Texas Program drafted by Hickey, Bell, and E. R. Meitzen, with an emphasis on local control and rotating leadership, provided the means for rank-and-file members to run the Texas SP in a more democratic fashion. On one hand, the party overcame the ideological purity of its ultraleft that advocated the collective ownership of land. On the other, the Texas SP took on the national leadership by the party's right wing. Once Meitzen was elected state secretary, he did not retaliate against previous opponents by expelling them. Instead, the party in Texas openly debated diverse points of view derived from a general commitment to work toward socialism.

The Texas Program opened the way to adopt a land plank that focused on the needs of sharecroppers and tenant farmers, who made up the greater part of the state's farmers. With an organizational structure in place that matched its democratic working-class ideology, the Texas SP became the main vehicle of Progressive Era reform in Texas and posed a direct challenge to the state's economic and political elites.

5 *Tierra y Libertad*

By 1911, the Texas Socialist Party had brought the farmer-labor bloc to a new stage of its political evolution. Growing wealth inequality and a government in the pocket of big business convinced agrarian radicals that the entire economic system needed to be replaced, not reformed. The Meitzens and their allies united the Texas SP around a revolutionary socialist program to address the needs of workers and farmers, but they now faced internal opposition from conservative Socialist leaders at the national level. At the same time, the Texas SP cut itself off from large sections of farmers by viewing the issue of growing land tenancy as principally a problem for white farmers. Just as the transnational influence of the 1848 German Revolution provided the spark for farmer-labor radicalism in Texas, the Mexican Revolution impelled the Texas SP to confront its racial divisions and broaden its organizational base.

To organize and champion the demands of tenant farmers, Socialists created the Renters' Union in 1911. At its founding convention in Waco in November, delegates called for lower rents, more legal and economic protection for tenant farmers, redistribution of land, and the end of the bonus system. They also declared "use and occupancy as the only just title to land." To lead them in this fight, they elected E. O. Meitzen to head the Renters' Union. Unlike the Populist movement and the Farmers' Union, which claimed to speak for all farmers, the Renters' Union represented the interests only of tenant farmers, who were now more than 52 percent of all Texas farmers.[1]

The Renters' Union was not immune to the prevalent racism of the era. At its first convention, membership was limited to "all white persons over 16 years of age who are tenant farmers." In the months leading up to the founding convention, the *Rebel* presented the need for a Renters' Union in stark racialized terms.

Its front page of September 9, 1911, printed highlights of the US Department of Commerce and Labor's census bulletin on Texas agricultural conditions for 1910. The document backed up the Socialists' claims that conditions of tenant farmers were worsening. It also showed that, although the number of nonwhite tenant farmers was increasing, the number of white tenant farmers was increasing even more. Two out of every three tenants were white. In the view of the *Rebel*, the problem therefore was primarily a white one.[2]

The *Rebel*'s appeals to join the Renters' Union were made to "Mr. White Renter." Not only were more whites becoming tenants but, according to the paper, landlords were renting to blacks and ethnic Mexicans over whites. A landlord in south Texas, according to the *Rebel*, stated to a prospective white tenant, "Nothing doing for you. . . . [W]e are going to cultivate this land with Mexicans. We want Mexican renters as we can make more out of them even though they are not as good farmers as the white farmers." The *Rebel* followed with another example from Milam County where a landlord had recently removed most of his white tenants and "In their place he put negroes and it is believed that this year the remainder of his white tenants will go where their brothers went last year, out on the country road with the earth for a bed, the stars for light, and the sky for a blanket." The *Rebel* concluded, "Now it was not because [the landlord] would prefer the odor of a male or female negro's skin that caused him to make this change from Caucasian to negro. He would prefer the Aryan to the Ethiopian. Save for one thing and that is the sons of Ham are as easily exploited as the sons of Montezuma so between the stove polish and copper-colored brethren the white man is being ground to dust. Do you ask then if the white renters should not organize?"[3] Comments like these led black socialist Hubert Harrison to ask whether southern socialists were for "Southernism or Socialism—which?"[4]

The racially exclusive membership policy of the Renters' Union did not last long. According to the SP's official position, capitalism debased African Americans and injected notions of racial superiority into white workers to keep them divided on class issues. The party offered no specific proposals to address the immediate needs of oppressed minorities within the working class. Socialism was the solution for the entire working class. Ultimately, though, it was the example of interracial unionism practiced by the Brotherhood of Timber Workers (BTW) that helped changed the racial membership policy of the Renters' Union.[5]

Founded in June 1910, the BTW organized black, white, and Mexican lumberjacks and mill hands in the Louisiana-Texas piney woods. The Southern Lumber Operators' Association, under the heavy hand of lumber baron John Henry Kirby, responded to the formation of the BTW by locking out workers and importing scabs. Pushed to the brink during the winter of 1912, the BTW at its April 1912 convention voted to affiliate with the Industrial Workers of the World (IWW). The convention began with black and white delegates meeting in separate halls, but, guided by "Big Bill" Haywood, who was in attendance, and Louisiana socialist Covington Hall, the delegates decided to buck regional racial norms and met together in one hall. The IWW's direct-action tactics and interracial inclusiveness reenergized the BTW, resulting in modest gains in Louisiana. But the near-feudal control Kirby had over east Texas lumber towns left very little room for the IWW and BTW to make headway into Texas.[6]

The BTW's militancy and cross-racial solidarity inspired Texas Socialists and farmers. At the Renters' Union's second convention in 1912, delegates eliminated the word *white* from its membership requirements and called for African Americans to organize separate local unions. Little evidence, however, has been discovered to suggest African Americans organized their own locals.[7]

After 1912, however, large numbers of Mexican Americans were drawn to the Renters' Union. If the Meitzens and Tom Hickey were surprised with the large number of Mexican Americans joining the Renters' Union, they should not have been. In November 1910, ten months prior to the founding of the Renters' Union, the Mexican Revolution broke out. Just as the land issue stood central for Texas tenant farmers, so did it too for many Mexican revolutionaries. The violence of the Mexican Revolution, in which an estimated 1 to 2 million people were killed, and the pull of an expanding southwest economy, pushed many Mexicans into Texas. From 1910 to 1920, the number of Mexican immigrants living in Texas doubled from 125,016 to 251,827.[8] Many brought their revolutionary aspirations tied to the land with them. The once disconnected trajectories of US agrarian radicalism and Mexican anarchism were now set to collide in Texas.

Separated only by a river, farmers in Mexico and Texas in the early twentieth century increasingly lost their land to banks, corporations, and wealthy landowners. Though sharing the land issue with Mexicans, many white Texas farmers held racist views of Mexicans, which prevented an alliance of all exploited workers of the land. Since 1876, Porfirio Díaz had ruled Mexico. In that year, with the aid of US capitalists, large Texas landowners, and landholding elites in Mexico, Díaz had led a revolt and seized control of the Mexican presidency; for the next thirty-five years he would be Mexico's de facto ruler. He centralized governmental power in Mexico City and guided efforts to promote industrialization. It was not, however, internal Mexican capital but an inflow of capital from the US and Europe that drove industrialization there. The result was the emergence of an oligopoly made up of Díaz supporters in Mexico City and foreign investors.[9]

Many of the foreign investors in Mexico were Americans with substantial economic investments in the US Southwest, a veritable "who's who" of US political and business leaders and corporations. Among them were Jay Gould,

J. P. Morgan, the Rockefellers, the Guggenheims, Phelps Dodge, Cargill, the Texas Oil Company, Cyrus McCormick, New Mexico senator Albert Bacon Fall, Texas governors Hogg and Culberson, and Albert S. Burleson, a member of Congress turned postmaster general and presidential adviser to Woodrow Wilson. Americans and Europeans controlled around 90 percent of Mexico's incorporated capital.[10]

The modernization campaign of Díaz and his cohort had adverse effects on Mexico's laboring classes in the field and factory. During the 1880s and 1890s, a movement resembling enclosure converted untitled land equaling one-fifth of Mexico's surface area into private property. Landownership moved from communal villagers, individual villagers, and smallholders to *hacendados*, local political bosses, and rancheros (to a large degree, foreigners) while most Mexicans became landless.[11]

Díaz's rule not only had a detrimental effect on Mexico's laboring classes, it also alienated many elites not directly tied to Díaz. Among disaffected elites and middle-class professionals, a sentiment grew for effective suffrage and free local governments. In the summer of 1900, liberal clubs formed that in early 1901 launched a campaign against the Díaz regime by organizing protests and distributing radical literature. Joining the agitation were socialists and anarchists, including the brothers Ricardo and Enrique Flores Magón. A political process of uniting cross-class forces of alienated regional elites, radical intellectuals, workers, and peasants began, which led to the Mexican Revolution. In turn, Díaz began a counter campaign of repression against revolutionary activity by jailing and assassinating democratic activists and shutting down insurgent presses.[12]

By 1903, the repressive climate under Díaz became so severe that many Mexican revolutionaries decided to organize their activities in exile. In January 1904 the Flores Magón brothers crossed the border into Laredo, Texas, hoping to establish a base of operations to foment revolution in Mexico. The Flores Magóns stayed briefly in Laredo before moving to San Antonio and starting the newspaper *Regeneración*, first published in November 1904. After facing police harassment in San Antonio, in 1905 the Flores Magóns moved to Saint Louis, Missouri. In Saint Louis, they and a small group of fellow exiles organized the Partido Liberal Mexicano (PLM), which by 1907 had more than 350 clubs across Mexico in addition to clubs in the United States. The Flores Magóns began a process in which Mexican revolutionaries had a radicalizing effect on labor relations in the US Southwest—and a significant influence on US radicals too.[13]

At the outbreak of the Mexican Revolution, Texas Socialists' views on the revolution were basically synonymous with those of their Right SP counterparts. The SP took a noninterventionist stance toward it, issuing a national proclamation in March 1911 that demanded the US government withdraw the troops President William Howard Taft sent to the Mexican border and condemned any incursion into Mexico as done on the behalf of US capitalists' investment and property interests in the country. Victor Berger's socialist daily the *Milwaukee Leader* ran editorials against US intervention in Mexico but, for the most part, covered the Mexican Revolution no differently from any other major news event.[14]

The first public display of outright support for the Mexican Revolution in Texas did not come from Socialists, but rather from a committee of citizens of Hall County in the Panhandle. In February 1911 the committee sent a resolution to the state legislature expressing sympathy with Mexican insurgents, their "fellow human beings," and applauding "their struggle for emancipation." Invoking the American Revolution, the resolution called on the legislature to support the revolutionaries' right to armed revolt and to oppose US intervention in Mexico. The legislature did not respond favorably to the resolution, as earlier in the session both houses had passed resolutions in support of Díaz's administration. One senator even called the Hall County resolution treason against the US government.[15]

Following the lead of the Hall County committee, Texas Socialists began campaigning against US intervention in Mexico and in support of Mexican revolutionaries. After the legislature emphatically rejected the Hall County resolution, Hickey wrote a paraphrased version of Irish nationalist Thomas Meagher's "On Abhorring the Sword" (1846). Hickey's "A Defense of the Insurrecto's Sword" appealed to religious sentiments and Texas patriotism:

> I do not condemn the use of arms in the hands of the Mexican *insurrectos* as immoral, nor do I conceive it to be profane to say that the Kingdom of Heaven, the Lord of Hosts, the God of battles has forever bestowed his benedictions upon those like the Mexican insurrectos who unshield [*sic*] the sword to gain their freedom and establish a nation's honor.
>
> From that evening on which, in the valley of Bethulia, He nerved the arm of the Jewish girl to smite the drunken tyrant in his tent, down to this, our day, in which he has blessed the insurgent chivalry of a Magon....
>
> No, Mr. President, the spirits of Crockett and Bowie, of Johnson and Houston, blesses [*sic*] this hall with their presence today and shudders at the degenerate sons of the Lone Star state who would decry the sword that leaps from the scabbard to install freedom and to assert the right of a free people.[16]

This passage encapsulates the transnational influences on Texas agrarian radicalism. Inspired by a group of rural Texans, Hickey comes to the defense of Mexican revolutionaries by invoking an Irish nationalist, who led a rebellion animated by the French and German Revolutions of 1848, and references the Old Testament and the Texas Revolution.

In an effort coordinated by the Meitzens, Hickey embarked on a speaking tour of Texas in the spring of 1911 as part of the Texas SP's statewide campaign to oppose a possible US war against Mexico. Hickey addressed meetings in both English and Spanish. In a March 1911 letter to his fiancée, Clare, he revealed his hopes that a revolution would soon take place in Texas: "Hard-times are ahead for all of us. The Revolution on this side of the Rio Grande cannot be much longer delayed."[17]

The cry "Tierra y Libertad" of the Mexican Revolution appealed to debt-ridden farmers who constituted the majority of the membership of the Texas SP. As Texas Socialists campaigned against US intervention in Mexico, their proximity to Mexico put them in direct contact with PLM militants. Many Texas Socialists, though not adopting anarchism, felt a common affinity with the direct-action philosophy of Ricardo and Enrique Flores Magón also being advocated by Haywood.[18]

Convergence on the land issue between Mexican revolutionaries and Texas Socialists opened the way for Mexican immigrants and Tejanos to join the Renters' Union and the Texas SP. In the summer of 1912, editors of the *Rebel* began to reprint articles from the PLM newspaper, *Regeneración*. The *Rebel*, calling *Regeneración* "the official organ of the Mexican revolution,"[19] frequently reported on revolutionary developments in Mexico and printed articles by Ricardo Flores Magón. It would be hard to call any newspaper the official organ of the Mexican Revolution, but this statement shows where Texas Socialists obtained their initial understanding of the revolution. Though critical at times of the *Rebel* for not fully understanding the internal dynamics of Mexican society, *Regeneración* reciprocated the friendly coverage, reporting favorably on the Renters' Union and covering political happenings in Texas.[20]

Differing political reactions to the Mexican Revolution, appearing even before differences over World War I and the Bolshevik Revolution, led to the initial fracturing of the Socialist Party in the United States during the 1910s. Texas Socialists had long been at odds with the dominant rightwing of the SP headed by Berger over the organization of the party. But once Mexican revolutionaries began interacting with Texas Socialists, the fight expanded from one of internal party organization to how a socialist transformation of the United States should be conducted. The Berger wing of the SP called for step-by-step reforms to achieve socialism and took a noninterventionist stance toward revolutionary Mexico. The Texas SP went further in calling for the emulation of the Mexican Revolution. As the Mexican Revolution politically radicalized white farmers in the Texas SP, it also challenged their white supremacist views toward Tejanos, Mexican Americans, and Mexicans. Through common political struggle, many white Texas Socialists no longer viewed ethnic Mexicans as slavish peons but as fellow fighters.

As Texas Socialists were forging a political relationship with the PLM in the fall of 1912, their faction fight with the right wing of the SP was coming to a head. At the SP's May 1912 national convention in Indianapolis, E. R. Meitzen and Hickey planned to introduce parts of the Texas Program into the SP's constitution. They were optimistic, for the Texas Program had the support of Eugene Debs and other leaders of the party's left wing. Upon arriving in Indianapolis, their plans for democratic structural changes became secondary to the larger political battles at hand. Forced to spend their time on the issues of industrial unionism and the party's choice for presidential candidate, Meitzen and Hickey's motions suffered defeat.[21]

Although the SP was at its height in terms of membership and political influence as delegates gathered in Indianapolis, it was torn by deep divisions. Left Socialists wanted the party to be more revolutionary by building mass struggles against capitalism through propaganda and direct action. In particular, they supported industrial unionism over the craft union orientation of the AFL. The Right, on the other hand, sought to organize the party for electoral action to win votes for Socialist candidates and support reforms that were often less than socialistic. They also felt the SP should work primarily within the current AFL structure and not organize independent industrial unions.[22]

The final compromise resolution put economic and political action on equal footing. It appeased the Right by not specifically endorsing industrial unionism and satisfied the Left by calling for attention "to the vital importance of the task of organizing the unorganized, especially the immigrants and unskilled laborers."[23] Meaning many things to many people, the labor resolution passed unanimously. After its passage, the Right proposed an amendment to the party constitution to make sure its meaning carried on after the convention. The amendment read "Any member of the party who opposes political action or advocates crime, sabotage, or other methods of violence as a weapon of the working class to aid in its emancipation, shall be expelled from membership in the party."[24]

Delegates engaged in a heated debate over the meaning of the word *sabotage*. Left Socialists made clear what they meant by *sabotage* by citing the examples of ancient Hebrews in Egypt spoiling bricks and southern slaves putting stones and dirt in their cotton bags to make them heavier.[25] "This is the time to draw the line between a real Socialist revolution on one side and anarchy, murder and sabotage on the other," railed Berger from the floor for the Right.[26] For Left Socialists, the debate over sabotage and direct action was not one of semantics, but one of whether the SP would be a party run by workers who embraced trade-union militancy or a party controlled by office seekers pushing gradual reforms of capitalism. Their views would not carry; the convention voted for the antisabotage clause 191 to 90.[27] The Right gained a powerful tool to wield against Left supporters of industrial unionism.

The Right also maneuvered to prevent the nomination of Debs for president in favor of either Charles Frances Russell, of New York, or Milwaukee mayor Emil Seidel, but Debs came out on top. Upon receiving word of his nomination, Debs acknowledged efforts by Hickey, Meitzen, and other Texas delegates to place him at the top of the ticket. "I shall never forget your personal loyalty and devotion," wrote Debs to Hickey. "This confidence and affection of you and other devoted comrades is my most sacred possession beyond my immediate family. I shall never forget you and Ed Green, and Meitzen, and Noble, and the rest of the Texas warriors, wheel-horses everyone [sic] of them. You four alone, above mentioned, represent nearly 25 feet of the revolution. When you see or write these comrades send your love along with mine."[28]

On the final day of the convention, after six days of charged debate, most of the exhausted delegates headed home. The Right, though, saw the remaining sparse delegation as one last opportunity for a power grab. In the final hour of the convention, Morris Hillquit of New York City, a Right member of the NEC, nominated J. Mahlon Barnes as chairman of the SP's National Campaign Committee. Barnes, a stalwart of the party Right, had been the party's national secretary from 1905 to 1911. He was a masterful organizer going back to his time in the SLP, though he was a personal scourge for many of his comrades. Before Hickey knew his first wife, Jean Keep, Barnes, a married man, had drugged and raped Keep. When the assault resulted in pregnancy, Barnes forced her to have an abortion. After Keep married Hickey, Barnes continued to pursue and psychologically terrorize her until she left Hickey and became his mistress. Later, while Barnes served as the SP's national secretary he fathered a child with Keep and misused party funds to support the child. Barnes also defrauded Mother Jones of money she had lent him. These final transgressions prompted Christian Socialists in the party and Mother Jones to force Barnes's resignation from his leadership position. Barnes was no friend of the party Left either: As national secretary, he oversaw the expulsion and suspension of numerous Left SP locals. When Hillquit nominated Barnes, he did so in a way that made it appear that Barnes had the support of the NEC and the Committee on Constitution. Barnes's nomination, though, had no such support, because Left members, such as Haywood, who had already left the convention, on each committee vehemently despised Barnes. Hillquit's ruse worked, though, and the remaining convention delegates elected Barnes chair of the Campaign Committee.[29]

Debs was enraged in hearing that Barnes would oversee his presidential campaign. In a rare instance of Debs forcefully injecting himself into an interparty conflict, he attended an NEC meeting to discuss the Barnes issue. Hillquit and Berger brushed aside the objections of Debs and other party members. They went as far as to say that those who refused to work under Barnes should quit the party. According to Debs biographer Ray Ginger, "Debs was so furious that he was literally screaming. With his long body leaning across the table, he waggled his finger under Hillquit's nose and shouted that the objections to Barnes had come from Socialists "just as good as you, Comrade Hillquit." The Right-controlled NEC kept Barnes as national campaign manager.[30]

Never shy of taking on the party's national leadership, the Texas Left jumped into the fray over Barnes. In July 1912 the Texas SP local of Branon, just a few miles southwest of Hallettsville, proposed a national referendum to remove Barnes as chairman of the Campaign Committee. The Branon local charged that Barnes was "foisted upon the party against its will, through the machinations of a few old-time members of the N.E.C." The Right leadership countered by making the accusation that the Branon proposal was a fraud and launched an investigation against E. R. Meitzen for forging the proposal. The Branon local submitted the proposal, but Meitzen did draft it. He emphasized that he asked the Branon local to approve and submit the proposal because he did not want the national membership to dismiss the proposal outright because it came from the Hallettsville local. The investigation cleared Meitzen of wrongdoing. Haywood, a member of the NEC, supported Meitzen through the entire ordeal. Believing the matter settled, Haywood excused himself from the NEC meeting and left town, but when the NEC reconvened the next day without Haywood, the NEC moved to discredit Meitzen anyway by adopting a report against him that "denounces the methods employed in securing [the referendum] as dishonest trickery, not to be tolerated in the Socialist movement."[31]

The connections between the SP faction fight and the Mexican Revolution would come through at a subsequent meeting of the NEC. At this meeting, Haywood sought to defend Meitzen from the report adopted in his absence. He made clear that "in spite of irregularity in the proceedings, . . . there is no evidence of any fraud" against Meitzen and that "no charge of forgery in connection with the motion can be sustained." Berger responded by moving that no further party speakers be sent to southern states. The motion, clearly aimed at Meitzen and his southern supporters, was defeated.[32] Berger's motion indicated his determination to stop the decentralizing campaign of Texas Socialists, even if it meant seriously harming SP organizing in the South.

While points on an agenda have distinct beginnings and endings in the printed minutes, in the actual meetings political debates (especially when heated) are rarely so delineated and frequently carry over to the next agenda point regardless of the topic. After Berger's defeated motion, Haywood proposed that the SP take immediate steps to prevent the United States from declaring war on Mexico. Such steps included calling a general strike should war be declared. The Right, insisting that the SP did not "have any right to attempt to declare a general strike," defeated Haywood's resolution. During the discussions, Haywood in frustration retorted that the Mexican revolutionists "might be in a far better position today if the Socialist party had not steadily refused to do its duty."[33]

Haywood, as the leader of the party's revolutionary Left, had long been an impediment to the Right's vision of the SP as a party of gradual reform that appealed to middle-class sensibilities. The convention's recently adopted antisabotage clause gave the Right the means to be done with Haywood. In December 1912, the Right-controlled New York SP submitted a motion for a national referendum to remove Haywood from the NEC. The motion charged that he violated the party constitution by stating "in public meetings in New York city that he never advocated the use of the ballot by the workers, and instead advised them to use direct action and sabotage." On February 26, 1913, Haywood was recalled by a vote of 22,495 for expulsion (mainly from Pennsylvania, Massachusetts, New York, New Jersey, and Wisconsin) and 10,944 against, mostly from Texas, Ohio, and western states.[34]

Despite vicious infighting, the SP carried out its most successful presidential campaign in 1912. The presidential field was crowded, with Theodore Roosevelt running on the Bull Moose ticket, President Taft seeking reelection, and Woodrow Wilson representing Democrats. Debs embarked on an exhausting campaign tour across the country. After years of scarcely regulated industrialization, confirming much of what the farmer-labor bloc had been arguing about the corrupting influence of capital on democracy, the country was ripe for reform. Roosevelt and Wilson incorporated much of the antimonopoly language of the farmer-labor bloc into their platforms, leaving them to battle it out for the reform vote. A vote for Debs would be a clear vote for socialism. More than nine hundred thousand people voted for Debs, representing 6 percent of the total vote.[35]

Although the Socialist vote reached new heights, the SP's membership declined as frustrated left-wing radicals left the party as a result of Berger's machinations and use of the antisabotage clause against Haywood. For many Texas Socialists, Haywood's expulsion came as bitter news. "Things will not get better unless we have a Haywood in every county, instead of expelling this hero from the party!" wrote Maria Boeer to her daughter Clare and son-in-law Hickey.[36] For many struggling Texas farmers like Boeer, Haywood's revolutionary syndicalism had more appeal than Berger's sewer socialism.

On March 1, 1913, in response to the Right's capture of the NEC, E. R. Meitzen published the first issue of the *Decentralizer*. "The Decentralizer stands for a form of party organization that is simple instead of complex," he pledged, "that breeds peace instead of internal and eternal [sic] warfare, that is decentralized instead of centralized, and therefore democratic, and efficient."[37] The paper defended Haywood, insisting that the recall showed "how little regard for law and decency a bureaucracy has when it wants to 'get' a man it can't control." The paper pointed out that Haywood had no hearing or trial on the charges brought against him by a "clique in control of the national machinery." In a dark, racist reference to lynching that likened Haywood's expulsion to the recent overthrow and assassination of Mexican president Francisco Madero by the counterrevolutionary forces of Victoriano Huerta, Meitzen intoned that Haywood "must not be Maderoed by political Huertas. Even though Haywood were the blackest scoundrel unhung, the gorge must rise to the throat of every Socialist who has any sense of justice at all . . . over the damnable treatment that has been given him."[38]

The collapse of Mexico's short-lived attempt at bourgeois democracy in Mexico under Madero, who was elected president in 1911 after the overthrow of the Díaz dictatorship, sparked an increase in revolutionary violence. Madero's assassination on February 21, 1913, galvanized revolutionary forces against the new dictatorship of Huerta. The widening struggle gave more authority to the radical demands of Mexico's landless farmers and working class.

No longer feeling any fidelity to the SP's conservative national leadership, the Texas SP moved closer to what it understood to be the politics of the Mexican Revolution. The *Dallas Morning News*, in reporting on the 1913 state convention of the Texas SP, declared, "Socialists Hold Up Mexico as Warning."[39] If the government did not address the growth of economic inequality, workers and farmers in the United States would be forced—like their comrades in Mexico—to resort to revolutionary violence. The convention marked a change in attitude of Texas Socialists toward Mexicans and Tejanos. Before, white tenant farmers saw Mexicans as what not to become—servile peons. Now, they held up the Mexican Revolution and its agrarian reforms as an example of what needed to be done.

While the SP was embroiled in an internal faction fight, Mexican revolutionary forces were even more splintered. In northern Mexico, Venustiano Carranza, a politician and rancher from Coahuila, led the fight against Huerta. Carranza's forces, calling themselves Constitutionalists, demanded the restoration of the 1857 constitution. Also in the north, Pancho Villa's División del Norte, at this time aligned itself with the Constitutionalists against Huerta. In southern Mexico, the peasant forces of Emiliano Zapata fought independently to advance radical agrarian demands of land redistribution. The Magonistas aided the Zapatistas because of their agrarian radicalism and opposed the Constitutionalists, whom they viewed as representative of bourgeois interests.

Operating out of Texas, "Magonista guerrilla chieftain" Jesús M. Rangel served as the PLM emissary to Zapata. In September 1913, Rangel organized a small group of sixteen radicals and syndicalists, which included IWW member and

BTW veteran Charlie Cline, to leave from Texas to join the PLM's armed struggle in Mexico. On September 11 Texas lawmen ambushed the band as they prepared to cross the border near Carrizo Springs. After a gunfight and two days on the run, two of Rangel's group and a Dimmit County deputy sheriff were dead before the group was captured and jailed. The fourteen survivors, including Rangel and Cline, received sentences ranging from six years to life imprisonment.[40]

After the arrests of the Rangel-Cline group, the PLM, IWW, and SP cooperated in a national defense campaign to free its members. The *Rebel* frequently covered the campaign. Spearheading the defense efforts in Texas was PLM activist José Ángel Hernández. Born in 1884 in Tepic, Mexico, Hernández emigrated to the United States in 1909, settling in Houston. He worked as a brick mason and a laborer on the sewer system. He reportedly became a socialist in 1912 after "reading Mexican Socialist Papers." After the Rangel-Cline prisoners were moved to San Antonio, Hernández moved there in October 1913 to work for their release.[41]

To benefit the Rangel-Cline Committee, Hernández organized a Saturday night dance in San Marcos on November 15, 1913, north of San Antonio. At the dance, attended by area Mexican Americans, Hernández made available radical literature and information on the Rangel-Cline case. Out of this gathering, 128 men and women sent a telegram to Texas governor Oscar Colquitt protesting what they called the "barbarous" imprisonment of "men loyal to the human race and the liberty of oppressed people." The telegram concluded with a warning that if any of the Rangel-Cline group were hanged, "your state will answer before the whole Mexican community."[42]

During the same period the San Marcos telegram was sent, Governor Colquitt heard rumors and received an anonymous tip that Mexicans in Texas were buying rifles in preparation for an uprising. Colquitt responded to signers of the San Marcos telegram in a letter emphasizing that he was committed to upholding the law. He warned that he regarded their threat as "a brazen one, and if any violence should come to American citizens as a result of your threat each of you will be held personally responsible under the law." He quickly unleashed the Texas Rangers to investigate the signers and the rumors that Mexicans were arming themselves.[43]

The rumors of greater arms sales to Mexicans proved false, but the governor and Texas Rangers went after signers of the San Marcos telegram. On November 21, 1913, authorities arrested Hernández in San Antonio and brought him before a grand jury. During his testimony, Hernández confirmed that he was a member of the PLM and espoused his anarchist beliefs of opposition to government by any state. Unable to detain him for sending a telegram and holding a dance, the authorities released Hernández after eight days but kept him under surveillance. The other 127 signers, most of whom were farmers from the San Marcos area, were also investigated. Judge W. C. Linden, head of the Hernández grand jury, feared that something along the lines of a bombing of the *Los Angeles Times* building in 1910 might happen in Texas if Mexican radicals were "not checked." Colquitt consulted with the state attorney general's office to figure out how to deal with "persons like J. A. Hernandez." They decided that Mexican radicals could be prosecuted under vagrancy laws long used in the South to control labor and remove undesirables. On December 28, 1913, Hernández organized another Rangel-Cline defense meeting in Houston. The local sheriff broke up the meeting, and Hernández was detained on a vagrancy charge. Presumably feeling the heat, Hernández moved to Indianapolis in 1914, where he continued his political activism.[44]

After the San Marcos telegram incident, Governor Colquitt expanded the mission of the Texas Rangers to include suppressing radical Mexican political activities in the state and stopping violations of the US Neutrality Act along the border, which forbids US citizens from waging war against a country at peace with the United States. Historians Charles Harris and Louis Sadler believe that this shift came about because "the telegram made Colquitt mad."[45] A deeper analysis of geopolitical and economic factors, however, illuminate the true motivation: to repress Mexican radicals and consequently the Texas SP.

On October 21, 1913, shortly before the San Marcos telegram, Colquitt returned to Austin from a month-long trip to Panama, Costa Rica, and Cuba.[46] According to the *Dallas Morning News*, Panama Canal Zone officials and the presidents of these countries received Colquitt and his party with much ceremony. "The United Fruit Company ... also did much to make the trip particularly pleasant."[47] On the canal, Colquitt stated, "I think the Panama Canal will bring a world of commerce to New Orleans and other Gulf ports. It will put us, as it were, on the crossroads of the high seas."[48]

The city of Houston was in an ideal position to benefit from the economic stimulus brought about by the interocean commerce of the Panama Canal. With seventeen railroad lines already converging in Houston, in 1910 construction began on the Houston Ship Channel to ensure the city's rise as a major Gulf and world port. Finished almost simultaneously with the Panama Canal in the summer of 1914, the Houston Ship Channel, traveling fifty miles inland, made Houston a major outlet for exporting products from the central west of the United States.[49]

Colquitt took an active part in securing federal funding for the ship channel, and Kirby and Jesse H. Jones played leading roles in getting the project off the ground and completed. By 1915, the annual traffic through the Houston Ship Channel totaled $53 million. Lumber and the booming oil industry were large parts of the total. The greatest item of commerce to pass through the channel, however, was cotton—picked in the main by tenant farmers, many of whom were becoming radicalized by the Mexican Revolution and the propaganda of the PLM and the Texas SP.[50]

The San Marcos telegram was not the only message of protest to greet Colquitt upon his return to Texas. In late August 1913, the Renters' Union and the Texas SP began a petition drive demanding that Colquitt call a special session of the legislature to address the land issue. Specifically, they demanded that the state hold a public referendum on a single-tax constitutional amendment to create "a tax equal to the full rental value on all land held for speculation—excepting homestead reservations."[51] If approved, the amendment would make holding land for speculation unprofitable, and it was hoped it would force speculators to sell their land to landless farmers.

The Texas land petition campaign was directly inspired by the revolutionary land reform in Sonora, Mexico, of July 1913, in which large estates were broken up and given to the landless. "The significance of this move," wrote the *Rebel*, "just across the Texas line from El Paso can scarcely be estimated by the landless Texans."[52] In promoting the petition, the paper urged, "Join the army of petition circulators and help start a peaceful revolution in Texas this fall that will lay Sonora in the shade."[53]

From the end of August until the beginning of December 1913, supporters of the land petition secured about fifty thousand signatures from 172 counties. Petitioners carried out their work in English, Spanish, German, and Czech, mostly during and after the historic Flood of 1913 in which the Guadalupe, Trinity, Brazos, and Colorado rivers overflowed from high rainfall, causing 177 known deaths. In Robertson County, the flooding hit black sharecroppers and tenants especially hard. The demands of the petition gained the endorsement of the Texas State Federation of Labor (TSFL).[54]

On December 20, E. R. Meitzen, representing the Renters' Union, met with Colquitt in Austin and presented him with the petition. In a terse thirty-minute meeting, Colquitt dismissed the land petition derogatorily as "visionary" and refused to call a special session to address the land question.[55] Though the petition failed in its direct objective of getting a constitutional land amendment put before voters, it did succeed in drawing substantial attention to the land question. Making clear the goal of the Renters' Union, Meitzen reaffirmed, "Our goal is to utterly wipe out landlordism in Texas, so that no one may have a 'comfortable income' but the man who himself tills or uses the land he occupies, without exploiting his fellowman."[56] Before the petition campaign, prohibition was the main issue debated by the candidates for governor. Now, because of the Renters' Union's land petition, any aspirant for the governor's office who ignored the land issue would do so at their peril.

At a time of greater attention to the land issue, the *Rebel* expanded its coverage of the Mexican Revolution, praising Pancho Villa. On January 31, 1914, while Villa was the de facto ruler of Chihuahua, the *Rebel* ran an article, "Villa as Socialist." The newspaper predicted that Villa would be the next president of Mexico and that he would confiscate the great estates of William Randolph Hearst and Harrison Gray Otis, "our alleged American patriots." The *Rebel* also reprinted an article from the *Literary Digest* detailing the "socialistic" policies of Villa's government to run the streetcar system, public utilities, a brewery, and gambling houses.[57]

Editors of the *Rebel* promoted a romanticized appraisal of Villa and his politics at a time when Villa enjoyed celebrity and folk-hero status in the United States. John Reed's widely read articles on Villa and the Mexican Revolution appeared in *Metropolitan* magazine toward the end of 1913. Reed's articles helped craft the image of Villa as the Robin Hood of his day. D. W. Griffith's film, *The Life of General Villa*, released in May 1914, furthered Villa's heroic image in certain American circles.[58]

Although some of Villa's policies during his rule in Chihuahua could be described as socialistic, he was hardly a socialist, even if the Texas SP viewed him as a comrade. Historian Friedrich Katz described Chihuahua under Villa in 1914 as a "revolutionary society" that witnessed the "redistribution of food and other goods (but not land) to the lower classes of society." Chihuahua was by no means a democracy, for sole governmental and military power resided in Villa. He did expropriate the land of Chihuahua's Mexican oligarchy for the use of his army, but despite the *Rebel*'s expectations, he left the vast estates of Hearst, Otis, and US Senator Albert Fall intact in order not to provoke US intervention. In contrast, a wide-ranging land redistribution program was underway and political power returned to local villages in the state of Morales under Zapata. The Texas SP's bandwagon admiration of Villa must have raised the ire of its allies in the PLM who opposed Villa and Carranza.[59]

Texas Socialist farmers saw similarities between their conditions and the land problem in Mexico. The *Rebel* confidently observed, "Things are rapidly shaping themselves for a similar revolution in Texas where four-fifths of the tillable land is held out of cultivation by . . . landlords who raise fake issues to distract the minds of our people."[60] A letter to the *Rebel* from Mercedes noted, "And the Mexicans, unable to read and write, are setting an example to the world, in solving the economic problem, which after all is the most important of problems."[61] The *Rebel* continued to take a solid stance against US intervention in Mexico: "All talk of intervention in Mexico comes from a bunch of industrial pirates who have offices in Wall Street."[62]

Besides looking across the border, the *Rebel* began to concern itself with the plight of Mexicans in Texas. E. O. Meitzen illustrated this in the advice he offered in the Renters' Union column: "We have a serious complaint from Fayette county brothers. Many landlords are importing Mexican renters who work on the halves and live in tents and shanties a white man's family would not stay in. The white renters are thus at a 'discount' and a very serious conditions [*sic*] confronts them. What is to be done? We would say: 'Organize, both American and Mexican renters."[63] The advice seems to have taken, as indicated by a letter from a certain Waelder to the *Rebel* a few months later. "I have been talking to the Mexicans as per your suggestion and find them willing and anxious to throw off the despot's yoke."[64] In May 1913 the Renters' Union arranged to have its "Constitution and Catechism" printed in Spanish, although not until *El Liberador* in December 1915 began publication in Taos, New Mexico, did socialists in the US Southwest have a Spanish-language paper modeled after the *Rebel*.[65]

Although white Socialists "talking to the Mexicans" surely recruited some Mexicans to the Renters' Union and SP, the person responsible for recruiting the most Mexicans was F. A. Hernández, a Tejano tenant farmer from Nordheim. Hernández, born around 1875 in Texas to parents who were also born in Texas, described himself as a Spanish American. He was the father of two teenage daughters and two teenage sons.[66] With a stated personal belief in "universal justice for all," Hernández's own life and that of his neighbors as impoverished tenant farmers led him to the socialist cause.[67] He was elected to the executive committee of the Renters' Union in 1913 and then to the position of assistant state organizer. In 1915, he was appointed to a leadership position in the Texas SP as a member of the Committee on Literature and Propaganda.[68]

The organizing efforts of F. A. Hernández for the Renters' Union and the Texas SP contributed to bridging the racial divide, and a two-day Renters' Union "celebration" held in Nordheim on September 5 and 6, 1913, demonstrated that interracial solidarity. Speakers addressed the crowd in German, English, and Spanish. The *Rebel* reported, "The meetings were well attended and with a spirit of solidarity not often met was manifested."[69]

The *Rebel* was also willing to come to the defense of Mexican Renters' Unions. When a prominent Yorktown merchant threatened that he and others would come with a wagon and take members of the town's Mexican Renters' Union to jail if they held another meeting, the *Rebel* responded by telling the Yorktown local, "Don't get scared. The Rebel is behind this move and friends of justice and righteousness need only be notified and there will be trouble in the air for Mr. Would-be-plutocrat [the merchant].... Better act decent: This is no child's play." Mexican Americans joining the Renters' Union were organized into Spanish-speaking locals, following the SP model of distinct ethno-language federations for Finns, Poles, Ukrainians, Russians, and so on. In Texas, for example, besides the numerous Spanish-language locals, in October 1915, E. R. Meitzen organized a German local of the SP in Houston's Third Ward.[70]

The years 1914 and 1915 would mark the pinnacle of socialist organization and influence in Texas. In February 1914, the Texas SP had forty-one hundred dues-paying members. Thousands more read its press, attended socialist encampments, voted for Socialist candidates, and looked to the party for political

Tierra y Libertad

Constancio Cirilo, circa 1940. Cirilo (born March 11, 1885, Tamaulipas, Mexico; died June 14, 1979, Houston, Texas) was secretary and treasurer of the Yorktown Renters' Union. Photo courtesy of Lotus Cirilo.

guidance. The highlight of this period for the SP was its 1914 gubernatorial campaign.[71]

In a referendum vote of the Texas SP's membership conducted via mail, members selected E. R. Meitzen as their 1914 candidate for governor. Meitzen distinguished himself as a leader of the struggle to root the SP in the struggles of working farmers by addressing the smallholding landownership aspirations of tenant farmers. As the party's state secretary, Meitzen accomplished this by putting control into the hands of local branches through the Texas Program. He also had gained a degree of general statewide recognition as a former leader of the Farmers Union.[72] An able office organizer and editor, Meitzen, according to Hickey, also "found that he has a natural talent for speaking." Meitzen applied his talent with the new organizing tool of the automobile to visit community barbecues in Lavaca County and other parts of the state to discuss socialism and build the Renters' Union during the summer of 1913.[73]

Joining Meitzen on the state SP ticket as a candidate for lieutenant governor was W. S. Noble, a forty-six-year-old veteran farmer-labor radical and farmer from Rockdale. At an early age, Noble joined the Farmers' Alliance. As a Populist, he was elected by the people of Eastland County as their deputy sheriff with his brother, J. L. Noble, as sheriff. He volunteered for a time as a lay Christian preacher and remained part of the faith as he joined and helped to organize the early SP in Texas. The Meitzen-Noble ticket, more than any previous Texas SP slate, embodied conjoined farmer-labor radicalism. Meitzen based himself in the struggles of farmers, but he also was a member of the International Typographical Union who organized the union's first local between Houston and San Antonio. He also organized a clerk's union and carpenter's union. Noble, before farming, was a wage laborer on the railroad and a trade unionist.[74]

Declaring itself "the expression of the economic interests of the working class," the 1914 platform of Texas SP was its most detailed and comprehensive to date. Upholding their view of farmers as part of the working class, the Texas SP endorsed industrial unionism and urged "the wage earners, the working farmers and all other useful workers everywhere to organize . . . on industrial lines, all to the ends that class divisions in the ranks of labor be abolished."[75] The Texas SP persevered to be a unifying force between the field and factory, urban and rural, while many trade unions, farm organizations, and even the right wing of the SP continued to view the interests of the two as separate.

In May 1914, three months before the outbreak of World War I, opposition to military intervention in Mexico remained a primary focus of the Texas SP's platform. Referring to Mexico as "our sister republic," Texas Socialists advocated "a policy of hands off the internal affairs of Mexico" from "war crazed nations" acting in "the interests of international capitalists."[76] Texas Socialists provided an early model of working-class internationalism and anti-imperialism for others to draw on when war in Europe began.

In addition to endorsing industrial unionism and opposing US intervention in Mexico, the Texas SP platform offered a wide array of proposals designed to advance the economic and political interests of the working class. After the Socialist call for the means of production and distribution to be "socially owned and democratically controlled," the platform advanced specific proposals. Predating the modern welfare state, the platform called for old-age pensions, "free medical attendance," workplace insurance, employer liability for workplace accidents, child labor laws, and free public education. Political and labor reforms included the repeal of vagrancy laws and blacklists, ending the use of convict labor, eliminating the poll tax, woman suffrage, a mail-in ballot for elections, and abolition of the Senate and veto power of the governor.[77]

Still, with the vast majority of the Texas working class being farmers, the Texas SP sought to make land the main issue of the 1914 election campaign. They made this abundantly clear with the campaign slogan "For Land and Liberty," taken directly from the Mexican Revolution's cry of "Tierra y Libertad." Specifically, Socialists demanded that all of the state's uncultivated land be made available to landless farmers, and called for high taxes on land held for speculative purposes.[78]

The land question did become the main issue of the campaign, but in a way that caught the Texas SP off guard. Within the Texas Democrat Party, prohibition was the dominant and most divisive issue, with progressive drys holding a slight edge over wets by 1914. Before the primary campaign, most expected the former congressman and Houston attorney Thomas Ball to receive the Democratic nomination for governor. As an ardent prohibitionist, connections to railroads and other corporate clients through his legal practice, and a longtime promoter of the Houston ship channel, Ball seemed the sure-win candidate. Texas Socialists eagerly anticipated a general election campaign in which they could offer a clear working-class alternative, centered on the land issue, in opposition to the corporate attorney. This was not to be.[79]

Into the fray of the Democratic primary stepped James Ferguson, relatively unknown at the time. Defying traditional political categories, Ferguson pursued an egocentric brand of politics based on advancing his own political power and influence. He was a formidable politician who became a major force in Texas politics for the next two decades. Born in 1871 in Bell County, Ferguson was the son of a Methodist minister who died when he was four. Ferguson spent his youth working the family farm. As a young adult, he roamed from job to job until he entered law school and passed the bar in 1897. In 1899 he married Miriam Wallace, a well-off farmer's daughter, who became not only his wife but his political partner. After his marriage, Ferguson began his rise among the area's financial elites. He first ventured into real estate and insurance, and in 1907 he opened the Temple State Bank. When he entered politics, his personal wealth—over $400,000—afforded him the luxury of financing his own campaigns.[80]

Unlike establishment Democrats who ignored the problem of land tenancy and Socialists who viewed it as a reason for class struggle, Ferguson saw it as a political opportunity. As wets and drys debated prohibition, Ferguson launched his campaign, emphasizing that he would veto any prohibition legislation and instead focus his administration on the problem of land tenancy. Specifically, Ferguson put forth a plan to limit rent to the prevailing thirds and fourths system and half if the landlord provided tools and supplies. Renting on the thirds and fourths meant that tenants gave landlords a third of their grain crop and a fourth of their cotton crop as rent. Ferguson's rent proposal maintained the status quo, though it would halt the growing number of landlords who squeezed tenants by asking for halves of both grain and cotton.[81]

The initial Socialist response to Ferguson was dismissive. *The Rebel* called him a joker, referring to him often as the "Fake Ferguson" in response to the "Farmer Jim" persona Ferguson donned for rural audiences to pose as a simple farmer. Socialists pointed out that his rent-limiting plan was unenforceable without radical changes to usury laws—changes that he would not make because they would hurt his banking business. In a nutshell, they felt Ferguson was attempting to steal their land plank after the success of their land petition campaign.[82]

Texas Socialists pointed out the hypocrisy of Ferguson's claims that he represented farmers. As a banker, he did not treat farmers particularly well. He charged them the same high interest rates as other bankers. While Ferguson called for limiting rent, Socialists demanded the abolition of landlordism and tenancy altogether. Socialists viewed Ferguson's call for rent limiting as a plan to transition agricultural labor in the state from tenancy to wage labor. This, after all, Socialists pointed out, was what Ferguson had done on his own thousand-acre farm in Bell County, where he worked the land not with tenants, but with wage laborers.[83]

Socialists did not believe Ferguson would survive the Democratic primary. Ball had the support of lumber baron Kirby, the growing oil industry, railroad corporations, and numerous big-business clients of his law firm. Democratic opponents of Ferguson even attacked his rent-limit plan as socialistic. So sure were Socialists of Ferguson's defeat that a month before the primary, a banner headline appeared in the *Rebel*: "Meitzen or Ball—Which?"[84] Both establishment Democrats and Socialists were in for a surprise.

Economic realities made the troubles of struggling tenant farmers particularly pressing. The average price of cotton per pound during 1913 was 12.48 cents. By the start of 1914, prices tumbled to 7.33 cents per pound. Improved agricultural techniques resulted in the largest cotton crops ever for many southern states.[85] The excess cotton, already driving prices down, became a glut on the market with the outbreak of war in Europe and the disruption of trade and export markets. Such low prices made it impossible for tenant farmers to escape tenancy and threatened small farm owners with slipping into tenancy. Many farmers no longer cared about who drank what and where, but instead concerned themselves with their own economic survival.

The land issue relegated prohibition to a secondary campaign issue for the first time in ten years. Establishment Democrats scrambled to draft a land position for Ball. He proposed that the state limit taxes on homestead improvements and assist in providing loans to farmers to purchase homes and land. To fund these proposals, Ball proposed to use one million dollars a year from the state's school fund. Socialists scoffed at Ball's land proposals. Besides defunding public education, which socialists vehemently opposed, Ball's proposal offered tenants very little. With 250,000 tenant farm families in Texas, Ball's scheme to drain a million dollars from the state school fund would amount to only $4 per family—hardly enough to buy a farm, let alone pay one's poll tax and bonus rent.[86]

Socialists were not the only ones who scoffed at Ball's proposal. So did primary voters. With corporate backing and the endorsements of most of the state's major newspapers, Ball had not planned on much of a campaign. Ferguson, on the other hand, conducted a vigorous campaign with daily campaign speaking stops that drew large crowds. He supplemented his public speaking with a dishonest "whispering campaign" that claimed Ball was a drunken adulterer who contracted a sexually transmitted disease.[87]

Ferguson also had no qualms injecting race into the campaign through an unscrupulous twisting of Ball's positions. During the campaign, Ball stated his desire to reform state election laws. He called for the repeal of the Terrell Election Laws, which established the primary system and allowed for the exclusion of many blacks, Mexicans, and poor whites from the electoral process. This call drew the support of some African American organizations. Ball's opposition to the Terrell laws, however, hardly stemmed from a position of racial and class equality, but instead flowed from his concern that the law allowed a candidate to win a primary with a plurality of the vote instead of a majority. This aspect of the laws had allowed Colquitt, an antiprohibitionist, to win the Democratic governor's nomination in 1910, without a runoff, over a field of divided prohibition candidates.[88] To replace the Terrell laws, Ball proposed requiring an educational prerequisite for voting—a Jim Crow legislative tool used in other southern states. Ferguson attacked Ball's education prerequisite as taking the vote away from Confederate veterans and giving it to blacks. "He wants to cut out from voting these brave men who fought that this state might be here today and were fighting when they might have been studying and acquiring an education," Ferguson declared. "He wants to let the niggers vote who have been educated at the public expense... by the taxes even these old soldiers may have paid."[89] Ferguson's devious political mind turned Ball's Jim Crow proposal into a position favoring educated blacks over Confederate veterans.

Not reliant on corporate backers to get his message out, Ferguson spent more than $31,000 on his campaign, an unheard-of amount in Texas at the time. National brewing companies, intent on preventing prohibition, buttressed his campaign funds. The liquor lobby expended resources to turn out the German vote in central Texas, the Mexican vote in south Texas, and the labor vote in the larger cities. Boosting his Farmer Jim credentials, Ferguson gained the endorsement of the Farmers' Union, which by this time was but a shell of its former self after many agrarian radicals left it for the SP around 1908. (The Farmers' Union now primarily served the interests of its merchant and banker sponsors.) On primary day, Ferguson registered a dramatic defeat of Ball by a vote of 237, 062 to 191,558.[90]

Texas Socialists' interactions with Mexican and Tejano radicals had chipped away at prevailing racist attitudes by 1914, but only to a very limited extent. When addressing fellow Socialists and members of the Renters' Union, agrarian radicals called for the organizing of Mexican workers. But when it came to public campaign appearances, Socialists still bowed to the racial norms of the era, if not with the same fierceness as their Democratic opponents. In Meitzen's campaign against Ferguson, he often couched his appeals to white farmers in racist terms. Meitzen throughout his campaign often made his appeals to white farmers who feared that tenancy would pull them down to the levels of poor Mexicans and African Americans. "Many white renters of good old southern stock have worked the land for many years," he began in a reference to conditions in Rockwell County. "These white renters helped to build one of the largest and best equipped rural high schools in the state. . . . Then the landlords moved to town, plantations were established and negroes and Mexicans were placed in the homes that the white renters once used."[91]

Meitzen and Noble carried out a grueling campaign throughout the state. From the end of May until the end of October, Meitzen made campaign appearances every day with only two interruptions. Toward the end of the campaign, heavy rains on the night of October 23 washed out the railroad bridges, preventing him from making a stop in Victoria. This gave Meitzen in his words, "a quiet day away from the battle and strife of a five months [sic] gubernatorial campaign." The other interruption came in mid-July when his father was shot![92]

On the morning of July 15, E. O. Meitzen, accompanied by Rev. J. W. Brice, a fellow Socialist, left the Hallettsville Post Office after purchasing postal cards. On the sidewalk outside the Post Office, City Marshall O. T. East approached Meitzen. East was upset at Meitzen for sending a letter to the city council requesting an investigation of the city's finances after Meitzen discovered that $13,000 of the city's budget was unaccounted for. Meitzen refused to talk to East and walked away. Just the day before, East had accosted Hickey on the street, threatening him and demanding that Meitzen keep silent about calling for an investigation. On this day, East refused to be ignored. East, a much smaller man than the fifty-nine-year-old former blacksmith, came at Meitzen from behind and slapped him. Standing his ground, Meitzen responded by striking East. East then pulled out his automatic pistol and fired at Meitzen, hitting him in the right groin. Meitzen lunged at East, putting him in a bear hug, causing East's second shot to miss. To prevent further firing, Meitzen bit down on East's pistol hand, severely injuring his thumb.[93] As Meitzen later recalled, "I was a bit dazed after the bullet hit and the thought struck me I was chewing on one of my friends who were around, so I spit out his hand. Confound him, I should have chewed it off."[94]

Hearing gunfire, nearby townspeople rushed to the scene and separated East and Meitzen as they wrestled on the ground. Fortunately, the bullet did not hit Meitzen's femur or any arteries, but it still created a nasty wound. Other than Meitzen's bullet wound, East came out of the struggle worse for the wear, badly bruised and bitten. East received medical treatment and, after posting a $500 bond, authorities allowed him to go home. Meitzen's son Arnold was one of the first to arrive at the scene. Leaning on his son's arm, E. O. walked to a nearby drugstore, where his wound was dressed.[95] From the table, Meitzen reportedly cried out "Print the news, keep the fight going."[96] When leaving the drugstore for his home, Meitzen told the gathered crowd, "Good-bye boys, it takes more bullets than this to kill old Meitzen."[97]

The news of Meitzen's shooting spread rapidly and shocked his family, friends, and comrades. E. R. immediately left the campaign trail to attend to his father. Feelings of shock quickly turned to anger. For two hours, Hickey fielded telephone calls from "angry men, who had armed themselves and were prepared to come to town on horseback, in autos, buggies, and wagons to our assistance." He and E. O. Meitzen implored for peace, and cooler heads prevailed. They insisted that East was not a "bad man at heart; he was the victim of a vicious system."[98]

Instead of arms, the people of Lavaca County flooded the Meitzen home with gifts to aid the respected agrarian radical's recovery. E. O.'s daughter, Frieda, recalled, "feasting on fruit cake, roast turkey, dewberry cobble, mill ground corn meal bread, etc. for weeks, while papa soon recovered and the marshal had near 'blood poison.'"[99] The "vicious system" never brought charges against East.[100]

Eugene Debs with Texas and Oklahoma socialists, circa 1910–14. Debs, top row center; E. O. Meitzen, center with gray beard; directly above Meitzen, Theodore Debs; to left of Meitzen, Tom Hickey (with dark beard); to left of Hickey, Oklahoma Socialist Party leaders Patrick Nagle (with mustache) and Fred Holt (partially cut off). Photo courtesy of Ann Meitzen.

The high points of the 1914 Socialist election campaign were the summer encampments. Conducted in July and August at various locations throughout the state, the encampments were some of the liveliest and best-attended the Socialists had ever organized, despite a heat wave with temperatures as high as 117 degrees. The encampments, which usually lasted three days, featured speakers such as E. R. Meitzen, W. S. Noble, Stanley Clark, Eugene Debs, and Kate Richards O'Hare.[101] In addition to Socialist speakers, the encampments featured evening entertainment and other attractions, as well as "plenty of wood, water and shade for camping purposes."[102]

Debs called the 1914 summer encampments of Texas and Oklahoma "the most extraordinary and significant of the kind I have ever attended." He described how eight thousand people, mainly tenant farmers, arrived at the encampment in Golden, Texas. "They came in processions and all the highways were filled with their wagons. Every man, woman and child of them carried a red flag. . . . Far as the eye could reach along all the roads there was the stream of farmers' wagons, filled with their families, and all of them waving red flags. It looked as if the march to the Socialist Republic had actually begun." Through interaction with encampment attendees, Debs concluded, "The most class-conscious industrial workers in the cities are not more keenly alive to the social revolution nor more loyal to its principles or more eager to serve it than are these farmers." Attendees were at the encampments for more than a temporary respite from the daily drudgery of farm life. As Debs observed, "These are Socialists, real Socialists, and they are ready for action, and if the time comes when men are needed at the front to fight and die for the cause, the farmers of Texas and Oklahoma will be found there and their wives and children will not be far behind them."[103]

The militancy of many tenant farmers at the encampments gave Texas Socialists optimism heading into the November elections, but they had realistic expectations in what they sought to achieve at the polls. They knew winning the governorship was unlikely but believed a respectable Socialist vote would put working-class pressure on the government. "The more we reduce the vote in the Democratic primaries," wrote E. R. Meitzen, "and the higher the Socialist vote goes next November, the more hesitant will big business be about putting over on the people their raw deals and steals through their legislative and state official tools." While partially conceding the governor's race, the Texas SP aspired to win a few state congressional elections. "If the Socialist party succeeds in securing a hundred thousand votes in Texas this year," editors of the *Rebel* began, "it will mean that we will carry many counties and representative districts; that the voice of the people will be heard on the floor of the Texas legislature for the first time and that the few husky Socialists with the bull whip of knowledge will lash the rascals through the halls of the legislature."[104]

Ferguson, by campaigning on the land issue, handily won the general election. The antiestablishment Democrat received 176, 599 votes to Meitzen's 24, 977. Meitzen's totals were more than the Republicans', at 11,411. The Socialist vote for governor was 281 votes less than they received in 1912, but the percentage of the SP vote increased from 8.4 percent in 1912 to 11.6 percent in 1914. After the election, Hickey complained that Ferguson stole much of the Socialists' thunder. According to Hickey, the consensus of newspaper people was that the SP had helped elect Ferguson by making the land issue the central one of the campaign. The Texas SP failed in its goal of reaching one hundred thousand votes, but the party shaped the political issues of the campaign and in so doing achieved its highest percentage of the vote ever—a total that did not include much of the SP's main constituency of tenant farmers who could not afford to pay the $1.75 poll tax. In addition, contemporary federal and university researchers found that there was widespread intimidation of tenants by landlords to dissuade them from voting for Socialists. In many areas, the secret ballot was a farce because Democrats controlled the election process.[105] The Texas SP was not purely an electoral party, and its struggle to improve working-class economic and political conditions did not pause between election cycles. Undeterred and even emboldened, Socialists headed with confidence into the new year.

By 1915, further radicalization of the Mexico Revolution exerted greater influence on the Texas SP. In September 1914 Villa broke with Carranza and shortly after formed an alliance with Zapata. By this time, the Texas SP had moved beyond the romantic view of Villa to embrace the land reform carried out by Zapata. The *Rebel* reprinted Zapata's August 1914 Manifesto to Mexicans, which attacked the limited land reforms of Carranza and called for deepening the agrarian revolution. Closer political collaboration with Mexican revolutionaries and immigrants brought about a more nuanced understanding of the Mexican Revolution within the Texas SP.[106] In December the *Rebel* printed a lengthy article by Ricardo Flores Magón, who condemned Carranza and also Villa for not committing to the agrarian revolution and praised Zapata as "a sincere and valiant" revolutionist.[107] In contrast, Berger's *Milwaukee Leader* ran an article calling Zapata "the blood thirsty rebel leader" as it scaled back its coverage of the revolution.[108]

The high point of Socialists' organizing among Mexicans in Texas came in 1915 when they were joined by Mexican revolutionary Lázaro Gutiérrez de Lara. In 1906 he had played a leadership role in the copper mine strike in Cananea, Mexico. The strike forged an early political partnership between the PLM, the IWW, and the SP. From a base in San Antonio, Gutiérrez de Lara took to the lecture circuit as an advocate of socialism before returning to southern Arizona to lead a wave of strike activity by Mexican miners. His activities and the organizing campaign by F. A. Hernández, who coordinated twenty locals in Texas, helped to push Mexican membership totals in the Texas SP to nearly one thousand. Locals in New Braunfels and Seguin claimed a combined total of 215, composed mainly of German and Mexican Americans.[109]

The integration of large numbers of Mexican immigrants and Tejanos into the Texas socialist movement brought dynamic changes to the Texas SP, both in its actions and in its political philosophy. For a week in early January 1915, the unemployed of Waco held mass meetings every day and night. At one of these meetings, when a man insisted that the unemployed demand that "the employers . . . discharge Mexicans from jobs and give [them] to Americans," a Waco socialist spoke up, "The man must be demented to advise going after the poor Mexicans . . . and not try to trample over other workers, regardless of color."[110] In a change of tone, the *Rebel* demanded that people have "the common decency to quit referring to the Mexicans as a lot of 'Damned Greasers!'"[111]

Multiethnic collaborations in the Texas SP increased. In Dallas, where the SP local led the unemployment movement, the SP cosponsored an antiwar demonstration with the Jewish organization the Arbeiter Ring on July 18, 1915. At the demonstration, five hundred people listened to speeches in Yiddish and English in opposition to war and militarism. The Arbeiter Ring was a socialistic anti-Zionist workers' mutual aid organization founded by secular Jewish immigrants from Eastern Europe with branches across the country.[112]

The land issue continued as the main spark to Socialist activism in Texas. When Socialists changed the name of the Renters' Union to the Land League of America in mid-November 1914, it indicated an effort to expand the party's base. The new organization took its name from the Irish National Land League founded by Irish republican Michael Davitt in October 1879. Like the Texas Renters' Union, the Irish National Land League strove to end landlordism and secure for tenant farmers the right to own the land they worked. The new Land League in Texas had a much broader focus, however, than its Irish namesake and the Renters' Union it absorbed. The new organization sought to increase the scope of the land issue beyond tenant farmers to town renters and small landowners.[113]

Besides widening its membership base, the Land League reoriented its political tactics. Although the Renters' Union emulated the IWW's model of industrial unionism as one big union for all tenant farmers, the Land League focused on gaining legislative reforms guided by the single-tax philosophy. The single-tax movement originated with radical reformer Henry George, which he developed in his widely read book *Progress and Poverty*, first published in 1879. George argued that the growth of extreme economic inequality was the result of the monopolies that capitalists held over natural resources, especially land. By holding land for speculative purposes, he stressed, economic elites increased their wealth and power at the expense of the laboring classes. To remedy the problem,

George advocated that taxes on producers, such as those on land improvements and personal property, be eliminated and replaced by a *single* tax at a rate of 100 percent on profits from land and other resources held for speculative purposes.[114]

After a brief heyday in the 1880s, the single-tax movement experienced a revival in the second decade of the twentieth century. The single-tax movement gained traction in the Lone Star state from the prominence of the land issue. Texas Socialists had long called for a tax on land held for speculative purposes. Its appeal was not limited to landless agrarians but extended to middle-class reformers who were not socialists and were sometimes even antisocialist. In February 1913 Lavaca County state senator Paulus introduced a single-tax measure on land in the Texas legislature. Though Paulus's bill failed, it did bring statewide attention to the single-tax movement.[115]

Texas Socialists viewed the popularity of the single-tax movement as a way to keep drawing attention to the land issue. As Hickey noted in a letter to William S. U'Ren, a leader of the single-tax movement in Oregon, "The powerful landlord organization that absolutely controls the politics and policies of this state are seeking through prohibition channels to play down the land question. Accordingly we are fighting back through the Socialist party and the Single Tax organization to keep the land issue in first place."[116]

The single-tax philosophy was popular with the nationwide labor movement. After the Portland (Oregon) Central Labor Council initiated a single-tax campaign and California's state labor federation began a similar movement, the Texas SP introduced a resolution to the TSFL's 1916 convention calling for it to endorse a single-tax land amendment to the Texas state constitution. Hickey, with the aid of J. J. Pastoriza, who was elected mayor of Houston on a single-tax platform in 1917, drafted the resolution. The TSFL unanimously endorsed the resolution, hoping that such an amendment would lower land values and thus lower rents for laborers.[117]

Though the Texas SP joined the single-tax movement, it did not do so uncritically. In a series of cowritten articles, E. R. Meitzen and Hickey carefully pointed out that the Texas SP "does not believe that the Single Tax is a cureall, for the ills that beset the nation." Although the single tax in its purest form would eliminate rent, Meitzen and Hickey asked, "What about interest and profit?" They were critical of the single-taxer belief that under a single tax "interest will be natural interest" and "that profit is legitimate." They recognized that single-taxers were still beholden to a capitalist system.[118]

The Texas SP offered critical support to the single-tax movement, but other state Socialist parties across the nation took a different approach. Viewing the single-tax movement as unsocialistic and led by middle-class reformers, many Socialist state organizations either abstained from it or were openly hostile, often for reasons of ideological purity.[119] The Texas SP took a less sectarian approach. Its leaders saw the movement as an opportunity to engage in a popular movement and draw its participants to socialism and working-class revolution. Citing German socialist revolutionary Wilhelm Liebknecht, Meitzen and Hickey were open about their reasons for involving the Texas SP in the single-tax movement. "Was it not Liebknecht," they wrote, "who said that in the course of the struggle between the classes the working class could draw to itself great divisions of the middle class and could use them to great advantage in their struggle against the great exploiters."[120]

By involving themselves in the Texas single-tax movement, Texas Socialists reached broader audiences and formed valuable relationships with the TSFL and middle-class reformers. With the Single Tax League and TSFL, the Texas SP fought for higher wages, lower rents, union rights, and landownership for landless farmers. At the same time, they maintained their socialist principles of independent political action. For example, the Texas SP refused to endorse its close ally, Pastoriza, because he ran as a Democrat in his campaign for mayor.[121] Yet, after his victory, the *Rebel* commented favorably, "The revolution has started and can't stop, using all kinds of instruments to attain its end, and Pastoriza is one of those instruments."[122]

Because early-twentieth-century US socialists exerted much of their efforts on basic bread-and-butter issues of the working class, some historians have characterized them as not Marxists or unsocialistic. Some scholars even go as far as to consider many Progressive Era socialists as part of America's capitalist-oriented liberal tradition.[123] All too often, the historiography of socialism demonstrates an overall lack of knowledge of basic socialist theory and practice. When historians portray socialists as non-Marxist liberals, the characterization can come from seeing tactics as strategy, or seeing the how as also the what. When both progressive liberals and socialists called for higher wages and lower rents (the how), each has a different strategy (the what) in mind. Progressive liberals make such demands to reform the capitalist system. Socialists, on the other hand, join with workers in their immediate demands to defend their basic interests against capitalists to advance working-class self-consciousness and draw workers closer to socialist revolution. Texas Socialists utilized the tactic of campaigning on the land issue and working with progressive reformers and organizations as part of their strategy for socialist revolution. Similar efforts had long been practiced by socialists around the world. Socialists would formularize these tactics during the Third and Fourth Congresses of the Communist International in 1921 and 1922 as transitional demands (slogans) and the united front.[124] Through the Texas SP's use of transitional demands and united-front-like tactics, they pulled the political spectrum in Texas significantly to the left.

In the aftermath of Ferguson's electoral victory, Texas Socialists sought to pressure the state government on the land issue. The US Commission on

Industrial Relations, known more popularly as the Walsh Commission, presented such an opportunity. In the midst of growing labor unrest, and after the shock of the 1910 *Los Angeles Times* building bombing, progressive reformers called for the creation of a federal commission to investigate industrial violence. In 1912 Congress passed a bill authorizing the creation of the commission. The act continued the government's long practice of holding public hearings and creating commissions to redirect public outrage from seeking working-class-based solutions to labor disputes into ineffectual bureaucratic commissions. President Taft signed the bill creating this latest commission, and in addition to representatives of industry and the public, he nominated three labor leaders to the nine-seat commission. His desire was to draw progressive support to his faltering reelection campaign. Congress refused to confirm Taft's appointments before Wilson succeeded him in the White House. Wilson kept Taft's labor and industry nominations and added Frank Walsh to chair the commission, all of whom gained congressional approval. Walsh was a Kansas City labor lawyer whom Wilson had not known for very long. Walsh helped Wilson's presidential campaign in Missouri, but he proved to be anything but just another head of a placid federal commission.[125]

Instead of glossing over class conflict, as many reformers did, Walsh drew out and sharpened class conflict as the way to address the causes of industrial unrest. As Walsh wrote to George Creel, "if our investigation results in placing our whole industrial system upon trial and endorsing or condemning it, . . . this Commission ought to do so [in] some brave and definite terms."[126] The Walsh Commission traveled the country from 1913 to 1915 making headlines wherever they went, both locally and nationally. Walsh and his fellow panel members held notable lengthy hearings on the Paterson silk strike, a New York City garment workers strike, an Illinois railroad strike, and the Colorado Coalfield War and the subsequent Ludlow Massacre. The Commission's hearings and findings were quite damning to the captains of industry in their treatment of laborers by exposing harsh working conditions and poverty wages. "Every great fortune," Walsh said, "is a fundamental wrong. . . . Every man with a fortune must at some time have crossed the line of ethics and of criminal law." Many moderate reformers, establishment politicians, and owners of industry felt the Walsh Commission had overstepped its bounds by attempting to polarize class relations.[127] When Walsh called for a $2.50 per day minimum wage for unskilled workers, one Georgia newspaper editor stated Walsh was "well worthy of a straitjacket!"[128]

On the other hand, working-class radicals praised the Walsh Commission. "There must have been some mistake on the part of the gentlemen who govern this country in allowing Frank P. Walsh to become chairman of the federal commission on industrial relations," wrote Debs. "Not only has Chairman Walsh been thorough in his investigation," continued Debs, "but he has been fearless and outspoken in his condemnation of the causes of poverty and misery, of slavery and degradation among workers."[129]

Agrarian radicals in Texas received an important boost when the Walsh Commission held hearings in Dallas on the conditions of agricultural workers in the Southwest. The Commission marked a departure from previous commissions, whose investigations did not include agricultural labor. Originally, the Walsh hearings were set to begin on December 16, 1914. The timing put pressure on Governor Ferguson to carry through on his land-reform campaign pledge when he assumed office in January. But, when investigation of the Ludlow Massacre took longer than anticipated, the Dallas hearings were rescheduled for March 1915. The postponement gave Ferguson time to act before the hearings began.[130]

When the state legislature convened in mid-January 1915, Ferguson declared its first responsibility was to pass land-reform legislation. "To charge more than a third and fourth rent . . . means a condition of the tenant farmers of Texas not but little better than the peons of Mexico," wrote Ferguson in his opening letter of instruction to the legislature. Ferguson continued in his comparison of tenant farmers on each side of the Rio Grande. "He [the tenant farmer of Texas] can expect nothing but a mere existence and no financial advancement of his condition. The peon of Mexico is getting the same. And the only difference is that the Mexican is now trying to destroy the government that permits such a condition to exist . . . while the tenant farmer of Texas is still loyal to his government and has appealed to reason."[131] The Mexican Revolution loomed large as a warning in both the Socialist and Democratic camps—for Socialists it was a threat aimed at capitalists, for Democrats a danger to avoid.

On March 3, 1915, less than two weeks before the Walsh hearings began in Dallas, the Texas legislature approved Ferguson's landlord and tenant proposal. The House passed the bill overwhelmingly. On paper, tenant farmers seemed to have won a degree of relief from rising rents, but many Democratic legislators voted for the bill with only feigned interest in improving the economic plight of tenant farmers. During Ferguson's election campaign, Socialists criticized his proposed land reform as being unenforceable without major changes to usury laws.[132] Many Democratic legislators voted for the act well aware of this. "I vote for the bill because it is a platform demand . . . yet I am doubtful of its constitutionality," emphasized a representative.[133] Others who earlier opposed such a bill now voted for it cynically. As another Democratic member of the legislature insisted, "I vote for the bill, although I am opposed to such legislation and do not believe it will stand the test before the courts and believe the whole thing to be a farce."[134] Another representative was even blunter: "I vote 'yea' on this bill. . . . At the same time I don't think it is worth the paper it is written on."[135] After passing the act, Democrats could say, rather hypocritically, that they had passed a land reform measure while at the same time maintaining the economic status quo. In fact, the state never enforced Ferguson's land-reform law, with courts eventually declaring the measure unconstitutional in 1921.[136]

Socialists sought to use the Walsh Commission to expose the duplicitous nature of the Democratic Party and further the struggle for true land reform. Walsh appeared earnest in his efforts to learn as much as possible about the conditions of agricultural workers in the Southwest. He called witnesses from various political persuasions and sent field agents to gather evidence months in advance of the hearings. One agent spent three days in Hallettsville, and another interviewed E. R. Meitzen and Noble while they were campaigning as heads of the SP's 1914 electoral ticket.[137]

The Walsh Commission began its hearings in Dallas on March 16, 1915. From the beginning, the hearings demonstrated Walsh's tactic of advancing progressive change by exposing class conflicts. To reveal class tensions in agricultural labor, Walsh had no qualms about utilizing socialists. Between the testimonies of landlords, bankers, merchants, and real-estate agents, Walsh placed those of well-known agrarian socialists and radicals. In Dallas, the Commission heard testimony from Arthur LeSueur, the former Socialist mayor of Minot, North Dakota, at the time dean of the socialistic People's College in Fort Scott, Kansas; Noble, the first president of the Land League; Oklahoma Socialists Patrick Nagle and W. L. Thurman; single-taxer J. J. Pastoriza; Emilio Flores, secretary of the Mexican Protective Association; and E. O. Meitzen.[138]

While the landlords and bankers espoused the virtues of self-improvement and class harmony and the supposed general contentment of tenant farmers, Walsh's radical witnesses laid bare the cruel realities of agricultural labor in the Southwest. The Commission also heard from various professors of economics, sociology, and agriculture, whose statistical facts backed up many of the radicals' claims. The testimony that drew the most media attention nationally was provided by the Texas tenant farm family of Levi and Beulah Stewart.[139]

Before the hearings began, the Commission tasked Noble with finding a typical tenant farm family, and he produced the Stewarts, who detailed their life as tenant farmers caught in an endless chain of poverty. Originally from Arkansas, they married at a young age, hoping to have a farm of their own someday. Instead, they found themselves trapped in the system of renting on the thirds and fourths. They moved from farm to farm, in debt to merchants as they struggled to feed eleven children. The Stewarts described a life of chronic poverty and hunger in which their children died from lack of proper medical care or faced a future without hope of a formal education.[140]

The testimony of E. O. Meitzen provided further evidence that the Stewarts were representative of most tenant farmers. In the months leading up to the hearings, the staff of the *Rebel* and the Land League gathered letters and testimonials for Meitzen to present as evidence in Dallas. He submitted to the Commission more than 150 letters from tenant farmers. In these letters, farmers described how landlords subjugated them to serflike conditions. Crop diversification would have made tenant farmers more self-sufficient and less vulnerable to the whims of the market, but landlords refused to allow tenants to grow anything but cotton. Some landlords did not even allow tenants to have a personal garden. Others claimed half the produce from the tenants' gardens. Tenant farmers, already in debt as a result of low cotton prices, were often forced to mortgage their few meager possessions such as tools, furniture, and a horse or mule in order to obtain credit for food and clothing.[141]

Ill-fed and ill-clothed, tenant farmers suffered from equally dire housing conditions. Landlords rarely provided adequate housing for tenant families. In the letters Meitzen submitted, tenant families with at least six members wrote of their houses that were only fourteen feet long and fourteen feet wide. In some cases, the houses were even fourteen by eleven in size with miserable living conditions. The drafty houses featured dirt floors, few windows, and leaky roofs. "If you try to harmonize the interest of exploiter and exploited," testified Meitzen in response to such conditions, "but still permit anyone to receive interest and rent and profit—all graft—or permit able bodied men to live without work, it means that you are trying to harmonize the interests of the hawk and dove." For Meitzen, the solution was "to stop any man from living from the toil of another," which in his view could be done only by "taking the power from landlordism and placing it in the people, where it justly belongs."[142]

Meitzen exposed the direct complicity of Texas Democratic leaders in the systematic exploitation of tenant farmers. He brought to light Governor Ferguson's past practice of charging farmers exorbitant interest rates, sometimes as high as 40 percent. He also told the Walsh Commission about an incident on a ranch owned by Postmaster General Burleson, the first Texan appointed to a Cabinet position and a key Wilson adviser. Thirty tenant families on Burleson's land had lived there for a few years, renting on the thirds and fourths. They laid down roots, building a schoolhouse and a church with a cemetery. Then, shortly before Christmas one year, armed guards at the behest of Burleson's managers moved prison convicts onto the land. Without notice, the tenant families were forced to vacate the land without anywhere to go, leaving behind the loved ones they buried on the land. Burleson's managers used the convict's labor to harvest the cotton crop planted by the tenants. Meitzen's revelation was a national embarrassment that followed Burleson for many years.[143]

The Walsh Commission also brought to light routine political and racial discrimination. A manager who worked for one of the biggest landlords in Coleman County removed socialist tenants from the lands he supervised and organized an Anti-socialist League in response to growing socialist activism.

Another revelation was that local law enforcement agencies at the start of the cotton-picking season in Texas invoked vagrancy laws to compel "lazy" and "idle" African Americans to work in the cotton fields, "instead of lying around the streets and refusing to do anything," as a wealthy landlord put it. Black workers often did refuse to work in the fields, though not because of laziness, but because of low and discriminatory wages. Through the use or threatened use of vagrancy laws, law enforcement officials at the behalf of landowners forced black workers to pick cotton for poverty wages.[144]

Among the letters Meitzen submitted to the Walsh Commission were several describing the exploitation of Mexican and Tejano labor. F. A. Hernández appears to have done much of the legwork to make sure their voices were included. Gutiérrez de Lara also contributed to this effort, stating, "I have heard of cases of the most brutal peonage to which Mexicans are subjected by the feudal exploiters of Caldwell [County], of this state, and how the Mexicans are shot and sent to prison or to the penitentiary under trumped-up charges for refusing to be peonized."[145] Hernández provided examples of how landlords used courts, where language barriers and often citizenship hindered Mexican laborers, to uphold high rents and interest rates to defraud Mexican laborers of their wages. Emilio Flores, secretary of the Mexican Protective Association, testified that in San Antonio, Mexican American laborers are often not "given work unless they produce a poll-tax receipt paid for the present year." Political cliques then direct them how to vote.[146]

The Texas SP succeeded in bringing the land issue to the forefront of Texas politics, but by 1915, continued admiration of the Mexican Revolution by Hickey and the Meitzens put the party in a precarious position. Some rank-and-file members and other farmer-labor radicals wanted to follow the Mexican path and engage in more direct action tactics. Much like the national party's right wing, however, many of the Texas SP's progressive allies looked disparagingly on many aspects of the Revolution. Emilio Flores, whose testimony at the Dallas hearings disclosed the racist and exploitive treatment of Mexican American laborers, blasted Ricardo Flores Magón as "the worst kind of anarchist" and called his newspaper, *Regeneración*, a "filthy paper," complaining that it was "disgraceful to let such a thing be transmitted through our mails."[147]

Around the time the Dallas hearings were wrapping up, the type of anarchism Flores detested came to fruition. In early 1915 a group of ethnic Mexicans, believing that the disruptions in south Texas caused by the Mexico Revolution made the area ripe for radical social and political change, drafted the Plan de San Diego. The plan, influenced by anarchist beliefs, called for an army of Mexicans, blacks, and Native Americans to kill all white males over the age of sixteen and overthrow US rule in Texas, Colorado, New Mexico, Arizona, and California in order to create an independent republic in the liberated territory.

Adherents of the plan were reacting to the vast changes the south Texas borderlands had experienced over the previous thirty years. For generations, small farmers and ranchers on both sides of the Rio Grande in northern Mexico and south Texas lived as they were accustomed as the region changed hands from Spain to Mexico to the Republic of Texas and then to the United States. In the fifty years after the end of the Mexican War in 1848, Anglos remained a small minority, but by the late nineteenth century, the use of barbed wire, better irrigation techniques, and the arrival of the railroad in Brownsville began to transform the economic and social order of the region. Agribusinesses and Anglo migrants used dubious legal means to seize land from longtime ethnic Mexican residents in the area. Many of the new arrivals were from southern states and expanded Jim Crow into Juan Crow, segregating Tejanos and Mexicans from Anglos. The new social order was enforced by violence, vigilante lynchings, and ruthless law enforcement by local police and Texas Rangers who targeted ethnic Mexicans.[148]

Beginning in July 1915, ethnic Mexican insurgents in south Texas began carrying out the Plan de San Diego by raiding and burning white-owned farms and settlements, killing around twenty-one residents and soldiers. In retaliation, Texas Rangers functioned as a Death Squad along the border and engaged in a campaign of ethnic cleansing. By year's end, hundreds of area Mexicans and Tejanos may have been killed. When a Dallas reporter came upon a Texas Ranger standing over three dead Mexicans and asked what happened, the grinning Ranger answered, "It's been pretty hot today—maybe they died of sunstroke." Federal troops were sent in to secure the border during this so-called "Bandit War." These same federal troops, once the border was secured, were redeployed to the Panama Canal Zone—demonstrating a direct link between the military component of US imperialism in the borderlands and the Canal Zone.[149]

In this climate of fear, sweeping rumors, and sanctioned murder by Texas Rangers, the Texas SP never wavered in its support of the Mexican Revolution. Texas Socialists continued their support, despite the fact they knew full well that federal and state authorities were fishing for ways to connect the SP, IWW, and PLM to the Plan de San Diego, and federal and state agents were questioning SP members and allies.[150] In November E. R. Meitzen traveled to Kingsville near the Mexican border, an area embroiled in "Bandit War" hysterics. In a socialist stump speech, Meitzen declared that the real thieves were the "bank bandits" of the bank of Kingsville (owned by King Ranch interests) that charged working people 33 percent interest. "Mexican bandits may be the scum of the earth," Meitzen remarked, "but they are gentlemen and scholars beside the bank bandits that rob only the poor."[151]

The PLM did not endorse the raids, and the Texas SP had scant connections with the Plan de San Diego, which did not prevent repercussions from coming their way. Emboldened by federal and state repression along the border, local authorities felt empowered to take on farmer-labor radicals. Such was the case of José Ángel Hernández, who returned to Texas from Indianapolis in

February 1915. In August he had received a commission from the Land League to organize locals in the San Antonio area, apparently joining the SP around the same time. On August 30 Hernández gave a public speech advocating socialism and membership in the Land League at Market Square in the center of San Antonio in front of a thousand spectators.[152] After the speech, local police arrested him for "inciting a rebellion and insurrection" and turned him over to federal authorities.[153] Two of Hernández's companions were also arrested as they distributed the San Antonio PLM newspaper, *Lucha de Clases*. An additional twenty-three spectators were arrested on vagrancy charges and held without bond for two days. Hernández's companions were fined $100 and $200 and the arrested spectators were released after paying $10 fines and promising not to attend similar meetings in the future.[154] The San Antonio chief of police boasted to reporters, "They have been taught a good lesson. From now on the Plan of San Diego will have little success here."[155]

Having aligned themselves with the Mexican Revolution, Texas Socialists were now receiving the blowback from the ruling elites' campaign against the revolution. The SP began a vigorous campaign in defense of Hernández. E. R. Meitzen and another comrade personally posted the $1,000 bail for Hernández.[156] The *Rebel* opined that Hernández "had committed the crime of organizing a very large League," noting "that there is a general conspiracy between the landlord and political machine of the San Antonio congressional district to stop the mouth of a man who was on the point of bringing thousands of Mexicans into the Land League and from thence into the party of the working class."[157] Hernández was acquitted and given a hero's welcome at the Texas SP and Land League conventions later in the year. His arrest was not an isolated incident, as more Land Leaguers and socialists faced jail and harassment.[158]

Agrarian working-class militants attracted to direct action continued to be the heart and base of the Texas SP. Proclaiming that the party's "historic mission is to abolish landlordism," Texas Socialists continued to draw inspiration from the Mexican Revolution. Early in 1916, the *Rebel* reviewed what it understood to be the great achievements of the Mexican Revolution—equity in the taxing of land, labor legislature in favor of the working class, the reformation of the judicial system, and the abolition of monopolies over natural resources.[159] When the *Rebel* ran a full-page front-page article under the banner headline "The Land Revolution in Yucatan," it praised the revolutionary government's proposal to confiscate land from wealthy landlords, making use and occupancy the basis of land titles. To reiterate its continued support for the Revolution, the *Rebel* reprinted the article three months later, calling it "the most special issue that has come off our press."[160]

6 From the Cooperative Commonwealth to the Invisible Empire

Transnational experiences with Mexican, as well as German, Irish, and Bolshevik revolutionaries strengthened the working-class movement built by the SP. In doing so, the Texas SP posed a serious threat to the capitalist nation-state. Socialists laid bare the social and economic injustices of capitalism. Through its electoral campaigns and propaganda, the Texas SP had attracted a small, but growing, number of militantly committed members. Though Texas Socialists primarily sought to bring about a revolution through education and the ballot, they did so during a time of intense political tensions. Revolution was not an abstract proposition in this moment. It was happening in neighboring Mexico and brewing in Ireland and the Russian Empire. At the same time in the United States, labor disputes and strikes persisted with no abatement in sight. As the US government militarily intervened in the Mexican Revolution and prepared for and then entered World War I, it waged a nationalist campaign of repression against working-class radicalism in the United States. The SP never fully recovered from this campaign of repression; the result was the forcible removal of working-class economic radicalism from the mainstream of US political culture.

Economic and political elites had acted to repress the Populist movement, but when they moved against the SP, they had assistance from the federal government. In Texas, during the Populist revolt, elites relied mainly on voter suppression and fraud to derail agrarian radicalism. When they utilized physical repression, it was local and not systematic. The socialist challenge to the economic status quo differed from that of the Populists, and it occurred during dramatically different historical circumstances. During this era of world war, revolution, and labor unrest, the state moved in a systematic manner never before seen to crush working-class radicalism throughout the nation. The state had previously used courts and the National Guard to halt individual strikes, but never had the government engaged in anything as wide-ranging as during the Red Scare of 1917–21. Using court injunctions, censorship, denial of mail service, arrests, deportations, and conniving at vigilante violence, the government suppressed and moved to the political margins the farmer-labor bloc and other strains of economic radicalism across the nation. In the Lone Star state, agrarian radicals faced the added menace of the Texas Rangers. In response to official repression, the farmer-labor bloc adopted tactics less threatening to the economic and political structures of capitalism. In doing so, the farmer-bloc compromised its organizational independence, resulting in its eventual collapse.

In Texas, Socialists confronted not only preparations for war in Europe, but also higher tensions along the Texas-Mexico border. Political collaboration between US and Mexican radicals posed a direct threat to US capital interests in Mexico and Texas. By 1914, US investments in Mexico totaled $580 million.[1] Maintaining land and labor conditions that ensured a maximum rate of profit stood high on the agenda for capitalist financiers and politicians. Quelling labor disputes on both sides of the border and preventing political collaboration between Mexican and US radicals was crucial for maintaining profits.

As the *Rebel* continued to report on revolutionary gains in Mexico, reports of radical Mexican American activities in Texas declined dramatically. After the first few months of 1916, the pages of the *Rebel* were devoid of any mention of F. A. Hernández or José Ángel Hernández or celebratory reports of Mexican activism that once frequented its columns. There were also fewer and fewer reports on the Land League and its significant number of Mexican American members. Repression and the drumbeat of preparedness took a toll. Without the activism of its ethnic Mexican members, the Land League ceased to exist except on paper.

The patriotic fervor surrounding the US involvement in World War I put immense pressure on working-class radicals. Political repression surely prompted many Mexican Americans to leave the socialist movement. Also, some Mexicans returned to Mexico to avoid the draft. At the same time, many Mexican Americans viewed the war as a struggle for democracy, leading them to enlist or participate in war savings and bond drives. Each of these pressures help explain the disappearance of reports of Mexican Americans from the pages of the *Rebel*. The individual examples of José Ángel Hernández and F. A. Hernández departures from the SP's milieu also casts light on the dramatic decline of Mexican American involvement in the Texas SP. That said, each Hernández had a different reaction, sending them in opposite directions.[2]

F. A. Hernández's political commitment to his comrades seems to have collapsed from the stress of wartime. He wrote three letters to the Committee on Public Information in August, October, and November 1918. In these letters, he documented his collaboration with government officials, beginning in 1915 after the German sinking of the British passenger ship RMS *Lusitania*. Hernández regularly informed on German and Mexican Americans who voiced opposition to the war and conscription or openly supported Germany. He also brought to the authorities' attention incidents of discrimination against Mexicans, insisting that such discrimination made them open to antiwar opinions. In the conclusion of one of the letters, Hernández wrote, "I have done all this for love of America. And not for the matter [sic] dollar: even when I am discriminated against and is such prejudice against Spanish American in Texas that we not allowed to go in a restaurant, hotel, barber shop or at cold drinks [sic]—even our children are separated in the school." Hernández maintained his basic socialist political beliefs that opposed the corrupting influence of money in politics. Once the SP was labeled as anti-American by the government, however, Hernández chose to inform on comrades and others he deemed anti-American while still struggling against discrimination and for a more just society as a loyal US citizen.[3]

While F. A. Hernández reconciled himself with US nationalism, José Ángel Hernández moved further toward working-class revolution. After the mass arrests at Market Square, many socialists in San Antonio ceased meeting out of fear of being jailed. Local socialists also knew an undercover informant was in their midst. With a halt in socialist activism in San Antonio, José Ángel Hernández now moved more within anarchist and syndicalist groups. In August 1917 he worked as a day laborer at the construction site of Camp Travis, being built to train troops for the war in Europe. Along with Cuban anarchist Antonio Ortiz, he organized Mexican and black construction workers to strike for better conditions and to oppose the war. In the grand plan, area tenant farmers would join them by stopping cotton production as well. After an undercover informant tipped off authorities, Hernández and Ortiz were arrested before the strikes could be carried out. The evidence against the two was "very weak," however, and to put them in front of a grand jury, the Bureau of Investigation would have had to expose its informant. Instead, the bureau agents convinced Hernández and Ortiz to choose deportation. Ortiz was put on a train to Galveston to catch the next ship bound for a foreign port. On August 31, authorities took Hernández to the international bridge in Laredo and ordered him to cross into Mexico.[4]

As the Texas SP struggled to hold onto its Mexican and Tejano members, it was seeking to reach more African Americans. The first Socialist meeting for black Texans occurred in Fort Worth on April 2, 1915, but it is unclear how far the commitment went. E. R. Meitzen in May 1916 urged blacks in Lavaca County to join the SP, but little evidence exists about how many joined.[5] The SP chairman of Rusk County did report in October 1916 that black Socialist R. Lane, of Greenville, was "stirring up the colored folks in the right way."[6]

In 1916 the conflict between the left-oriented Texas SP and the increasingly right-dominated national SP came to an impasse. The first disappointment for the Texas rebels came with the national party's candidates for president and vice president. The Meitzens, like most Texas Socialists, were strong supporters of Eugene Debs, the party's candidate for president in every election since its founding. By 1915, however, Debs had passed his physical limits. In the spring, he suffered a major collapse, leaving him bedridden for six weeks from torn muscles and exhaustion. Although better by summer, he remained in a sanitarium to regain his health. Despite pleas from the party's rank and file, Debs announced in November 1915 that because of ill health he would not accept the party's nomination for president in 1916.[7] He did, though, seek to set the tone of the coming campaign. "The issue," he wrote, "is socialism against capitalism, imperialism and militarism." Expressing lack of faith in the party's right-wing leaders to carry out this clear position, he continued: "There has been a tendency in our party for some years, and it has been quite marked, to obscure the class character of our party to make it more acceptable to the middle class, and on this account many . . . working-class revolutionists . . . have deserted the party."[8]

In the absence of Debs, the Meitzens put their support behind Arthur LeSueur for president and Kate Richards O'Hare of Missouri for vice president. Citing LeSueur's agrarian credentials, the *Rebel* proclaimed "that the hope of the Socialists of America rests today as it did at the birth of the republic on militant farmers." LeSueur was a veteran of the socialist movement who in the early days helped organize the state party in North Dakota. The *Rebel* thought it was especially important to place a woman on the Socialist ticket as a way to demonstrate the party's support for woman suffrage. In the end, the national party membership chose two uncharismatic antimilitarist writers as its standard bearers—Allan Benson of New York for president and George Kirkpatrick for vice president.[9]

More disappointing for Texas Socialists than the party's choice of presidential ticket was the new composition of the National Executive Committee. Victor Berger and Morris Hillquit, the national leaders of the party's right wing, were elected on the first ballot. Joining Berger and Hillquit on the NEC were fellow right-wing leaders John Work and John Spargo and the centrist Anna Maley. Adolph Germer of Illinois, a centrist who was moving increasingly to the right, was elected national secretary. After World War I, Germer would lead the fight to expel from the SP the left-wing ethnic federations and other socialists who supported the Bolshevik Revolution. Large support from party members in the Midwest and Northeast now placed the SP in the firm control of its right wing.[10]

Although Texas Socialists grew severely disillusioned with the national SP, they still had much enthusiasm for their own state organization. Operating independently of the national office, the Texas SP established the Southern

Socialist Lecture System. The lecture system organized daily engagements for Socialist speakers. The Boeer women once again provided finances to get the lecture system started. Their motivation for continuing to fund the socialist movement came in part from the failed Easter Rebellion of April 1916, in which Irish militants launched an insurrection to end British rule in Ireland. When the uprising failed, the British army executed many of its leaders, including the socialist James Connolly. "The shocking defeat of the Irish heroes affected us deeply," wrote Maria Boeer to her daughter Clara and Irish son-in-law Tom Hickey. "I have to think of our good Tom who may have known most of Irish martyrs personally. And those noble martyrs died because the masses were too lazy, cowardish, stupid and oblivious to contribute to their own salvation."[11]

In 1916 the Texas SP mounted a vigorous election campaign. A statewide membership referendum selected E. R. Meitzen once again as the party's candidate for governor. The party selected Clarence Nugent, son of Thomas Nugent, the Populist candidate for governor in 1892 and 1894, as its candidate for state attorney general. Meitzen and lieutenant governor nominee W. S. Noble embarked on a two-month speaking tour of central and west Texas. "The Red Automobile Tour," as they called it, began in May and continued through June with the slogan "For Land and Liberty." Using Noble's automobile, the two candidates spoke three times a day, at 11 a.m., 3 p.m., and 8:30 p.m., on the issues of land, money, cotton, and trusts.[12]

As the Red Automobile Tour progressed, however, the flotsam of war began to wash ashore on the American continent. By the summer of 1916, calls for preparedness and US involvement in the war in Europe had become deafening. When E. O. Meitzen and Hickey carried out a July socialist speaking tour of Texas, they added antipreparedness to their list of topics to discuss along with land and finance. E. R. Meitzen continued his campaign for governor with "War: Its Cause and Cure" as one of his main stump speeches. As part of the same effort, Socialists across the state initiated nonpartisan antipreparedness clubs in their towns.[13]

Texas Socialists campaigned for Benson at the top of their ticket with greater zeal because of his antipreparedness credentials. After all, he owed his selection to those credentials.[14] Benson himself, however, did not put as much effort into his campaign as party members in the field did. In fact, he avoided the field and ran his campaign primarily by writing articles in his office.

As the nation entered the summer campaign season in 1916, President Woodrow Wilson made two key moves to mollify critics and gain votes. To appease farmers, he supported and signed into law the Federal Farm Loan Act, which provided government loans to farmers. It was virtually the same act he opposed in 1914, which had drawn the ire of farmers. Now Wilson was attempting to appear as a champion of small farmers.[15] The other move was perhaps even more important to his reelection. In response to growing antiwar sentiment fomented in large part by socialists, he adopted the campaign slogan "He Kept Us Out of War."

In Texas, now that the Wilson administration had appeased farmers and those opposed to war, the Democratic election campaign returned to the persistent issue of prohibition. After their setback in the 1914 election, drys reorganized their state organization and were once again a major factor in state politics. Prohibition became the main issue of the 1916 Texas elections. To counter resurgent prohibition forces, Governor James Ferguson formed an alliance with archconservative Joseph Bailey based on shared opposition to prohibition and woman suffrage.[16]

Texas Socialists saw the writing on the wall. "We should say that in spite of the tremendous campaign that has been waged . . . the natural gain in the Socialist vote is not likely to be as great as we have been inspired to hope for," conceded the *Rebel* shortly before the election. "He kept us out of war" was a "powerful slogan," it admitted. The slogan, along with Wilson's support for the child labor act, caused "an undertow away from our party." Wilson won the support of many radicals and pacifists who "might otherwise have given an ear to the Socialist message," but instead voted "the lesser evil" over Republican candidate Charles Evan Hughes, who called for an increase in preparedness. Nationally, Benson received only two-thirds the number of votes Debs polled in 1912. In Texas, the Socialist vote dropped nearly ten thousand votes from the previous election. Ferguson handily won reelection. Looking to the future, the *Rebel* concluded its election analysis: "Let us remember whether we gain or lose, that the Socialist party is not a mushroom growth . . . that a loss in vote is not a loss. It merely means that our gains in the past have frightened the powers-that-be into 'reforms' that for a time lull the people to sleep. . . . '[R]eforms' only get the people deeper into the mind and mire of capitalism and that REVOLUTION is the only way out."[17]

In August 1916 the *Rebel* began promoting a new organization founded in 1915 called the Farmers and Laborers' Protective Association (FLPA). "Membership," according to a FLPA organizer, "was confined to working farmers and wage-workers. . . . [T]he purpose of the organization . . . is an industrial co-operative and educational union, taking in all workers." The FLPA toward the end of 1916 gained between five and eight thousand members organized in two hundred locals in northern and western Texas.[18]

Before the fall of 1916, the FLPA was largely inactive as a cooperative venture that established a few stores for the bulk purchasing of potatoes and flour. But the continual slide of west Texas farmers into tenancy, the influence of the Mexican Revolution, and the nation's movement toward war, radicalized its members. The radicalization was also due, in no small part, to the increasing prominence of SP members in the FLPA. Party member George T. Bryant, of Lueders, who also had ties to the IWW, became the FLPA's national organizer. W. T. Webb, of Cisco, elected by Socialists as their state secretary in January 1916, also joined. After an organizing tour of central and east Texas, the FLPA held a state convention in Cisco in February 1917. The convention adopted strong resolutions against conscription and US entry into the world war. Reportedly, members were encouraged to arm themselves to resist conscription "to the death." The FLPA also decided to organize "negro lodges" and to form an antidraft alliance with the IWW in nearby Rotan.[19]

The Texas SP's role in the FLPA put it in direct confrontation with the position of the national party's Right on trade unions. The right wing advocated working within the existing craft union structure of the AFL, but to do so left out scores of industrial and agricultural workers. The AFL aligned itself with the preparedness campaign and then the war effort. The FLPA, on the other hand, was open to skilled and unskilled alike and agricultural as well as industrial workers. It also reached out to workers of all races and took a militant stance against war.

As the threads tying farmer-labor radicals in Texas to the SP were fraying, a new form of agrarian radicalism burst onto the scene, drawing attention to the far northern reaches of the Great Plains. While the SP suffered serious setbacks at the polls in 1916, the Nonpartisan League (NPL) in North Dakota swept into power. The NPL called for state-supported and state-controlled grain elevators, mills, banks, and farm insurance—longstanding demands of the farmer-labor bloc, especially its socialist component. North Dakota voters put NPL majorities in the state's house of representatives and supreme court (it would take the senate in 1918), elected NPL candidate Lynn Frazier governor with 80 percent of the vote, and sent NPL member John Miller Baer to the US House of Representatives.[20]

The NPL began as the brainchild of Albert Bowen Jr., who grew up on a North Dakota farm and became a teacher at a one-room schoolhouse. North Dakota faced economic conditions similar to those in Texas. In 1915 more than two-thirds of the farms in North Dakota were mortgaged and a quarter of the farmers were tenants. These conditions led Bowen to join the North Dakota SP. In 1912 he ran as its candidate for governor. Just as the Meitzens helped move the Texas SP away from its old collective farming position, Bowen and LeSueur did the same for the North Dakota SP. At the 1912 SP national convention, Bowen joined the efforts of E. R. Meitzen, Hickey, and LeSueur to make the party more responsive to farmers.[21]

By late 1914, Bowen had become dissatisfied with the SP's continual focus on industrial workers to the detriment of working farmers. He quit the party in February 1915 and immediately set to the task of organizing a "Non-Partisan

Political organization" for farmers.[22] Bowen's new organization drew on North Dakota's history of agrarian protest dating back to the Farmers' Alliance and Populist movement. He also solicited the support of the state's popular cooperatives, through which prominent Fargo attorney William Lemke joined the cause.[23]

Bowen originated the idea of the NPL, but much of its organizational growth has been credited to Arthur Townley. Born in 1880, Townley grew up on a farm in western Minnesota and taught school for two years before moving to North Dakota in 1904. He became a farmer but by 1913 had gone bust and was in debt for thousands of dollars. After joining the SP, Townley became one of its most successful organizers, working closely with Bowen. When Bowen quit the party, he reached out to Townley to take charge of building the new organization. Townley became president, and two other former SP members, Francis B. Wood and O. S. Evans, served as vice president and secretary, respectively. To help grow the NPL's membership, Townley hired former SP organizers to canvass the state. Membership in the NPL soon reached twenty-two thousand.[24]

The NPL decided to enter the electoral arena. Rather than establishing itself as an independent party, the NPL captured the North Dakota Republican Party. NPL leaders made Lemke the chair of the state Republican Party and used its statewide machinery to run NPL candidates on the Republican ticket.[25] This tactic, by forgoing independent working-class political action, led to the NPL's stunning early electoral successes but ultimately led to the collapse of the farmer-labor bloc.

After its victories in the 1916 elections, the NPL eyed expansion. It planned to establish state organizations across the Great Plains, the Mountain West, and the South. To do so, Townley called on many of his former Socialist comrades to join the NPL. LeSueur became an early agrarian promoter of the NPL, and so too did E. R. Meitzen, who wrote LeSueur to tell him he "wanted to get in on this Non-Partisan business. Suggesting plans as to how to save Texas." That Texas needed saving in Meitzen's mind shows how tenuous the SP's position had become among farmer-labor radicals in the state. LeSueur wrote Townley, suggesting that Meitzen come to North Dakota and Minnesota for two or three months. He emphasized to Townley that bringing Meitzen north might lead to the *Rebel*'s becoming the organ of the NPL in the South. Meitzen, not yet ready to make an open break from the SP, first suggested to Hickey "that in writing editorials" for the *Rebel*, "you pitch them along N.P. lines without directly citing it." He asked Hickey not to say anything about his trip. "I will have to mull over the best way to break the news to our readers." With Townley's approval, the NPL agreed to pay for Meitzen's expenses and put him on a speaking tour of the upper Great Plains. Hickey told E. O. Meitzen, "I figure he [E. R.] is on the biggest mission of his life. The result of his experience in North Dakota may revolutionize the politics of Texas."[26]

The NPL promoted Meitzen's North Dakota tour and gave him a big write-up in its paper, the *Nonpartisan Leader*. The article introduced Meitzen as a representative of "the Land League of Texas, the most vigorous expression of its people against . . . oppression."[27] Nowhere did the NPL mention that Meitzen was a prominent leader of the Texas SP. Although Townley actively sought out Socialist leaders and rank-and-filers to help organize and join the NPL, he and the NPL in general, publicly distanced themselves from any ties to socialism and the SP during this period of heightened nationalism and militarism. As for the defunct Land League, Meitzen told Hickey, "I will continue that Land League fiction for the present," calling the Land League a "handy old corpse."[28]

E. R. Meitzen's commitment to the SP had lessened, but not to socialism. His new embrace of the NPL, part of the same continuity of agrarian radicalism that dated back to the 1870s, was a break from the right wing of the SP. "Not only are its [NPL's] principles socialistic," wrote Meitzen to Hickey, "but most important of all, it is carrying out that vital fundamental principle of the Socialist movement which the American party (at least) has never done and will never do: organizing a class-conscious political movement of the workers for the purpose of calling the government in the interests of the workers." He concluded, "In other words . . . the revolution has gotten out of the hands of the Hillquit movement and is sweeping America like a prairie fire. We must get in on it not for profit; but because we two love to be where things are 'didding.'"[29]

As leaders of a once vibrant socialist movement in Texas, the Meitzens did not want to abandon the thousands of workers and farmers they had drawn to the SP. They still saw uses for the SP, as would become clear later. To avoid a potentially disruptive public break, they aimed to ease rank-and-file Socialists into the NPL slowly. The first mention of the NPL in the *Rebel* appeared on the back page of its January 13, 1917, edition with a brief report of the NPL electoral victories in North Dakota.[30]

To prepare readers for the new relationship with the NPL, the *Rebel* ran a highly critical article of the SP's national leadership as a way to erode further the ties of farmer-labor radicals to the SP and its leadership. "Wanted—a Socialist Party" was the title of an article written by one of Meitzen's closest allies, Covington Hall, who argued that the party's poor showing in the election of 1916 indicated "that it did not have the INTELLECTUAL COURAGE to grasp and face the tremendous issues confronting human society and to offer boldly and without compromise the only solution therefor—SOCIAL REVOLUTION." He lambasted Benson, blaming him for the party's electoral decline and casting him as a mere reformer, not a revolutionary. Hall pointed to Benson's speeches on economics that talked "of effects and not of causes." For Hall, reformers like Benson talked only about how to alleviate the ill effects of capitalism, while revolutionaries pointed to the elimination of the cause itself—capitalism. Hall then blamed the party's National Executive Committee for not conducting a campaign to empower the working class through industrial democracy.[31]

On January 20, 1917, in a bold, front-page headline, "The Revolution in the Northwest," the *Rebel* announced that "Socialism is coming not through the Socialist party alone if at all, although it is the driving power of that positive revolutionary force." The newspaper acknowledged the "positive revolutionary forces" of the SP but opened its readers to alternatives. "The fires of revolution in America are being fanned to flame from a thousand and one sources," continued the paper, which listed examples of the peons in Yucatan, the land revolution in Texas, and growing cooperative projects. Its editors praised "the drive through Socialist agitation to a more and more radical legislation." With this lead-up, the *Rebel* arrived at its destination: "Last, but not least, as an impetus to the impending Gigantic Change is the revolution of the actual farmers that began in North Dakota (started by Socialists) and is now sweeping the Northwest like a prairie fire."[32]

"I feel more love and respect for this movement and its leaders than I ever did for the SP, at least in late years," wrote Meitzen to Hickey from his northern visit. "They are beginning to put a lot of confidence in my ability and trustworthiness," he continued. Initially, the NPL took Meitzen on as an organizer for four months, paying his expenses and providing a salary.[33] Early in his four-month stint, Meitzen met with Townley and Joe Gilbert, a former leader of the Washington state SP who now headed the NPL's National Organization Department. Shortly afterward, Meitzen became one of the NPL's five national organizers.[34] He told Hickey he would return to Texas as "the 'man behind' the N.P. organization work in Texas and Oklahoma." Meitzen pointed out to NPL "head knockers" that the German-language edition of the *Nonpartisan Leader* was "badly in need of someone who knows a little more than merely to translate," and he convinced them to hire his father.[35] Soon E. O. Meitzen moved to Fargo and served as editor of the paper's German-language supplement.[36]

The Meitzens were not the only SP leaders who joined the NPL. "All the big Reds are flocking to this movement," wrote E. R. Meitzen to his parents. "The SP is dead. The name will never be first across the people. We must cut loose completely . . . and join what I conceive to be the most revolutionary movement for workers America has ever seen."[37] Many of the core members of the SP's agrarian base, including Hickey, LeSueur, George and Grace Brewer (Kansas), Walter Thomas Mills (Nebraska), H. H. Stallard (Oklahoma), Covington Hall (Louisiana-Texas), and Stanley Clark (Texas), left or would soon leave the party for the NPL.[38]

When the Executive Committee of the Communist International analyzed the political situation in the United States at its June 1923 plenum, it noted the movement of agrarian socialists from the SP to the NPL: "The Socialist Party of

America has also turned to the farming population but let itself to be persuaded to fuse with the Non-Partisan League and other similar parties, with the result that the Socialist Party has completely disappeared in several states."[39] In many ways, the Executive Committee description of agrarian socialists joining the NPL as a fusion is correct. The fusion, while not formal, represented more of a coming together of ideas rather than an ideological departure. Fusion, however, was not what Socialists in the NPL initially wanted. As seen in the proceedings of the SP's emergency convention of April 1917, Socialist NPLers sought to create distinct roles for the SP and NPL.[40]

As the United States moved quickly to the brink of joining the world war, the SP called an emergency national convention in St. Louis to discuss the party's position on the war. By the time the convention convened on April 7, Congress had declared war against Germany the day before. In this charged environment, Socialists debated the war and their stance toward the NPL as well. Historians who have examined the convention have understandably focused almost entirely on the war debate. The debate, though heated, ended with delegates by a large majority approving a resolution declaring that the United States' "entrance into the European war was instigated by predatory capitalists." The resolution denounced the Wilson Administration's decision "as a crime against the people of the United States and against the nations of the world." The convention called for active opposition to the war.[41]

Much more contentious and confusing to delegates was the discussion about the NPL. On the fourth day of the convention, delegates approved a resolution by LeSueur, "On Relation of Socialist Party to Non-Partisan League," by a vote of 114 to 56. The resolution at first glance opposed fusion with the NPL. Many delegates viewed and approved it as such, pointing to the final line of the resolution: "No compromise, no political trading." A closer reading, however, reveals that drafters of the resolution had two distinct roles for the SP and NPL in mind. The resolution noted that "large numbers of comrades have affiliated with the league in the hope of speedy economic reforms though political victory . . . with a fair promise of success." On the other hand, "the purpose of the Socialist movement," the resolution continued, is "the emancipation of the working class from economic servitude by the abolition of capitalist exploitation rather than the election to office of candidates for the purpose of speedy economic reform." The NPL would carry out the more immediate practical work of gaining elected office to enact "speedy economic reforms," while the SP would "maintain in the utmost possible vigor the propaganda of Socialism . . . [so it] may continue to lay the foundations for the social revolution."[42] In short, the NPL would be the electoral party and the SP the propaganda party.

In Texas, Hall was less amenable to keeping ties to the SP. When a split occurred in the Wisconsin SP between pro- and antiwar factions, Hall proclaimed, "The Socialist party is done for. The Republican party is done for. The Democratic party is done for. The Common People have no other choice but [to] organize a new party and a new union of their own." He concluded that "the most promising new political organization seems to be the Farmers Non-Partisan League" and, "as for the new Union, the Industrial Workers of the World is the only real thing in sight."[43] Whether Meitzen would have decided to carry out dual work in the NPL and SP or completely abandon the SP, however, we will never know. The government made the decision for him and others when it moved to repress the socialist movement in Texas in May 1917.

The Bureau of Investigation (BI) intensified surveillance of the Meitzens, monitoring their writings, correspondence, and movements. Agents took note when E. O. Meitzen left Hallettsville in May to assume his editorial position in North Dakota. What drew their attention was Meitzen's route. He did not head straight north. Instead, he headed west to Arizona. He stopped in the mining towns of Globe and Douglas, where he toured the mining and lumber districts and gave political speeches, which the BI found were for the purpose of assisting the IWW and promoting the NPL. Meitzen seemed to be following the line Hall advocated in the *Rebel*: to build the NPL as the new party and the IWW as the new union for the working class. His meetings appear to have been successful, for the Arizona NPL and the IWW were still collaborating in May 1920.[44]

The BI fished for ways to arrest Meitzen. The Lavaca County postmaster informed the BI that the Meitzens had printed an article in the *New Era* advising readers not to buy Liberty bonds. When the BI investigated the claim, though, they could find no such article. What BI agents did find was that the Meitzens had a long history in the Hallettsville area, and the political organizations they promoted over the years had, according to a report, "gained considerable strength." They also noted that the Meitzens have "a strong following among the lower class of people."[45]

Unable to find any evidence of the Meitzens hampering the war effort and wary of arousing the "lower class of people," authorities needed a more vulnerable target to go after in their mission to suppress antiwar radicalism. They found their man in Tom Hickey. Since November 1916, Hickey had been editing the *Rebel* in relative isolation at the Boeer family farm in west Texas. On May 17, 1917, Texas Rangers, without a warrant, forced Hickey into a car and kidnapped him, holding him incommunicado for two days. He was finally released on a $1,000 bond after his wife Clara secured a lawyer.[46]

The next day, federal authorities arrested eight members of the FLPA in nearby Snyder. The following day, US marshals and Texas Rangers arrested twelve more members in Rotan and nearly forty in the area around Abilene, Texas. Authorities brought federal indictments of "seditious uprising" against the FLPA members. Among those arrested were organizer Bryant and the Texas SP's state secretary Webb. After the dust settled, prosecutors brought to trial fifty-five people—fifty-three of them were members of the SP and fifty-one were tenant farmers. Prosecutors made the charges based on a claim that the FLPA was organizing an armed uprising against conscription. The arrests of Hickey and members of the FLPA were part of a government campaign to repress radicalism and stifle opposition to the war. This antidemocratic campaign had the backing of the US attorney general, Thomas Watt Gregory, and was carried out by US marshals, Secret Service agents, and Texas Rangers with the assistance of local, state, and federal courts.[47]

News of the arrests and alleged FLPA plot produced headlines and sensational stories across the state. The *El Paso Herald* ran a banner headline: "WEST TEXANS ARM TO FIGHT DRAFT?" Articles portrayed those arrested as anarchists under the influence of German money. Authorities used the arrests of Hickey and Socialist members of the FLPA to portray the SP as a treasonous and disloyal organization deserving of a government crackdown.[48]

Coincidently, on the same day as the mass arrests of the FLPA members occurred near Abilene, the *Rebel* printed the antidraft resolution passed by the 105 members of the FLPA lodge in Olney. "A majority of us voted for Wilson's Prosperity, Preparedness and Peace, and we object to being paid off in Blood, Bull and Bullets," read the resolution. "We are willing to fight to the last ditch for the protection of foreign commerce when we have some," it continued, "but so long as foreign commerce rests in the hands of Wall Street we insist that said Street furnish the blood and gold to protect it." In a warning, the resolution concluded, "The overwhelming majority of the working class is opposed to conscription, but if we are forced to stand for it, let the God of 10 percent beware lest the worm turneth which he is sometimes wont to do."[49]

The government carried out a six-week show trial of the FLPA members beginning in September. Numerous community members, including the mayor of Snyder, joined Socialists in testifying to their innocence. Prosecutors failed to produce any tangible evidence of any plot and the jury found all but three of the defendants either not guilty or innocent. Despite a lack of evidence, the jury received enough pressure from government authorities to pass guilty verdicts on Bryant and two other FLPA leaders, who were sentenced to serve six years at the federal penitentiary in Leavenworth, Kansas.[50]

The arrest of the FLPA members and Hickey served the government's purpose of fanning public opinion against the SP and antiwar activism. But the arrests also had an unintended effect. "We have been rushed with letters pouring in here," wrote Arnold Meitzen to Hickey after his release, "wanting to know all about it and the [subscriptions] are pouring [in]."[51] Arnold ran the daily operations of the *Rebel*, which before Hickey's arrest was in dire financial straits. A week later, Arnold wrote Clara Hickey, "Today we received about two hundred new ones [subscriptions] and every day the past week from 100 to 200. If that keeps up much longer we may get out of debt and then can begin to live like human beings instead of slaves. It seems it takes war and such horrible things to wake up the fool people."[52]

Arnold Meitzen and the *Rebel* staff were emboldened by the flood of new subscribers and letters of support. On the front page of their June 2, 1917, issue, they brazenly printed the blurb "DON'T BUY BONDS" on the front page—just the type of statement authorities were looking for. On the same page, Hickey promised readers that "the real story" of his arrest would appear in the next issue. Hickey never got to tell readers his story and none of the new subscriptions was ever filled.

On June 9, Postmaster General Albert Burleson made the *Rebel* the first periodical to be barred from the US mail under the Espionage Act, which he and Attorney General Gregory drafted. Both men had axes to grind with the *Rebel*. The paper had exposed Burleson when he replaced tenants on his land with convict labor, and it had regularly attacked Gregory for not fully enforcing antitrust legislation. Burleson was so eager to suppress the *Rebel* that he did so six days before the new act became law.[53]

Government repression crushed the Texas SP and greatly hindered efforts to build the NPL in Texas. The previous year, violent state repression in south Texas quashed expressions of Mexican radicalism in the area. Persistent harassment and intimidation resulted in the disappearance of Mexican American locals of the SP and the Land League in south and central Texas. The mass arrests of Socialist and FLPA members in west Texas dried out an area that had been a wellspring of Socialist strength. Shortly after those arrests, US marshals also hauled in five members of the Texas SP in east Texas, curtailing Socialist activism in the area. Instead of expending resources to grow their movement as the main organization against the war, Texas Socialists had to devote almost all of their time and energy fighting legal challenges and getting comrades out of jail.[54]

With the government waging a campaign against radicalism, the NPL trod lightly. Townley acknowledged the imperialist origins of the war begun by governments serving the profit motives of "gigantic corporations." Yet the NPL did not campaign directly against it, conceding that they hoped the war could be used for the collective good of the people. The NPL demanded that the government as "a war measure take over the railroads and distribution of food into their hands."[55] Opponents of the NPL cared little for critical nuances and attacked Townley and the NPL as treasonous. Throughout the war, NPL leaders would face numerous indictments related to the Espionage Act.[56]

E. R. Meitzen moved away from the SP's official antiwar position and closer to that of the NPL's. "I for one think that the war will do good," wrote Meitzen to Hickey in May 1917, "even though it looks like a lunatic asylum." Meitzen cited the revolution in Russia, which overthrew the czar, and "the steps toward collectivism everywhere" as evidence of the good the war was doing. He did not view his approval as a capitulation but as a pragmatic back door to a revolution. He expressed to Hickey that "We can do this and that is what the Russian rebels did—take advantage of the discontent caused by the war gamblers." Meitzen further assured Hickey: "The tactic we are now taking politically it is best to let things alone so far as going directly against the war machine; we can't stop it; let's ride it out instead."[57]

In August Hickey wrote Meitzen that he noticed a positive buzz for the NPL among Texas's farmer-labor radicals. Meitzen wrote in reply, "The enthusiasm you speak of was partly due to 15,000 'composite' editions of the *Nonpartisan Leader* that I had sent to a select list of Texas and Oklahoma radicals and progressives. It was my opening gun."[58] One of the items in the edition Meitzen sent out was a Townley speech against war profiteers. Meitzen's "opening gun" had its desired effect. Some of the radicals and progressives on Meitzen's list wrote to the *Nonpartisan Leader* voicing their agreement with the paper and wanting more. A sampling of the letters read as follows: "I received from some unknown source a copy of your paper. . . . [H]ope that you will grow . . . and finally overflow clear down here in Texas." "Go to them boys. . . . I wish you could come here." "I received a copy of the special composite edition. . . . [I]t is surely a humdinger. Paid close attention to Townley's speech. . . . [It] is true in every respect. . . . But as long as we have a capitalist congress we cannot expect anything else. Your movement is good . . . so that America may have a government of the people, by the people and for the people instead of for the capitalist class." Another Texas farmer wrote in, stating he had been a county secretary of the Farmers' Alliance and now "wanted to see Texas North Dakotaized."[59]

With such a positive response from farmer-labor radicals in Texas, the NPL moved E. R. Meitzen back to Texas as an organizer in early September 1917. Joining him as NPL organizers were Hickey and Stanley Clark. Both Clark and Hickey had reputations as organizers who went off script and enjoyed a good drink. As their comrades and friends, the Meitzens tolerated such behavior while they organized the Texas SP, but the NPL ran a much tighter ship, especially in the political environment of wartime repression.[60] The NPL national office agreed to hire Hickey and Clark as paid organizers, but offered these words of caution: "In order to obtain the results we are after, we must be a little circumspect and not go as far as to give our opponents an opportunity of putting a quietus on our work."[61]

Meitzen and Hickey followed the advice—Clark did not. In a September 1917 organizing speech, Clark did not hold back. "If profiteering does not stop and the lumber barons do not cease to rob and deport the Industrial Workers of the World, the United States will need 750,000 soldiers to keep the rest of the west quiet."[62] He was referring to the mass deportation of more than a thousand IWW organized striking miners in Bisbee, Arizona, in July 1917. Authorities arrested Clark for speaking out against conscription. Clark denied opposing conscription, though he freely admitted speaking out against the deportations. Federal prosecutors included Clark in the mass trial in Chicago of 166 IWW members charged with conspiracy to sabotage the war effort. Clark was found guilty and sent to Leavenworth, where he remained jailed until July 21, 1922, when his sentence was commuted.[63]

The Wilson administration conducted an unrelenting drive to suppress all forms of radicalism. Other radical periodicals were barred from the mail, and Socialists who were elected were prevented from taking their seats in state and federal legislative bodies. Thousands of working-class militants were arrested and sentenced to jail. Debs in November 1918 was sentenced to ten years in prison for an antiwar speech he gave at Canton, Ohio, in June 1918. In July 1917 Kate Richards O'Hare was arrested for giving an antiwar speech in Bowman, North Dakota, to a crowd composed largely of NPL members. O'Hare never quit the SP or joined the NPL, but she was an active supporter of the NPL.[64] "My arrest and conviction is but an incident in the great human drama that is being enacted on the plains of the great northwest," she wrote after being sentenced to five years in jail, "and nothing more thrilling and dramatic has ever been enacted than the drama of the rise of the Non-Partisan League."[65]

With the SP pushed to the brink through repression and internal disputes, Meitzen and Hickey made their public declaration for the Texas NPL in December 1917. "Dear Comrade: This is possibly the most important letter you have ever received," wrote Hickey in a letter to Meitzen's list of radicals and progressives. "I believe that the Socialist Party cannot function in any agricultural state in the nation, while the present unpleasantness is on." Hickey acknowledged that the SP "may make great progress in the great industrial centers," but he insisted that farmers needed an organization of their own. The letter included the platform of the NPL with its call for state run mills, grain elevators, and insurance.[66]

The Texas farmer-labor bloc's embrace of the of NPL broke its decades-long practice of independent political action. "Texas being a Democratic state," the letter explained, "no doubt, all or nearly all, of the candidates nominated will make the race in the Democratic primaries."[67] Trying to break working-class people's alliance with the "party of their fathers" had been one of the more frustrating tasks of farmer-labor radicals. The election tactics of the NPL appealed to E. R. Meitzen. "We Southerners were born Democrats you know. We can't quite get over that," E. R. acknowledged in an interview with the *Nonpartisan Leader*. "But," he went on, "we can still be Democrats and also be Nonpartisans. That is the beauty of your organization—that we can bring together the irreconcilable."[68]

The climate of deepening repression put added pressure on German Texans. Not only were radicals at risk, but others suspected of disloyalty as well. "They are arresting people right and left these days for even so much as singing 'The Wacht am Rhein,' or eating 'German fried potatoes,'" observed E. R. Meitzen.[69] For German Texans, to engage in daily practices related to their heritage and culture that once were commonplace now made their loyalty suspect in the eyes of authorities.

On April 4, a mob brutally beat four NPL organizers in the east Texas town of Mineola, where E. R. Meitzen had given a public talk on March 23 on behalf of the NPL. Before Meitzen's arrival, the area head of the Red Cross, E. Gentry, denounced the NPL at the town's Methodist church: "The Nonpartisan League is another form of German propaganda financed by German money." The minister of the church, Charles V. Hughes, then threatened violence. The NPL "shan't organize the farmers. I have a Winchester, and it will pop, too." On the day of Meitzen's talk, a group of "leading citizens" from Mineola and nearby Tyler showed up. Among them were the local postmaster, the mayor's father, local business owners, newspapermen, and a district attorney. They arrived at the meeting with intent to break it up. The farmers in attendance kept them from doing so, but while Meitzen gave his talk, the owner of a local restaurant stood three feet from him brandishing a knife. Refusing to be intimidated, Meitzen and other NPL organizers vowed to carry on their work in the area.[70]

After hearing about what happened to Meitzen, M. M. Offut, an area stock farmer who was the first NPL organizer in Texas, visited Rev. Hughes, an acquaintance of his. Offut hoped to reassure him that the NPL was a loyal organization composed mainly of Democrats. According to Offut, Hughes refused to listen and said he was "going to fight it [the NPL] in every way I can." Offut told him that was his privilege as long as he kept within the law. To this, Hughes replied, "I care nothing for the law. I would rather die and go to hell than turn this government over to a lot of dirty red Socialists, and your League is nothing but the Socialist Party under another name." Offut saw he was getting nowhere and went to leave, but a group of ruffians grabbed him. With a pair of sheep sheers, they hacked off his long gray beard and hair after they kicked and beat him. Afterward, they threw him on a train leaving town.[71]

Local police rounded up three other NPL organizers in the area and placed them in jail. Shortly before midnight, a mob broke them out of jail and drove them to the woods just outside town. The organizers recognized their captors as many of the same "leading citizens" who attempted to break up Meitzen's meeting. The leading citizens stripped the organizers, forced them on their stomachs, beat them with a blacksnake whip twenty-five to thirty times each, and poured salt and water into their wounds. The organizers were then allowed to get up and run away as guns fired in their direction to hurry them on their way. All three eventually made it back to NPL headquarters in Waco.[72]

The Mineola attack deeply shook the NPL leaders from North Dakota who came to Texas to oversee organizing. They had heard the stereotypes of Texas as a rough-and-tumble lawless land, and now they believed them. Unfortunately for the NPL, similar violence against the NPL became commonplace in the upper Great Plains (even more so than in Texas), especially once the 1918 campaign season heated up. Opponents of the NPL hired and deputized thugs to break up NPL meetings from Minnesota to Washington. Vigilantes beat and in a few cases tarred and feathered NPL organizers.[73]

The mob violence in Mineola, although it set back the NPL's growth in Texas, did make news across the state and drew people's attention to the organization. The NPL capitalized on the attention when John Canada joined the NPL. Canada was the publisher of the *Southland Farmer*, a respected agricultural newspaper based in Houston with a large circulation that extended across the entire South. Canada made the paper an official organ of the NPL.[74]

Facing repression in the South, the NPL diverted most of its resources to election campaigns in the upper Great Plains and Idaho. In July 1918 E. R. Meitzen traveled to St. Paul, Minnesota, to assist the NPL election campaign. In a bitterly contested election, the NPL candidate for governor in Minnesota, Charles A. Lindbergh, failed to win the Republican primary in June. After the primary defeat, the NPL joined leaders of organized labor and Thomas Van Lear, the Socialist mayor of Minneapolis, to form an independent slate of farmer-labor candidates seeking to unite urban and agrarian workers. Most of the farmer-labor candidates lost. The effort, however, laid the groundwork for the Minnesota State Federation of Labor to pledge itself to independent political action the next summer.[75]

The 1918 elections registered impressive gains for the NPL, especially in North Dakota, where it solidified control of the state government. In no other state, however, did the NPL seize control of one of the major parties as it did in North Dakota. Still, voters elected NPL candidates to state legislatures, state supreme courts, and local offices in Minnesota, Montana, South Dakota, Idaho, Colorado, and Nebraska. Meitzen stayed up north and became a prominent organizer for the league. He returned to Texas infrequently as he crisscrossed the Great Plains and western states. By early 1919, the NPL, at the height of its power and influence, had more than two hundred thousand members in thirteen states.[76]

The 1918 election results in Texas registered the opposite for farmer-labor radicalism. During a time of extreme political repression, the Texas SP defiantly ran

W. P. Simpson for governor. Simpson received only 1,660 votes, however—the party's lowest total since 1902. Once again, the main race played out in the Democratic primary. The race was between incumbent governor William P. Hobby and Ferguson (who had been impeached and convicted in 1917). Ferguson's opposition to prohibition and woman suffrage put him at odds with the state's Democratic leaders, who solidly backed Wilson. They used Ferguson's veto of a popular appropriations bill for the University of Texas to start a successful campaign to impeach and remove him from office in September 1917. As part of his impeachment, Ferguson was disqualified from holding any office "under the State of Texas."[77]

Afterward, Ferguson maintained a high political profile by creating his own newspaper, the *Ferguson Forum*, and by speaking out against prohibition and woman suffrage. Ferguson felt women did not belong in politics and were "contented with the exalted position which the Creator of the universe gave them when he made them ruler of the home."[78] He continued to appeal to his tenant farmer base that helped him win the governorship in 1914, and he sought the support of organized labor by addressing the Texas State Federation of Labor (TSFL) convention in March 1918. He did so in an effort to reclaim the governorship in 1918, notwithstanding the terms of his impeachment that barred him from holding a state office. The terms included nothing, however, that prevented him from running in the primary. In Ferguson's view, to win the primary was the best way to challenge his being barred from state office.[79]

Hobby had been lieutenant governor and succeeded Ferguson in 1917 after the latter's removal. Hobby secured the allegiance of progressive Wilson Democrats because of his support for prohibition and woman suffrage. During his time as governor, he signed legislation to give women the right to vote in primaries. Women voters proved decisive in the 1918 Democratic primary. Ferguson polled 217,012 votes, a total similar to the one that won him the primary in 1916, but with women's voting support, Hobby easily defeated him, with 461,479 votes, and cruised to victory in the general election.[80]

Although progressive Wilsonian Democrats rejoiced in Hobby's victory and Ferguson supporters took heart in the latter's healthy showing, a third faction within the Texas Democratic Party, the conservatives, were deeply troubled by the election results. Conservative Democrats vehemently opposed prohibition, woman suffrage, and just about every other Progressive Era reform that encroached on state's rights. Some of their worst fears came true when the Eighteenth Amendment was ratified in January 1919 and when Texas became the first southern state to approve the Nineteenth Amendment in June 1919. In reaction, they encouraged former US senator Joseph Bailey to run for governor in 1920.[81]

Six days after the 1918 election, an armistice was signed, ending World War I. The AFL and the railroad brotherhoods hoped their wartime cooperation with the government and its truce with capital would be rewarded. They sought to restart the prewar campaign against the open shop and achieve formal recognition of unions organized during the war. The decrease in production demands after the war, however, led to a sharp rise in unemployment and an increase in wholesale prices. The war had brought about more business opportunities and patriotic cooperation with corporations, but the wartime truce between labor and capital came to an immediate end. More than four million workers across the United States went on strike, demanding higher wages, shorter hours, and union recognition.[82]

From early in its existence, much of organized labor had tied itself to the Democratic Party. In these immediate postwar years with Democrats pursuing a more open probusiness agenda, organized labor began to consider a more independent path. The NPL, acting on this new political openness, formed successful political partnerships with organized labor in North Dakota, Minnesota, Montana, and Washington.[83] A similar opening presented itself in Texas. To make the most of it, the NPL sent E. R. Meitzen back to Texas.

In early 1920, the Texas governor called a special election to replace the Houston area's state senator. The Texas NPL used it as an opportunity to duplicate the farmer-labor electoral alliances it had formed in the north. In January, Meitzen and another NPL organizer began canvassing Harris County to build the NPL and promoting the idea of a farmer-labor political coalition. Their efforts paid off when the Houston Labor and Trade Council agreed to hold a mass meeting in downtown Houston in conjunction with the Harris County NPL on February 6. The stated purpose of the meeting was to bring organized workers and farmers together to vote on a proposal of organized labor working with the NPL and, if approved, to select delegates for a farmer-labor convention to be held the next day.[84]

Unionized machinists, teamsters, musicians, city employees, telegraphers, and shipbuilders, among others, along with NPL organized farmers, attended the meeting. Meitzen addressed the attendees, detailing the gains the NPL had made in the Great Plains. "The hayseeds have shown us union men the way," declared a Houston unionist, "and we ought to be more willing to follow them in politics up to the neck." At the convention the next day, delegates adopted a platform calling for reaffirming the rights of collective bargaining that were under sharp attack by open-shop forces. The platform also defended the rights of free speech, press, and assembly and called for the initiative and referendum, state inspection and grading of agricultural products, abolition of the poll tax, and equal wages for equal work for women. The platform included a plank calling for a tax on speculative land holdings similar to the single-tax demand that helped elect J. J. Pastoriza mayor of Houston in 1917. The convention selected Charles Murphy, a state representative from Houston, as its candidate for state senate and two farmers and a railroad engineer as candidates for state representative.[85]

The *Houston Chronicle* noted in its coverage of the convention: "behind the movement as a state organizer is E. R. Meitzen." The paper then reminded readers that he was the SP candidate for governor in 1914. In this seemingly innocuous observation, the paper opened the door to making the NPL's alleged socialism the focus of its election coverage. Two weeks later, the *Chronicle* launched a full-blown attack: "Meitzen, leader of the non-partisan league in Texas, formerly ran on the socialist ticket for governor and the main planks of the non-partisan league are rank socialism . . . its aims and ends are destructive of all constitutional government." The *Houston Post* joined in the attack with a banner headline: "Bolshevism Snarle [sic] at Gates of Houston." The paper in shrill but predictable tones unloaded: "The old socialistic crew of Texas are trying to put this un-American, undemocratic, unrepublican and unspeakable scheme of Leninism and Trotzkyism across. . . . [V]ote for the Democratic ticket and against SOCIALISM and the menace of RUSSIAN BOLSHEVISM and SOVIET-ISM." Charles Murphy's opponent, Lynch Davidson, a politically connected lumber businessman, announced that his campaign was opposed to all forms of radicalism. The weekly *Houston Labor Journal* tried to respond by running articles touting the NPL's gains for workers and farmers in North Dakota, but the labor journal could not keep pace with the barrage of anti-NPL articles from the city's two daily newspapers.[86]

Organized labor in Houston remained undeterred in its support for NPL candidates, convinced that its coalition with farmers gave it a chance of victory. Union members and working farmers did go to the polls in Harris County, which Murphy carried by 400 votes. The senatorial district, however, included Fort Bend and Waller counties. When the votes of these counties were added to the total, Murphy lost the election by 75 votes. The NPL put so much of its effort into organizing the much larger Harris County that it left the two rural counties unorganized. Still, the NPL and organized labor felt heartened by the election results. With only two months of organizing and in the face of a well-financed red-baiting campaign, they came within a hair's breadth of winning. "A new order in Texas politics is inevitable and imminent," wrote the *Houston Labor Journal*, "that and nothing else is the portent of the showing made by the Farmer and Labor Non-Partisan Leagues. . . . [T]hrough surprising solidarity at the polls they served notice to the special privilege brood."[87]

Before the budding coalition could build any momentum, two important developments altered the course of farmer-labor politics in Texas in 1920—the repression of the Galveston dockworker strike and the emergence of James Ferguson's American Party. Ferguson, no longer eyeing the governorship, set his sights on the US Senate seat up for grabs in 1922. To win, he needed additional political allies beyond his electoral base of two hundred thousand poor farmers. Just as he did in 1916, Ferguson courted Bailey and his conservative followers.[88] On June 12, 1919, the front page of the *Ferguson Forum* featured a lengthy editorial by Ferguson: "I Am for Joe Bailey for President—Why." Ferguson depicted Bailey as a defender of Jeffersonian democracy against progressive Democrats who hold "the idea that the government should do everything ... as though it were an apple tree that could be plucked at will and in time replenished by nature."[89]

Bailey and Ferguson opposed woman suffrage and equality, as well as black equality. As Ferguson put forth in his newspaper, the legal voters of Texas "do not want woman suffrage, and its attendant train of social equality with negroes, feminism, domination of elections by hypocritical political preachers and union of church and state in an unholy alliance."[90] The chairman of a Fort Worth conference of conservative Democrats made it clear: "This is a government of white men for white men and by white men."[91]

While Bailey and his conservative supporters had designs to recapture the Democratic Party, Ferguson and his supporters had other plans. Always the shrewd politician, Ferguson knew that his chances of winning an election in the Democratic primary were doomed. With Hobby and Wilson Democrats in control of the party machinery and the suffrage vote lined firmly against him, Ferguson's group hoped to enlist Bailey and conservative supporters in the creation of a new party.[92]

In a bit of political maneuvering, Ferguson organized a meeting of four hundred supporters to launch the American Party before Bailey's address to the Fort Worth conference. Though the Bailey and Ferguson forces held many similar conservative positions on social issues and state's rights, when it came to the labor question, they stood opposed. Ferguson's electoral support came from poor farmers. To this end, Ferguson called for changes in the Federal Farm Loan Act to help poor, landless farmers. He also sought the labor vote by supporting the closed shop and the eight-hour workday, but Bailey adamantly called for the open shop and opposed the eight-hour workday. By December, Bailey and Ferguson's brief courtship ended when Bailey made clear his intentions to run for governor in the Democratic primary on an antilabor platform. With Bailey forces no longer in the equation, Ferguson tweaked his platform to appeal more directly to poor farmers and laborers.[93]

The new American Party platform stated, "Instead of a continual row about what we shall drink, let us think about something to eat and something to wear." The platform "demanded the right of labor to form a union" and to strike, denouncing the use of court injunctions "to make labor work, as a crime against human liberty." Calling the "land question the biggest question before the American people," the platform called for government-issued tax-exempt loans for farmers at rates of interest not to exceed 5 percent. Additional planks called for the enforcement of antitrust laws against "that class that never labor, reap or sow . . . and [to] send them to jail"; opposition to compulsory military training; a pardon for Debs; greater funding for public education; and a pay raise for postal workers.[94]

The response of farmer-labor activists to the American Party transformed the party from a disgruntled faction of the Democratic Party, made up of Ferguson and his closest allies, into a farmer-labor protest organization. Farmers and laborers enthusiastically responded to the new American Party platform, as evidenced by the organization of party units in the agricultural areas north of Austin, where the Farmers' Alliance was born, and in Galveston, with its concentration of union workers. The same was true in Fayette and Lavaca counties, longtime hotbeds of Populist and socialist activities and home counties of the Meitzens.[95]

As historian James Green pointed out, "Socialists had not created the southwestern class struggle; they had simply politicized it. Therefore, the destruction of the Socialist party did not put an end to class conflict or remove class issues from the region's politics."[96] Hence when the American Party directly appealed to class issues, radical-minded farmers, laborers, and middle-class sympathizers responded and turned the party into their own.

What allowed the American Party to supplant the NPL in Texas as the leading vehicle of farmer-labor radicalism was its immediate response to the Galveston dockworker strike. On March 12, 1920, longshoremen in New York City went on strike demanding higher wages. The strike rapidly spread to ports along the Atlantic Ocean and the Gulf of Mexico. The strike reached Galveston on March 19, when 1,600 dockworkers and screwmen from eleven white and eleven black locals of the International Longshoremen's Association walked out against the Mallory and Morgan shipping companies demanding higher wages. After an initial bout of violence, when strikers attempted to block strikebreakers, the Galveston strike proceeded with relatively little violence. The lack of violence did not keep local business associations from urging the governor to declare martial law to end the strike. Galveston business leaders desired state intervention because they felt the city government, including the police department, was prolabor and was doing little to stop the strike. In the 1919 elections, a prolabor political coalition that included black and white dockworkers, under the name of the City Party, had swept the Galveston elections. The local government stood as at least a neutral force during the strike.[97]

Yielding to business interests, Governor Hobby on June 7 declared martial law in Galveston. He sent more than a thousand state militiamen to Galveston Island to enforce a ban on public gatherings and loitering and to protect strikebreakers. Galveston city commissioners protested Hobby's action and continued to support and enact prolabor demands such as higher taxes on the city wharfs. Seeing that the city government was overly sympathetic to the black and white striking dockworkers, Hobby on July 14 suspended the mayor, commissioners, city attorney, city recorder, and the police force and put the Texas National Guard in control of the city. In October 1920 Hobby and state Democrats further infuriated organized labor by enacting an open-port law that banned any actions that might hinder the free passage of trade within the state. Supporters of labor and the American Party correctly viewed the open port law for what it was, a piece of antistrike legislation, and denounced it as such.[98]

The American Party was not a regional anomaly, but rather part of the nationwide farmer-labor political movement at that time. In July 1920 Ferguson represented the American Party at a conference in Chicago instigated by John Fitzpatrick, president of the Chicago Federation of Labor. The conference brought together a wide array of political organizations for the purpose of creating a national labor party. Éamon de Valera attended as part of his mission to gain international recognition for the Republic of Ireland. Political and tactical disputes kept the conference from producing a true national party, but it was the first in a series of conferences that paved the way for Robert La Follette's run for the presidency in 1924.[99]

Immediately upon returning to Texas, Ferguson ended the American Party's affiliation with the Chicago conference. He claimed that he did so because of "the lack of vision on the part of its leaders, the provincialism of its platform ideas, and the restriction of its political geography."[100] More likely, however, Ferguson found that he could not use the conference to advance his personal ambitions. That Ferguson attended the conference at all was undoubtedly the result of the influence of individuals from the Texas farmer-labor bloc that transformed the character of the American Party. For more than a year before the conference, the Meitzens, Hickey, and Hall were in dialogue with the Committee of Forty-Eight about Texas and NPL representation at the Chicago conference. The Committee of Forty-Eight was formed in 1919 by progressive reformers seeking to create a new national political party from the then existing forty-eight states. Even after Ferguson ended his affiliation with the Chicago conference, E. R. Meitzen and Hickey organized a meeting in Dallas between representatives the NPL, SP, the Union Labor Party, the American Party, and the Committee of Forty-Eight to continue political collaboration.[101]

In August the American Party held a national convention in Fort Worth. The convention confirmed former Democratic state senator T. H. McGregor, of Austin, as its candidate for governor and the prolabor platform adopted earlier in the year. To keep up appearances as a national party, the American Party nominated Ferguson as its candidate for president of the United States. Ferguson, however, with his sights on the US Senate seat coming up for election in 1922, used the nomination merely as a vehicle to keep himself before the Texas electorate. He did not campaign outside Texas, and even within the state he electioneered only on a small scale.[102]

Ferguson's campaign for president was a fake, but the American Party ran an extensive campaign for McGregor for governor. His campaign received a major boost when the TSFL endorsed him. After Hobby signed the open-port bill, McGregor quickly denounced it. On October 13, the TSFL executive board issued a statement announcing a parting of ways with the Democratic Party, charging that it betrayed wageworkers. In a historic break from the party, the TSFL executive board endorsed McGregor over the open-shop Democratic candidate for governor, Pat Neff.[103]

While white trade unionists were growing disenchanted with the Democratic Party, the same was happening with black trade unionists and the Republican Party. In Galveston, the black Republican newspaper offered no public support to the striking longshoremen, and state Black and Tan leaders endorsed the open shop. Shortly afterward, they lost control of the state Republican Party to the Lily Whites. When McGregor declared his opposition to martial law in Galveston, he rapidly gained the support of labor on the island.[104]

In Galveston, a public meeting was called for the night of June 28 for the purpose of organizing the American Party in the city and nominating candidates for office. The Texas National Guard broke up the meeting, but supporters of the American Party persisted and later nominated a slate of local candidates supported by black and white unionists. The party endorsed McGregor for governor, and Galveston unionist supporters campaigned throughout the summer of 1920. By October, however, Galveston supporters of the American Party decided to no longer run their candidates for state representatives on the American Party ticket. Instead, they opted to run them on the nonpartisan Independent Citizen's Ticket.[105]

The reasons for the sudden switch to the Independent Citizen's Ticket are not entirely clear, but they might be explained by actions taken at the top of the American Party. The October 14 issue of the *Ferguson Forum* featured the front-page appeal "Republican Brethren; Let Us Dwell Together!" "The first thing to be done to make political reform possible in Texas," Ferguson announced, "is to beat the democrats and forever drive them from power as a state or national organization." To achieve this, Ferguson called upon Republicans who want a "new deal in Texas government" to vote for the American Party as the Republican Party stood no chance of defeating the Democrats on their own.[106]

A few days later, Black and Tan Republicans publicly exposed a deal between Ferguson and the Lily Whites that had been in the works for three months. A Black and Tan leader revealed that the Lily Whites agreed to endorse American Party candidates in "certain districts" and in return the American Party agreed to endorse Lily Whites in the ninth and fourteenth congressional districts. The fourteenth district was southwest of Houston, along the coast to Calhoun County and headed inland. The area had a large population of African Americans who supported the Black and Tan faction. The ninth district was west of the fourteenth to Nueces County and went further inland north to include San Antonio. In 1920 the ninth district elected Black and Tan Republican Harry Wurzbach to Congress, the only representative from Texas to vote for the Dyer Anti-lynching Bill in 1922. Ferguson's political deal with Lily Whites, which might explain why Galveston's black and white workers left the American Party, compromised the biracial unionism and interracial political alliance between the city's black and white workers.[107]

Democrats and open-shop supporters stepped up their campaign against the American Party, which was now weakened by Ferguson's chicanery. Despite the official endorsement of organized labor, McGregor came in a distant third for governor. Lee Rhodes, an old standard-bearer of the Socialist Party, received only 6,796 votes. When the American Party and SP votes are combined, 15.8 percent of voters chose a labor-based alternative to the two major parties. The 1920 election also revealed a conservative bloc of nearly 39 percent of the electorate. In this reconfigured electoral map, progressive Wilsonian Democrats no longer held a majority, only a slim plurality. For the record, Ferguson received 47,968 votes (9.9%) for president in his Texas-only campaign. He drained farmer-labor support from Debs, who, although still in prison, received 8,121 votes in Texas. Nationally, Debs received his highest vote total ever.[108]

The American Party, though defeated in the big races, could take heart in a few victories. For a party in existence for only a year, it significantly reduced the margin of Democratic victory in statewide offices. It also won four counties—Austin, Fayette, Lavaca, and Washington—in the highly populated area of central Texas. These counties held large German populations, and blacks made up 44 percent of Washington County, which elected H. J. Neinast to the state legislature on the American ticket. The 127th District of Fayette and Austin counties did the same when Otto Memking, of Ellinger, defeated a prominent Democratic member of the state House, Leonard Tillotson, a banker from Sealy. This gave the American Party two representatives in the House. In the Meitzen territory of Fayette and Lavaca counties, the American Party defeated every Democratic candidate it ran against for county office. The offices won by the American Party in Lavaca County included county judge, the offices of county clerk, sheriff, tax collector, and tax assessor, as well as a seat on the four-member county commission. Austin County also elected an American Party sheriff. With Prohibition in effect, to have a county sheriff opposed to Prohibition, and thus more likely to look the other way, was important to the drinking culture of area Germans.[109]

Although some Texas farmers might be able to hide their drink, none could hide from the deteriorating economic conditions. The national value of crops dropped from around $15.4 billion in 1919 to $7 billion in 1921. Cotton, the principle cash crop, cost between 20 and 35 cents per pound to grow, but much of the 1920 crop sold only for 10 cents per pound. Cattle, bought earlier for $40 a head, were worth a mere $8 a head in 1921. Just about everything farmers produced sold at less than the cost of production, while prices for consumer products remained at high wartime levels.[110]

Following a now old Texas tradition, sixty-nine farmers of Fannin County got together and formed a protest organization to address their economic grievances. On October 30, 1920, they founded the Farm-Labor Union of America (FLUA). One of the founding farmers acknowledged its roots in the tradition of agrarian protest: "The Farm-Labor Union of America is the heir of all the good points of the . . . other farmers' organizations that have gone before."[111] Another farmer emphasized the grassroots nature of the new organization: "I belonged to the Farmers' Alliance until it passed away and to the Farmers' Union as long as it lasted, but the Farm-Labor Union is the only dirt farmers' organization we ever have had and I feel proud of its principles. I am 66 years of age and do not miss a meeting."[112]

The FLUA, the product of a direct line of farmer-labor protest organizations in Texas dating back to the 1870s, soon grew to 125,000 members in Texas and spread into Oklahoma, Arkansas, Louisiana, Alabama, Mississippi, and Florida. Its national membership reached 300,000 members. In comparison with other agricultural organizations, the FLUA was unique in that only working farmers could join. The Farm Bureau allowed lawyers, merchants, and bankers into its ranks. Many of the leading organizers and supporters of the FLUA were old Populists and socialists such as Covington Hall, E. R. Meitzen, and Lee Rhodes.[113]

Like the Farmers' Alliance, the FLUA fashioned itself as a nonpartisan organization with no political or religious affiliations. The FLUA, however, followed a different political trajectory. The Farmers' Alliance contained many members who advocated independent political action outside the two-party system. They helped develop a movement culture that led to the creation of the People's Party and shaped some of its leaders as they transitioned into the SP. Although economic issues stood paramount for Populists and socialists, they also addressed social issues. Populists supported woman suffrage, and the SP had a strong record of championing women's rights. Both movements made limited but genuine attempts to reach out to and organize African Americans and later Mexican Americans, even though such efforts were often tenuous and strained by a more paternalistic form of white supremacy. The FLUA, however, never developed the movement culture of its predecessors or formed an independent political party. As a quasi-business organization, the FLUA focused overwhelmingly on economic issues and remained virtually silent on social issues. Its purely economic objectives left it ill prepared to combat the revival of the Ku Klux Klan in the 1920s.[114]

Three weeks before the creation of the FLUA, the United Confederate Veterans wrapped up their annual reunion in Houston with a parade on October 9, 1920. In the parade was William Simmons, the Imperial Wizard of the Georgia KKK, followed by a float and white-robed Klansmen. The Klan had arrived in Texas. Before heading back to Georgia, Simmons laid the groundwork for the Texas KKK, which grew to as many as eighty thousand members. Before the Klan's just-as-swift implosion after 1926, the Texas KKK gained partial or complete control of every major Texas city except San Antonio and Galveston, and elected a US senator and very nearly a governor.[115]

The Klan drew almost everyone's attention with large torch-lit parades of hooded men carrying US flags and burning crosses, but the FLUA attracted the attention of organized labor. TSFL president George Slater noticed that the FLUA campaigned against the Industrial Domestic Court Bill in the Texas legislature. Industrial courts, popular with Progressive reformers of this period, were adopted by a few states as supposedly neutral courts to mediate conflicts between labor and capital. Such courts, however, nearly always sided with capital and were opposed by organized laborers and farmers. Acknowledging Slater's interest, the FLUA invited him to its May 1921 convention. He reciprocated by inviting FLUA president W. W. Fitzwater to address the TSFL's convention, where Fitzwater was warmly received. A month later, Samuel Gompers promoted political alliances between organized labor and farm organizations as part of the AFL's national policy strategy. FLUA members in Texas became regular participants in local labor councils, and in turn trade unionists participated in FLUA meetings.[116]

The Depression of 1921 devastated farmers and workers. In the spring, the Railroad Labor Board gave approval for railroad corporations to cut wages at nearly one hundred railroads, even though railroad unions pointed out that the average rail worker earned an average of $157.46 a month while incurring $153.50 a month in subsistence expenditures. The open-shop campaign was also in full swing, threatening the very existence of unions. Pushed to the brink of economic ruin, farm and labor organizations put their proclamations of farmer-labor political unity into action in the 1922 elections. They had to do so, however, without the American Party. The farmer-labor bloc in Texas had used the American Party as a vehicle to advocate demands, but Ferguson still held control of the party machinery. On January 28, 1922, the executive committee of the American Party officially disbanded. At the same time, Ferguson announced his candidacy for the US Senate as a Democrat.[117]

The NPL, also in tatters, soon faded away. In March 1920 the NPL gained approval of an amendment to the North Dakota constitution that allowed recall of elected officials. Elites orchestrated a successful special election to recall NPL officials Governor Lynn Frazier, attorney general William Lemke, and commissioner of agriculture John Hagen in 1921. The NPL was ousted from power by its own democratic measures as voters made elected NPL leaders the first statewide officeholders to be recalled in US history. Four days after the election, Townley entered a jail in Jackson, Minnesota, to serve a ninety-day sentence after being found guilty of disloyalty during the war. E. R. Meitzen and Hall, who campaigned against the recall, returned to Texas in December 1921.[118]

Meitzen continued efforts to bring organized labor and farmers together for joint political action in Texas.[119] Under the umbrella of the Nonpartisan Political Conference, representatives of the FLUA, TSFL, NPL, and the big four railroad brotherhoods met five times from late 1921 to April 1922 to discuss an electoral strategy. Out of these meetings came a declaration of principles: exemption from taxation of farm and city homestead improvements, establishment of a state-owned bank, "the elimination of profiteering and all forms of fictitious future dealing in necessities of life," abolition of the poll tax, a women's minimum wage law, the rights of collective bargaining, improvement of the educational system, and opposition to convict labor. The conference chose Bonham lawyer Fred S. Rogers as its candidate for governor. The Nonpartisan Political Conference decided to work within the Democratic Party on a state level but left it to local conferences to determine a strategic approach to municipal elections.[120]

The political tactics of the NPL made a farmer-labor political alliance in Texas more palatable to organized labor than it had been in the 1890s. Until the 1920s, organizations of the farmer-labor bloc agitated for their political demands through independent political parties while the main bloc of organized labor affiliated with the AFL worked within the two-party system. Because agrarian radicals in Texas now sought to run candidates in the Democratic primary, organized labor joined them in a political coalition. The TSFL's endorsement of the American Party in 1920 caused internal dissension, but now the decision not to create a new party was in line with the stance of national AFL leaders. Slater, president of the TSFL, denied that the goal of the Nonpartisan Political Conference was to create a labor party. The railroad brotherhoods, too, did not want to cut ties with Democrats, because they were backing William Gibbs McAdoo, former head of the US Railroad Administration, as the Democratic presidential nominee in 1924.[121]

After E. R. Meitzen orchestrated the merger of the Texas NPL and FLUA sometime between April and December 1922, the FLUA adopted the political strategy of the Nonpartisan Political Conference. As editor of the FLUA's newspaper, the *Farm Labor Union News*, Meitzen promoted the links between the organization and the TSFL. Although the FLUA did adopt a producerist critique of early twentieth-century capitalism and endorsed political candidates, its overriding concern was the economic plight of farmers. The new organization's business union orientation eased its political coalition with organized labor and Gompers's brand of "pure and simple unionism."[122]

When the Klan entered politics in 1922, its opponents in the farmer-labor bloc and black community had few effective ways to fight them at the ballot box. The purely economic focus of the FLUA left it ill equipped to combat the social, cultural, and racist appeals of the KKK. In fact, both the KKK and the FLUA endorsed former Populist-turned-Klansman "Cyclone" Davis in his 1922 bid for US Congress. At the July 1922 meeting of the Anderson County FLUA, on the other hand, whether one believed in unionism took precedence over whether one belonged to the KKK as the decisive factor in choosing candidates for county office.[123]

With the lack of primary source materials on the FLUA, it is hard to get specific evidence on its relationship with black farmers. A letter from a black FLUA farmer that appeared in the only extant copy of its newspaper indicates the problematic, restricted political choices that confronted African Americans in Texas in the early 1920s. In an extremely repressive, racist political climate, George Starks, who identified himself as a member of a colored local of the FLUA of Independent Springs, wrote this to the *Farm Labor Union News*:

> I am a colored man, one hundred per cent union and I am with you white people to the last ditch. I joined this F.L.U. of A., from a business standpoint and consider it the last resort for freedom. Our race never asks for anything, but we surely will take anything you white people will give us. Now you have given me the Union fever and I can not get set well until we get every man in office we want and carry out all the purposes of the Union.[124]

When the axis of Texas politics tilted on pro- versus anti-Klan as it did beginning in 1922, the economic issues of the farmer-labor bloc received little attention.

Rogers, who received 195,941 votes in the Democratic primary, finished behind Klan-backed incumbent Governor Neff, who drew 289,188 votes. Though the combined farmer-labor vote failed to propel Rogers into the governor's mansion, the farm vote did turn out, as local FLUA-supported candidates won thirty state Senate and House races. In seven counties, practically the entire FLUA slate was elected. In Lavaca County, residents elected E. O. Meitzen county surveyor, a position he held until 1929.[125]

While the election results show that farmers supported Rogers, the same could not be said for unionized workers. There are a few factors that might explain the lack of labor's support at the polls. During the campaign, the *Dallas Morning News* reported that, in the 1920 primary election, Rogers supported Joseph Bailey for governor and attacked organized labor. A few trade union officials came to the defense of Rogers as a supporter of organized labor. They insisted he made no antilabor statements and that his speech in support of Bailey was "along the line of Jeffersonian Democracy and urging people to stand by a man who believed in state rights." Bailey's endorsement of Rogers did not help his case.[126]

Another factor that limited labor's support for Rogers was the 1922 railroad strike. On July 1, a few weeks before the Texas Democratic primary, the railroad brotherhoods, in response to railroad corporations cutting wages, went out on a national strike. In the lead-up to the primary election, Governor Neff refused to call out the Texas Guard against strikers and remained quiet about the strike. His strategic silence seems to have won him the faith of organized labor. Once he won the primary, however, he declared martial law in strike centers and sent the Texas Guard and Texas Rangers to put down the strike.[127]

The FLUA remained by the side of striking railroad workers, condemned Neff's declaration of martial law, and lent material aid to strikers. FLUA president Fitzwater assured strikers in Childress that the FLUA stood behind them: "Your fight is our fight, and you have got to win. . . . I want to tell you that we are with you to the finish. If you need food, remember that we have bulls in the pasture, hogs in the pen, and peas and corn in the field. When you need it come and get all you need—it's free." After a federal injunction, however, the strike quickly collapsed to the detriment of workers with union locals negotiating regional rather than national contracts.[128]

Whereas the 1922 primary election produced a gubernatorial candidate for Democrats in Neff, the US senatorial race required a runoff. Former state senator and Texas railroad commissioner Earle Mayfield received the full support of the Klan in his bid for the US Senate. Mayfield, a widely suspected member of the KKK, faced Ferguson in the runoff. The hotly contested campaign was waged almost solely on the Klan issue. Though Ferguson held white supremacist beliefs, he was firmly against the Klan. He believed in the rule of law and opposed vigilantism. He called a Klan member a "foolish fanatic" who is "wasting all them sheets and pillow cases to cover yourself up . . . scaring women and children and ignorant colored people." As a state's-rights Jeffersonian, Ferguson supported the separation of church and state against the Klan's Christian Invisible Empire. Further, he opposed Klan-supported federal Prohibition. Mayfield defeated Ferguson by a vote of 273,308 to 228,701. Ferguson, who courted the labor vote, blamed his defeat on union workers who, he claimed, voted for Mayfield. Ferguson offered little proof for his accusation. In fact, the Nonpartisan Political Conference endorsed Ferguson. Mayfield's victory, though, could not have been achieved without working-class votes, and he went on to win the general election.[129]

After the 1922 election, it became clear that Black and Tans lost their fight against the Lily Whites for control of the Republican Party. Clifton F. Richardson Sr., secretary of the Houston NAACP and editor and owner of the *Houston Informer*, lambasted the election campaign: "Neither the republicans nor independent democrats made any concerted effort to secure the colored vote, and thus the black man took only passing notice of the grand political parade." Richardson also noted the growing national trend of African Americans to vote Democratic. This was due in part to the failure of the Republican-controlled US Senate to support the Dyer antilynching bill. As a result, northern Democrats began to actively court black votes and, in Texas, African Americans began to vote for anti-Klan Democrats. Ferguson, who, despite his racism, ran an anti-Klan campaign, reportedly received 3,500 black votes in Bexar County in the primary. In the general election, the anti-Klan candidate for US Senate achieved the significant feat of obtaining 130,744 votes as a write-in.[130]

Though Texas Democrats won the 1922 elections, they feared the latent possibility of a unified farmer-labor and black voting bloc. Blacks, where allowed, were now voting in the Democratic primary and the FLUA was encouraging its members and allies to run in the Democratic primary. White-supremacist Democrats saw the writing on the wall. With the white vote now divided, the black vote could be the deciding factor in elections. The 1903 Terrell Election Law proved inadequate in stopping blacks from voting. This law empowered parties' county executive committees to decide who voted in local elections. In many counties, Democrats prevented blacks from voting. In others, they allowed blacks to vote, often in order to manipulate the vote. In theory, if farmer-labor activists gained control of a county's Democratic Party machinery, they could allow blacks to vote.[131]

With pro-Klan legislators now in control of both Texas houses after the 1922 elections, they acted to stop farmer-laborer control from ever happening. Representative Douglas Davenport introduced a primary-election bill called the "white man's primary law," barring blacks from voting in the Democratic primary. Passed by a large majority in May 1923, the new law effectively disenfranchised black Texans. A few weeks before its passage, an editorial by Richardson expressed the bitterness felt by black voters: "This paper believes that both the republican and democratic parties, as such have outlived their days of usefulness and that sooner or later they must pass off the scene or be politically rejuvenated and renovated."[132]

The farmer-labor bloc of Texas, by fighting under the banner of the American Party in the 1920 election, abandoned its often tenuous but at times progressive history of support for women's rights and organizing across racial lines. The attempts by farmer-labor activists over the decades to unite poor farmers and workers across the racial divide led to violence against their movements by white supremacists and state repression. By the 1920s, many white farmer-labor activists found it easier to ignore racial and other social issues and focus purely on economic matters in hopes of no longer incurring the wrath of white supremacists.

The bridge connecting the farmer-labor bloc to social conservatives was a shared belief in Jeffersonian democracy. Throughout this period, Jefferson democracy was invoked by both archconservatives, such as Joseph Bailey, and radical southern socialists, like the Meitzens. At the core, they shared an opposition to centralized authority. What divided the two was the farmer-labor bloc's producerist ideology, which stood in opposition to conservatives' faith in free-market liberalism. The farmer-labor bloc of the 1890s–1910s also still believed that the state could play a positive role if controlled by producers. This belief was manifested in the call for a Cooperative Commonwealth.[133]

The seeds of social conservatism and a diluted producerism had long existed in the farmer-labor bloc. It took the state-sponsored repression of labor and agrarian radicals in the years surrounding World War I for them to germinate. Being an outspoken radical became a danger that could lead to jail, deportation, or even death. After the war, the farmer-labor bloc in Texas avoided the outward appearance of the radicalism its members had previously embraced.

In the increasingly sophisticated consumer society of the 1920s, a pronounced shift from a producerist to a consumerist worldview occurred among many farmer-labor intellectuals. The germ causing the transition from producerism to consumerist liberalism were the consumer cooperatives advocated by labor and agrarian organizations dating back to the Farmers' Alliance. The FLUA also advocated for consumer cooperatives, and it and the TSFL began to employ more consumerist than producerist language. As editor of the *Farm Labor Union News*, E. R. Meitzen became the leading voice of the FLUA's cooperative plans. He entered the ultimate halls of power, testifying in February 1925 before a congressional committee in Washington in favor of the creation of a federal cooperative marketing board.[134]

Consumerism took many intellectuals of the farmer-labor bloc down the slope from Marxism to Adam Smith. In this era when being a radical was dangerous, for many, a worker cooperative, devoid of class struggle, seemed like an easier path to better the conditions of the working class than revolution. The shift helped pave the way for the coming New Deal of the 1930s, which took more of a consumerist than a producerist ideology, where workers were regarded as consumers rather than producers.

The Bolshevik Revolution played a factor in the farmer-labor bloc's changing view of the state. Workers and peasants in the Soviet Union faced colossal obstacles in their efforts to implement a soviet form of government. The ever-changing news from the Soviet Union left many in the farmer-labor bloc wondering about their own demands for a producerist-run society. The FLUA did explore ways to sell cotton to the Soviet Union and FLUA president Fitzwater planned a visit to Moscow in August 1923. Neither happened. After Vladimir I. Lenin's death in January 1924 and the rise of Joseph Stalin, the Soviet Union resembled more of a nightmare than a model workers' state.[135]

Within Jeffersonian ideology sits a basic contradiction—democracy versus individualism. Jeffersonian ideology champions the yeoman and artisan free from restraints of a centralized government, while it also advocates democracy— as in the common good of the people. Producers' control of a regulatory state was the main contradiction in the farmer-labor bloc's devotion to Jeffersonian democracy. The farmer-labor bloc had experienced how a capitalist-controlled state could crush its dreams for a Cooperative Commonwealth through court injunctions, martial law, industrial courts, and the Federal Reserve. A Stalinized Soviet Union made them question whether the state could ever be used to the benefit of workers and farmers. Ferguson and others like him held no contradictions in their interpretation of Jeffersonian democracy when it came to the role of government. They opposed what they saw as an excessive use of federal intrusions by the Wilson administration in the form of prohibition, woman suffrage, the Federal Reserve, and support for a global centralized authority in the League of Nations. The Jeffersonian beliefs of Ferguson bear a striking resemblance to the antistate beliefs of the early-twentieth-first century's Tea Party and right-wing libertarians.[136]

The farmer-labor bloc of Texas, in adopting the election tactics of the NPL and losing, was now left without an independent political party of its own. The White Primary Law completely prevented African Americans from participating in the only meaningful election in Texas—that of the Democratic primary. When white agrarian radicals abandoned the black working class, a rejuvenated interracial political alliance reminiscent of the Populist era became an improbability. Instead, the farmer-labor bloc led itself into a Democratic Party dominated by socially conservative, antistatist Jeffersonian Democrats. Texas ceased being a hotbed of economic radicalism and instead became one of social conservatism—a transition that has had lasting political ramifications on the entire nation. At the time, farmer-labor radicals still held out hope that the new alliance of labor and working farmer organizations would bring about the Cooperative Commonwealth in the near future.

Conclusion

Descent into New Deal Liberalism

Heading into 1923, it seemed as if decades of exhausting work by the farmer-labor bloc might finally culminate in the creation of a working-class-based political party that could contend for power nationally. In the three years since John Fitzpatrick's Chicago convention failed to produce a nationally cohesive Farmer-Labor Party in July 1920, conditions had changed dramatically. The election tactics of the NPL after the recall election in 1921 were no longer the pole of attraction they had once been. The NPL did leave behind, however, lasting organized farmer and labor political coalitions in the West and upper Great Plains. Similar coalitions were being built elsewhere, such as the one in Texas headed by E. R. Meitzen. The probusiness attitudes of leading Democrats created more space for trade union leaders who supported independent political action.

Sensing the sea change, Fitzpatrick once again called a national convention to meet in Chicago in July 1923 to build a national party based on an alliance of workers and farmers. He sent out invitations far and wide to those interested in building a farmer-labor party. He did not realize, however, how much the sea had changed. In western states, where the farmer-labor party idea had gained the most traction, communists dominated the movement. Coming out of the left wing of the SP after it was expelled in 1919, the communist Workers Party adopted the tactic of building a broad-based farmer-labor party as a step toward a working-class revolution. Many members of the Workers Party, particularly in the West and upper Great Plains, had made the political journey from the SP to the NPL and now to the Workers Party. E. R. Meitzen had longstanding political relationships with many of them.[1]

Fitzpatrick realized many liberal and progressive unions and organizations would not want to form a new party with communists. At the last minute, he made an unsuccessful attempt to change the character of the convention from forming a new party to just discussing a platform for a future party. As expected, the liberals and progressives did not attend, but the radical farmers did. "The farmers and the Communists found common ground at the convention almost at once," wrote historian Lowell Dyson. Together they cheered the cooperative plans of the Soviet Union, called for producer control of the economy, and urged nationalization of basic industry. The communists compromised and agreed to adopt agrarian demands they viewed as too Populist. Over the objections of Fitzpatrick, who thereupon quit, delegates founded the Federated Farmer Labor Party (FFLP).[2]

When FFLP organizers went into the field, they discovered that in states that had existing variations of a farmer-labor party, activists were unwilling to merge with the FFLP. The FFLP continued to play a role in the growing farmer-labor party movement but would not lead it. Stepping into the leadership role was the farmer-labor coalition of Minnesota that the NPL had started and E. R. Meitzen helped organize. In November 1923, Minnesota farmer-laborers organized a small conference of progressives and farmer-labor organizations, including the FFLP. The conference decided to call a convention in St. Paul in mid-1924 to form a new Farmer Labor Party (FLP) that could rally around Wisconsin senator Robert La Follette for president.[3]

While western farmer-labor radicals were organizing for the 1924 election, so too was the Conference for Progressive Political Action (CPPA). The railroad brotherhoods created the CPPA and organized its first conference in February 1922 in Chicago, which was attended by representatives of various unions and farm organizations, the Committee of Forty-Eight, the SP, and advocates of a farmer-labor party. Chicago unionists and the SP wanted the creation of a third party. The CPPA decided, however, not to create a new party but instead to support friends of labor within the two dominant parties. Moreover, the railroad brotherhoods saw the CPPA as an instrument to promote William Gibbs McAdoo Jr.'s candidacy for the Democratic presidential nomination. The railroad brotherhoods' hope for a McAdoo presidency came to a halt in February 1924 when he was implicated in the Teapot Dome scandal. The CPPA then got behind La Follette.[4]

With farmer-labor radicals and the CPPA supporting La Follette, all seemed set for an independent working-class party to break the two-party system, make a real challenge for the White House, and play a lasting role in US political culture. Instead, the whole configuration imploded. FLP supporters saw the 1924 election as the first campaign of a new party, but the CPPA saw LaFollette's campaign as a one-time-only independent campaign and opposed creating a new party. They hoped La Follette would win, though what was more important was that they saw the campaign as a way to pressure the two main parties to be friendlier to organized labor. An aging Samuel Gompers also intervened, voicing his opposition to the creation of a new party. Most important, La Follette himself refused to be a part of creating a new party. As part of the CPPA coalition, the SP did seek an American Labor Party but eventually conceded that the campaign would only lay groundwork for a future labor party.[5]

The CPPA also disparaged the presence of communists in the FLP, citing the leading role of the Workers Party in organizing the approaching St. Paul convention. The SP also engaged in a sectarian campaign against what it claimed was a communist-controlled FLP. Communists did have a large presence in the FLP, but if all the delegations that organizers expected arrived in St. Paul, communists would have been in the minority. Under mounting pressure, though, La Follette on May 28 released a letter in which he disavowed the St. Paul convention as communist-riddled. He encouraged his supporters not to attend. The letter had its desired intent. Many progressive organizations previously committed to attending the convention pulled out. Not all heeded LaFollette's warning, however. E. R. Meitzen, who represented the FLUA of Texas, and others described by Dyson as "some dogged Farmer Laborites" from South Dakota, Nebraska, and Minnesota, disregarded La Follette and arrived in St. Paul intent on creating a new national party. Without the presence of organizations warned away by LaFollette, the communists were firmly in control.[6]

The FLP adopted resolutions endorsing the Women's Equal Rights Amendment, demanding the release of political prisoners, and opposing the Ku Klux Klan. The platform called for public ownership of basic industries, protections for organized labor, the end of land tenantry, full political and economic rights for women and Negros, diplomatic recognition of the Soviet Union, independence for the Philippine Islands, the right of self-determination for Puerto Rico and other US colonies, and the withdraw of US troops from Central America and the Caribbean. Undoubtedly as a result of communist influences, the platform had stronger anti-imperialist demands than any previous platform of the farmer-labor bloc. Delegates approved the platform and created a national committee, to which Meitzen was elected.[7]

Some delegates wanted to nominate La Follette regardless of his public rebuke of the convention. In the end, though, the FLP selected Duncan McDonald, a former president of the United Mine Workers of Illinois, as its candidate for president. Many delegates, and even McDonald himself, thought his nomination would serve only as a placeholder. They hoped La Follette would eventually accept the FLP's endorsement. More, though, was at play than most noncommunist delegates realized in McDonald's nomination.[8]

After the death of Lenin in January, a power struggle erupted for leadership of the Soviet Union and the Third International, each faction trying to out-"left" each other. In the midst of this power play, the Third International directed the US Workers Party to demand of La Follette, as a condition of FLP's endorsement of him, that the FLP be given total control of his campaign. They knew full well that he would reject such a demand, thus allowing the FLP to nominate, in its view, a true revolutionary. When La Follette rejected the FLP even before the St. Paul convention, communists maneuvered to have McDonald nominated as a placeholder for their own Workers Party candidate.[9]

After the Republican convention overwhelmingly went for Calvin Coolidge over La Follette as expected, La Follette accepted the backing of the CPPA for president on condition he be allowed to run as an independent without creating a new party. Since La Follette refused backing from the FLP, the Workers Party withdrew their support from McDonald and announced its own presidential candidate—the communist labor organizer William Z. Foster. After La Follette refused the nomination and the communists exited, the FLP was stillborn.

After the FLP disintegrated, E. R. Meitzen put his support behind La Follette's independent campaign. Meitzen stood as an elector for him in Texas, along with fellow old-timer farmer-labor radicals Lee Rhodes and M. A. Smith. LaFollette lost the election, but his national vote total was the highest any presidential candidate supported by the farmer-labor bloc had ever garnered. He received 17 percent of the popular vote, winning Wisconsin and coming in second in eleven Western states.[10] The farmer-labor bloc seemed to be at the zenith of its political influence and a serious oppositional force to the status quo of the US political system. Without a political party, though, it was in a nebulous state.

In Texas, the state of the farmer-labor bloc was especially bleak. Repression and deep internal divisions had wracked the SP, moving it further to the fringes of Texas political culture. As a result of the NPL's strategy, which E. R. Meitzen endorsed, to channel farmer-labor radicalism into the two-party structure, farmer-labor radicals in Texas no longer had a popular party of their own. In the fall of 1924, Meitzen moved the editorial offices of the *Farm Labor Union News* from Bonham to Texarkana. In nonelection years, the FLUA devoted most of its energy to promoting its cooperative plans. After faring poorly in the political campaigns of 1922 and 1924, the FLUA in 1925 put extra efforts into making its cooperative marketing plan for cotton a success. The market plan failed. Some of its state officials felt they could create a better marketing plan and left with a portion of the FLUA's membership to found a rival organization, the Southern Farmers Co-operative Marketing Association.[11]

Meitzen was already planning for the next political battle. He told his old comrade Covington Hall that he was dreaming of establishing a new radical paper "and making a fight to build up a Farmer-Labor party in Texas, Oklahoma, and Arkansas." Hall wrote to Lemke about the plan: "This I believe we could easily do once we get the paper going, for we stand in pretty strong with the rebel farmers all thru those states." He acknowledged the challenges of such a fight: "It will be hard sledding at the start, but the pendulum is bound to swing ere long against the reactionaries now in office."[12]

When the FLUA held its state convention in Dallas in December 1925, Meitzen organized the first convention of the Texas Labor Party to take place concurrently. With representatives from the Texas State Federation of Labor and the railroad brotherhoods in town for the FLUA convention, he sought to reinvigorate the Texas farmer-labor political coalition that began in 1920. This time, however, Meitzen's plan was not to run in the Democratic primary, but instead to return to independent political action by running candidates through the new Texas Labor Party.[13]

The FLUA and labor unions balked at the notion of joining the Texas Labor Party. The FLUA's involvement in political campaigns was always contentious among its members. Some even viewed its political activities as the cause of the split that led some of its members to form the new marketing association. In hopes that avoiding politics would save their organization, FLUA leaders formally announced in January 1926 that "political activities will be left in the hands of individuals" and would no longer be a function of the organization.[14] The FLUA soon collapsed.

Moving on without the FLUA, the band of farmer-labor radicals around Meitzen formed the Texas Labor Party in Dallas and elected him to lead it. He resigned from the FLUA. On December 9, the same day that the Texas Labor Party was formed, a similar convention in Arkansas also created a labor party. Delegates there chose an old-time member of the Knights of Labor, the socialist J. C. Thompson, as their state chairman. At the time, Thompson was president of the Arkansas FLUA, but not for much longer.[15]

The Texas Labor Party moved forward with some unexpected allies, especially in light of the fate of the 1924 Farmer-Labor Party. The Workers Party decided, after its miserable showing in the 1924 elections, that it made a tactical mistake in derailing the FLP. In 1925 it returned to its original tactic of building farmer-labor parties as a way to break workers away from the twin parties of capitalism. To organize farmers in a fight against capitalism and build farmer-labor parties, the Workers Party created the United Farmers Educational League (UFEL) in March 1926. Alfred Knutson, of North Dakota, one of the NPL's best-known former organizers, served as national secretary of the UFEL and edited its paper, the *United Farmer*. Since joining the Workers Party as a member of the NPL, he had been a leader of the party's work among farmers. The UFEL, though under the control of the Workers Party with a clear anticapitalist message, fashioned itself as a broad-based organization seeking to build farmer-labor parties. It worked with cooperatives and called for traditional farmer-labor demands such as nationalization of basic industries, land for the farmers who worked it, and the end of the tenant system. To invoke an air of nonpartisanship, Knutson created a national committee that included a sizable minority of noncommunists. The most recognizable noncommunist on the committee was E. R. Meitzen. Other well-known longtime farmer-labor radicals joined the UFEL's efforts to build the Texas Labor Party, including Covington Hall, M. A. Smith, Lee Rhodes, Stanley Clark, and the two Meitzens. Missing from this list is Meitzen's longtime friend and comrade Tom Hickey, who died on May 7, 1925, of throat cancer. A partnership of many years had passed.[16]

As the movement continued, Workers Party leader James Cannon also enlisted E. R. Meitzen to serve on the national committee of the International Labor Defense (ILD)—an organization dedicated to defending working-class political prisoners. Cannon and Meitzen had worked together on various committees at the 1924 St. Paul convention. They also shared a common friend and comrade, William Haywood. Cannon, Haywood, and Rose Karsner initially discussed the idea of the ILD in Moscow in March 1925. A later trip to Moscow would find Cannon becoming a leader of the Left Opposition against Stalinism.[17] As noted by historian Bryan Palmer, during this struggle, "Cannon converted the ILD into his own political fortress."[18]

By 1926, it was painfully clear that the Texas Labor Party was going nowhere. E. R. Meitzen's new newspaper, the *Toiler*, was unable to help the Texas Labor Party grow because of government interference with his mailing rights. Of more pressing concern to Meitzen was providing for a growing family. Sometime in the early 1920s, Meitzen had married Lillie Carson McCullough, a war widow who married a soldier right before he was sent to war. Three months after the marriage, her husband was killed in France. In 1923 Lillie and E. R. had their first child, Ernest Jr., and their second, Johanna Lula, in 1927. Throughout his working life, Meitzen had worked only as a paid political organizer and a newspaperman. He was now a socialist without a party and a newspaperman without a newspaper. A move was needed.[19]

After Lillie became pregnant with Jo-Lou, Meitzen purchased a newspaper in Live Oak, Florida. Upon Jo-Lou's birth, the family moved to their new home in Florida. The Texas economy was in a rut, and Florida was experiencing a boom fueled by real-estate speculation. For the Meitzens, a new start in Florida seemed like a great opportunity. Shortly after Meitzens arrived in Florida, however, the bubble burst. Meitzen adjusted by moving the paper to the larger nearby town of Lake City. The new paper, the *Columbia Gazette*, eventually became Columbia County's paper of record, but it still was a struggle for the family financially, as it was for just about everyone, as the country entered the Great Depression.[20]

For a brief period, Hall moved in with the Meitzen family in Lake City and helped run the paper. The Meitzen children affectionately called Hall "Uncle Covington," and soon the Meitzen brood grew to five with the birth of John.

Hall did not stay in Florida long. He stayed in regular contact with Meitzen as the two of them, along with Lemke, corresponded over what course of action to take to advance their lifelong commitment to fight for the working class.[21]

After being recalled as the NPL's attorney general of North Dakota, Lemke joined in the efforts to create a national farmer-labor party. By the end of the 1920s, Lemke came to a conclusion: "With regard to the political situation," Lemke wrote Hall in 1929, "I believe a new party would be impossible at this time. We tried it for six years without success." He now was considering a return to the old NPL tactic: "it seems to me that we ought to be able to take over the Democratic party if it is worth taking over."[22]

Hall, the old Wobbly, was not completely convinced at first: "Personally, I believe there is as much chance to launch a new Party as there is to take over the Democratic. For this reason: The Democrat party is split wide open."[23] It took the extra convincing of Meitzen, who had gone over to Lemke's position, to win him over. "I think I told you," Hall wrote Lemke, "I was attempting to launch a national weekly[,] . . . the purpose of which would be to take over the Democratic party through its liberal wing. . . . [Y]ou and Ernest Meitzen put the idea in my head."[24] Hall was correct in his analysis of the Democratic Party as "split wide open." The party was in shambles after its utter defeat in 1924 and had not recovered in time for 1928. There was, however, another dynamic at work. The defeats resulted in a politically reconfigured Democratic Party that capitalized on the efforts of farmer-labor radicals.

The 1924 La Follette campaign had brought together a diverse coalition of farmer-labor radicals, liberals, and progressive-minded Democrats and Republicans. This coalition came together as a result in large part of years of work by farmer-labor activists. Just as the defeated 1964 Barry Goldwater campaign assembled a new conservative coalition that led to Republican near-dominance of the White House for more than two decades beginning in 1969, the failed La Follette campaign brought together the political elements that would make up the rank-and-file support for Franklin Roosevelt's presidential victory in 1932 and his New Deal programs of the early 1930s. The New Deal coalition would hold the White House until 1953 and have a strong presence in Congress through the 1980s.

After the Democratic Party's electoral disaster in 1924, Roosevelt sought to reorient the party along more progressive lines. He felt Democrats had to make themselves "by definite policy, the Party of constructive progress, before we can attract a larger following." Roosevelt actively courted the Bryan-McAdoo wing of the party to form an alliance with his northeastern base of support. In 1928 the hopes of Roosevelt's budding progressive coalition were set back when presidential candidate Alfred Smith allowed his campaign to run on probusiness lines.[25]

Roosevelt's efforts did not go unnoticed by former members of the farmer-labor bloc who held Meitzen's, Lemke's and Hall's vision of a left-wing takeover of the Democratic Party. Lemke was looking for a Democrat who would support legislation he drafted to assist economically struggling farmers. Roosevelt seemed like the Democrat he needed. Senator Burton Wheeler of Montana, who ran as La Follette's candidate for vice-president in 1924, was also looking at Roosevelt as a possible candidate to move the Democratic Party to the left. Wheeler became the first nationally known Democratic leader to endorse Roosevelt for president. Both Lemke and Wheeler played key roles in garnering support for Roosevelt from the farmer-labor bloc. This support helped Roosevelt win the Democratic nomination against conservative Democrats, and then the Midwest against Herbert Hoover in the general election. Roosevelt used his sweeping electoral mandate to implement the early programs of the New Deal.[26]

The nature of agriculture also dramatically changed by the 1930s, greatly affecting the social and political base of the old farmer-labor bloc. Agribusiness came to dominate farming; as farm sizes grew, the number of farmers decreased. Technological developments and government policies greatly assisted the rise of agribusiness to the detriment of tenant farmers. Cost-effective and labor-saving tractors lessened landowners' need to have a large number of tenant families working their land, leading to the "tractoring out" of many tenant farmers from the land. Roosevelt's New Deal agricultural programs provided generous subsidies to landowning farmers, but tenants and sharecroppers, many of whom were African American, received no such payments and were displaced. At the height of the farmer-labor bloc, farmers and rural people were the majority of the population. After the rapid descent that began in the 1920s, farmers today comprise only 2 percent of the population.[27] They have moral weight as the growers of our food, but they lack the physical numbers to be anything more than a special-interest group. These changes have moved the heart of the battle between labor and capital from the field to the factory. Economic radicalism, within a few short years, came to reside almost solely in the domain of industrial unionism amid the battles of the CIO through the 1940s until the Treaty of Detroit of 1950, when labor bureaucrats made peace with capitalism. After 1950, US political culture would not witness a large movement based on economic radicalism for more than sixty years.

To be sure, the United States has seen many movements since the 1930s—civil rights, women's rights, immigrant rights, and gay rights. Other movements have revolved around a single issue, such as opposition to a particular war. Economic issues were a factor in each of these movements, especially the civil-rights movement, but they were secondary within the general call for social equality or winning the issue at hand. This does not mean that economic radicalism has not been present within US political culture—it has. Just that, since the 1950s, economic radicalism has been primarily advocated by small, mainly Marxist-influenced, parties and organizations that have been pushed to the margins.

In the midst of the changes in agriculture, Hall left Florida and an elderly E. O. Meitzen moved in with his son and family in Lake City. E. R. gave his father a desk in his paper's newsroom. At home, E. O. enjoyed playing with his grandchildren. He cheered the election of Roosevelt and watched with satisfaction the implementation of the early New Deal programs that resembled many of the farmer-labor planks he promoted all his life. After all, was this not what he wanted? If the farmer-labor bloc could not get elected itself, then its secondary objective had always been to put left working-class pressure on the state.[28]

Now entering his seventies, E. O. Meitzen had made a long political trek. He grew up on stories from his father and uncle of their struggles during the 1848 Revolution in Germany. Entering adulthood, he became the learned blacksmith who joined the Greenback Labor Party. For the rest of his life, he remained a dedicated farmer-labor radical committed to the vision of a Cooperative Commonwealth, a true political and economic democracy run by workers and farmers who produced its wealth. After Johanna, his wife of nearly forty-six years, died in 1923, he remained active in politics as Lavaca County's elected surveyor for the next few years. He lent his well-respected name to causes such as the UFEL and wrote occasional letters to the editor of the *Dallas Morning News* to champion workers and farmers' rights.[29]

E. O. spent about four years in Florida before returning to Texas to live with his daughter Frieda and her family. Frieda had married a descendant of Sam Houston and they lived in Houston with their six children. Frieda's family fixed up a shack in their backyard for her father to live in. Years of activism and constant campaigning were now taking their toll. He spent the last year of his life with a persistent illness, although he remained jolly to the end. A week before he died at the age of seventy-nine on February 24, 1935, he told his daughter, "Frieda, go to your two babies, as they need you more than I do. My parents are here with me. So are others whom I haven't seen for fifty years or more. They will help me across." E. O. crossed—and so ended a grand chapter of farmer-labor radicalism.[30]

E. O. Meitzen did not live long enough to see Roosevelt's second term as president. After Roosevelt's first term, the New Deal entered a new, more conservative phase. The more conservative phase of the New Deal would eventually turn Lemke, and some other farmer-laborites, against Roosevelt. But through New Deal programs, Roosevelt had won the allegiance of much of the old farmer-labor bloc, wedding them to the Democratic Party—E. R. Meitzen included. The farmer-labor bloc collapsed into New Deal liberalism.

E. R. had become a New Deal Democrat, but this did not mean he was right with the establishment. He actively participated in the campaign to repeal the poll tax in Florida. In sections of the state with large white populations, the fight for repeal was not too contentious. Florida Democratic senator Claude Pepper, who supported the campaign to gain poor white support for New Deal programs, used class-based arguments to push for repeal of the tax. In 1938 Florida became the first southern state to repeal the poll tax—a longtime goal of the Meitzens.[31]

E. R.'s role in the repeal efforts, however, did not go uncontested by white supremacists. He lived in Columbia County, where race loomed large in political issues. The county bordered the southern Black Belt with an African American population of nearly 40 percent.[32] In Texas, Meitzen had always walked the political tightrope of championing political and economic rights for the entire working class while taking care not to upset racial norms for fear of a violent backlash. In Florida, however, his prominent opposition to the poll tax ran directly afoul of the KKK.

Meitzen, as one of his sons recalled, got into "a writing war against the KKK." Meitzen used his paper to expose the local chief of police as a Klan member. The chief, forced to resign, was not the only member of the Invisible Empire unmasked by Meitzen, who used his paper to publicly identify Klansmen. At church, an upset Klansman challenged him to a fight. As Meitzen's children remembered, "Daddy knocked him down." The Klan in turn escalated its campaign of intimidation against Meitzen. As his son William recalled, "Another time the Klan burned a cross in our front yard. My mother and sisters were all afraid but daddy didn't worry about it and went to bed!"[33] His daughter Jo-Lou remembered another time when the Klan rode outside their home at night. Her father stood watch, and she hid under the bed.[34]

The Klan attempted to extend their assaults to those nearest the family. Fortunately, word reached Meitzen that the Klan was preparing to ride on the home of the hired black woman who watched his children and helped clean the house. Meitzen moved her family to his home while the Klan carried out their night riding. Having been continually foiled, the Klan intended to inflict real harm on Meitzen. One night while Meitzen was walking home, the postmaster (apparently in the Klan as well) pulled a knife on Meitzen. It was not the first time someone had pulled on knife on him and Meitzen escaped unharmed. When word reached Meitzen that the Klan planned to tar and feather him, he borrowed a six-shooter, and the Klan finally backed down.[35]

These were harrowing experiences for the Meitzen family, who missed their friends and loved ones in Texas. As a New Deal Democrat, Meitzen stood for election as an at-large delegate to the 1940 Democratic national convention, but he was not selected.[36] Shortly thereafter, the family packed up and moved back to Texas. They settled in Yoakum, where Meitzen ran the *Yoakum Times* and continued the tradition of exposing corrupt government officials. During World War II, he sold war bonds to assist the Allied war effort against fascism. Later, his daughter, Jo-Lou, married a German immigrant who, along with his family, narrowly escaped Nazi persecution.[37]

Meitzen made one more move. In 1943 he moved to Dickinson on the mainland of Galveston County. He ran first the *Galveston County Press* and then, using the old family newspaper name, the *Dickinson New Era*. When asked whether her mother was politically active, Jo-Lou said she volunteered at the polls for elections and was very active in their local Methodist church. When asked whether her father was religious, she said no. He did, however, enjoy the choir and often sat in the back of the church by himself and listened to choir practice. He seemed to be reflecting. Like his father, E. R. had come a long way. When he was four, his father joined the Grange and from his childhood he watched him join the Populist revolt. E. R. joined his father in the Farmers Union and thus himself became a part of the continuity and evolution of agrarian radicalism in the farmer-labor bloc. By 1948, the farmer-labor bloc was a fading memory. At the age of sixty-seven, E. R. Meitzen passed away at his home on November 27, 1948. Another Red Scare was on hand, and with it, the example of the farmer-bloc would be temporarily erased from public memory.[38]

One of the main reasons the farmer-labor bloc had such a forceful influence on Texas political culture was the guiding influence of the Meitzens. They and those they brought around them, such as Maria Boeer, Tom Hickey, and Covington Hall, built democratic organizations from the ground up that responded to and represented the needs of the working class. Workerist dogmas and schemes cloaked in pseudo Marxism were replaced with plain-folk language and transitional demands. The Meitzens realized that such language, and such demands, were not always purely socialistic, yet they hoped they would lead to the Cooperative Commonwealth.

While serving as a model for reaching working-class people at their own level, the Meitzens unfortunately do not provide a useful model for today in fighting racial injustice. Too often, the prevailing norms of white supremacy informed their actions. The Meitzens did, though, probe the limits of white supremacy. Even if the Meitzens did not break down those barriers, they did weaken them.

Most of all, and what is much more promising, the Meitzens' and their comrades' internationalism greatly distinguished them not only from the liberals of their time, but from those of today as well. Although many liberals have well-meaning concerns about the plight of the downtrodden and poor of the United States, they have a blind spot when it comes to imperialism. From nineteenth-century gunboats to twenty-first-century drones, Democrats and Republicans have engaged in a bipartisan foreign policy that carries out the interests of

US big business in toppling foreign democratic governments and causing immeasurable misery, death, and destruction to those outside the Western world. In contrast, transnational influences critically, and continually, informed the Meitzens' worldview. The 1848 German Revolution gave them a revolutionary heritage. Contact with Mexican revolutionaries challenged their previously held racial beliefs and galvanized tenant farmers into action. They did not oppose the Russian Revolution, but rather sought to learn from its experiences. In his 1914 campaign for governor of Texas, E. R. Meitzen declared our "only gauge of battle shall be the principles of International Socialism."[39] Or, in more classic terminology: "Workers of the World Unite!"

At home, the protest movements of the farmer-labor bloc achieved their highest levels of success when organized politically outside the two-party system. When farmer-labor activists worked inside the two-party system, Democrats and Republicans could engage in empty talk about reforms without paying a political price. Yet, upon deciding to contest for power independently, farmer-labor activists forced Democrats and Republicans to respond with meaningful reforms or risk losing power. As the *Rebel* saw it in 1916: "One vote for Socialism will do more to scare the ruling class into granting concessions and 'reforms' and into calling off war dogs, than a thousand votes for even the most radical (non-Socialist) party. This is seen in the acts of both Wilson and Roosevelt who have frankly stated that if they were not permitted to make 'reforms' the Socialist party would march into power with ten league boots."[40]

Many of the most significant Progressive Era and later New Deal reforms were long championed by the farmer-labor bloc. Indeed, many had their roots stretching back to the plebeian agrarian radicalism of Tom Paine: the eight-hour day, the secret ballot, direct election of senators, a progressive income tax, public education, public-works projects, state and federal departments of labor, workplace safety, food and drug safety, the right to join a union, anti-child-labor laws, unemployment compensation, a minimum wage, and social security. Democrats and Republicans would simply not have enacted these reforms without protest movements creating substantial outside political pressure. To be sure, the enactment of the reforms in question came about most prolifically when the farmer-labor bloc was in its most independent phases, particularly through the vehicles of the People's and Socialist Parties. Moreover, New Deal reforms flowed from the militant struggles of industrial unionists led and influenced in large part by the Communist Party, the Socialist Workers Party, and their immediate predecessors and allied organizations. After initially granting reforms, the ruling elites' responses to the People's and Socialist Parties serve as an additional, albeit cruel, measure of their success. To hinder further independent working-class reform movements, they unleashed two of the most reactionary campaigns in US history with the implementation of Jim Crow and the first Red Scare. Decades later, both the Communist Party and Socialist Workers Party fell victim to a second Red Scare.

To this day, the US political landscape has not seen a long-lasting political coalition, dedicated to radical economic reform and functioning outside the two-party system, like the farm-labor bloc of the 1870s to the 1920s. The civil-rights movement of the 1960s did make a turn to address poverty, helping to inspire reforms such as Medicaid and Medicare. Yet its turn toward economic radicalism and even outright anticapitalism, caused the movement to suffer severe repression from the FBI. Not until the brief Occupy movement of 2011–12 would a movement based on economic radicalism appear in the United States. Up until that moment, radical critiques of capitalism for more than three generations had focused on the concerns of industrial workers such as wages, workplace safety, and union rights. Industrial concerns do remain, but deindustrialization and the ascendancy of neoliberal economic policy since the 1970s significantly changed the economic landscape for working and middle-class Americans. Occupy, in turn, responded to debt, interest, speculation, Wall Street corruption, the influence of money in politics, corporate greed, and wealth inequality. In other words, Occupy activists most aggressively protested the inequalities inherent in finance capitalism. In historical perspective, then, Occupy therefore harked back to the radical agrarian critique of finance capitalism that spurred the creation of the farmer-labor bloc. Differing from the farmer-labor bloc, which organized itself politically to contest for power, Occupy was hindered by an overreliance on anarchistic horizontal forms of organizing that, although raising political and even class consciousness among young people, never effectively organized large sections of the working class. In the end, Occupy suffered the same fate as the farmer-labor bloc when the Obama administration orchestrated a coordinated crackdown on the movement.[41]

After the repression of Occupy, working-class activists continued the age-old debate: if we are to advance our demands in the electoral arena, should it be done within or independent of the Democratic Party? The path many radicals have taken by running as Democrats was the same the Meitzens took many times. Yet the Meitzens did so as a tactic they thought could lead the working class to power. Even then, each time they took that turn, it proved wrong and came with dire consequence for the farmer-labor bloc. For the Meitzens and other farmer-labor radicals, the tactic of running in the Democratic primary or dissolving their organization into a campaign without a party was new—or at least something tried only a few times before and thus worth attempting again. The tactic, however, has persisted for so long, and with results not much different than from the era when the Meitzens used it, that the lessons of its futility should have become clear long ago.

In the twenty-first century, just as in the past, working-class activists face ridicule and attack for choosing an independent political course. In 2004 antiwar activists were told to vote Democratic because George W. Bush was a "fascist" and "war criminal" for leading the United States to invade Iraq, even though Democratic presidential candidate John Kerry had voted to authorize war with Iraq. Later in 2020, when environmental and racial justice activists questioned voting for Democratic candidate Joe Biden because of his poor environmental record and his prominent role as an architect of mass incarceration in authoring the 1994 Crime Act, they were told they were enabling fascism by withholding their vote for Biden and against Donald Trump.[42]

These tropes echo the attacks on Abolitionists during the 1856 and 1858 elections and socialists during World War I. When the Republican Party did not call for the immediate end of slavery, many Abolitionists put their support behind the defiantly uncompromising abolitionist Liberty Party. For doing so, Abolitionists were told "Don't Throw Away Your Votes!" The *New York Daily Times* even proclaimed, "in the approaching canvass, as always heretofore, Radical Abolitionism will be found fighting on the side of Slavery."[43] Who will now say that the Abolitionists were wrong for not choosing the lesser evil and instead uncompromisingly calling for the immediate end of slavery and pushing Lincoln toward abolition? During the 1916 presidential election, while war raged in Europe, the Socialist Party ran a clear antiwar campaign, despite Wilson's candidacy as the one "Who Kept Us Out of War." Wilson won and led us into war.

E. O. Meitzen understood that taking the path of independent political action over the lesser evil would not be easy. In trying to convince farmers in the Farmers Union to join the socialist movement in 1907, he wrote in the FU's national paper, "The speculator is linked with the capitalist class, as a whole, and every exploiter of human labor must see in this great uprising of the working class of farmers their ultimate dethronement.... '[T]he trouble lies in our government being in the hands of the very enemies of the great plain, common working people.... If you have a thorn in your foot poultices may do some good, but removing the thorn would be a much better, although for a moment it might be more intensely painful."[44] In other words, voting a lesser evil might temporarily soothe the pain. But if one really wants to solve the foundational problem, an independent anticapitalist course is necessary, in spite of the short-term pain. In a world of rapidly growing economic inequality, systematically murderous racism, and environmental destruction, a return of the farmer-labor bloc of the Meitzen type may well be our only hope of transforming our political culture into one that fulfills the promise of genuine democracy.

Notes

Introduction

1. US Congress, *Senate Commission on Industrial Relations*, vol. 10, 9143.
2. See Sperber, *European Revolutions*, and Hahn, *1848 Revolutions*.
3. Demshuk, review of *Nation and Loyalty*.
4. Lause, *Long Road to Harper's Ferry*, 144–45, 159, 176–77; Lause, *Young America*, 34, 102.
5. Omar Ali successfully shows the existence of a separate and distinct Black Populist movement in *In the Lion's Mouth*.
6. Green, *Grass-Roots Socialism*, xi, xiv; Kyle Wilkison provides a cultural history of agrarian protest in central and eastern Texas in *Yeomen, Sharecroppers, and Socialists*.
7. Throughout this book, a capital "S" Socialist refers to a member of the Socialist Party. A lower case "s" refers to a socialist or socialism in general.
8. Lansing, *Insurgent Democracy*, 16, 25, 27.
9. Hine, *Black Victory*, 43.
10. Charles Postel argues in *The Populist Vision* that the Populist movement was guided by a modern business orientation. Along with Postel, see Walter Nugent's *Tolerant Populists* for a counter to the argument that Populists were backward-looking and reactionary.
11. De Leon, *American Labor Who's Who*, 157.

Chapter 1. What Was Lost in Germany Might, in Texas, Be Won

1. "A list of Passengers arrived from foreign countries at the Port of Galveston during the quarter ending March 31, 1850," National Archives; Williams, "German Pioneers in Texas," 70; Williams, *History of the Meitzen Family* [unpaged]; *Nonpartisan Leader*, September 20, 1917; Hahn, *1848 Revolutions*, 64. *Achtundvierzieger* is German for 48er, the term used to describe those who participated in the German Revolution of 1848.
2. Davies and Moorhouse, *Microcosm*, 11, 54–55, 61–103, 407–32.

3. Holmgren, *Family Tree Book*, 12; Blackbourn, *Long Nineteenth* Century, xiii, 93–96; Davies and Moorhouse, *Microcosm*, 212–13.

4. Henderson, *Rise of German Industrial Power*, 25, 28; Davies and Moorhouse, *Microcosm*, 163, 210, 219.

5. Holmgren, *Family Tree*, 12; Williams, *History of the Meitzen Family*, unpaged; Hildebrandt et al., Siebmacher's, 29: 14, 30: 191. Translations throughout this book are by the author.

6. Holmgren, *Family Tree Book*, 12, 15; Carsten, *History of the Prussian Junkers*, 79; U.S. Census, *Census Reports*, 1860; Boethel, *Big Guns of Fayette*, 79; *Verzeichnis der Hausbesitzer Breslaus*, Archiwum Panstwowe we Wroclawiu.

7. Berding, *Soziale Unruhen*, 243; Blackbourn, *Long Nineteenth Century*, 50–51; Davies and Moorhouse, *Microcosm*, 220; "Silesian Weavers Uprisings," *Great Soviet Encyclopedia*; Carsten, *History of the Prussian Junkers*, 77–78.

8. Blackbourn, "Discreet Charm of the Bourgeoisie" in Blackbourn and Eley, *Peculiarities of German History*, 176–77; Bramsted, *Aristocracy*, 20, 32, 36; Goethe, *Wilhelm Meister's Apprenticeship*, 151; Noyes, *Organization and Revolution*, 18.

9. Weyland and Wade, *Early History of Fayette County*, 56–57; Holmgren, *Family Tree Book*, 12; Henderson, *Rise of German Industrial Power*, 73–74.

10. Jennie Holmgren was born September 16, 1818 (Holmgren, *Family Tree Book*, 7, 8; I HA Rep. 93 Ministerium der öffentlichen Arbeiten, Nr. 637 Konduitenlisten der Baubeamten im Regierungsbezirk Liegnitz, vol. 1, Adhib, 1834–1837, Geheimes Staatsarchiv Preußischer Kulturbesitz Berlin [hereafter, GStAPK]; I HA Rep. 93 B Ministerium der öffentlichen Arbeiten, Nr. 638 Konduitenlisten der Baubeamten im Regierungsbezirk Liegnitz, Bd. 2, 1839–1856, GStAPK; Hildebrandt, Siebmacher's, 28: 19).

11. Williams, *History of the Meitzen Family*, unpaged; Weyland and Wade, *Early History of Fayette County*, 56; Holmgren, *Family Tree Book*, 15; Geue, *New Homes*, 106. The trade of machine builder, which Otto Meitzen worked as, was not organized by a guild at this time in Prussia (Noyes, *Organization and Revolution*, 29).

12. Henderson, *Rise of German Industrial Power*, 13, 27, 71–72.

13. Henderson, *Rise of German Industrial Power*, 26, 56; *Neue Rheinische Zeitung*, December 9, 1848.

14. Henderson, *Rise of German Industrial Power*, 56, 63.

15. Schmidt, et al., *Illustrierte Geschichte der deutschen Revolution*, 33–35; Blackbourn, *Long Nineteenth Century*, 113.

16. Blackbourn, *Long Nineteenth Century*, 138; Kitchen, *Cambridge Illustrated History of Germany*, 179; Schmidt, et al., *Illustrierte Geschichte der deutschen Revolution*, 36, 43–44; Davies and Moorhouse, *Microcosm*, 223.

17. Schmidt, "Moritz Eisner," 27–28, 46–47.

18. Schmidt, *Wilhelm Wolff*, 58, 66–68.

19. Schmidt, *Wilhelm Wolff*, 21, 50, 76–77, 88–89; Schmidt, "Matthäi-Brüder," 326–27, 334; Engels, "Wilhelm Wolff," *Marx and Engels Collected Works* [hereafter, *MECW*]), 24: 132.

20. Schmidt, *Wilhelm Wolff*, 76–77, 88–89; Schmidt, "Matthäi-Brüder," 326–27, 334; Engels, "Wilhelm Wolff," 24: 132.

21. Schmidt, *Schlesische Demokratie*, 2:90, 92, 152.
22. Schmidt, *Wilhelm Wolff*, 156–57; Schmidt, *Schlesische Demokratie*, 2: 152.
23. Henderson, *Life and Times*, 247; Schmidt, *Wilhelm Wolff*, 170–71.
24. Henderson, *Life and Times*, 249; Schmidt, *Schlesische Demokratie*, 2: 152.
25. Henderson, *Life and Times*, 249; Schmidt, *Schlesische Demokratie*, 2: 152; Schmidt, *Wilhelm Wolff*, 172–73; Engels, "Wilhelm Wolff," 135.
26. Engels, "Wilhelm Wolff," 131, 136; Henderson, *Life and Times*, 250; Marx, "Notes on the Arrest, Maltreatment and Expulsion of Wilhelm Wolff," *MECW*, 6: 581–82; Marx and Engels, "Demands of the Communist Party in Germany," *MECW*, 7: 3–7; Schmidt, *Schlesische Demokratie*, 2: 152; Marx and Engels, *Communist Manifesto*, 38–39.
27. Marx and Engels, *Communist Manifesto*, 28, 33.
28. Marx, "Preface to the First German Edition," *MECW*, 35: 7. Wolff remained a steadfast ally of Marx and Engels until his death in Manchester on May 9, 1864.
29. Schmidt, *Schlesische Demokratie*, 2: 94; Schmidt, "Matthäi-Brüder," 341–43. Rudolph Matthäi became one of the leading figures of "true socialism." Marx and Engels critiqued true socialism in *The German Ideology* in *MECW*, 5: 470; *Der Bote aus dem Katzenbachthale*, February 1846; Schmidt, *Wilhelm Wolff*, 185–86; Davies and Moorhouse, *Microcosm*, 223.
30. Schmidt, et al., *Illustrierte Geschichte der deutschen Revolution*, 58; quote from Engels, *Revolution and Counter-revolution in Germany*, 15.
31. Davies and Moorhouse, *Microcosm*, 216; Hahn, *1848 Revolutions*, 64–65.
32. *Nonpartisan Leader*, September 20, 1917.
33. Schmidt, *Schlesische Demokratie*, 1: 9.
34. Schmidt, et al., *Illustrierte Geschichte der deutschen Revolution*, 109–10.
35. Höpfner, "Ness von Esenbeck," 69–71; Schmidt, *Schlesische Demokratie*, 1: 14.
36. Schmidt, *Schlesische Demokratie*, 1: 15; *Neue Rheinische Zeitung*, June 8, 14, 1848.
37. Noyes, *Organization and Revolution*, 223–24; Henderson, *Rise of German Industrial Power*, 93; Hahn, *1848 Revolutions*, 57; Henderson, *Life and Times*, 250; *Neue Rheinische Zeitung*, June 1, 1848.
38. Noyes, *Organization and Revolution*, 254; Mattheisen, "Voters and Parliaments," 10.
39. Noyes, *Organization and Revolution*, 92, 128–37, 152–60, 322–25.
40. *Neue Rheinische Zeitung*, June 25, July 30, 1848.
41. *Der Demokrat*, Probeblatt, July; no. 4, August 1848; Kraffert, *Geschichte des evangelischen Gymnasiums zu Liegnitz*, 129; Schmidt, *Schlesische Demokratie*, 1: 64; 2: 163; marriage licenses, Fayette County Archives, 1838–1923.
42. *Der Demokrat*, Probeblatt, July 1848; Marx and Engels, "Demands of the Communist Party in Germany," *MECW* 7: 3–4; Schmidt, *Schlesische Demokratie*, 1: 64.
43. *Der Demokrat*, no. 1, July; no. 3, July; no. 4, August 1848.
44. Schmidt, *Schlesische Demokratie*, 1: 81, 114, 116–18; 2: 101, 155.
45. *Der Demokrat*, no. 10, September 1848; Bleiber, "Germany, September Crisis 1848," in Chastain, *Encyclopedia of 1848 Revolutions*; *Neue Rheinische Zeitung*, September 14, 27, 1848.
46. *Neue Rheinische Zeitung*, November 9, 12, 15, 1848; Sperber, *European Revolutions*, 218–19.

47. Schmidt, *Schlesische Demokratie*, 1: 169, 225; *Der Demokrat*, no. 13, October 1848.
48. Wolff, *Schlesische Milliarde*, 24–25; Engels, "Wilhelm Wolff," 146, 148–49.
49. Engels, "Wilhelm Wolff," 146, 148–49; Wolff, *Schlesische Milliarde*, 26–27. From March 22 to April 25, 1849, Wolff wrote a series of eight articles collectively titled *Die schlesische Milliarde*, in which he detailed how the "robber-knights" extracted their feudal dues and calculated the total financial amount taken from peasants. Wolff concluded that for the previous thirty years the peasantry of Silesia had paid feudal lords approximately 240 million thalers. His articles appeared in the *Neue Rheinische Zeitung*.
50. *Neue Rheinische Zeitung*, May 8, 9, 10, 11, 17, 19, 1849; Hahn, *1848 Revolutions*, 161, 163; Schmidt, *Schlesische Demokratie*, 1: 280, 282, 345; *Neue Kölnische Zeitung*, May 17, 1849; Engels, "Campaign for the German Imperial Constitution," *MECW* 10: 154, 206, 208, 215, 234–37.
51. Engels, *Revolution and Counter-revolution in Germany*, 54.
52. Levine, *Spirit of 1848*, 15–16; Hahn, *1848 Revolutions*, 197; Lich, "Goethe on the Guadalupe," in Lich and Reeves, *German Culture in Texas*, 38.
53. *Neue Rheinische Zeitung*, June 7, 1848; Hahn, *1848 Revolutions*, 143; Honeck, *We Are the Revolutionists*, 14.
54. Hall quoted in Nichols, *The "S" Word*, 36; Kistler, "German-American Liberalism," 82–83.
55. Lause, *Young America*, 12.
56. Lause, *Young America*, 35.
57. Lause, *Young America*, 9, 16–17, 34–35. Quote on pp. 16–17.
58. Marx and Engels, *Communist Manifesto*, 27.
59. Marx and Engels, *Communist Manifesto*, 43.
60. Jordan, *German Seed in Texas Soil*, 40–41.
61. Gish, "Introduction," in Bracht, *Texas in 1848*, vii; Reichstein, *German Pioneers on the American Frontier*, 27, 36.
62. Jordan, *German Seed*, 41–45; Reichstein, *German Pioneers*, 20.
63. Lich, "Goethe on the Guadalupe," 37, 58; Biesele, *History of the German Settlements*, 7–9; Reichstein, *German Pioneers*, 20–21, 48, 58; Lich, "Bettina, TX," *Handbook of Texas Online*, https://www.tshaonline.org/handbook/entries/bettina-tx.
64. Guthrie, "Cabet, Étienne (1788–1856)," *Handbook of Texas Online*, https://www.tshaonline.org/handbook/entries/cabet-etienne; Davidson, "La Réunion," *Handbook of Texas Online*, https://www.tshaonline.org/handbook/entries/la-reunion.
65. Geue, *New Homes*, 94, 124; Williams, "German Pioneers in Texas," 70; Weyland and Wade, *Early History of Fayette County*, 56.
66. Biesele, *History of the German Settlements*, 135; Geue, *New Homes*, 37; Weyland and Wade, *Early History of Fayette County*, 56; Supak, Hensel, and Dippel, "German Settlers in Fayette County," in Williams, *Fayette County*, 22; Carter and Ragsdale, *Biegel Settlement*, 47; 1852 Fayette County, Texas, tax rolls, Texas State Library and Archives Commission, Austin, Texas.
67. Weyland and Wade, *Early History of Fayette County*, 58; Supak, Hensel, and Dippel, "German Settlers in Fayette County," 22; Williams, *History of the Meitzen Family*, unpaged; "Killen, Ida," *Texas Death Certificates, 1890–1976*, 1918, Tarrant-Howard Counties.

Notes to Chapter 1

68. U.S. Census, *Census Reports*, 1860, 1880, 1920; Surviving ship passenger lists are reprinted in Geue, *New Homes*, 70–108; Jordan, *German Seed*, 32; Biesele, *History of the German Settlements*, 60–63; Baker, *First Polish Americans*, 3. The majority of Czech immigrants to Texas were Moravian. During the nineteenth century, however, many Moravians in Texas were incorrectly identified as Bohemian. Throughout this book when a source uses Bohemian that is the identifier that will be used. Otherwise, Czech will be used to include both Bohemians and Moravians ("Czech Texans," *Texas Almanac*, online, https://texasalmanac.com/topics/culture/czech/czech-texans).

69. Lotto, *Fayette County*, 294–95; Schmidt, *Schlesische Demokratie*, 1: 88–89; 2: 36; Buenger and Kamphoefner, *Preserving German Texan Identity*, 48–49; Buckingham, "Red Tom" Hickey, 193; Baker, *First Polish Americans*, 15–16, 165; marriage licenses, Fayette County Archives, 1838–1923; Holmgren, *Family Tree Book*, 15; US Census, *Census Reports*, 1860; 1861 county tax rolls, Fayette County, Texas, Texas State Library and Archives Commission, Austin, Texas; *Nonpartisan Leader*, September 20, 1917.

70. Schmidt, *Schlesische Demokratie*, 2: 36; Marriage licenses, 1838–1923, Fayette County Archives; Holmgren, *Family Tree Book*, 15; U.S. Census, *Census Reports*, 1860; 1861 county tax rolls, Fayette County, Texas, Texas State Library and Archives Commission, Austin, Texas; *Nonpartisan Leader*, September 20, 1917.

71. Garrett, "Fayette County," *Handbook of Texas Online*, https://www.tshaonline.org/handbook/entries/fayette-county.

72. Levine, *Spirit of 1848*, 67; Walker, "Old Homeland and the New," in Lich and Reeves, *German Culture in Texas*, 76–77.

73. *Texas Monument*, January 11, 1854; Biesele, *History of the German Settlements*, 210.

74. Randers-Pehrson, *Adolf Douai*, 189; Lause, *Long Road to Harper's Ferry*, 144–45; Lause, *Young America*, 31; Lich, "Goethe on the Guadalupe," 58, 62.

75. Biesele, "Texas State Convention," 248–49; Tolzman, "A German-American Position Statement," in Tolzman, *German-American Forty-Eighters*, 97.

76. *Louisville Platform*, reprinted in Tolzman, *German-American Forty-Eighters*, 99–102.

77. *Louisville Platform*, 103–4.

78. *Louisville Platform*, 103–4; Biesele, "Texas State Convention," 251; 1848 and 1852 Free Soil Party platforms and Republican Party Platform of 1856, contained in McKee, *National Conventions and Platforms*, 66–69, 80–83, 97–99.

79. Levine, *Spirit of 1848*, Buhle, *Women and American Socialism*, 3–4, 11.

80. Levine, *Spirit of 1848*, 102; *San Antonio Zeitung*, March 25, 1854.

81. Biesele, "Texas State Convention," 249–51.

82. *San Antonio Zeitung*, May 20, 1854.

83. Ibid.

84. Buhle, *Women and American Socialism*, 9.

85. Biesele, "Texas State Convention," 254–55; Sass, "Man and His Environment," in Lich and Reeves, *German Culture in Texas*, 92.

86. Biesele, *History of the German Settlements*, 199; *San Antonio Zeitung*, May 20, 1854.

87. *Texas Monument*, June 28, August 1, 1854; Biesele, *History of the German Settlements*, 199–202.

88. Biesele, *History of the German Settlements*, 202; Olmsted, *Journey through Texas*, viii, 133, 140–42, 202–9; Honeck, *We Are the Revolutionaries*, 61, 64, 68. *Tejano* is a term used to identify persons born in Texas of Mexican or Spanish ethnicity.

89. Honeck, *We Are the Revolutionaries*, 51, 61–64; Olmsted, *Journey through Texas*, 436–39; Siemering, *Deutschen in Texas*, 9; Douai, "Labor and Work," *Workmen's Advocate*, April 23, 1887; Levine, *Spirit of 1848*, 161, 247; Randers-Pehrson, *Adolf Douai*, 289, 299. For informative accounts of the political activism of German 48ers in the North, see Levine's *Spirit of 1848* and Honeck's, *We Are the Revolutionaries*. In April 1872, a Galveston section of the First International, Section 44, was founded. The section only lasted until June 1872, however, as a result of divisions over whether to invite the participation of black workers (Messer-Kruse, *Yankee International*, 206–7).

90. Kamphoefner, "New Perspectives on Texas Germans," 442–43; 1854 and 1855 county tax rolls, Fayette County, Texas, Texas State Library and Archives Commission, Austin, Texas.

91. Wooster, "Analysis of Texas Know Nothings," 414, 416.

92. Griffin, "American Party," *Handbook of Texas Online*, https://www.tshaonline.org/handbook/entries/american-party; Buenger, "Whig Party," *Handbook of Texas Online*, https://www.tshaonline.org/handbook/entries/whig-party; (La Grange) *True Issue*, February 23, 1856; *La Grange Paper*, June 16, 1855, quoted in Biesele, *History of the German Settlements*, 203; *Washington American*, September 3, 1856; *Der Demokrat*, no. 1 July, 1848; *True Issue*, February 23, 1856.

93. Wish, "Slave Insurrection Panic," 207.

94. Addington, "Slave Insurrections," 414–16; Wish, "Slave Insurrection Panic," 208. A result of this forced removal of Mexicans, coupled with an earlier expulsion during the 1840s of many ethnic Mexicans from central and east Texas by Anglos in a racist reaction to attempts by the Mexican government to reclaim Texas, was that ethnic Mexicans would not play a significant role in farmer-labor politics until the late nineteenth century.

95. Wish, "Slave Insurrection Panic," 208; Addington, "Slave Insurrections," 417.

96. Baggett, "Constitutional Union Party," 236; *Colorado Citizen*, May 28, 1859.

97. Baum, *Shattering of Texas Unionism*, 33; *Colorado Citizen*, May 28, 1859; *San Antonio Texan*, May 28, 1859; *True Issue*, July 23, 1859.

98. Baum, *Shattering of Texas Unionism*, 37; Reynolds, *Texas Terror*, 12; *Colorado Citizen*, May 28, 1859.

99. Baum, *Shattering of Texas Unionism*, 38.

100. *New Orleans Daily Picayune*, September 8, 10, 13, 1860; Addington, "Slave Insurrections," 426, 433.

101. Reynolds, "Texas Troubles," *Handbook of Texas Online*, https://www.tshaonline.org/handbook/entries/texas-troubles; Baggett, "Constitutional Union Party," 248–49; Whitman, "Year of Meteors [1859–60]."

Chapter 2. Inheritors of the Revolution

1. US Congress, *Industrial Relations, Final Report and Testimony*, 9143.

2. Buenger, "Secession," *Handbook of Texas Online*, https://www.tshaonline.org/handbook/entries/secession; *States Rights Democrat*, February 21, 1861.

3. Kamphoefner, "New Perspectives on Texas Germans," 444–45.

4. US Census, *Census Reports, 1860*; *States Rights Democrat*, March 21, 1861.

5. Bynum, *Long Shadow*, x, 26; Kamphoefner, "New Perspectives on Texas Germans," 449. Otto Meitzen at fifty-one years old was exempt from the draft.

6. *Der Demokrat*, no. 1 July, 1848; US Census, *Census Reports*, 1860; 1860, 1861, 1862 county tax rolls, Fayette County, Texas.

7. "Cunerth, Otto, Twenty-fourth Cavalry," Compiled Service Records of Confederate Soldiers, National Archives; Baker, *First Polish Americans*, 69–71; Smith, "Battle of Arkansas Post," *American Battlefield Trust*.

8. Smith, "Battle of Arkansas Post"; Baker, *First Polish Americans*, 71.

9. "Cunerth, Otto, Twenty-fourth Cavalry," *Compiled Service Records*; quote from Baker, *First Polish Americans*, 71–72. Included in the Poles joining the Sixteenth Illinois was Peter Kiołbassa; Lundberg, *Granbury's Texas Brigade*, 79, 242; McCaffrey, *This Band of Heroes*, 80, 88, 99, 115, 124; Bradley, "Granbury's Texas Brigade," *Handbook of Texas Online*; Kamphoefner, "New Americans or New Southerners?" in *Lone Star Unionism, Dissent, and Resistance*, ed. de la Teja, 123.

10. Abernethy, "Deutschtum in Texas," in Lich and Reeves, *German Culture in Texas*, 213; McGowen, "Battle or Massacre?" 67–70, 75–80, 83, 85; "Nueces, Battle of the," *Handbook of Texas Online*, https://www.tshaonline.org/handbook/entries/nueces-battle-of-the.

11. Bellville *Countryman*, March 26, 1863; Kamphoefner, "New Perspectives on Texas Germans and the Confederacy," 450; *Houston Tri-Weekly Telegraph*, January 14, 1863.

12. Garrett, "Fayette County," *Handbook of Texas Online*, https://www.tshaonline.org/handbook/entries/fayette-county; Williams, *History of the Meitzen Family*, 13.

13. Williams, "German Pioneers in Texas," 71.

14. Johnson, *History of Texas and Texans*, 1916–917; Boethel, *Big Guns of Fayette*, 79; Holmgren, *Family Tree Book*, 15; US Census, *Census Reports*, 1870.

15. Moneyhon, *Republicanism*, xvi; Kamphoefner, "New Americans or New Southerners? Unionist German Texans," in de la Teja, ed., *Lone Star Unionism, Dissent, and Resistance*, 126, 130.

16. US Census, *Census Reports, 1870*; Kamphoefner, "New Americans or New Southerners?" 126–28.

17. US Census, *Census Reports, 1870*; *States Rights Democrat*, April 5, 1867, February 14, 1868, November 12, 1869; Kamphoefner, "New Americans or New Southerners?" 123; Johnson, *History of Texas and Texans*, 1916.

18. *States Rights Democrat*, October 29, 1869.

19. *States Rights Democrat*, March 21, 1861, May 1, 1868, October 29, 1869; Baum, *Shattering of Texas Unionism*, 58.

20. *True Issue*, December 15, 1855, February 23, 1856; Baum, *Shattering of Texas Unionism*, 149; Moneyhon, *Republicanism*, 58, 181.

21. Moneyhon, *Republicanism*, 82, 85, 91.

22. Moneyhon, *Republicanism*, 90, 103, 134; Casdorth, *History of the Republican Party in Texas*, 5–6, 40.

23. *States Rights Democrat*, November 26, 1869; *Weekly Democratic Statesman*, September 25, October 2, 1873, March 23, 1876; Martin, "Greenback Party," 169; Miller, "Franke,

Louis," *Handbook of Texas Online*, https://www.tshaonline.org/handbook/entries/franke-louis; *Journal of the House of Representatives of the State of Texas*, thirteenth legislature. Franke was elected as a representative of the Twenty-sixth District in 1872, but he was murdered on the capitol grounds on February 19, 1873.

24. *Bastrop Advertiser*, October 18, 1873.

25. "Cunerth, Otto," Passport Applications, 1795–1905, National Archives.

26. Schmidt, *Schlesische Demokratie*, 2: 35–36; Nietsche, *Geschichte der Stadt Gleiwitz*, 709. There is evidence to suggest that Cunerth lived longer. An "Otto Cunerth" is cited as the director of a teacher's training school for women in Thorn, Germany (now Torun, Poland), for the academic year 1886–87. This is consistent with his career as a teacher and previous work at a girl's school. Otto Cunerth, *Jahresbericht über das Städtiche Lehrerinnen-Seminar, die höhere- und Bürger-Mädchenrschule zu Thorn für das Schuljahr 1886/87*, https://kpbc.umk.pl/dlibra/publication/218564/edition/217456/content.

27. *Rebel*, July 25, 1914; Johnson, *History of Texas and Texans*, 1917; Meitzen-Williams, *New Breslau*, 2.

28. McMath, *American Populism*, 39.

29. Pearsons et al., "Business and Financial Conditions Following the Civil War in the United States," 17; Barnes, *Farmers in Rebellion*, 50–51; Cohen, *Reconstruction of American Liberalism*, 123.

30. Goodwyn, *Populist Moment*, 21–22.

31. Cohen, *Reconstruction of American Liberalism*, 30.

32. McMath, *American Populism*, 45, 51.

33. Moneyhon, *Texas after the Civil War*, 133, 152; *Weekly Democratic Statesman*, June 5, 1873.

34. Moneyhon, *Texas after the Civil War*, 155–56.

35. *Journal of the House of Representatives of the State of Texas: Being the Session of the Thirteenth Legislature*, 273, 1351–53; *Weekly Democratic Statesman*, September 25, 1873; Moneyhon, *Texas after the Civil War*, 203; *Journal of the Senate of Texas: Being the Session of the Thirteenth Legislature*, 860, 1147.

36. Quote of *Victoria Advocate* in *Weekly Democratic Statesman*, July 24, 1873.

37. *Weekly Democratic Statesman*, July 31, August 7, 14, September 25, 1873; *Bastrop Advertiser*, August 16, 1873.

38. *Bastrop Advertiser*, August 23, September 6, 20, October 11, 18, 1873; *Weekly Democratic Statesman*, October 30, 1873.

39. *Weekly Democratic Statesman*, October 18, 1873.

40. Ibid.

41. *Weekly Democratic Statesman*, August 2, 23, September 6, October 18, 1873.

42. Dobie, *Coronado's Children*, 15–16.

43. *Weekly Democratic Statesman*, August 2, 9, November 29, 1873. Quotes in November 13, 1873, issue.

44. *Weekly Democratic Statesman*, November 27, 1873, quote in October 30, 1873 issue; *Bastrop Advertiser*, October 18, November 1, 1873; Largent, "Ledbetter, William Hamilton," *Handbook of Texas Online*, https://www.tshaonline.org/handbook/entries/ledbetter-william-hamilton. Because of a dearth of sources, little else is known about

the People's, or Farmers,' Party. It was common practice among Democratic newspapers to belittle challenges from reformers and then deny them coverage.

45. *Bastrop Advertiser*, October 18, November 1, 1873; *Weekly Democratic Statesman*, October 30, 1873; Barr, *Reconstruction to Reform*, 64–65.

46. *Weekly Democratic Statesman*, October 9, November 6, 20, 1873.

47. *Weekly Democratic Statesman*, July 3, 1873; Smith, "Grange Movement," 297; Martin, "Grange," 366–68.

48. *Weekly Democratic Statesman*, July 3, September 18, 1873. Quote from July 3, 1873, issue.

49. *Weekly Democratic Statesman*, October 17, 1873.

50. *Weekly Democratic Statesman*, September 25, 1873.

51. Moneyhon, *Texas after the Civil War*, 197.

52. *Weekly Democratic Statesman*, July 18, 1873.

53. *Weekly Democratic Statesman*, October 30, 1873.

54. *Bastrop Advertiser*, December 6, 20, 1873; Moneyhon, *Texas after the Civil War*, 197; *Directory of the Members and also the State Officers of the Fourteenth Legislature of the State of Texas*, 2–6; *Journal of the Senate of Texas: Being the Session of the Fourteenth Legislature*, 297.

55. *Weekly Democratic Statesman*, October 16, quote from November 16, 1873.

56. Barr, *Reconstruction to Reform*, 9; *Bastrop Advertiser*, December 6, 1873.

57. Martin, "Grange," 367; *Bastrop Advertiser*, March 28, April 11, 18, 1874; Goodwyn, *Populist Moment*, 32.

58. Martin, "Grange," 373.

59. Martin, "Grange," 374; Cardwell, *Sketches of Legislators*, 107–9.

60. Martin, "Grange," 370, 374; *San Antonio Express* quoted in *Galveston Daily News*, May 8, 1878. The paper stated that "the name of the author is withheld."

61. Martin, "Grange," 370, 374; Dixon, "Roberts, Oran Milo (1815–1898)," *Handbook of Texas Online*, https://www.tshaonline.org/handbook/entries/roberts-oran-milo; Barr, *Reconstruction to Reform*, 75.

62. Smith, "Grange Movement," 300.

63. Barnes, *Farmers in Rebellion*, 51; Hungate quote in McMath, *Populist Vanguard*, 5.

64. Martin, "Greenback Party," 169.

65. Foner, *Great Labor Uprising*, 224–27; Barr, *Reconstruction to Reform*, 44; Randers-Pehrson, *Adolf Douai*, 301–2.

66. *Galveston Daily News*, July 28, 31, 1877.

67. *Galveston Daily News*, July 31, 1877.

68. *Galveston Daily News*, August 1, 1877; Foner, *Great Labor Uprising*, 199.

69. *Galveston Daily News*, August 1, 1877; Cuney was born on a plantation near Hempstead, Texas, in 1846, the son of a wealthy white slaveowner and a slave mother. In 1859 he went to Pittsburgh, Pennsylvania, where he received a formal education. Afterward he returned to Texas and became a leader of the Republican Party (Casdorth, *History of the Republican Party in Texas*, 46).

70. F. Johnson, *History of Texas*, 1916; Meitzen-Williams, *History of the Meitzen Family*, np.

71. Holmgren, *Family Tree Book*, 13; Meitzen-Williams, *History of the Meitzen Family*, np.

72. Williams, *History of the Meitzen Family*, np; *Rebel*, July 25, 1914; US Congress, *Senate Commission on Industrial Relations*, vol. 10, 9142.

73. US Congress, *Senate Commission on Industrial Relations*, vol. 10, 9142–43; Holmgren, *Family Tree Book*, 13.

74. Johnson, *History of Texas and Texans*, 1916; 1879 and 1881 county tax rolls, Fayette County; Holmgren, *Family Tree Book*, 13; *La Grange Journal*, May 4, 1882.

75. Barr, *Reconstruction to Reform*, 44–45, 47; Martin, "Greenback Party," 3; McGuire, "Kuechler, Jacob," *Handbook of Texas Online*, https://www.tshaonline.org/handbook/entries/kuechler-jacob.

76. Barr, *Reconstruction to Reform*, 48; *Galveston Daily News*, August 25, 1878; Casdorth, *History of the Republican Party in Texas,* 38–40; *Norton's Union Intelligencer*, October 12, 1878.

77. Barr, *Reconstruction to Reform*, 51, 54–55; Moneyhon, *Republicanism*, 79.

78. *Texas Capital*, July 4, 1880.

79. *Texas Capital*, May 23, 11, 1880; Barr, *Reconstruction to Reform*, 56, 60; *La Grange Journal*, November 10, 1880; Lambert, *Pocket Directory of the Seventeenth Legislature of Texas*, 3.

80. *Galveston Daily News*, July 1, 1882.

81. Barr, *Reconstruction to Reform*, 27–28, 64–65, 69; Miller, "Zapp, Robert," *Handbook of Texas Online*, https://www.tshaonline.org/handbook/entries/zapp-robert; Casdorth, *History of the Republican Party in Texas,* 45.

82. Martin, "Greenback Party in Texas," 8; *Texas Capital*, May 23, 1880; Foner, *Great Labor Uprising*, 227.

83. *Rebel*, July 25, 1914.

84. US Congress, Senate, Industrial Relations, Final Report and Testimony, submitted to Congress by the Commission on Industrial Relations, created by the Act of Congress, August 23, 1912 (Washington, DC: GPO, 1916), vols. 9 and 10, 9143; *Rebel*, July 25, 1914; *La Grange Journal*, May 8, June 5, September 18, 1884; Williams, *History of the Meitzen Family*, np.

85. *La Grange Journal*, June 17, 1886.

86. McMath, *American Populism*, 74–75; Maroney, "Great Southwest Strike," *Handbook of Texas Online*, https://www.tshaonline.org/handbook/entries/great-southwest-strike; Hild, "Knights of Labor," 25, 28, 31; *Rebel*, March 6, 1915.

87. Barnes, *Farmers in Rebellion*, 39; Goodwyn, *Populist Moment*, 26–27.

88. Barnes, *Farmers in Rebellion*, 34, 52; Goodwyn, *Populist Moment*, 33.

89. Maroney, "Great Southwest Strike," *Handbook of Texas Online*, https://www.tshaonline.org/handbook/entries/great-southwest-strike; Hild, "Knights of Labor," 28.

90. Hild, "Knights of Labor," 29–31,

91. Hild, *Greenbackers*, 74, 77–78; McMath, *Populist Vanguard*, 25.

92. Case, *Great Southwest Railroad Strike*, 32, 38, 39, 154.

93. Goodwyn, *Democratic Promise*, 59–60, quote on 59; Goodwyn, *Populist Moment*, 36.

94. Goodwyn, *Populist Moment*, 37–39; Goodwyn, *Democratic Promise*, 57, 62; *Rural Citizen*, March 18, 1886, as quoted in Goodwyn, *Democratic Promise*, 62.
95. Goodwyn, *Populist Moment*, 51; McMath, *Populist Vanguard*, 26; Hild, *Greenbackers*, 86; quote from Dunning, *Farmers' Alliance*, 41.
96. Hild, *Greenbackers*, 3–4, 86; McMath, *American Populism*, 79–80; quote from *Galveston Daily News*, August 8, 1886.
97. Wiedenfeld, "Gay, Bettie Munn," *Handbook of Texas Online*, https://www.tshaonline.org/handbook/entries/gay-bettie-munn; Postel, *Populist Vision*, 75–76, 83–85, Gay quote on 75; McMath, *American Populism*, 126–27.
98. Goodwyn, *Populist Moment*, 51–52; Hild, *Greenbackers, Knights of Labor, and Populists*, 86; Palmer, "Southern Mercury," *Handbook of Texas Online*, https://www.tshaonline.org/handbook/entries/southern-mercury; *La Grange Journal*, November 4, 1886, April 28, 1887.
99. *La Grange Journal*, July 22, 1886.
100. *Rebel*, July 25, 1914; Barnes, *Farmers in Rebellion*, 39; *La Grange Journal*, November 4, 1886.
101. Hofstadter, *Age of Reform*, 62.

Chapter 3. Populist Revolt

1. Goodwyn, *Populist Moment*, 43, 53; Barnes, *Farmers in Rebellion*, 78–80.
2. Goodwyn, *Populist Moment*, 66; *La Grange Journal*, November 3, 1887.
3. *La Grange Journal*, April 14, 1887.
4. *La Grange Journal*, July 7, 1887.
5. McMath, *Populist Vanguard*, 46, 59.
6. Grand State Farmers' Alliance, *Constitution and By-laws Adopted*, 7; Grand State Farmers' Alliance, *Constitution and By-laws Approved*, 8; Abramowitz, "Negro in the Populist Movement," 257.
7. US Congress, *Senate Commission on Industrial Relations*, vol. 10, 9143; *La Grange Journal*, October 13, 1887; Williams, *History of the Meitzen Family*, np.
8. *Hallettsville Herald*, January 17, 1889; Williams, *History of the Meitzen Family*, np.
9. *Hallettsville Herald*, May 10, 24, 1888; *Southern Mercury*, April 19, 1888; *Galveston Daily News*, May 16, 1888.
10. *Hallettsville Herald*, May 24, 31, July 19, 1888.
11. *Hallettsville Herald*, May 24, 1888.
12. Barnes, *Farmers in Rebellion*, 83–86; *La Grange Journal*, June 14, 1888; *Hallettsville Herald*, June 14, 1888.
13. Barnes, *Farmers in Rebellion*, 86–87.
14. *Hallettsville Herald*, July 5, 1888; *Southern Mercury*, July 12, 1888; Hild, *Greenbackers*, 113–14.
15. *Hallettsville Herald*, July 5, 19, 1888.
16. Barnes, *Farmers in Rebellion*, 94; *Hallettsville Herald*, August 9, September 6, 1888.
17. *Hallettsville Herald*, August 30, 1888, translation: played out or finished.
18. *Hallettsville Herald*, August 16, November 15, 1888.
19. Goodwyn, *Populist Moment*, 84–87.

20. *Hallettsville Herald*, November 15, 1888, March 7, 14, 1889, and August 11, 1892.
21. McMath, *Populist Vanguard*, 86–89; McMath, *American Populism*, 109.
22. McMath, *American Populism*, 109; McMath, *Populist Vanguard*, 88, 109.
23. McMath, *Populist Vanguard*, 88.
24. *Southern Mercury,* January 9, May 3, 1890; Hild, *Greenbackers*, 136; McMath, *Populist Vanguard*, 99.
25. Hart, *Revolutionary Mexico*, 148–51.
26. Barnes, *Farmers in Rebellion*, 121; *Southern Mercury,* April 10, 1890.
27. *Galveston Daily News*, March 10, August 13, 1890; quote from *The Rebel*, July 25, 1914.
28. *Southern Mercury* quoted in Barnes, *Farmers in Rebellion*, 119; *Hallettsville Herald*, November 27, 1890.
29. Goodwyn, *Populist Moment*, 148.
30. Hild, *Greenbackers*, 137–38.
31. Goodwyn, *Populist Moment*, 157–59.
32. *Hallettsville Herald*, February 5, 1891; Hild, *Greenbackers*, 164.
33. *Hallettsville Herald*, July 30, 1891; Barnes, *Farmers in Rebellion*, 124.
34. *Hallettsville Herald*, April 9, 16, 23, August 27, 1891; *Galveston Daily News*, September 22, 1891.
35. Martin, *People's Party*, 36–37.
36. *Hallettsville Herald*, April 16, 1891.
37. *Hallettsville Herald*, April 9, 30, May 7, 1891. Quote from April 30, 1891, issue.
38. McMath, *Populist Vanguard*, 107; Hild, *Greenbackers*, 139; *Hallettsville Herald*, May 21, 1891.
39. *Hallettsville Herald*, June 11, 1891; Martin, *People's Party*, 40–41.
40. Martin, *People's Party*, 39–40.
41. *Hallettsville Herald*, November 19, 1891.
42. *Dallas Morning News*, November 25, 1891.
43. *Dallas Morning News*, February 11, 1892.
44. *Hallettsville Herald*, January 14, 21, February 11, 1892; McMath, *Populist Vanguard*, 106, 130–31.
45. *Hallettsville Herald*, March 3, 1892.
46. *Hallettsville Herald*, 11, 1892.
47. Quote from *Hallettsville Herald*, March 31, 1892; *Southern Mercury*, April 21, 1898.
48. *Dallas Morning News*, April 12, 1892.
49. *Hallettsville Herald*, April 14, 28, 1892.
50. *Hallettsville Herald*, March 18, 31, 1892. Quote from *Hallettsville Herald*, March 31, 1892.
51. *Hallettsville Herald*, June 9, 1892.
52. *Hallettsville Herald*, May 26, 1892.
53. *Dallas Morning News*, June 24, 1892; *Hallettsville Herald*, June 23, 30, 1892.
54. *Hallettsville Herald*, July 7, 1892; McMath, *American Populism*, 168, 170–71.
55. Goodwyn, *Populist Moment*, 171–72; *Hallettsville Herald*, July 7, 1892.
56. *La Grange Journal*, June 16, 1892; *Hallettsville Herald*, August 4, 11, 1892. Quote from *Dallas Morning News*, August 1, 1892.

Notes to Chapter 3

57. *Hallettsville Herald*, August 18, September 1, 22, 1892.
58. Cantrell, "Our Very Pronounced Theory," 667–70.
59. *Hallettsville Herald*, September 15, 1892.
60. *Galveston Daily News*, September 4, 1892.
61. *Galveston Daily News*, September 6, 1892.
62. *Hallettsville Herald*, September 29, 1892.
63. *Hallettsville Herald*, October 13, 1892.
64. *Dallas Morning News*, November 2, 6, 1892; *Hallettsville Herald*, November 10, 17, 1892.
65. Barnes, *Farmers in Rebellion*, 138–39.
66. *Dallas Morning News*, November 11, 1892; *Hallettsville Herald*, November 17, 1892; Baumgartner and Vollentine, "Gonzales County," *Handbook of Texas Online*, https://www.tshaonline.org/handbook/entries/gonzales-county; Odintz, "Colorado County," *Handbook of Texas Online*, https://www.tshaonline.org/handbook/entries/colorado-county.
67. Barnes, *Farmers in Rebellion*, 142; Martin, *People's Party*, 210–11.
68. *Hallettsville Herald*, December 1, 15, 1892.
69. *Dallas Morning News*, January 8, 1893; *Hallettsville Herald*, February 23, May 11, August 3, 1893.
70. *Hallettsville Herald*, January 5, July 27, August 31, November 9, 1893; Martin, *People's Party*, 162, 191–93; McMath, *Populist Vanguard*, 148; *Dallas Morning News*, August 5, 1893; *Texas Advance*, November 18, 1893; Boethel, *LaBaca*, 37; US Congress, *Senate Commission on Industrial Relations*, vol. 10, 9143. Unfortunately, issues of the *New Era* before March 1899 have been lost to history.
71. *Hallettsville Herald*, January 4, 1894; McMath, *American Populism*, 181.
72. *Texas Advance*, July 14, 1894; Yellen, *American Labor Struggles*, 114, 125, 136.
73. Pierce, *Striking with the Ballot*, 3–5, 107–8.
74. *Southern Mercury*, October 25, 1894.
75. *Texas Advance*, July 7, 1894; *Southern Mercury*, August 30, 1894.
76. *Dallas Morning News*, June 22, 1894.
77. *Texas Advance*, April 7, June 30, 1894; *Texas Vorwärts* quote in Martin, *People's Party*, 108; *Dallas Morning News*, June 22, 1894.
78. McMath, *American Populism*, 183; *Hallettsville Herald*, November 2, 1893.
79. *Hallettsville Herald*, August 24, 1893.
80. Durden, *Climax of Populism*, x.
81. Goodwyn, *Populist Moment*, 179.
82. McMath, *American Populism*, 200; Goodwyn, *Populist Moment*, 217–18; *Hallettsville Herald*, August 10, 1893.
83. *Dallas Morning News*, November 8, 17, 1894; *Galveston Daily News*, November 15, December 22, 1894; Barnes, *Farmers in Rebellion*, 156; Martin, *People's Party*, 106; *Hallettsville Herald*, October 25, November 22, 1894; Texas Secretary of State, Lavaca County election results, 1894, Texas State Library and Archives Commission, Austin, Texas.
84. *Southern Mercury*, December 6, 1894; *Hallettsville Herald*, November 15, 1894; quote in *Dallas Morning News*, November 22, 1894; Martin, *People's Party*, 178, 236.
85. *Southern Mercury*, December 6, 1894, January 3, 1895.

86. *Galveston Daily News*, September 8, 1892.

87. Goodwyn, *Populist Moment*, 218, 241; *Southern Mercury*, March 7, 1895. The antifusionists called themselves middle-of-the-roaders because of their refusal to take either the Democratic or Republican side.

88. *Southern Mercury*, February 7, 1895.

89. *Southern Mercury*, March 14, 1895.

90. *Dallas Morning News*, May 30, 1895.

91. *Dallas Morning News*, May 30, 1895.

92. *Dallas Morning News*, May 30, 1895; *Hallettsville Herald*, February 6, 1896.

93. *Hallettsville Herald*, January 16, 1896.

94. *Southern Mercury*, November 12, 1896; Barnes, *Farmers in Rebellion*, 170; McMath, *American Populism*, 202; Goodwyn, *Democratic Promise*, 462.

95. *Southern Mercury*, March 26, 1896.

96. *Southern Mercury*, July 9, 1896.

97. Green, "Socialism," 7; *Appeal to Reason*, August 31, 1895.

98. Green, *Grass-Roots Socialism*, 17–19; *Laborer*, October 31, 1908.

99. *Appeal to Reason*, December 21, 1895; *Southern Mercury*, September 19, December 26, 1895, July 16, 1896.

100. *Appeal to Reason*, March 14, 1896.

101. Goodwyn, *Democratic Promise*, 466.

102. *Southern Mercury*, July 9, 1896; Goodwyn, *Democratic Promise*, 447; Green, *Grass-Roots Socialism*, 15.

103. Woodward, *Tom Watson*, 218–19.

104. *Southern Mercury*, July 23, 1896.

105. As quoted in Woodward, *Tom Watson*, 290.

106. *Southern Mercury*, July 16, 1896.

107. *Southern Mercury*, July 23, 1896; *Hallettsville Herald*, June 11, 1896; *Galveston Daily News*, August 8, 1896.

108. *Appeal to Reason*, July 18, 1896.

109. *St. Louis Globe-Democrat*, July 24, 1896.

110. *St. Louis Globe-Democrat*, July 21, 1896.

111. *St. Louis Globe-Democrat*, July 23, 1896.

112. *St. Louis Globe-Democrat*, July 22, 1896; Goodwyn, *Democratic Promise*, 478.

113. Goodwyn, *Democratic Promise*, 484.

114. *St. Louis Globe-Democrat*, July 26, 1896; Salvatore, *Eugene V. Debs*, 158; Goodwyn, *Democratic Promise*, 491.

115. *St. Louis Globe-Democrat*, July 28, 1896.

116. *Galveston Daily News*, July 27, August 5, 1896; Cantrell, *Kenneth and John B. Rayner*, 232–37.

117. *Galveston Daily News*, August 5, 1896.

118. *Galveston Daily News*, August 6, 8, 1896; *Dallas Morning News*, August 7, 8, 1896; Hild, *Greenbackers*, 28.

119. *Galveston Daily News*, August 7, 1896; Cantrell and Barton, "Texas Populism and the Failure of Biracial Politics," 678.

120. *Galveston Daily News*, August 6, 7, 9, 1896; Cantrell, *Kenneth and John B. Rayner*, 232–37; *Southern Mercury*, August 13, October 22, 1896; *Chicago Defender*, July 17, 1920; *Houston Informer*, February 7, 1920, January 19, 1924.

121. Hild, *Greenbackers*, 194; *Dallas Morning News*, November 25, December 20, 1896; Lavaca County election results, 1894, Texas State Library and Archives Commission, Austin, Texas; *Hallettsville Herald*, November 12, 1896; Martin, *People's Party*, 210–11, 243.

122. *Dallas Morning News*, December 10, 1896; *Southern Mercury*, September 17, 1896.

123. *Southern Mercury*, December 17, 1896.

124. *Southern Mercury*, November 26, 1896.

125. Debs quoted in Salvatore, *Eugene V. Debs*, 161–62.

126. *Dallas Morning News*, February 21, 1897.

127. *Memphis Commercial Appeal*, February 21, 1897.

128. *Memphis Commercial Appeal*, February 21, 23, 24, 25, 1897. Quotes from February 25, 1897, issue.

129. Goodwyn, *Democratic Promise*, 559–60; *Austin Daily Statesman*, July 25, 1897; Martin, *People's Party*, 194, 208.

130. Barnes, *Farmers in Rebellion*, 190–91, 194; Hicks, *Populist Revolt*, 384, 398–400; *Dallas Morning News*, June 18, 1898; *Cincinnati Enquirer*, September 6, 7, 1898, May 9, 10, 11, 1900; Martin, *People's Party*, 246; *Hallettsville Herald*, December 30, 1897, November 17, 1898, November 15, 1900; *Southern Mercury*, November 24, 1898. Early in 1898, Meitzen and his family moved to Austin to join forces with G. W. Mendell, the socialist leader of the Travis County People's Party. They ran an independent slate of candidates for county offices in 1898, including Meitzen for superintendent of public education. All candidates lost and the Meitzens returned to Hallettsville late in 1898 (*Rebel*, July 25, 1914; *People's Advocate*, December 22, 1893; Green, *Grass-Roots Socialism*, 15; *Austin Daily Statesman*, July 8, November 1, 8, 10, 1898; *Hallettsville New Era*, May 4, 1900).

131. US Census, *Census Reports*, 1890; Wagner, "Boll Weevil," *Handbook of Texas Online*, https://www.tshaonline.org/handbook/entries/boll-weevil; Green, "Tenant Farmer Discontent and Socialist Protest in Texas," 133–34.

132. *Southern Mercury*, December 15, 1898.

Chapter 4. The Battle for Socialism in Texas, 1900–11

1. *Hallettsville New Era*, April 7, 1905.

2. *Appeal to Reason*, November 24, 1898.

3. *Houston Daily Post*, December 4, 1898; Allen, *Chapters in the History of Organized Labor in Texas*, 25.

4. Green, *Grass-Roots Socialism*, 15–21; Hild, *Greenbackers*, 194; *Southern Mercury*, November 24, 1898; Wilkinson, *Yeomen*, 174.

5. *Shiner Gazette*, June 13, 1906; *Hallettsville New Era*, March 10, 1899.

6. *Southern Mercury*, November 29, 1900.

7. *Rebel*, November 4, 1916.

8. Bellamy, *Looking Backward*, iii.

9. Green, *Grass-Roots Socialism*, 151–75; Wilkinson, *Yeomen*, 125–60.

10. Edwards, unpublished autobiography, 46, Edwards Collection, Texas Labor Archives, Library Special Collections, University of Texas at Arlington.

11. Wilkinson, *Yeomen*, 125, 127, 136 (Smith quote), 139; *Rebel*, July 8, 1911.

12. *Rebel*, September 6, 1913.

13. *Rebel*, October 25, 1913.

14. *Rebel*, June 13, 1914, April 10, 1915, March 11, 1916; Jo-Lou Gaupp, interview by the author, video recording, Arlington, Texas, July 12, 2008. See also Stephen Burwood, "Debsian Socialism through a Transnational Lens," *Journal of the Gilded Age and Progressive Era* 2, no. 3 (July 2003): 253–82.

15. *Kansas City Star*, September 17, 19, 1901; *Louisville Courier-Journal*, April 2, 3, 4, 1902.

16. As quoted in *Louisville Courier-Journal*, April 3, 1902.

17. Quoted in Green, *Grass-Roots Socialism*, 22.

18. Miller, "Building a Progressive Coalition in Texas," 164.

19. Miller, "Building a Progressive Coalition in Texas," 169.

20. US Census, *Census Reports*, 1900.

21. *Hallettsville Herald*, April 24, May 29, 1902.

22. *Texas Almanac and State Industrial Guide, 1904*, 35, 37.

23. Quoted in Buenger and Kamphoefner, *Preserving German Texan Identity*, 23.

24. Buenger and Kamphoefner, *Preserving German Texan Identity*, x.

25. Quoted in Buenger and Kamphoefner, *Preserving German Texan Identity*, 140.

26. Quoted in Buenger and Kamphoefner, *Preserving German Texan Identity*, 141.

27. *Houston Post*, July 11, 1904; US Congress, *Senate Commission on Industrial Relations*, vol. 10, 9143. In Texas, county judges preside over a five-member commissioners court and hold broad judicial and administrative authority over county government functions.

28. *Hallettsville New Era*, October 21, 1904; *Cuero Daily Record*, May 29, 1904.

29. *Hallettsville New Era*, August 19, 26, December 2, 1904, March 24, April 7, 1905; *Rebel*, July 25, 1914; *Socialist Party Official Bulletin*, October 1904. In the 1904 presidential election, Debs received 400,939 votes (2.83 percent)—up from the 87,769 votes he received in 1900.

30. *Hallettsville New Era*, February 17, 1905.

31. *Hallettsville New Era*, May 5, 1905; Sanders, *Roots of Reform*, 150; Hunt, *History of Farmers Movements*, 45–48, 51.

32. Hunt, *History of Farmers Movements*, 64, 69; Sanders, *Roots of Reform*, 150; *Southern Mercury United with the Farmers Union Password*, May 4, 1905.

33. *Hallettsville New Era*, July 14, 28, 1905; Sanders, *Roots of Reform*, 152.

34. Hunt, *History of Farmers Movements*, 55, 69.

35. Greene, *Pure and Simple Politics*, 217.

36. *Hallettsville New Era*, April 7, September 8, 1905.

37. *Hallettsville New Era*, March 9, 1906.

38. *Vindicator* (town unknown), June 1, 1891, clipping in Hicks Family Papers, Texas Labor archives, Library Special Collections, University of Texas at Arlington [hereafter, Hicks Papers].

Notes to Chapter 4

39. Wilkinson, *Yeomen*, 141; *National Rip-Saw*, March 1908, clipping in Hicks Papers; *Hallettsville New Era*, September 8, 1905.
40. *Hallettsville New Era*, January 20, October 20, 1905.
41. *Hallettsville New Era*, January 12, 1906; Hunt, *History of Farmers Movements*, 82–84; *Schulenburg Sticker*, September 13, 1906; *National Co-operator and Farm Journal*, April 10, 1907.
42. *Hallettsville New Era*, January 12, 1906.
43. *Hallettsville New Era*, March 9, April 13, 1906.
44. *Hallettsville New Era*, June 15, 1906.
45. *Hallettsville New Era*, July 27, 1906; *Shiner Gazette*, July 18, October 16, 1906; *Schulenburg Sticker*, October 11, 1906.
46. *Hallettsville New Era*, August 17, 1906; *Hallettsville Herald*, September 20, 1906; Wiedenfeld, "Gay, Bettie Munn," *Handbook of Texas Online*, https://www.tshaonline.org/handbook/entries/gay-bettie-munn.
47. *Hallettsville New Era*, August 3, 1906.
48. *Hallettsville New Era*, August 31, 1906.
49. *I and N Reporter*, Winter 1977–78, 41; *Hallettsville Herald*, September 20, 1906; Lavaca County Naturalization Records, Vol. 2, 1899–1903, Vol. 3, 1904–1906, Vol. 4, 1906; *Hallettsville New Era*, July 28, 1905; *Obzor*, June 1, September 15, 1906.
50. *Hallettsville New Era*, November 23, 1906; *Hallettsville Herald*, November 8, 1906.
51. *Hallettsville New Era*, November 23, 1906.
52. *Hallettsville New Era*, February 17, 1905.
53. *Hallettsville New Era*, November 16, 1906.
54. *International Socialist Review*, November 1903, 258.
55. Ibid.
56. *Hallettsville New Era*, November 16, 1906.
57. *Socialist Party Official Bulletin*, February, March, April, May 1906.
58. *Socialist Party Official Bulletin*, October 1904; Wilkinson, *Yeomen*, 175; "Election of Texas Governors, 1845–2010," *Texas Almanac* online, https://texasalmanac.com/topics/elections/elections-texas-governors-1845%E2%80%932010.
59. Green, *Grass-Roots Socialism*, 40–41; "Big Encampment" flyer, Thomas A. Hickey Papers, Southwest Collection/Special Collections Library, Texas Tech University, Lubbock, Texas [hereafter, Hickey Papers].
60. Wilkinson, *Yeomen*, 177; *Socialist Party Official Bulletin*, October 1904; Winkler, *Platforms*, 471–72; "Election of Texas Governors, 1845–2010," *Texas Almanac* online, https://texasalmanac.com/topics/elections/elections-texas-governors-1845%E2%80%932010.
61. Winkler, *Platforms*, 484.
62. Winkler, *Platforms*, 485; *Socialist Party Official Bulletin*, August 1906; *Laborer*, September 1, 1906.
63. Edwards, unpublished autobiography, 43, 45–46; Wilkinson, *Yeomen*, 179; "Election of Texas Governors, 1845–2010," *Texas Almanac* online, https://texasalmanac.com/topics/elections/elections-texas-governors-1845%E2%80%932010.
64. Winkler, ed., *Platforms*, 493–96; Green, *Grass-Roots Socialism*, 56.

65. Green, *Grass-Roots Socialism*, 56–57; *Socialist Party Official Bulletin*, October 1905, February 1906; *Provoker*, December 2, 1909; Bell to Morgan, October 19, 1909, Thomas J. Morgan Papers, Special Collections Research Center, Joseph Regenstein Library, University of Chicago [hereafter, Morgan Papers].

66. *National Co-operator and Farm Journal*, April 10, 1907; *San Antonio Daily Express*, June 12, 1908; *Dallas Morning News*, August 5, 1908.

67. Hunt, *History of Farmers Movements*, 84, 86; *Journal of the House of Representatives of the Regular Session of the Thirtieth Legislature of Texas*, 130, 485, 572, 602, 625, 660, 681.

68. Hunt, *History of Farmers Movements in the Southwest*, 87, 100, 123.

69. *1908 Socialist Party National Convention*, 14–15.

70. *1908 Socialist Party National Convention*, 178–79. During the discussion, C. W. Barzee, a delegate from Oregon and a farmer, accepted an amendment to his resolution replacing "of his class" with "of the working class"—an important change for Left Socialists who considered farmers part of the working class (183).

71. *1908 Socialist Party National Convention*, 183, 186.

72. *Socialist Party National Convention*, 301–2; Foner, "Introduction," in Foner, ed., *Clara Zetkin: Selected Writings*, 30–31.

73. Buhle, *Women and American Socialism*, 145, 147–48; *Socialist Woman*, June 1907; *1908 Socialist Party National Convention*, 306.

74. *Socialist Party National Convention*, 302.

75. Basen, "'Jennie Higginses' of the 'New South in the West,'" in Miller ed., *Flawed Liberation*, 99; *Dallas Morning News*, February 19, September 7, 1906; *Socialist Party Official Bulletin*, September 1906, April 1908.

76. *1908 Socialist Party National Convention*, 305; On the Dallas suffrage movement see Prycer, "'Not Organizing for the Fun of It.'"

77. See issues of the monthly *Socialist Woman*, June 1908-December 1908. In 1909 the *Socialist Woman* changed its name to *Progressive Woman*; *Progressive Woman*, October 1909. Within a couple of years after the 1908 convention, Payne's activism turned more toward radical syndicalism. She moved to San Diego and at some point joined the Industrial Workers of the World. While in San Diego she participated in numerous labor struggles and helped lead the 1912 San Diego free-speech fight. She was frequently attacked by right-wingers, jailed by the police, and harassed and surveilled by the Bureau of Investigation. *San Francisco Chronicle*, May 28, 1912; Gershon report May 8, 1918, Watson reports July 12, December 14, 1918, Buck reports May 23, 24, 1919, Blanford reports May 24, June 17, 1919, Bureau of Investigation Files (BI).

78. Winkler, ed., *Platforms*, 513–14; *Provoker*, December 2, 1909; "Election of Texas Governors, 1845–2010," *Texas Almanac* online, https://texasalmanac.com/topics/elections/elections-texas-governors-1845%E2%80%932010.

79. Bell to Morgan, October 19, 1909, Morgan Papers; *Provoker*, December 2, 1909; *Dallas Morning News*, February 25, March 9, April 2, 8, 1908.

80. *Houston Post*, July 16, August 1, 6, 8, 1909; *Provoker*, December 9, 23, 1909, January 6, 13, 20, 1910; Bell to Morgan, October 19, 1909, E. R. Meitzen to Morgan, July 30, 1910, Morgan Papers; Clark to Comrades, December 14, 1908, Hickey Papers; *Socialist Party Official Bulletin*, March, June 1907; Kipnis, *American Socialist Movement*, 180.

81. Hickey, biographical sketch, Hickey Papers; "New York, Passenger Arrival Lists (Ellis Island), 1892–1924," database, *FamilySearch*; Allen, "Notes, undated," Allen Papers

82. Buckingham, *"Red Tom,"* 114, 138, 166; *Dallas Morning News*, November 15, 1905, July 23, 1910.

83. Hardy, "Texas Program," *International Socialist Review*, April 1911, 623.

84. Hardy, "Texas Program," 622–23.

85. Ness and Azzellini, "Introduction," *Ours to Master and to Own*, 7; Hardy, "Texas Program," 623.

86. Hardy, "Texas Program," 623.

87. Marx wrote, "Political economy confuses, on principle, two different kinds of private property, one of which rests on the labor of the producer himself, and the other on the exploitation of the labor of others. It forgets that the latter is not only the direct antithesis of the former, but grows on the former's tomb and nowhere else" (*Capital*, 1: 931).

88. *National Congress of the Socialist Party, 1910*, 212–35.

89. Winkler, *Platforms*, 527–28; *Dallas Morning News*, August 8, 14, 1910.

90. Wilkinson, *Yeomen*, 173; Green, "Tenant Farmer Discontent," 133.Winkler, ed., *Platforms*, 529.

91. *New Era* article reprinted in *Dallas Morning News*, June 19, 1910; King, "Andrews, Reddin, Jr.," *Handbook of Texas Online*, https://www.tshaonline.org/handbook/entries/andrews-reddin-jr; "Andrews, A R, Sixteenth Cavalry," *Compiled Service Records*, US National Archives; Wilkinson, *Yeomen*, 150.

92. *Dallas Morning News*, August 5, 1909.

93. Hickey to Clara Boeer, January 5, 1910, Hickey Papers; *Dallas Morning News*, July 23, 1910.

94. *Abilene Reporter*, June 19, 1911, clipping in Hicks Papers; *Rebel*, July 1, 1911; Hickey to Clara Boeer, February 16, May 16, June 20, 1911, Hickey Papers; Hall, *Labor Struggles*, 200–201.

95. *Rebel*, July 1, 1911; Buckingham, *"Red Tom" Hickey*, 53.

96. Green, *Grass-Roots Socialism*, 138; Weinstein, *Decline of Socialism*, 94–102, table 1; Hickey to Clara Boeer, February 16, 1911, and Redmond to Alma Boeer, February 16, 1916, Hickey Papers.

97. "Maria Boeer," Texas Death Certificates, 1890–1976, Texas Department of Health Services; "Texas, Marriages, 1837–1973," database, *FamilySearch*; US Census, *Census Reports*, 1860, 1910; Maria Boeer to Clara and Tom Hickey, May 24, 1916, Hickey Papers; 1864, 1865, 1866, 1867, 1874, 1879, 1882 county tax rolls, Colorado County, Texas.

98. See Boeer/Wolf Families Papers; Clara Boeer to Hickey, November 28, 1910, Maria Boeer to Clara Hickey, March 18, 22, 1913, Hickey Papers. Boethel, *Lavacans*, 67. The Meitzens also published a Czech-language socialist paper, *Pozor*. *Habt Acht* is German for take heed.

99. Hardy, "Texas Program," 622; Bell to Boeer Sisters, March 25, 1909, Crider to Boeer Sisters, March 25, 1909, June 12, 1911, Hickey to Clare Boeer, February 16, 1911, Hickey to Carl Wolf, June 4, 1913, Hickey Papers; US Census, *Census Reports*, 1930; *Sangerton News*, May 20, 1910.

100. *Dallas Morning News*, August 14, 1910.

101. *Rebel*, March 17, 1917.
102. Winkler, *Platforms*, 613.
103. E. R. Meitzen to Lowe, October 19, 1910, Hickey Papers; *Progressive Woman*, October, 1911, June, July, 1912, June–July, 1913.
104. *Rebel*, March 18, 1916.
105. *Rebel*, September 23, 1916.
106. *Rebel*, March 18, 1916.
107. Ibid.
108. *Rebel*, November 25, 1916.
109. *Rebel*, December 2, 1916.

Chapter 5. Tierra y Libertad

1. *Dallas Morning News*, November 5, 1911. The bonus system charged tenants an extra bonus in rent from $1 to $3 for tenants to stay on the farm they rented the previous year (Hamilton, "Texas Farm Tenure Activities," 330).
2. *Rebel*, September 9, November 11, 1911.
3. *Rebel*, September 9, 1911.
4. *International Socialist Review*, July 1912, 67–68.
5. Shannon, *Socialist Party*, 51.
6. Hall, *Labor Struggles of the Deep South*, 120, 128; Green, *Grass-Roots Socialism*, 204–27.
7. Green, *Grass-Roots Socialism*, 223.
8. McCaa, *Missing Millions*; McWilliams, *North from Mexico*, 163.
9. Hart, *Revolutionary Mexico*, 6; Haber, *Industry and Underdevelopment*, 12.
10. Hart, *Revolutionary Mexico*, xi, 47, 132, 136–37, 148–51; Katz, *Pancho Villa*, 130; Raat, *Revoltosos*, 13.
11. Knight, *Mexican Revolution*, 1: 79, 95.
12. Knight, *Mexican Revolution*, 1: 30–32; Cockcroft, *Intellectual Precursors*, 91, 93; Gomez-Quiñones, *Sembradores*, 23–25; Raat, *Revoltosos*, 20–21.
13. Gomez-Quiñones, *Sembradores*, 23–25; Raat, *Revoltosos*, 20–21; MacLachlan, *Anarchism*, 18–19.
14. *Socialist Party Official Bulletin*, March 1911; *Milwaukee Leader*, February 14, 1913. For examples of news coverage, see *Milwaukee Leader*, February 17, 1912, and February 10, 1913, to cite only two.
15. *Dallas Morning News*, February 15, 1911.
16. "Defense of the Insurrecto's Sword," Hickey Papers.
17. Flyer, "Hickey Will Lecture on Socialism in Spanish," and Hickey to Clare Boeer, March 10, 1911, Hickey Papers.
18. *Socialist Party Official Bulletin*, March 1911; Hickey to Clare Boeer, March 10, 1911, Hickey Papers.
19. *Rebel*, June 15, 1912.
20. *Rebel*, June 22, November 12, 1912, May 10, 17, 1913; Foley, *White Scourge*, 11; *Regeneración*, November 13, 22, 1913, January 24, 1914, July 11, 1914. *Regeneración* ran an

article in its December 27, 1913, issue criticizing an article in the *Rebel* that simplified the Mexican Revolution as a revolt against the Roman Catholic Church. This was not the normal stance of the *Rebel*, which, agreeing with *Regeneración*, viewed economic exploitation as the main cause of the revolution. For examples of *The Rebel*'s coverage of the Mexican Revolution, see the *Rebel*, June 8, 15, 1912, December 20, 1913, July 7, 1915.

21. *National Convention of the Socialist Party, 1912*, 4, 121, 151, 159; E. R. Meitzen to Hickey, February 1911, Hickey Papers.

22. Kipnis, *American Socialist Movement*, 402.

23. *National Convention of the Socialist Party, 1912*, 195.

24. Quote from *National Convention of the Socialist Party, 1912*, 122. See also Kipnis, *American Socialist Movement*, 400–403; Ginger, *Bending Cross*, 309.

25. Bohn, "Some Definitions," *International Socialists Review* 12, no. 8: 747–49.

26. *National Convention of the Socialist Party, 1912*, 133.

27. *National Convention of the Socialist Party, 1912*, 137.

28. Debs to Hickey, May 21, 1912, Hickey Papers. Green at this time was the state secretary of the Texas SP.

29. *National Convention of the Socialist Party, 1912*, 164; Buckingham, *"Red Tom" Hickey*, 68, 82–84, 201; Kipnis, *American Socialist Movement*, 380.

30. Ginger, *Bending Cross*, 310–11.

31. *Socialist Party Monthly Bulletin*, July 1912.

32. *Socialist Party Monthly Bulletin*, October 1912.

33. Ibid.

34. *Socialist Party Monthly Bulletin*, January, March–April 1913.

35. Ginger, *Bending Cross*, 310–12.

36. Maria Boeer to Tom and Clare Hickey, undated, Hickey Papers.

37. *Decentralizer*, March 1, 1913.

38. *Decentralizer*, April 13, 1913. "Maderoed" refers to President Francisco Madero, who was assassinated during a right-wing military coup in Mexico led by Victoriano Huerta.

39. *Dallas Morning News*, November 11, 1913.

40. Raat, *Revoltosos*, 259; Green, *Grass-Roots Socialism*, 329; Hall, *Labor Struggles*, 151, 161; *Brownsville Herald*, September 12, 1913; Sanders to Hutchings, September 15, 1913, Texas Adjutant General's Correspondence, Texas State Library and Archives Commission [hereafter, Adjutant General's Correspondence]; Harris and Sadler, *Texas Rangers*, 134; Barnes Report, September 17, 1913, "Mexican Files," Bureau of Investigation, National Archives and Records Administration, Washington, DC [hereafter, BI].

41. In 1915, the committee succeeded in getting the prison sentences reduced. Raat, *Revoltosos*, 259; Green, *Grass-Roots Socialism*, 329; *Rebel*, May 30, 1914, February 20, May 8, August 7, September 18, 25, October 23, 1915; *International Socialist Review*, February 1914, 507; quote from "Voluntary Statement of J. A. Hernandez," Colquitt Papers, Center for American History, University of Texas at Austin [hereafter, Colquitt Papers, CAH].

42. Hughes to Hutchings, November 21, 1913, Adjutant General's Correspondence; telegram to Colquitt, November 15, 1913, Colquitt Papers, CAH.

43. "A Friend" to Colquitt, November 17, 1913, Harrison to Colquitt, November 17, 1913, Colquitt to Hernandez et al., November 17, 1913, Hughes to Colquitt, November 24, 1913, Tobin to Colquitt, November 22, 1913, Colquitt Papers, CAH; Lansing to Hutchings, November 17, 1913, Colquitt Papers, Texas State Library and Archives [hereafter, Colquitt Papers, TSL].

44. "Voluntary Statement of J. A. Hernandez"; Hughes to Colquitt, November 24, 1913, Colquitt Papers, CAH; Hughes, "List of Signers on Telegram to Governor Colquitt," December 14, 1913, Adjutant General's Correspondence; Linden quoted in Linden to Colquitt, December 3, 1913, Colquitt quoted in Colquitt to Linden, December 6, 1913, Colquitt Papers, TSL; *International Socialist Review*, February 1914, 507; Hernández to Colquitt, December 28, 1913, copy of letter in Needham Report, March 27, 1918, "Mexican Files," BI; Hernández to Pizana, November 24, 1914, "Mexican Files," BI. On October 1, 1910, the *Los Angeles Times* building was dynamited, killing twenty-one people.

45. Harris and Sadler, *Texas Rangers*, 135.
46. *Dallas Morning News*, October 22, 1913,
47. *Dallas Morning News*, November 2, 1913.
48. *Dallas Morning News*, September 24, 1913.
49. Bennett, *History of the Panama Canal*, 307–10.
50. Ibid.
51. *Rebel*, August 9, 1913.
52. *Rebel*, August 9, 1913.
53. *Rebel*, August 23, 1913.
54. *Houston Post*, May 17, 1914; Brazos River Authority, "Timeline of the Brazos River Basin,"; Doremus Jr. to Colquitt, December 9, 1913, Colquitt Papers, CAH; *Rebel*, November 15, 22, December 20, 1913.
55. *San Antonio Express*, December 21, 1913.
56. *Rebel*, January 3, 1914.
57. *Rebel*, January 31, 1914.
58. "Publisher's Note," in Reed, *Insurgent Mexico*, iii; Katz, *Pancho Villa*, 324–25.
59. Katz, *Pancho Villa*, 431.
60. Quoted in B. Johnson, *Revolution in Texas*, 65.
61. *Rebel*, March 14, 1914.
62. *Rebel*, June 8, 1912.
63. *Rebel*, May 24, 1913.
64. *Rebel*, August 16, 1913.
65. *Rebel*, May 3, 10, November 15, 1913, December 11, 1915.
66. *Rebel*, May 10, 17, 1913, November 20, December 4, 1915; US Census, *Census Reports 1910*; US Congress, *Senate Commission on Industrial Relations*, vol. 10, 9284–85, 9287–88; Foley, *White Scourge*, 111; F. A. Hernández to Committee of Public Information, October 4, 1918, "Old German Files," BI; *Dallas Morning News*, November 9, 1913.
67. F. A. Hernández to Committee of Public Information, October 4, 1918, "Old German Files," BI.
68. *Rebel*, May 10, 17, 1913, November 20, December 4, 1915; *Dallas Morning News*, November 9, 1913.

69. *Rebel*, September 27, 1913.
70. *Rebel*, June 7, 1913, February 21, 1914, October 16, 1915; *Yorktown News*, May 22, 1913.
71. *Rebel*, February 28, 1914.
72. "Platform of the Socialist Party of Texas," Socialism File; *Houston Post*, May 2, 1914.
73. Hickey to Clara Hickey, July 14, 1913, Hickey Papers.
74. "Platform of the Socialist Party of Texas."
75. Ibid.
76. Ibid.
77. Ibid.
78. *Rebel*, June 6, 1914.
79. Gould, *Progressives and Prohibitionists*, 124; *Rebel*, February 21, 1914.
80. Gould, *Progressives and Prohibitionists*, 130.
81. Gould, *Progressives and Prohibitionists*, 131.
82. *Rebel*, April 11, 25, 1914.
83. Gould, *Progressives and Prohibitionists*, 130; *Rebel*, April 11, 1914.
84. *Rebel*, June 13, 20, 1914.
85. US Census Bureau, *Cotton Production and Distribution*, 10, 19–23.
86. *Crockett Courier*, June 11, 1914; *Rebel*, July 11, 1914.
87. Gould, *Progressives and Prohibitionists*, 136.
88. *Temple Daily Telegram*, July 14, 1914; Gould, *Progressives and Prohibitionists*, 7.
89. *Temple Daily Telegram*, July 14, 1914.
90. *Rebel*, June 6, August 7, 23, 1914; Gould, *Progressives and Prohibitionists*, 137; Green, *Grass-Roots Socialism*, 294.
91. *Rebel*, October 31, 1914.
92. Ibid.
93. *Houston Post*, July 16, 1914; *Hallettsville Herald*, July 16, 1914; *Rebel*, July 18, 25, 1914; Williams, *History of the Meitzen Family*, n.p.
94. Williams, *History of the Meitzen Family*, n.p.
95. *Hallettsville Herald*, July 16, 1914; *Rebel*, July 18, 1914.
96. *Rebel*, July 18, 1914.
97. *Houston Post*, July 16, 1914.
98. *Rebel*, July 25, 1914.
99. Williams, *History of the Meitzen Family*, n.p.
100. *Rebel*, October 31, 1914.
101. *National Rip-Saw*, June, 1914.
102. *Childress Post*, August 12, 1914.
103. *National Rip-Saw*, June 1914.
104. *Rebel*, July 18, 1914; The ambitions of Texas Socialists did have some grounding. Oklahoma Socialists were waging an election campaign based on the land issue that was much like their Lone Star comrades' campaign. In the November 1914 elections, six Socialists were elected to the Oklahoma state legislature and close to one hundred were elected to local and county offices (Green, *Grass-Roots Socialism*, 293).

105. *Rebel*, November 21, 1914; Green, *Grass-Roots Socialism*, 297–98.

106. *Rebel*, November 7, 1914.

107. *Rebel*, December 26, 1914.

108. *Milwaukee Leader*, December 20, 1913.

109. Raat, *Revoltosos*, 47, 58–59, 78, 80; Gutiérrez de Lara to Hickey, March 8, 1915, US Congress, Senate, Industrial Relations, Final Report and Testimony, submitted to Congress by the Commission on Industrial Relations, created by the Act of Congress August 23, 1912(Washington, DC: GPO, 1916), vols. 9 and 10, 9272–73; *Rebel*, December 5, 1914; Zamora, *Mexican Worker in Texas*, 133, 146.

110. *Rebel*, January 16, 1915.

111. *Rebel*, February 12, 1916.

112. *Rebel*, June 6, 13, 20, 1914, February 13, 1915; *Dallas Morning News*, July 19, 1915.

113. *Rebel*, November 28, 1914; Green, *Grass-Roots Socialism*, 303.

114. *Dallas Morning News*, November 18, 1914; Johnston, *Radical Middle Class*, 159–61.

115. *El Paso Herald*, February 10, 1913; Green, *Grass-Roots Socialism*, 303.

116. Hickey to U'Ren, April 18, 1916, Hickey Papers.

117. *Houston Post*, March 1, April 11, 1911, February 24, July 10, 1917; Davis, "Joseph Jay Pastoriza," 61–62; *Rebel*, May 6, 1916.

118. *Rebel*, September 25, 1915.

119. U'Ren to Hickey, July 18, 1916, Hickey Papers.

120. *Rebel*, September 25, 1915.

121. Green, *Grass-Roots Socialism*, 303.

122. *Rebel*, March 3, 1917.

123. For a discussion of the historiography of US socialists as not Marxists, see Burwood, "Debsian Socialism."

124. Radek, "Theses on Tactics and Strategy," in Riddell, *To the Masses*, 936–38; Executive Committee of the Communist International, "December 1921 Theses on the Workers' United Front," and Riddell, "Editorial Introduction," both in Riddell, *Toward the United Front*, 5–13, 1164–73.

125. McCartin, *Labor's Great War*, 18–19, 166.

126. Stromquist, *Reinventing "The People*," 165; quote in Walsh to Creel, August 18, 1913, Walsh Papers.

127. Stromquist, *Reinventing "The People*," 166; McCartin, *Labor's Great War*, 13; *Times-Picayune*, March 9, 1915.

128. *Augusta Chronicle*, March 11, 1915.

129. *National Rip-Saw*, July 1915.

130. Brown to Walsh, November 28, 1914, Walsh to Aylward, November 30, 1914, Walsh to O'Brien, December 1, 1914, Walsh Papers.

131. *Journal of the House of Representatives* [Texas], 131.

132. *Journal of the House of Representatives*, 788–91; *Rebel*, April 11, 25, 1914.

133. *Journal of the House of Representatives*, 789.

134. *Journal of the House of Representatives*, 789.

135. *Journal of the House of Representatives*, 791.

136. Rumbo v. Winterrowd, 228 S.W. 258 (Tex. Civ. App. 1921); *Supplement to Vernon's Texas Civil and Criminal Statutes*, vol. 2, 1554.

137. US Congress, *Senate Commission on Industrial Relations*, vol. 9, iv; US Congress, *Senate Commission on Industrial Relations*, vol. 10, iii; *Rebel*, March 6, 1915.

138. US Congress, *Senate Commission on Industrial Relations*, vol. 10, iii.

139. US Congress, *Senate Commission on Industrial Relations*, vol. 9, 8956–82; *Washington Post*, March 19, 1915; *Nashville Tennessean*, March 18, 1915; *Louisville Courier Journal*, March 18, 1915.

140. US Congress, *Senate Commission on Industrial Relations*, vol. 10, 9005–44.

141. US Congress, *Senate Commission on Industrial Relations*, vol. 10, 9260–89.

142. US Congress, *Senate Commission on Industrial Relations*, vol. 10, 9146, 9282.

143. US Congress, *Senate Commission on Industrial Relations*, vol. 10, 9144; *New York World*, May 5, 1917; *Augusta Chronicle*, April 27, 1919.

144. US Congress, *Senate Commission on Industrial Relations*, vol. 10, 9001–2, 9107–25; *Dallas Morning News*, March 20, 1915.

145. US Congress, *Senate Commission on Industrial Relations*, vol. 10, 9272.

146. US Congress, *Senate Commission on Industrial Relations*, vol. 10, 9203, 9283–85.

147. US Congress, *Senate Commission on Industrial Relations*, vol. 10, 9201.

148. Martinez, *Injustice Never Leaves You*, 6-7.

149. B. Johnson, *Revolution in Texas*, 1–2, 70; Sandos, *Rebellion*, 172; *Dallas Morning News*, August 14, September 8, 1915; Henry to Barnes, February 2, 1917, in Barnes Report, February 13, 1917, "Mexican Files," BI.

150. Barnes to sheriff, Cameron County, October 30, 1915, Adkins to Barnes, November 4, 1915, in Breniman Report, November 5, 1915, Roll 856, BI.

151. *Rebel*, November 6, 1915.

152. In English, *Lucha de Clases* is class struggle. Barnes Report, September 1, 2, 1915, "Mexican Files"; *Dallas Morning News*, August 31, 1915; Zamora, *Mexican Worker in Texas*, 145.

153. *San Antonio Express*, September 1, 1915.

154. Zamora, *Mexican Worker in Texas*, 156–57; *San Antonio Express*, August 31, September 1, 1915; *Rebel*, October 23, 1915.

155. *San Antonio Express*, September 1, 1915.

156. *Rebel*, September 25, October 23, November 6, 1915.

157. *Rebel*, October 23, 1915.

158. *Rebel*, September 25, October 23, November 6, 1915.

159. *Rebel*, April 3, November 20, 1915, January 29, 1916.

160. *Rebel*, March 4, June 3, 1916.

Chapter 6. From the Cooperative Commonwealth to the Invisible Empire

1. Raat, *Revoltosos*, 13; Hart, *Revolutionary Mexico*, xi; *Rebel*, January 8, 1916.

2. The "Mexican Files" of the Bureau of Investigation contain numerous reports of Mexicans leaving the United States to avoid the draft. Johnson, *Revolution in Texas*, 158–60).

3. F. A. Hernández to Committee on Public Information, August 17, October 4, November 18, 1918, F. A. Hernández to Rolland, November 16, 1916, "Old German Files," BI. The Committee on Public Information was a government agency that used propaganda to influence public opinion in favor of the war and against antiwar activities.

4. Sorola Report, June 30, 1916, Lopez Report, June 11, 1917, Ramos Report, August 20, 1917, Wiseman Reports, August 23, 24, 1917, Barnes to Bielaski, August 27, 1917, Swift Report August 31, 1917, Farland Reports, August 30, 31, 1917, "Old German Files," BI; White, "Camp Travis," *Handbook of Texas Online*, https://www.tshaonline.org/handbook/entries/camp-travis.

5. Green, *Grass-Roots Socialism*, 96; *Rebel*, April 3, 1915, May 13, 1916; *Dallas Morning News*, June 29, 1915.

6. *Rebel*, October 14, 1916.

7. Salvatore, *Eugene V. Debs*, 275–76.

8. *American Socialist*, November 27, 1915, quoted in Ginger, *Bending Cross*, 335.

9. *Rebel*, February 19, March 18, 1916.

10. *Rebel*, December 25, 1915, March 25, 1916; Green, *Grass-Roots Socialism*, 136, 214, 221; *American Socialist*, May 27, 1916.

11. Maria Boeer to Clara and Hickey, May 24, 1916, Thomas A. Hickey Papers, Southwest Collection/Special Collections Library, Texas Tech University, Lubbock, Texas [hereafter, Hickey Papers]; *Rebel*, April 29, 1916; Bell to "Dear Comrades," July 1916, Bell to Hickey, July 27, 1916, Hickey Papers.

12. *Rebel*, April 3, November 20, 1915, April 29, 1916; Winkler, *Platforms*, 625–28; *Dallas Morning News*, November 12, 13, 1915.

13. *Rebel*, June 24, October 14, 1916; Hickey to Pastoriza, July 14, 1916, Hickey Papers.

14. *Rebel*, September 16, 1916.

15. Shannon, *Socialist Party*, 91–92; Green, *Grass-Roots Socialism*, 351.

16. Gould, *Progressives and Prohibitionists*, 166–71.

17. *Rebel*, November 11, 1916.

18. *Rebel*, August 5, November 25, 1916.

19. *Rebel*, November 25, 1916; Baulch, "Making West Texas Safe," 119–22, 126.

20. Lansing, *Insurgent Democracy*, 19, 39.

21. Lansing, *Insurgent Democracy*, 6, 11–13; *National Convention of the Socialist Party, 1912*, 4.

22. Lansing, *Insurgent Democracy*, 18.

23. Lansing, *Insurgent Democracy*, 18–20.

24. Lansing, *Insurgent Democracy*, 14–20, 30.

25. Lansing, *Insurgent Democracy*, 22, 38.

26. E. R. Meitzen to Hickey, March 1, 1917, Hickey to E. O. Meitzen, March 17, 1917, Hickey Papers.

27. *Nonpartisan Leader*, April 26, 1917.

28. E. R. Meitzen to Hickey, March 1, 1917, Hickey Papers.

29. E. R. Meitzen to Hickey, May 9, 1917, Hickey Papers.

30. *Rebel*, January 13, 1917.

31. *Rebel*, January 20, 1917.

32. *Rebel*, January 27, 1917.

33. E. R. Meitzen to Hickey, May 9, 1917, Hickey Papers.

34. De Leon, ed., *American Labor Who's Who*, 157.

35. E. R. Meitzen to Hickey, May 9, 1917, Hickey Papers.

36. *Nonpartisan Leader*, September 20, 1917.

37. E. R. Meitzen to Dear Folk, April 28, 1917, Hickey Papers.

38. Hickey to Clare Hickey, March 5, November 11, 14, 1918, Hickey to Comrades, December 22, 1917, Hickey Papers; Shannon, *Socialist Party*, 27–28; *Spokesman Review*, June 6, 1920.

39. Trachtenberg, "Executive Committee Report-Discussion, June 23, 1923," in *Communist Movement at the Crossroads: Plenums of the Communist International's Executive Committee, 1922–1923*, ed. Mike Tabor (Chicago: Haymarket, 2019), 446–47.

40. Socialist Party, *Emergency Convention of the Socialist Party of America, 1917*.

41. *Rebel*, April 21, 1917; Socialist Party, *Emergency Convention of the Socialist Party of America, 1917*, fifth day evening session, 3.

42. Socialist Party, *Emergency Convention of the Socialist Party of America, 1917*, fourth day evening session, 2; quotes are from *Milwaukee Leader*, April 12, 1917.

43. *Rebel*, May 19, 1917.

44. Lawrence Report, July 26, 1917, roll 399, BI; Breniman Report, May 29, 1920, roll 778, BI.

45. Lawrence Report, July 26, 1917, roll 399, BI.

46. *Dallas Morning News*, May 27, 1917; *Rebel*, May 26, 1917;

47. *Pearson's Magazine*, September 1917, 137; Baulch, "Making West Texas Safe," 120–21; *Abilene Daily Reporter*, May 21, 1917; Harris and Sadler, *Texas Rangers*, 25.

48. *El Paso Herald*, May 21, 1917; *Abilene Daily Reporter*, May 21, 1917; *San Antonio Express*, May 21, 1917; *Sherman Daily Democrat*, May 21, 1917; *Houston Post*, May 23, 1917; *Temple Daily Telegram*, May 23, 1917.

49. *Rebel*, May 19, June 2, 1917; Nugent to Hickey, August 29, 1917, Hickey Papers. "The God of 10 per cent" is in reference to the practice of tithing 10 percent to God. There are references in the Bible to bad things happening to those who do not contribute their share.

50. Baulch, "Making West Texas Safe," 123, 127.

51. Arnold Meitzen to Hickey, May 24, 1917, Hickey Papers.

52. Arnold Meitzen to Clara Hickey, June 1, 1917, Hickey Papers.

53. Green, *Grass-Roots Socialism*, 356; For only one example of the *Rebel* attacking Gregory, see *Rebel*, October 17, 1914.

54. Carl Rossen to Hickey, June 5, 1917, Hickey Papers.

55. *Nonpartisan Leader*, June 14, 1917.

56. Lansing, *Insurgent Democracy*, 129.

57. E. R. Meitzen to Hickey, May 21, 1917, Hickey Papers.

58. E. R. Meitzen to Hickey, August 25, 1917, Hickey Papers.

59. *Nonpartisan Leader*, July 12, August 30, September 6, 27, 1917.

60. E. O. Meitzen to Hickey, December 26, 1916, April 1, 1917; Hickey to Clara Hickey, April 12, 1917; E. R. Meitzen to Hickey, August 25, 1917—all in Hickey Papers; Green, *Grass-Roots Socialism*, 277.

61. Gilbert to Hickey, August 25, 1917, Hickey Papers.

62. *Daily Herald*, August 9, 1918.

63. *Daily Herald*, October 2, 1917, August 9, 1918; Hickey to Clara Hickey, November 17, 1917, Hickey Papers; Kohn, *American Political Prisoners*, 91.

64. *Social Revolution*, August 1917, March 1918.

65. *Social Revolution*, March 1918.

66. Hickey to Dear Comrades, December 22, 1917, Hickey Papers.

67. Ibid.

68. *Nonpartisan Leader*, April 26, 1917.

69. E. R. Meitzen to Hickey, May 21, 1917, Hickey Papers. The pressures of E. R. Meitzen's political activities dealt him a hard personal blow in April 1918. "E. R. is badly hit," Hickey wrote to Clara, "he has had a row with his girl. He is so sore he feels like joining the Army as a volunteer next July (I am not joking)." Meitzen did try to enlist, but medical examiners found he had a "defect" that kept him from volunteering (Hickey to Clara Hickey, April 4, 1918, and E. R. Meitzen to Hickey, July 19, 1918; both in Hickey Papers).

70. *Nonpartisan Leader*, April 29, 1918.

71. Ibid.

72. Ibid.

73. Hickey to Gilbert, May 14, 1918, E. R. Meitzen to Hickey, May 16, 1918, Hickey Papers; Lansing, *Insurgent Democracy*, 118–24; *Nonpartisan Leader*, May 27, 1918.

74. E. R. Meitzen to Hickey, May 16, 1918, Hickey Papers; *Nonpartisan Leader*, May 27, 1918.

75. E. R. Meitzen to Hickey, July 15, 1918, Grace Brewer to Clara Hickey, July 18, 1918, H. J. Greenwood to Hickey, October 12, 1918, Hickey Papers; Lansing, *Insurgent Democracy*, 176–77. H. J. Greenwood was the state secretary of Nebraska NPL. Charles A. Lindbergh was the father of the famous aviator Charles Lindbergh.

76. Lansing, *Insurgent Democracy*, 141–44; Hickey to Clara Hickey, November 24, 1918, Hickey Papers.

77. Gould, *Progressives and Prohibitionists*, 211–18.

78. *Ferguson Forum*, July 26, 1918.

79. *Ferguson Forum*, December 6, 1917, June 6, 1918; TSFL, *Twenty-First Annual Convention, 1918*, 13–15; Gould, *Progressives and Prohibitionists*, 236.

80. Brown, *Hood, Bonnet, and Little Brown Jug*, 8; Gould, *Progressives and Prohibitionists*, 246.

81. Brown, *Hood, Bonnet, and Little Brown Jug*, 8; *San Antonio Light*, August 11, 1919; *Brownsville Daily Herald*, August 14, 1919.

82. Montgomery, *Fall of the House of Labor*, 388, 395; Gould, *Progressives and Prohibitionists*, 250–51.

83. Lansing, *Insurgent Democracy*, 175–78.

84. *Houston Labor Journal*, January 10, February 14, 1920; *Houston Post*, February 5, 1920. The previous state senator accepted an appointment from the governor, creating the need for a special election. Three state representatives then resigned to run for the senate seat, creating a need to fill their seats as well. *Houston Chronicle*, February 28, 1920.

85. *Houston Labor Journal*, February 14, 1920; *Houston Post*, February 7, 8, 1920.

86. *Houston Chronicle*, January 25, February 8, 15, 21, 22, 27, 29, March 1, 4, 1920, quote from February 27, 1920 issue; *Houston Labor Journal*, February 21, 28, 1920 *Houston Post*, March 1, 1920.

87. *Houston Labor Journal*, February 28, March 13, 1920; *Nonpartisan Leader*, March 29, 1920.

88. *Galveston Daily News*, August 15, 1919; *Ferguson Forum*, June 12, 1919.

89. *Ferguson Forum*, June 12, 1919.

90. *Ferguson Forum*, June 19, 1919.

91. *Galveston Daily News*, August 15, 1919.

92. *Galveston Daily News*, August 15, 1919; *Denton Record Chronicle*, January 30, 1920.

93. *Ferguson Forum*, August 15, September 18, December 18, 1919, February 12, 26, April 15, 22, 1920; *Denton Record Chronicle*, August 15, 1919; Gould, *Progressives and Prohibitionists*, 270–71; *Galveston Daily News*, October 4, December 6, 1919; *Laredo Weekly Times*, August 17, 1919.

94. *Ferguson Forum*, April 22, 1920 (quotes); *Semi-weekly Farm News*, August 13, 1920.

95. *Ferguson Forum*, May 27, July 1, 22, 1920; *San Marcos Record*, July 30, 1920; Hickey to Flowers, March 15, 1920, Hickey Papers.

96. Green, *Grass-Roots Socialism*, 346–47.

97. Andrews, "Black Working-Class Political Activism," 628, 640, 646–48.

98. *Dallas Morning News*, June 8, 1920; Andrews, "Black Working-Class Political Activism," 640–48, 652; *Dallas Morning News*, August 12, 1920, October 9, 1920; *Ferguson Forum*, October 21, 1920.

99. *Dallas Morning News*, July 13, 1920.

100. *Dallas Morning News*, July 18, 1920;

101. Hopkins to Hall, May 1, 1919, Hickey Papers; Breniman Report July 24, 1920, BI.

102. *Semi-weekly Farm News*, August 13, 1920; *Ferguson Forum*, August 12, 1920.

103. *Dallas Morning News*, August 12, October 9, 1920; *Ferguson Forum*, October 21, 1920.

104. *Dallas Morning News*, August 11, 1920; Andrews, "Black Working-Class Political Activism," 636, 654; Casdorth, *History of the Republican Party in Texas*, 5–6, 40.

105. *Ferguson Forum*, July 1, August 19, 1920; Andrews, "Black Working-Class Political Activism," 655.

106. *Ferguson Forum*, October 14, 1920.

107. *Dallas Morning News*, October 20, 1920, January 27, 1922; "Wurzbach, Harry Mcleary," *Handbook of Texas Online*, https://www.tshaonline.org/handbook/entries/wurzbach-harry-mcleary; US Census, *Census Reports*, 1920.

108. *Ferguson Forum*, November 18, 25, 1920; *Dallas Morning News*, November 4, 5, 7, 1920. In December 1920, after nine months on strike, dockworkers returned to work with a modest raise, though without a union and with an open shop (Andrews, "Black Working-Class Political Activism," 656, 661–62).

109. *Ferguson Forum*, November 18, 25, 1920; *Dallas Morning News*, November 4, 5, 7, 1920; Kamphoefner, "Handwriting," 54, 61, 64.

110. Hunt, *History of Farmer Movements*, 147.

111. Hunt, *History of Farmer Movements*, 145; quote from *Dallas Morning News*, August 2, 1921.

112. *Farm-Labor Union News*, September 18, 1925, quoted in Hunt, *History of Farmer Movements*, 146.

113. Hunt, *History of Farmer Movements*, 146; *Dallas Morning News*, March 15, 1922; Farm-Labor Union of America, *Constitution and By-laws of the Farm-Labor Union of America, March 1, 1924*; *Semi-weekly Farm News*, December 12, 1922; *Nonpartisan Leader*, June 28, 1920; Hall to Lemke, April 26, 1924, Lemke Papers.

114. *Constitution of the Farm-Labor Union of America*; *Semi-weekly Farm News*, December 24, 1920.

115. Alexander, *Crusade for Conformity*, 1, 5, 9, 13.

116. *Semi-weekly Farm News*, May 24, 1921; TSFL, *Twenty-Fourth Annual Convention, 1921*, 97–98; *Dallas Morning News*, May 18, 1921; *Semi-weekly Farm News*, February 22, June 24, 1921, July 12, 1921, January 17, March, 24, 1922.

117. *Semi-weekly Farm News*, April 22, May 10, 1922; *Ferguson Forum*, February 2, 1922.

118. Lansing, *Insurgent Democracy*, 233–39.

119. Hall to Lemke, December 10, 1921, Lemke Papers; *National Rip-Saw*, January 1922.

120. *Dallas Morning News*, October 30, 1921; TSFL, *Twenty-Fifth Annual Convention, 1922*, 45–46, quote on 46; *Semi-weekly Farm News*, April 25, 1922; *Ferguson Forum*, May 4, 1922.

121. *Semi-weekly Farm News*, February 10, April 25, 1922; Sanders, *Roots of Reform*, 415.

122. Anderson, "History of the Farm Labor Union in Texas," 15–16, 59, 97; *Semi-weekly Farm News*, May 19, 1922; Hunt, *History of Farmer Movements in the Southwest*, 162–82.

123. *Farm Labor Union News*, July 22, 1922 (This is the only known copy of this newspaper in existence and is held at the UT-Arlington labor archive. A two-year run of the *Farm Labor Union News* was lost by the US Department of Agriculture's history archive.) *Dallas Morning News*, July 13, 1922.

124. *Farm Labor Union News*, July 22, 1922.

125. Anderson, "History of the Farm Labor Union," 57, 65–66; *Dallas Morning News*, July 28, August 29, 1922; *Semi-weekly Hallettsville Herald*, October 31, 1924, November 12, 1926.

126. *Southwestern Railway Journal*, May 1922, 10, 15.

127. *Semi-weekly Farm News*, July 15, 18, 28, August 11, 1922; TSFL, *Twenty-Sixth Annual Convention, 1923*, 90.

128. *Semi-weekly Farm News*, August 8, 11, 18, September 5, 1922; *Locomotive Engineers Journal*, August 1922, 575; Green and Boston, "Looking for Lefty," in *Texas Left*, ed. Cullen and Wilkison, 115–16. Quote from *Semi-weekly Farm News*, August 18, 1922.

129. *Semi-weekly Farm News*, July 18, August 22, 1922; quote from *Ferguson Forum*, September 14, 1922; Anderson, "History of the Farm Labor Union," 59; *Dallas Morning News*, August 4, 5, 10, 1922.

130. *Houston Informer*, November 11, December 23, 1922, April 21, 28, 1923; Brown, *Hood, Bonnet, and Little Brown Jug*, 150; *Semi-weekly Farm News*, August 15, 1922.

131. *Semi-weekly Farm News*, June 5, 1923; Brown, *Hood, Bonnet, and Little Brown Jug*, 144–45, 149.

132. *Houston Informer*, April 21, 1923; Texas Legislature, *Journal of the House of Representatives of the First Called Session of the Thirty-Eighth Legislature*, 41–42, 53, 376–78, 446.

133. *National Rip-Saw*, September 1922; *American Vanguard*, March 1923.

134. Donohue, *Freedom from Want*, 4, 27, 187, 191, 198; *Semi-weekly Farm News*, March 31, 1922; TSFL, *Twenty-Sixth Annual Convention, 1923*, 46, 74; *Ogden Standard Examiner*, February 19, 1925.

135. *Dallas Morning News*, August 24, 1923.

136. Beck, "On This Date in 1924 Woodrow Wilson Died"; Johnston, "Long Live Teddy," 411–43.

Conclusion

1. Dyson, *Red Harvest*, 11.
2. Dyson, *Red Harvest*, 12–13.
3. Dyson, *Red Harvest*, 15.
4. Dyson, *Red Harvest*, 17–18.
5. *Milwaukee Leader*, April 11, May 16, 1924; Dyson, *Red Harvest*, 19.
6. *Milwaukee Leader*, April 15, 17, May 16, 1924; Dyson, *Red Harvest*, 23.
7. Mahoney, "Report of the National Farmer-Labor-Progressive Convention, 1924," Mahoney Papers, Minnesota Historical Society, Saint Paul, MN.
8. Mahoney, "Report"; Dyson, *Red Harvest*, 22–24.
9. Dyson, *Red Harvest*, 22–23.
10. *Semi-weekly Hallettsville Herald*, October 31, 1924; *Washington Post*, January 20, 1925.
11. Hall to Lemke, April 26, September 17, 1924, March 20, 1925, Lemke Papers; Hunt, *History of Farmer Movements*, 190–91.
12. Hall to Lemke, May 19, 1925, Lemke Papers.
13. *Dallas Morning News*, December 10, 1925.
14. *Semi-weekly Farm News*, January 5, 1926.
15. *United Farmer*, March 1, 1926; De Leon, *American Labor Who's Who*, 228.
16. Palmer, *James P. Cannon*, 238–39; *United Farmer*, March 1, November 1926, June 1927; Dyson, *Red Harvest*, 10, 34; *Dallas Morning News*, May 3, 1925.
17. Palmer, *James P. Cannon*, 260–65; Mahoney, "Report"; *Labor Defender*, January 1926. Meitzen was never a public member of the Workers Party or the later Communist Party. Meitzen and party leaders could have decided to keep his membership secret as a method of drawing radical farmers closer to the communist movement—a tactic they were known to employ. Although such a possibility exists, the available evidence makes it seem unlikely. Meitzen was presumably just a fellow traveler.
18. Palmer, *James P. Cannon*, 265.
19. Peter Gaupp to Tom Alter, July 5, 2010, email in author's possession; "Texas, World War I Records, 1917–1920," database, *FamilySearch*; Williams, *History of the Meitzen Family*, np; Hall to Lemke, November 5, 1925, Lemke Papers.
20. Hall to Lemke, December 5, 1926, February 9, 1929, Lemke Papers; Wynne and Knetsch, *Florida in the Great Depression*, 7. Only two issues and a few scattered clippings of the *Columbia Gazette* still exist.
21. Hall to Lemke, February 9, 1929, Lemke Papers; Williams, *History of the Meitzen Family*, np; Jo-Lou Gaupp, interview by the author, video recording, Arlington, Texas, July 12, 2008.
22. Lemke to Hall, July 3, 1929, Lemke Papers.
23. Hall to Lemke, July 14, 1929, Lemke Papers.
24. Hall to Lemke, September 23, 1929, Lemke Papers.
25. Schlesinger, *Crisis of the Old Order*, 103, 276–77.

26. Blackorby, *Prairie Rebel*, 185–86; Schlesinger, *Crisis of the Old Order*, 277; MacKay, *Progressive Movement of 1924*, 13.

27. Conkin, *Revolution*, 15, 68; Clark, "Agrarian Context of American Capitalist Development" in Zakin and Kornblith, *Capitalism Takes Command*, 15.

28. Meitzen, *Meitzen Type*, 18; Gaupp interview.

29. US Census, *Census Reports*, *1920*; *Weimar Mercury*, August 3, 1923; *Dallas Morning News*, February 21, March 15, June 9, 1928.

30. Gaupp interview; Meitzen-Williams, *History of the Meitzen Family*, np; *Shiner Gazette*, February 28, 1935.

31. "Rites For E. R. Meitzen Held Sunday," 1948 newspaper clipping in author's possession, given to him by Jo-Lou and Peter Gaupp (source and date of clipping indeterminable); Farris, "Re-enfranchisement of Negroes in Florida," 267–69.

32. US Census, *Census Reports*, 1930.

33. Email communication from William Meitzen, June 13, 2011; John Meitzen, "My Family History," unpublished paper, 1992, copy in author's possession, n.p.

34. Gaupp interview.

35. Gaupp interview; J. Meitzen, "My Family History."

36. Florida Secretary of State, *Tabulation of the Official Vote, Florida Primary Elections*, 11–12.

37. *Weimar Mercury*, May 14, 1943; *San Antonio Express*, October 8, 1943; Gaupp interview; Meitzen-Williams, *History of the Meitzen Family*.

38. Gaupp interview; *Galveston News*, November 28, 1948.

39. Meitzen, "E. R. Meitzen's Letter of Acceptance," Socialism File, Center for American History.

40. *Rebel*, November 11, 1916.

41. Marina Sitrin, "Horizontalism and the Occupy Movements," *Dissent*, Spring 2012, https://www.dissentmagazine.org/article/horizontalism-and-the-occupy-movements; Naomi Wolf, "Revealed: How the FBI Coordinated the Crackdown on Occupy," *Guardian*, December 29, 2012, https://www.theguardian.com/commentisfree/2012/dec/29/fbi-coordinated-crackdown-occupy.

42. Colin McMahon, "Trampled by Partisans," *Chicago Tribune*, November 5, 2012; Jeremy Scahill, "The Moral and Strategic Calculus of Voting for Joe Biden to Defeat Trump—or Not," *Intercept*, April 20, 2020, https://theintercept.com/2020/04/20/donald-trump-joe-biden-2020-presidential-election-voting/; Caitlin Johnstone, "Don't Fool Yourself: Your Biden Vote Was Not a 'Vote against Fascism,'" *Scoop Independent News*, November 6, 2020, https://www.scoop.co.nz/stories/HL2011/S00039/dont-fool-yourself-your-biden-vote-was-not-a-vote-against-fascism.htm; Bob Buzzanco, "Hysteria about Fascism and Coups Hurts the Left," *Afflict the Comfortable (The Mind of Bob Buzzanco)*, November 18, 2020, https://afflictthecomfortable.org/2020/11/18/hysteria-about-fascism-and-coups-hurt-the-left/.

43. *Radical Abolitionist*, October, November 1858; *New York Daily Times*, April 12, 1856; Lause, *Long Road*, 181.

44. *National Co-operator and Farm Journal*, April 10, 1907.

Bibliography

Archives and Manuscripts

Archives of Labor and Urban Affairs, Wayne State University, Detroit, Michigan.
Archiwum Panstwowe we Wroclawiu, Wroclaw, Poland.
Austin History Center, Austin, Texas.
Cunningham Library, Indiana State University, Terre Haute, Indiana.
DeGolyer Library, Southern Methodist University, Dallas, Texas.
Dolph Briscoe Center for American History, University of Texas at Austin.
Elwyn B. Robinson Department of Special Collections, Chester Fritz Library, University of North Dakota, Grand Forks, North Dakota.
Fayette Public Library, Museum and Archives, La Grange, Texas.
Fred J. Reynolds Historical Genealogy Department, Allen County Public Library, Fort Wayne, Indiana.
Geheimes Staatsarchiv Preußischer Kulturbesitz, Berlin, Germany.
Houston Metropolitan Research Center, Houston, Texas.
Local History Center, La Retama Central Library, Corpus Christi, Texas.
Minnesota Historical Society, Saint Paul, Minnesota.
National Archives and Records Administration, Washington, DC.
New York Public Library, Manuscripts and Archives Division, New York, New York.
Research Collections and Preservation Consortium, Columbia University, New York, New York.
Special Collections Research Center, Joseph Regenstein Library, University of Chicago.
Southwest Collection/Special Collections Library, Texas Tech University, Lubbock, Texas.
State Library and Archives of Florida, Florida Department of State, Tallahassee, Florida.
Texas Department of State Health Services, Austin, Texas.
Texas Labor Archives, Library Special Collections, University of Texas at Arlington.
Texas State Library and Archives Commission, Texas Secretary of State, Archives and Information Services Division, Austin, Texas.
Universitätsarchiv, Humboldt Universität zu Berlin, Berlin, Germany.

Victoria Regional History Center, Victoria College/UH-Victoria Library, Victoria, Texas.

Newspapers and Organizational Publications

Abilene Daily Reporter
American Socialist (Chicago, Illinois)
American Vanguard (Leesville, Louisiana)
Appeal to Reason (Girard, Kansas)
Augusta (Georgia) *Chronicle*
Austin Daily Statesman
Bastrop (Texas) *Advertiser*
Der Bote aus dem Katzenbachthale (Liegnitz, Prussia)
Brownsville (Texas) *Daily Herald*
Chicago Defender
Childress (Texas) *Post*
Cincinnati Enquirer
Colorado Citizen (Columbus, Texas)
Columbia Gazette (Lake City, Florida)
Countryman (Bellville, Texas)
Crockett (Texas) *Courier*
Cuero (Texas) *Daily Record*
Daily Picayune (New Orleans, Louisiana)
Dallas Morning News
Decentralizer (Hallettsville, Texas)
Denton (Texas) *Record Chronicle*
Der Demokrat (Liegnitz, Prussia)
El Paso Herald
Farm Labor Union News (Bonham, Texas)
Ferguson Forum (Temple, Texas)
Galveston Daily News
Hallettsville (Texas) *Herald*
Hallettsville (Texas) *New Era*
Houston Chronicle
Houston Informer
Houston Labor Journal
Houston Post
Houston Review
I & N Reporter
International Socialist Review (Chicago, Illinois)
Kansas City (Missouri) *Star*
Labor Defender (Chicago, Illinois)
Laborer (Dallas, Texas)
La Grange (Texas) *Journal*
Laredo (Texas) *Weekly Times*
Liberator (New York, New York)

Locomotive Engineers Journal (Cleveland, Ohio)
Louisville Courier-Journal
Memphis Commercial Appeal
Milwaukee Leader
Nashville American
Nashville Tennessean
National Co-operator and Farm Journal (Dallas, Texas)
National Rip-Saw (Saint Louis, Missouri)
Neue Rheinische Zeitung
New York Daily Times
New York Herald
New York Times
Nonpartisan Leader/National Leader (Fargo, North Dakota; Saint Paul and Minneapolis, Minnesota)
Norton's Union Intelligencer (Dallas, Texas)
Obzor (Hallettsville, Texas)
Ogden (Utah) *Standard Examiner*
Pearson's Magazine (New York, New York).
People's Advocate (Austin, Texas)
Provoker (Chicago, Illinois)
Radical Abolitionist (New York)
The Rebel (Hallettsville, Texas)
Saint Louis Globe-Democrat
San Antonio Express
San Antonio Light
San Antonio Texan
San Antonio Zeitung
San Francisco Chronicle
Sangerton (Texas) *News*
San Marcos Record
Schulenburg (Texas) *Sticker*
Semi-weekly Farm News (Dallas, Texas)
Semi-weekly Hallettsville (Texas) *Herald*
Sherman Daily Democrat
Shiner (Texas) *Gazette*
Socialist Party Official Bulletin (Chicago, Illinois)
Socialist Woman (Chicago, Illinois; Girard, Kansas)
Social Revolution (St. Louis, Missouri)
Southern Mercury (Dallas, Texas)
Southern Mercury United with the Farmers Union Password (Dallas, Texas)
Southland Farmer (La Porte and Houston, Texas)
Southwestern Railway Journal (Fort Worth, Texas)
Spokesman Review (Spokane, Washington)
States Rights Democrat (La Grange, Texas)

Temple (Texas) *Daily Telegram*
Texas Advance (Dallas, Texas)
Texas Capital (Austin, Texas)
Texas Monument (La Grange, Texas)
Texas Vorwärts (Austin, Texas)
Times-Picayune (New Orleans, Louisiana)
True Issue (La Grange, Texas)
United Farmer (Bismarck, North Dakota)
Washington American (Washington, Texas)
Washington Post (District of Columbia)
Weekly Democratic Statesman (Austin, Texas)
Weimar (Texas) *Mercury*
Workmen's Advocate (New Haven, Connecticut)
Yorktown (Texas) *News*

Books, Articles, and Other Publications

Abramowitz, Jack. "The Negro in the Populist Movement." *Journal of Negro History* 38, no. 3 (July 1953): 257–89.

Addington, Wendell G. "Slave Insurrections in Texas." *Journal of Negro History* 35, no. 4 (1950): 408–34.

Alexander, Charles C. *The Crusade for Conformity: The Ku Klux Klan in Texas, 1920–1930*. Houston: Texas Gulf Coast Historical Association, 1962.

Ali, Omar H. *In the Lion's Mouth: Black Populism in the New South, 1886–1900*. Jackson: University of Mississippi Press, 2010.

Allen, Ruth. *Chapters in the History of Organized Labor in Texas*. Austin: University of Texas Press, 1941.

Anderson, Robert E. "The History of the Farm Labor Union in Texas." MA thesis, University of Texas–Austin, 1928.

Andrews, Gregg. "Black Working-Class Political Activism and Biracial Unionism: Galveston Longshoremen in Jim Crow Texas, 1919–1921." *Journal of Southern History* 74, no. 3 (August 2008): 627–68.

Baggett, James Alex. "The Constitutional Union Party in Texas." *Southwestern Historical Quarterly* 82, no. 3 (January 1979): 233–64.

Baker, T. Lindsay. *The First Polish Americans: Silesian Settlements in Texas*. College Station: Texas A&M University Press, 1979.

Barnes, Donna A. *Farmers in Rebellion: The Rise and Fall of the Southern Farmers Alliance and People's Party in Texas*. Austin: University of Texas Press, 1984.

Barr, Alwyn. *Reconstruction to Reform: Texas Politics, 1876–1906*. Dallas: Southern Methodist University Press, 2000.

Basen, Neil K. "'Jennie Higginses' of the 'New South in the West.'" In *Flawed Liberation: Socialism and Feminism*, edited by Sally M. Miller. Westport, CT: Greenwood, 1981.

Baulch, Joe R. "Making West Texas Safe for Democracy: The 1917 Farmers and Laborers Protective Association Conspiracy." *West Texas Historical Association Yearbook* 62 (1986): 119–30.

Baum, Dale. *The Shattering of Texas Unionism: Politics in the Lone Star State during the Civil War Era*. Baton Rouge: Louisiana State University, 1998.

Beck, Glenn. "On this Date in 1924 Woodrow Wilson Died." *GlennBeck.com*, February 03, 2012. http://www.glennbeck.com/2012/02/03/on-this-date-in-1924-woodrow-wilson-died/.

Bellamy, Edward. *Looking Backward: 2000–1887*. Boston: Ticknor, 1888.

Bennett, Ira E. *History of the Panama Canal, Its Construction and Builders*. Washington, DC: Historical Publishing, 1915.

Berding, Helmut, ed. *Soziale Unruhen in Deutschland während der französischen Revolution*. Göttingen, Ger.: Vandenhoeck and Ruprecht, 1988.

Biesele, Rudolph Leopold. *The History of the German Settlements in Texas, 1831–1861*. Austin: Von Boeckmann-Jones, 1930.

———. "The Texas State Convention of Germans in 1854," *Southwestern Historical Quarterly* 23, no. 4 (April 1930): 247–61.

Blackbourn, David. "Discreet Charm of the Bourgeoisie." In *Peculiarities of German History*, edited by David Blackbourn and Geoff Eley, 159–292. Oxford: Oxford University Press, 1984.

———. *The Long Nineteenth Century: A History of Germany, 1780–1918*. New York: Oxford University Press, 1998.

Blackorby, Edward C. *Prairie Rebel: The Public Life of William Lemke*. Lincoln: University of Nebraska Press, 1963.

Bleiber, Helmut. "Germany, September Crisis." In *Encyclopedia of 1848 Revolutions* [online], ed. James Chastain. https://www.ohio.edu/chastain/dh/germsept.htm.

Boethel, Paul C. *The Big Guns of Fayette*. Austin, TX: Von Boeckman-Jones, 1965.

———. *LaBaca*. Columbus, TX: Butler Office Supply and Printing Company, 1997.

———. *The Lavacans*. Columbus, TX: Butler Office Supply and Printing Company, 1991.

Bramsted, Ernest K. *Aristocracy and the Middle-Classes in Germany: Social Types in German Literature, 1830–1900*. Chicago: University of Chicago Press, 1964.

Brown, Norman D. *Hood, Bonnet, and Little Brown Jug: Texas Politics, 1921–1928*. College Station, TX: Texas A&M University Press, 1984.

Buckingham, Peter. *"Red Tom" Hickey, the Uncrowned King of Texas Socialism*. College Station: Texas A&M University Press, 2020.

Buenger, Walter L., and Walter D. Kamphoefner, eds., *Preserving German Texan Identity: Reminiscences of William A. Trenckman, 1859–1935*. College Station: Texas A&M University Press, 2018.

Buhle, Mari Jo. *Women and American Socialism, 1870–1920*. Urbana: University of Illinois Press, 1981.

Burwood, Stephen. "Debsian Socialism through a Transnational Lens." *Journal of the Gilded Age and Progressive Era* 2, No. 3 (July 2003): 253–82.

Buzzanco, Bob. "Hysteria about Fascism and Coups Hurts the Left." *Afflict the Comfortable (The Mind of Bob Buzzanco)*, November 18, 2020. https://afflictthecomfortable.org/2020/11/18/hysteria-about-fascism-and-coups-hurt-the-left/.

Bynum, Victoria E. *The Long Shadow of the Civil War: Southern Dissent and Its Legacies*. Chapel Hill: University of North Carolina Press, 2010.

Cantrell, Gregg. *Kenneth and John B. Rayner and the Limits of Southern Dissent.* Urbana: University of Illinois Press, 1993.

———. "'Our Very Pronounced Theory of Equal Rights to All': Race, Citizenship, and Populism in the South Texas Borderlands." *Journal of American History* 100, no. 3 (December 2013): 663–90.

Cantrell, Gregg, and D. Scott Barton. "Texas Populists and the Failure of Biracial Politics." *Journal of Southern History* 55, no. 4 (November 1989): 659–92.

Cardwell, John. *Sketches of Legislators and State Officers, 1876–1878.* Austin, TX: Democratic Statesmen Print, 1876.

Carsten, Frances Ludwig. *A History of the Prussian Junkers.* Aldershot, UK: Scolar, 1989.

Carter, Emily Suzanne, and Crystal Sasse Ragsdale. *Biegel Settlement: Historic Sites Research, Fayette Power Project.* Austin: Texas Archeological Survey/University of Texas at Austin, 1976.

Casdorth, Paul. *A History of the Republican Party in Texas, 1865–1965.* Austin, TX: Pemberton, 1965.

Case, Theresa A. *The Great Southwest Railroad Strike and Free Labor.* College Station: Texas A&M University Press, 2010.

Clark, Christopher. "The Agrarian Context of American Capitalist Development." In *Capitalism Takes Command: The Social Transformation of Nineteenth-Century America*, edited by Michael Zakin and Gary Kornblith, 13–37. Chicago: University of Chicago Press, 2012.

Cockcroft, James D. *Intellectual Precursors of the Mexican Revolution, 1900–1913.* Austin: University of Texas Press, 1968.

Cohen, Nancy. *The Reconstruction of American Liberalism, 1865–1914.* Chapel Hill: University of North Carolina Press, 2002.

Conkin, Paul K. *A Revolution Down on the Farm: The Transformation of American Agriculture since 1929.* Lexington: University Press of Kentucky, 2008.

Cullen, David O'Donald, and Kyle G. Wilkison, eds. *The Texas Left: The Radical Roots of Lone Star Liberalism.* College Station: Texas A&M University Press, 2010.

Davies, Norman, and Roger Moorhouse. *Microcosm: Portrait of a Central European City.* London: Pimlico, 2003.

Davis, Stephen. "Joseph Jay Pastoriza and the Single Tax in Houston, 1911–1917." *Houston Review* 8, no. 2 (1986): 56–78.

De Leon, Solon, ed. *The American Labor Who's Who.* New York: Hanford, 1925.

Demshuk, Andrew. Review of *Nation and Loyalty in a German-Polish Borderland: Upper Silesia, 1848–1960*, by Brendan Karch. *German Studies Review* 42, no. 3 (October 2019): 601–3.

Dobie, J. Frank. *Coronado's Children: Tales of Lost Mines and Buried Treasures of the Southwest.* Austin: University of Texas Press, 2011.

Donohue, Kathleen G. *Freedom from Want: American Liberalism and the Idea of the Consumer.* Baltimore, MD: Johns Hopkins University Press, 2003.

Dunning, Nelson A., ed. *Farmers' Alliance History and Agricultural Digest.* Washington, DC: Alliance, 1891.

Durden, Robert F. *The Climax of Populism: The Election of 1896*. Lexington: University Press of Kentucky, 1965.

Dyson, Lowell K. *Red Harvest: The Communist Party and American Farmers*. Lincoln: University of Nebraska Press, 1982.

Engels, Frederick. *Revolution and Counter-revolution in Germany*. Peking: Foreign Language Press, 1977.

Farris, Charles D. "The Re-enfranchisment of Negroes in Florida." *Journal of Negro History* 39, no. 4 (October 1954): 259–83.

Foley, Neil. *The White Scourge: Mexicans, Blacks, and Poor Whites in Texas Cotton Culture*. Berkeley: University of California Press, 1997.

Foner, Philip S. *The Great Labor Uprising of 1877*. New York: Pathfinder, 1991.

———, ed. *Clara Zetkin Selected Writings*. Chicago: Haymarket, 2015.

George, Henry. *Progress and Poverty: An Inquiry into the Cause of Industrial Depressions and of Increase of Want with Increase of Wealth; The Remedy*. New York: D. Appleton, 1879.

Geue, Ethel Hander. *New Homes in a New Land: German Immigration to Texas, 1847–1861*. Baltimore, MD: Clearfield, 1970.

Ginger, Ray. *The Bending Cross: A Biography of Eugene V. Debs*. Chicago: Haymarket, 2007.

Gish, Theodore G. Introduction to *Texas in 1848*, by Viktor Bracht. San Marcos, TX: German-Texan Heritage Society, 1991.

Goethe, Johann Wolfgang von. *Wilhelm Meister's Apprenticeship and Travels*. trans. Thomas Carlyle. London: Chapman and Hall, 1893.

Gomez-Quiñones, Juan. *Sembradores, Ricardo Flores Magon y el Partido Liberal Mexicano: A Eulogy and Critique*. Los Angeles: Aztlan/University of California—Los Angeles Chicano Studies Center, 1973.

Goodwyn, Lawrence. *The Democratic Promise: The Populist Moment in America*. New York: Oxford University Press, 1976.

———. *The Populist Moment: A Short History of the Agrarian Revolt in America*. New York: Oxford University Press, 1978.

Gould, Lewis L. *Progressives and Prohibitionists: Texas Democrats in the Wilson Era*. Austin: University of Texas Press, 1973.

Green, James R. *Grass-Roots Socialism: Radical Movements in the Southwest, 1895–1943*. Baton Rouge: Louisiana State University Press, 1978.

———. "Socialism and the Southwestern Class Struggle, 1898–1918: A Study of Radical Movements in Oklahoma, Texas, Louisiana, and Arkansas." PhD diss., Yale University, 1972.

———. "Tenant Farmer Discontent and Socialist Protest in Texas, 1901–1917." *Southwestern Historical Quarterly* 81, no. 2 (October 1977): 133–54.

Greene, Julie. *Pure and Simple Politics: The American Federation of Labor and Political Activism, 1881–1917*. Cambridge: Cambridge University Press, 1998.

Haber, Stephen H. *Industry and Underdevelopment: The Industrialization of Mexico, 1890–1940*. Stanford, CA: Stanford University Press, 1989.

Hahn, Hans Joachim. *The 1848 Revolutions in German-Speaking Europe*. New York: Pearson Education, 2001.

Hall, Covington. *Labor Struggles of the Deep South & Other Writings*, edited by David R. Roediger. Chicago: Charles H. Kerr, 1999.

Hamilton, C. Horace. "Texas Farm Tenure Activities." *Journal of Land and Public Utility Economics* 14, no. 3 (August 1938): 330–33.

Harris, Charles H., and Louis R. Sadler. *The Texas Rangers and the Mexican Revolution: The Bloodiest Decade, 1910–1920*. Albuquerque: University of New Mexico Press, 2004.

Hart, John Mason. *Revolutionary Mexico: The Coming and Process of the Mexican Revolution*. Berkeley: University of California Press, 1987.

Henderson, William Otto. *The Life and Times of Friedrich Engels*. Vol. 1. London: Frank Cass, 1976.

———. *The Rise of German Industrial Power, 1834–1914*. Berkeley: University of California Press, 1975.

Hicks, John D. *The Populist Revolt: A History of the Farmer's Alliance and the People's Party*. Lincoln: University of Nebraska Press, 1961.

Hild, Matthew. *Greenbackers, Knights of Labor, and Populists: Farmer-Labor Insurgency in the Late-Nineteenth-Century South*. Athens: University of Georgia Press, 2007.

———. "The Knights of Labor and the Third Party Movement in Texas, 1886–1896," *Southwestern Historical Quarterly* 119, no. 1 (July 2015): 25–43.

Hildebrandt, Adolf Matthias, Maximilian Gritzner, and Gustav A. Seyler, eds. *Siebmacher's Grosses und Allgemeines Wappenbuch*. 82 vols. Nuremberg, Ger.: Bauer und Raspe, 1854–1967.

Hine, Darlene Clark. *Black Victory: The Rise and Fall of the White Primary in Texas*. New ed. Columbia: University of Missouri Press, 2003.

Hofstadter, Richard. *The Age of Reform: From Bryan to FDR*. New York: Vintage, 1955.

Holmgren, Ida. *Family Tree Book of the Holmgrens and the Meitzens*. Hallettsville, TX: New Era, 1901.

Honeck, Mischa. *We Are the Revolutionists: German-Speaking Immigrants and American Abolitionists after 1848*. Athens: University of Georgia Press, 2011.

Höpfner, Günther. "Ness von Esenbeck (1776–1858)—ein deutscher Gelehrter an der Seite der Arbeiter." In *Beiträge zur Nachmärz-Forschung*, 9–102. Schriften aus dem Karl-Marx-Haus No. 47. Trier, Ger.: Karl-Marx-Haus, 1994.

Hunt, Robert Lee. *A History of Farmer Movements in the Southwest, 1873–1925*. College Station: A. and M. Press, A. and M. College of Texas, 1935.

Johnson, Benjamin Heber. *Revolution in Texas: How a Forgotten Rebellion and Its Bloody Suppression Turned Mexicans into Americans*. New Haven, CT: Yale University Press, 2003.

Johnson, Frank W. *A History of Texas and Texans*. Chicago: American Historical Society, 1916.

Johnston, Robert D. "Long Live Teddy / Death to Woodrow: The Polarized Politics of the Progressive Era in the 2012 Election," *Journal of the Gilded Age and Progressive Era* 13, no. 3 (July 2014): 411–43.

———. *The Radical Middle Class: Populist Democracy and the Question of Capitalism in Progressive Era Portland, Oregon*. Princeton, NJ: Princeton University Press, 2003.

Johnstone, Caitlin. "Don't Fool Yourself: Your Biden Vote Was Not a 'Vote against Fascism.'" *Scoop Independent News*, November 6, 2020, https://www.scoop.co.nz/stories/HL2011/S00039/dont-fool-yourself-your-biden-vote-was-not-a-vote-against-fascism.htm.

Jordan, Terry G. *German Seed in Texas Soil: Immigrant Farmers in Nineteenth-Century Texas*. Austin: University of Texas Press, 1966.

Kamphoefner, Walter D. "The Handwriting on the Wall: The Klan, Language Issues, and Prohibition in the German Settlements of Eastern Texas." *Southwestern Historical Quarterly* 112, no. 1 (July 2008): 52–66.

———. "New Americans or New Southerners? Unionist German Texans." In *Lone Star Unionism, Dissent, and Resistance: The Other Civil-War Texas*, edited by J. Frank de la Teja, 101–22. Norman: University of Oklahoma Press, 2016.

———. "New Perspectives on Texas Germans and the Confederacy." *Southwestern Historical Quarterly* 102, no. 4 (April 1999): 440–55.

Katz, Friedrich. *The Life and Times of Pancho Villa*. Stanford, CA: Stanford University Press, 1989.

Kipnis, Ira. *The American Socialist Movement, 1897–1912*. Chicago: Haymarket, 2004.

Kistler, Mark O. "German-American Liberalism and Thomas Paine." *American Quarterly* 14, no. 1 (Spring 1962): 81–91.

Kitchen, Martin. *Cambridge Illustrated History of Germany*. Cambridge: Cambridge University Press, 2000.

Knight, Alan. *The Mexican Revolution*. 2 vols. Lincoln: University of Nebraska Press, 1986, 1990.

Kohn, Stephen M. *American Political Prisoners: Prosecutions under the Espionage and Sedition Acts*. Westport, CT: Praeger, 1994.

Kraffert, Adalbert Herman. *Geschichte des evangelischen Gymnasiums zu Liegnitz*. Legnica, Pol.: DrückVon H. Krumbhaar, 1869.

Lambert, Will. *Pocket Directory of the Seventeenth Legislature of Texas*. Austin, TX: Swindells' Book and Job Office, 1881.

Lansing, Michael. *Insurgent Democracy: The Nonpartisan League in North American Politics*. Chicago: University of Chicago Press, 2015.

Lause, Mark. *Long Road to Harper's Ferry: The Rise of the First American Left*. London: Pluto, 2018.

———. *Young America: Land, Labor, and the Republican Community*. Urbana: University of Illinois Press, 2005.

Levine, Bruce. *The Spirit of 1848: German Immigrants, Labor Conflict, and the Coming of the Civil War*. Urbana: University of Illinois Press, 1992.

Lich, Glen E., and Dona B. Reeves, ed. *German Culture in Texas: A Free Earth; Essays from the 1978 Southwest Symposium*. Boston: Twayne, 1980.

Lotto, Frank. *Fayette County: Her History and Her People*. Schulenburg, TX: self-published, 1902.

Lundberg, John R. *Granbury's Texas Brigade: Diehard Western Confederates*. Baton Rouge: Louisiana State University Press, 2012.

MacKay, Kenneth Campbell. *The Progressive Movement of 1924*. New York: Columbia University Press, 1947.

MacLachlan, Colin M. *Anarchism and the Mexican Revolution: The Political Trials of Ricardo Flores Magón in the United States*. Berkeley: University of California Press, 1991.

Martin, Roscoe. "The Grange as a Political Factor in Texas." *Southwestern Political and Social Science Quarterly* 6 (1925–1926): 363–83.

———. "The Greenback Party in Texas." *Southwestern Historical Quarterly* 30, no. 3. (January 1927): 161–77.

———. *The People's Party in Texas: A Study in Third-Party Politics*. Austin: University of Texas Press, 1933.

Martinez, Monica Muñoz. *The Injustice Never Leaves You: Anti-Mexican Violence in Texas*. Cambridge, MA: Harvard University Press, 2018.

Marx, Karl. *Capital*, vol. 1. Translated by Ben Fowkes. New York: Vintage, 1977.

Marx, Karl, and Frederick Engels. *Collected Works*. 50 vols. Moscow: Progress, 1977, 1989.

———. *The Communist Manifesto*. New York: Pathfinder, 1990.

Mattheisen, Donald J. "Voters and Parliaments in the German Revolution of 1848: An Analysis of the Prussian Constituent Assembly," *Central European History* 5, no. 1 (March 1972): 3–22.

McCaa, Robert. *Missing Millions: The Human Cost of the Mexican Revolution*. Minneapolis: University of Minnesota Population Center, 2001.

McCaffrey, James M. *This Band of Heroes: Granbury's Texas Brigade, C.S.A.* Austin, TX: Eakin, 1985.

McCartin, Joseph A. *Labor's Great War: The Struggle for Industrial Democracy and the Origins of Modern American Labor Relations, 1912–1921*. Chapel Hill: University of North Carolina Press, 1997.

McGowen, Stanley S. "Battle or Massacre?: The Incident on the Nueces, August 10, 1862," *Southwestern Historical Quarterly* 104, no. 1 (July, 2000): 64–86.

McKee, Thomas. *The National Conventions and Platforms of All Political Parties, 1789 to 1904*, fifth ed. Baltimore, MD: Friedenwald, 1904.

McMahon, Colin. "Trampled by Partisans," *Chicago Tribune*, November 5, 2012.

McMath, Robert C. Jr. *American Populism: A Social History, 1877–1898*. New York: Hill and Wang, 1992.

———. *Populist Vanguard: A History of the Southern Farmers' Alliance*. New York: W. W. Norton, 1975.

McWilliams, Carey. *North from Mexico: The Spanish-Speaking People of the United States*. New York: Greenwood, 1968.

Meitzen, John. "The Meitzen Type: The Texas Socialist Party and E. O. Meitzen." unpublished paper, University of Texas–Austin, 2001.

Messer-Kruse, Timothy. *The Yankee International: Marxism and the American Reform Tradition, 1846–1876*. Chapel Hill: University of North Carolina Press, 1998.

Miller, Robert Worth. "Building a Progressive Coalition in Texas: The Populist-Reform Democrat Rapprochement, 1900–1907." *Journal of Southern History* 52, no. 2 (May 1986): 163–82.

Moneyhon, Carl H. *Republicanism in Reconstruction Texas*. College Station: Texas A&M University Press, 1980.

———. *Texas after the Civil War: The Struggle of Reconstruction*. College Station: Texas A&M University Press, 2004.

Montgomery, David. *The Fall of the House of Labor: The Workplace, the State, and American Labor Activism, 1865–1925*. Cambridge: Cambridge University Press, 1987.

Ness, Immanuel, and Dario Azzellini, eds. *Ours to Master and to Own: Workers' Control from the Commune to the Present*. Chicago: Haymarket, 2011.

Nichols, John. *The "S" Word, a Short History of an American Tradition . . . Socialism*. New York: Verso, 2015.

Nietsche, Benno. *Geschichte der Stadt Gleiwitz*. Gliwice, Pol : Paul Raschdorff, 1886.

Noyes, P. H. *Organization and Revolution: Working Class Associations and the German Revolutions of 1848–1849*. Princeton, NJ: Princeton University Press, 1966.

Nugent, Walter. *Tolerant Populists: Kansas Populism and Nativism*. Chicago: University of Chicago Press, 1963.

Olmsted, Frederick Law. *A Journey through Texas: Or a Saddle-Trip on the Southwestern Frontier*. Lincoln: University of Nebraska Press, 2004.

Palmer, Bryan D. *James P. Cannon and the Origins of the American Revolutionary Left, 1890–1928*. Urbana: University of Illinois Press, 2007.

Pearsons, Warren M., Pierson M. Tuttle, and Edwin Frickey. "Business and Financial Conditions following the Civil War in the United States." *Review of Economics and Statistics* 2, suppl. 2 (July 1920): 5–21.

Pierce, Michael. *Striking with the Ballot: Ohio Labor and the Populist Party*. Dekalb: Northern Illinois University Press, 2010.

Postel, Charles. *The Populist Vision*. Oxford: Oxford University Press, 2007.

Prokhorov, Alexander, ed. *Great Soviet Encyclopedia*. 3rd ed. New York: Macmillan, 1973.

Prycer, Melissa. "'Not Organizing for the Fun of It': Suffrage, War, and Dallas Women in 1918." *Legacies* 31, no.1 (Spring 2019): 26–35.

Raat, W. Dirk. *Revoltosos: Mexico's Rebels in the United States, 1903–1923*. College Station: Texas A&M University Press, 1981.

Radek, Karl. "Theses on Tactics and Strategy." In *To the Masses: Proceedings of the Third Congress of the Communist International, 1921*, edited by John Riddell, 936–38. Chicago: Haymarket, 2015.

Randers-Pehrson, Justine Davis. *Adolf Douai, 1819–1888: The Turbulent Life of a German Forty-Eighter in the Homeland and the United States*. New York: Peter Lang, 2000.

Reed, John. *Insurgent Mexico*. New York: International, 2006.

Reichstein, Andreas. *German Pioneers on the American Frontier: The Wagners in Texas and Illinois*. Denton: University of North Texas Press, 2001.

Reynolds, Donald E. *Texas Terror: The Slave Insurrection Panic of 1860 and Secession*. Baton Rouge: Louisiana State University Press, 2007.

Riddell, John, ed. *To the Masses: Proceedings of the Third Congress of the Communist International, 1921*.Chicago: Haymarket, 2015.

———. *Toward the United Front: Proceedings of the Fourth Congress of the Communist International, 1922*. Chicago: Haymarket, 2011.

Salvatore, Nick. *Eugene V. Debs: Citizen and Socialist*. Urbana: University of Illinois Press, 1984.

Sanders, Elizabeth. *Roots of Reform: Farmers, Workers, and the American State, 1877–1917*. Chicago: University of Chicago Press, 1999.

Sandos, James A. *Rebellion in the Borderlands: Anarchism and the Plan of San Diego, 1904–1923*, Norman: University of Oklahoma Press, 1992.

Scahill, Jeremy. "The Moral and Strategic Calculus of Voting for Joe Biden to Defeat Trump—or Not," *Intercept*, April 20, 2020, https://theintercept.com/2020/04/20/donald-trump-joe-biden-2020-presidential-election-voting/.

Schlesinger, Arthur M. Jr. *The Crisis of the Old Order, 1919–1933*. Vol. 1 of *The Age of Roosevelt*. Boston: Houghton Mifflin, 1957.

Schmidt, Walter. "Die Matthäi-Brüder: Lebenswege dreier schlesischer Burschenschafter im 19. Jahrhundert." In *Abhandlungen der Leibniz-Sozietät der Wissenschaften*. Vol. 25, *Von Aufklärung bis Zweifel*. Beiträge zu Philosophie, Geschichte und Philosophiegeschichte. Festschrift für Siegfried Wollgast. Edited by Gerhard Banse, Herbert Hörz, and Heinz Liebscher, 325–63. Berlin: Trafo, 2008.

———. "Moritz Eisner und die 1848er Demokratie in Schlesien." *Leibniz-Sozietät/Sitzungsberichte* 63 (2004): 19–53.

———. *Die schlesische Demokratie von 1848–49, Geschichte und Akteure*. 2 vols. Berlin: Trafo, 2012.

———. *Wilhelm Wolff: Kampfgefährte und Freund von Marx und Engels, 1846–1864*. Berlin: Dietz, 1979.

———. *Wilhelm Wolff: Sein Weg zum Kommunisten, 1809–1846*. Berlin: Dietz, 1963.

Schmidt, Walter, Gerhard Becker, Helmut Bleiber, Rolf Dlubek, Siegfried Schmidt, and Rolf Weber. *Illustrierte Geschichte der deutschen Revolution 1848–49*. Berlin: Dietz, 1975.

Shannon, David A. *The Socialist Party of America*. Chicago: Quadrangle, 1967.

Siemering, August. *Die Deutschen in Texas waehrend des Buergerkrieges/The Germans in Texas during the Civil War*, edited by William Paul Burrier Sr. Plantation, FL: Llumina, 2013.

Sitrin, Marina. "Horizontalism and the Occupy Movements." *Dissent*, Spring 2012. https://www.dissentmagazine.org/article/horizontalism-and-the-occupy-movements.

Smith, Ralph A. "The Grange Movement in Texas, 1873–1900." *Southwestern Historical Quarterly* 42, no. 4 (April 1939): 297–315.

Smith, Sam. "Battle of Arkansas Post." *American Battlefield Trust*. https://www.battlefields.org/learn/articles/battle-arkansas-post.

Sperber, Jonathan. *The European Revolutions, 1848–1851*. Cambridge: Cambridge University Press, 1994.

Stromquist, Shelton. *Reinventing "The People": The Progressive Movement, the Class Problem, and the Origins of Modern Liberalism*. Urbana: University of Illinois Press, 2006.

Taber, Mike, ed. *The Communist Movement at the Crossroads: Plenums of the Communist International's Executive Committee, 1922–1923*. Chicago: Haymarket, 2019.

Texas, State of. *Directory of the Members and Officers of the Fourteenth Legislature of the State of Texas and also the State Officers of the State of Texas*. Austin: Caldwell and Walker, 1874.

———. *Journal of the House of Representatives of the State of Texas: Being the Session of the Thirteenth Legislature Begun and Held at the City of Austin, January 14, 1873.* Austin: John Cardwell, 1873.

———. *Journal of the House of Representatives of the Regular Session of the Thirtieth Legislature of Texas Convened at the City of Austin January 8, 1907 and Adjourned without Day, April 12, 1907.* Austin: Von Boeckmann-Jones, 1907.

———. *Journal of the House of Representatives of the Regular Session of the Thirty-Fourth Legislature, Convened January 12, 1915, and Adjourned March 20, 1915.* Austin: Von Boeckmann-Jones, 1915.

———. *Journal of the House of Representatives of the First Called Session of the Thirty-Eighth Legislature, Begun and Held at the City of Austin, March 15, 1923.* Austin: Von Boeckmann-Jones, 1923.

———. *Journal of the Senate of Texas: Being the Session of the Thirteenth Legislature Begun and Held at the City of Austin, January 14, 1873.* Austin: John Cardwell, 1873.

———. *Journal of the Senate of Texas: Being the Session of the Fourteenth Legislature Begun and Held at the City of Austin, January 13, 1874.* Austin: Cardwell and Walker, 1874.

———. *Texas Almanac and State Industrial Guide, 1904.* Galveston: A. H. Belo, 1904.

Thompson, E. P. *The Making of the English Working Class.* New York: Penguin, 1991.

Tolzman, Don Heinrich, ed. *The German-American Forty-Eighters, 1848–1998.* Bloomington: Indiana University Printing Services, 1997.

US Bureau of the Census, Department of Commerce. *Cotton Production and Distribution, Season of 1914–15.* Bulletin 131. Washington, DC: Government Printing Office, 1915.

———. Eighth Census of the United States Taken in the Year 1860. Census Reports. Washington, DC: US Bureau of the Census, 1864.

———. Ninth Census of the United States Taken in the Year 1870. Census Reports. Washington, DC: US Bureau of the Census, 1871.

———. Tenth Census of the United States Taken in the Year 1880. Census Reports. Washington, DC: US Bureau of the Census, 1888.

———. Eleventh Census of the United States Taken in the Year 1890. Census Reports. Washington, DC: US Bureau of the Census, 1891.

———. Twelfth Census of the United States Taken in the Year 1900. Census Reports. Washington, DC: US Bureau of the Census, 1901.

———. Thirteenth Census of the United States Taken in the Year 1910. Census Reports. Washington, DC: US Bureau of the Census, 1911.

———. Fourteenth Census of the United States Taken in the Year 1920. Census Reports. Washington, DC: US Bureau of the Census, 1921.

———. Fifteenth Census of the United States Taken in the Year 1930. Census Reports. Washington, DC: US Bureau of the Census, 1931.

US Congress. Senate. *Industrial Relations, Final Report and Testimony. Submitted to Congress by the Commission on Industrial Relations, Created by the Act of Congress August 23, 1912,* vols. 9 and 10. Washington, DC: GPO, 1916.

Weinstein, James. *The Decline of Socialism in America, 1912–1925.* New York: Vintage, 1969.

Weyland, Leonie Rummel, and Houston Wade. *An Early History of Fayette County.* La Grange, TX: La Grange Journal, 1936.

Whitman, Walt. "Year of Meteors [1859–60.]" *Leaves of Grass*. New York: Modern Library, 2001.

Wilkison, Kyle G. *Yeomen, Sharecroppers, and Socialists: Plain Folk Protest in Texas, 1870–1914*. College Station: Texas A&M University Press, 2008.

Williams, Frieda Meitzen. "German Pioneers in Texas." *Frontier Times* 13, no. 1 (October 1935): 70–72.

———. *History of the Meitzen Family*. Hallettsville, TX: privately printed, 1958.

———. *New Breslau (Oil Town Later)*. Houston: privately printed, 1969.

Williams, Marjorie L., ed. *Fayette County: Past and Present*. N.p., 1976.

Winkler, Ernest W. ed. *Platforms of Political Parties in Texas*. Austin: Bulletin of the University of Texas No. 53, 1916.

Wish, Harvey. "The Slave Insurrection Panic of 1856." *Journal of Southern History* 5, no. 2 (May 1939): 206–22.

Wolf, Naomi. "Revealed: How the FBI Coordinated the Crackdown on Occupy." *Guardian*, December 29, 2012. https://www.theguardian.com/commentisfree/2012/dec/29/fbi-coordinated-crackdown-occupy.

Wolff, Wilhelm. *Die schlesische Milliarde*. Zurich: Volksbuchhandlung, 1886.

Woodward, C. Vann. *Tom Watson: Agrarian Rebel*. New York: Oxford University Press, 1938.

Wooster, Ralph A. "An Analysis of Texas Know Nothings." *Southwestern Historical Quarterly* 70, no. 3 (January 1967): 414–23.

Wynne, Nick, and Joseph Knetsch. *Florida in the Great Depression*. Charleston, SC: History Press, 2012.

Yellen, Samuel. *American Labor Struggles, 1877–1934*. New York: Pathfinder, 2004.

Zamora, Emilio. *The World of the Mexican Worker in Texas*. College Station: Texas A&M University Press, 1993.

Index

Abilene, Texas, 182–83
Abilene Farmers Journal (newspaper), 115–16, 130
abolitionists, 30, 35, 40, 42–43, 50, 218
Adelsverein (Society for the Protection of German Immigrants in Texas), 31–33
African Americans, 6, 35, 91, 94, 116, 148, 167, 173, 200, 214; and 1877 Railroad Strike (Galveston), 62–64; and Democratic Party, 202; disenfranchisement, 103, 112, 113, 117, 154, 202, 204; and dockworkers, 52, 62, 193–95; and Farmers' Alliance, 76, 79; and FLP, 207; and FLPA, 177; and FLUA, 10, 200; and German Texans, 43, 51, 58, 73, 112–13; and GLP, 66–67; and People's Party, 6, 84, 86–88, 92, 94, 96–97, 101–3, 107, 197; and political independence, 58; and Republican Party, 6, 9, 59, 64, 88, 90, 101–2, 112, 195–96, 202; and SP, 117–19, 136–37, 155, 173, 197; women, 63. *See also* Colored Farmers' National Alliance
agribusiness, 168, 212
Alabama, 9, 48, 72, 76, 114–15, 197
Alamo, 57
Allied People's Party, 111
American Bimetallic League, 97
American Federation of Labor (AFL), 9, 92, 115, 126, 141, 177, 189, 199. *See also* Texas State Federation of Labor
American Party (Texas), 8–9, 191–95, 199, 202
American Protective Association, 96
American Railway Union, 91, 99
American Revolution, 14, 26, 29, 73, 86, 92, 139

anarchism, 137, 146, 167, 173, 183, 217
Anderson County, Texas, 200
Andrews, Reddin, 129–30
Anglos, 57, 96, 112, 168, 224n94
Antimonopoly Party, 70
Anti-socialist League, 166
Appeal to Reason (newspaper), 98–99, 108–9
Arbeiter Ring, 160
Arizona, 159, 167; and IWW, 182, 186; and NPL, 182; and SP, 127
Arkansas, 9, 47–48, 69, 76, 165, 197, 208–9
Arthur, Chester, 67
Ashby, Harrison "Stump," 89, 94, 102
Asian immigration, 65
Atwood, E. Francis, 123
Austin, Texas, 39, 42, 46, 56, 58, 62, 102, 147–48, 193–94, 233n130
Austin County, Texas, 31, 34, 40, 49, 65, 88, 113, 196
Austin Democratic Statesman (newspaper), 56, 58–60
Austin Workingmen's Club, 62

Baer, John Miller, 177
Bailey, Ben, 87
Bailey, Joseph, 115, 176, 189, 192, 201
Baird, J. A., 111
Baird, R. A., 58
Ball, Thomas, 152–55
Ballard, James, 94, 103
Baptist, 129
barbed wire, 168
Barker, Wharton, 105
Barnes, J. Mahlon, 142–43

Index

Bartsch, Robert Julius, 19
Barzee, C. W., 236n70
Bastrop Advertiser (newspaper), 57
Battle of Arkansas Post, 47–48
Battle of Leipzig, 14
Battle of San Jacinto, 57
Baylor University, 129
Bell, John, 43
Bell, W. J., 122, 126–27, 134
Bellamy, Edward, 109, 121
Bell County, Texas, 58, 153–54
Benson, Allan, 174–76, 179
Benson, George, 110
Berger, Victor, 111, 123, 126, 130, 139–44, 159, 174
Bexar County, Texas, 46, 48, 202
Biden, Joe, 218
Biegel, Joseph, 33–34
Billingsley, Jesse, 57
birth control. *See* Sanger, Margaret
Bisbee, Arizona, 186
Blum, Robert, 24, 36
Boeer, Alma (Maria's daughter), 132–33, 175
Boeer, Clara (Maria's daughter). *See* Hickey, Clara
Boeer, Louise (Maria's daughter), 132, 175
Boeer, Maria Wolf, 34–35, 109, 130–32, 144, 175, 182, 215
Boeer, Wilhelm, 131
Bohemian, 14, 53, 86, 117, 223n68
boll weevil, 105
Bolshevik (Russian) Revolution, 7, 140, 171, 174, 185, 191, 203, 216
Bonham, Texas, 108, 199, 208
Bowen, Albert, Jr., 177–78
Bowie, James, 139
Branon, Texas, 143
Brazoria County (Texas), 86, 88
Breslau, Prussia, 22; during 1848 Revolution, 21–23, 25; Meitzens in 3–4, 13
Breslauer Demokratische Verein (Breslau Democratic Club), 21
Breslau Workers Club, 21, 25
Brewer, George, 180
Brewer, Grace, 180
Broiles, H. S., 69
Brotherhood of Timber Workers, 136–37
Brown, John, 43
Brownsville, Texas, 168
Bryan, William Jennings, 81, 94, 99–104, 108, 211
Bryant, George T., 177, 182–83
Bull Moose Party, 144
Bund Freier Maenner, 36

Bureau of Investigation, 173, 182, 236n77
Burleson, Albert S., 138, 166, 184
Burleson County, Texas, 101
Bush, George W., 218
Butler, Marion, 104
Butte, Montana, 126–27

Cabet, Étienne, 32, 36
Caldwell County, Texas 58, 66, 167
California, 161, 167, 236n77
Camp Travis, 173
Campbell, R. F., 57, 59
Campbell, Thomas, 112, 121
Canada, John, 188
Cananea copper mine strike (1906), 159
Cannon, James, 10, 210
Cargill, 138
Caribbean, 207
Carranza, Venustiano, 145, 149, 159
Carrizo Springs, Texas, 146
Catholic, 35, 96, 118, 238–39n20
cattle industry, 34, 125, 138, 168, 197
Central America, 207
Charlemagne, 16
charity, 20
Chicago, 29, 35, 66, 91, 95, 98–99, 101, 186, 194, 205–6
Chicago Federation of Labor, 194
child labor, 128, 152, 176, 216
Childress, Texas, 201
Chilton, Horace, 111
Christianity, 109–10, 129, 151, 183, 201, 245n49
Christian socialism, 87, 109, 129, 142, 151
cholera, 30, 33
Cirilo, Constancio, 151
Cisco, Texas, 177
City Party (Galveston), 193
civil rights movement, 212, 217
Civil War (US), 45–49, 54, 61, 87, 112, 225n9
Clark, George, 90
Clark, Stanley, 110, 128, 158, 180, 185–86, 210
Cleburne Demands, 71–72
Cleveland, Grover, 61, 84, 92–94
Cline, Charlie, 146–47, 239n41
Coke, Richard, 60
Coleman County, Texas, 166
Colorado, 114, 163, 167, 188
Colorado County (Texas), 31, 34–35, 40–42, 49, 51, 72, 86, 88, 90, 131
Colored Farmers' National Alliance, 76, 79, 82, 85
Colored National Labor Convention, 52
Colquitt, Oscar, 130, 146–48, 155
Columbia County, Florida, 210, 214

Columbia Gazette (newspaper), 210, 249n20
Columbus, Texas, 41, 43
Comanche, 32, 42
Comanche County, Texas, 70; city of Comanche, 90
Commission on Industrial Relations, 1, 163–67
Committee of Forty-Eight, 194, 206
Committee on Public Information, 172, 243n3
communism (communists), 8, 10, 205, 207–10, 249n17
Communist International, 162, 180–81
Communist League, 20, 36
Communist Manifesto, 20–21, 31, 110, 120
Communist Party USA, 215–16
Compromise of 1850, 42
Confederacy, 40, 45–46, 80, 130; army, 40, 47–49; former Confederates, 50, 52–53, 61, 87–88, 129, 155; immigrants in military, 40, 46–48. *See also* United Confederate Veterans
Conference for Progressive Political Action, 206
Conger, Josephine, 124
Congress of Industrial Organizations (CIO), 212
Connolly, James, 130, 175
Considerant, Victor Prosper, 32
Constitutional Union Party, 43
consumerism, 203
convict labor, 65, 71, 87, 92, 152, 166, 184, 199
Cook County, Illinois, 99, 123
Coolidge, Calvin, 208
Cooperative Commonwealth, ix, 8, 10, 107, 129, 203–4, 213, 215; and Colored Alliance, 76; and Farmers' Alliance, 71; and socialism, 98, 109–10
cooperatives, 3, 60, 68, 70–71, 75–76, 80, 82, 91, 176, 180, 203, 208
Corpus Christi, Texas, 105, 128
Costa Rica, 147
cotton, 34–35, 54–55, 60, 69, 83, 91, 105, 141, 166–67; and Farmers' Alliance, 75–76; and FLUA, 204, 208; and FU, 122; price of, 54, 69, 154, 197; and SP, 175; and Soviet Union, 204; and tenant farming, 5, 147, 153, 173
Creel, George, 163
Crime Act (1994), 218
Crockett, David, 139
crop-lien system, 60, 68, 78, 82, 128. *See also* sharecropping; tenant farming
Cuba, 96, 147, 173
Culberson, Charles, 94, 103, 138
Cunerth, Carl Otto, 25–26, 35, 41, 46–48, 50–53, 226n25

Cuney, Norris Wright, 63–66, 227n69
Czechs, 34, 46, 51, 118, 148, 223n68. *See also* Bohemian; Moravians

Dallas, 104, 164–68, 194; and Farmers' Alliance, 69, 72, 76, 79, 84–86; and FLUA, 209; and GLP, 66; and People's Party, 84, 87–88, 92, 100, 102–3; and Republican Party, 57; and socialism, 110, 120–21, 124, 126–27, 160; and suffrage movement, 125; utopian colony, 32
Dallas Labor Journal (newspaper), 121
Dallas Morning News (newspaper), 86–87, 92, 103–4, 145, 147, 200, 213
Daniel, J. B., 105
Darmstädter group, 32, 36, 65
Davenport, Douglas, 202
Davidson, Lynch, 191
Davis, Edmund, 65
Davis, James "Cyclone," 89, 104–5, 200
Davitt, Michael, 160
Daws, S. O., 68, 102–3
Debs, Eugene, 3, 96, 186, 193, 234n29; and 1908 election, 125; and 1912 election, 176; and 1920 election, 196; and Populism, 21, 92, 98–101, 103–4; and Pullman strike, 91–92; and race, 119; and Social Democratic Party, 108; and SP, 111, 120, 141–44, 158, 174; on Walsh Commission, 163–64
Decentralizer (newspaper), 144
Degener, Edward, 50
DeLeon, Daniel, 98, 126–27
Democratic Clubs (Silesia), 18, 25
Democratic Party, 55–58, 80, 129, 144, 162, 164–66, 176, 182, 189, 211–18; and 1922 primary, 201; and African Americans, 6, 9, 96, 102, 202; and American Party, 193, 198; and anti-socialism, 191; in Fayette County, 51–53; and German Texans, 42, 93, 113; and Grange, 60, 64, 68; and GLP, 66–67; and Farmers' Alliance, 61, 70, 75, 78–79, 81–85, 89; and FU, 114–15; Jeffersonian Democrats, 52, 85, 203–4; and Mexican Americans, 88–89; and NPL, 186–87; and organized labor, 29–30, 69, 87, 190, 194–96, 199–201, 205–6; and People's Party, 86–87, 89–90, 94–95, 97, 99–100, 103, 121; and prohibition, 152–55; reform of, 107–8; and religion, 118; and slavery, 41–42; and suffrage, 133; and voter repression, 159; and white supremacy, 10, 59, 105, 111, 192. *See also* White Man's primary; White Primary Law
Demokrat, Der (newspaper), 25–27, 35
Deutsche Anzeiger, Der (newspaper), 96

De Valera, Éamon, 194
DeWitt County, Texas 42
Díaz, Porfirio, 137–39, 145
Dickinson, Texas, 215
Dickinson New Era (newspaper), 215
Dimmit County, Texas, 146
Dobie, J. Frank, 57
dockworkers, 63, 89, 247n108; and African Americans, 52, 63; Galveston strike (1922), 191
Donnelly, Ignatius, 105
Douai, Adolf, 36, 38–40, 62
Douglas, Arizona, 182
Dunlap, Andrew, 70–72
Dyer Anti-Lynching Bill, 196, 202
Dyson, Lowell, 206–7

East, O. T., 156–57
Easter Rebellion, 175
Eastland County, Texas, 151
economic determinism, 203
education, 38, 54, 57, 64–65, 67–68, 87, 152, 154, 193, 233n130; Texas public school fund, 84
Edwards, Sr., George Clifton, 110, 121
Eighteenth Amendment, 189
election fraud, 89, 94, 103, 113, 159
Ellinger, Texas, 196
El Paso, Texas, 148
El Paso Herald (newspaper), 183
Engels, Friedrich, 19–22, 28, 30–31, 36, 121, 221n28, 221n29
environmental activism, 218
Ernst, Friedrich, 31
Espionage Act, 184
evangelism, 109–10
Evans, George Henry, 30
Evans, O. S., 178

Fall, Albert Bacon, 138, 149
Fannin County, Texas, 197
Fargo, North Dakota, 178, 180
Farm Bureau, 197
Farmer, William, 108, 116
farmer-labor bloc, 2–3, 5–6, 9–11, 53, 144, 172, 199–200, 203–5, 208, 215–18; and American Party, 8, 194, 198, 202; and anti-imperialism, 207; and NPL, 8, 177–78; and New Deal coalition, 212–13; and People's Party, 87, 108; and SP, 7, 135; and white supremacy, 107
Farmer-Labor Party (FLP), 2, 9, 205–9
Farmers' Alliance, 4, 61–62, 75, 99, 114, 151, 184, 197, 203; and African Americans, 76, 79; Austin Manifesto, 83; and Democratic Party, 84; in Fayette County, 67, 73; and independent political action, 78–81; in Kansas, 80; and KOL, 68–71, 108; in Lavaca County, 91; in North Dakota, 80, 178; and People's Party, 86, 88–89, 102; and St. Louis platform, 80–81, 83; in South Dakota, 80; western Alliances, 82; and women, 72; "yardstick," 81–82. *See also* National Farmers' Alliance and Industrial Union
Farmers and Laborers' Protective Association (FLPA), 176–77, 182–83
Farmers' and Laborer's Union of America, 76
Farmer's Educational and Cooperative Union of America *see* Farmers' Union
Farmers' Mutual Benefit Association, 80
Farmers' Union (FU), 1, 107, 118, 121–23, 135, 151, 155, 197, 215, 218; and socialism, 114–16
Farm Labor Union News (newspaper), 199, 203, 208, 248n123
Farm-Labor Union of America (FLUA), 1, 9–10, 197–204, 207–9; and African Americans, 200; and KKK, 200
Farm Loan Act, 175, 192
fascism, 218. *See also* Nazis
Fayette County, Texas, 1, 35, 50, 64, 67, 72, 129, 131, 149; and American Party, 193, 196; and Civil War, 46, 48–49; and Democratic Party, 51–53, 55, 58; and Farmers' Alliance, 67, 73, 75–76, 78–80; German settlement, 31, 34, 39, 41; and Grange, 60, 67, 72–73; and People's Convention (1873), 57–59; and People's Party, 86, 193; and Reconstruction, 51; and Republican party, 58; slavery in, 40, 43, 45
Federal Bureau of Investigation (FBI), 217. *See also* Bureau of Investigation
Federal Reserve, 204
Federated Farmer Labor Party, 206
Ferguson, James, 8–9, 153–55, 159, 162, 164, 166, 176, 189, 201–2, 204; and American Party, 191–96, 198
Ferguson, Miriam Wallace (Ma), 153
Ferguson Forum (newspaper), 189, 192, 195
feudalism, 15–18, 22, 25–28, 137
Field, James, 88
Finley, N. W., 84
Fitzpatrick, John, 194, 205–6
Fitzwater, W. W., 198, 201, 204
Flood of 1913, 148
Flores, Emilio, 165, 167
Flores Magón, Enrique, 138–39, 140
Flores Magón, Ricardo, 138–39, 140, 159, 167

Index

Florida, 6, 9–10, 82, 197, 210–11, 213–14
Fort Bend County, Texas, 88, 103, 191
Fort Butler (Illinois), 48
Fort Worth, Texas, 69, 78–79, 124, 173, 192, 194
Forty-Eighters, 4–5, 13, 29, 31, 36–37; in Texas, 5, 32, 36–39, 45, 53, 56, 73, 112, 171, 219n1
Foster, William Z., 208
Fourier, Charles, 30, 32, 36
Fourteenth Amendment, 55
Franke, Louis, 52, 225–26n23
Frankfurt Assembly, 24–27, 29
Frazier, Lynn, 177, 199
Fredericksburg, Texas, 32, 33
Freedman's Bureau, 52
Freeman, W. W., 120
free silver, 67, 71, 84, 88, 90, 93–95, 97–99, 104
Free Soil Party, 31, 37
freethinkers, 36–38
Freier Verein (Sisterdale, Texas), 38
Freie Verein, Der (Free Society, Sisterdale, Texas), 36
Frémont, John, 41
French Immigrants (Texas), 32
French Revolution, 14, 17, 139
Friedrich Wilhelm IV, 13, 27
Fugitive Slave Law, 37

Gaines, Thomas, 90
Galveston, Texas, 13, 33, 35, 52, 62–64, 173, 193; dockworkers strike (1922), 191, 193–95; and First International, 224n89; and GLP, 66; and Know Nothings, 41; and People's Party, 88–90, 101–2. *See also* City Party (Galveston)
Galveston County, Texas, 215
Galveston County Press (newspaper), 215
Galveston Daily News (newspaper), 63, 83
Garrison, William Lloyd, 30
Gaupp, Jo-Lou (E. R. Meitzen's daughter), 110, 210, 214–15
Gay, Bettie Munn, 72, 89, 117
Gay, James Bates, 117
Gay, Rufus King, 72
gay rights, 212
Gentry, E., 187
George, Henry, 160
Georgia, 48, 76, 98–99, 163, 198
German Confederation, 15
German Revolution of 1848, 1, 4, 13–14, 16, 18, 20–29, 135, 139, 213, 216
German Social-Democratic Party, 124
German Texans, 29, 38–43, 45, 51, 56, 65, 118, 131, 196, 215; and African Americans, 43, 51, 58, 73, 112–13; and Comanche, 32; and Civil War, 5, 40, 45–49; and Democratic Party, 42, 113, 155; early settlement in Texas, 31, 35; and FU, 115; and 1873 People's Party, 5, 56–59, 73, 92–93, 96; and racism, 112–13; and religion 77–78; repression of, 40, 173, 187; and Republican Party, 50, 112; and SP, 35, 109, 130–32, 148, 150, 160, 237n98. *See also Adelsverein*
Germer, Adolph, 174
Gibbs, Barney, 105
Gilbert, Joe, 180
Ginger, Ray, 143, 182
Globe, Arizona, 127
Golden, Texas, 158
Goldwater, Barry, 211
Gompers, Samuel, 92, 115, 198, 200, 206
Gonzales County (Texas), 79, 86, 90
Goodwyn, Lawrence, 69
Gould, Jay, 68–69, 137
Granbury's Texas Brigade, 48
Grand Saline, Texas, 120
Grange (Patrons of Husbandry), 2, 5, 58–61, 66–68, 70, 72–73, 76, 98, 215; and religion, 72
Great Depression, 210
Great Railroad Strike of 1877, 62–64
Green, Ed, 142
Green, James, 7, 98, 120, 193
greenback ideology, 70–71, 80, 104, 108
Greenback Labor Party, 2, 39, 52, 58, 62, 64–67, 78, 88, 108, 213; and African Americans, 66; and interracial alliance, 65
Greenville, Texas, 173
Gregory, Thomas Watt, 183–84
Gresham, Newt, 114
Gresham, Walter, 90, 92
Griffith, D. W., 149
Guggenheims, 138
Gutiérrez de Lara, Lázaro, 159, 167

Habt Acht (newspaper), 131
Hagen, John, 199
Hall, Covington, 137, 179–82, 194, 197, 199, 208, 210–11, 213, 215
Hall County, Texas, 139
Hallettsville, Texas, 117–18, 130, 156, 165, 182, 233n130; and Colored Alliance, 79; and Farmers' Alliance, 79–80; and People's Party, 84–88, 96; and socialism, 107, 114–15, 143
Hallettsville Herald (newspaper), 83, 85–87. 89, 96, 117–18
Hallettsville New Era (newspaper), 91, 96, 109, 114, 117–18, 129–30, 182

Handweker-Bund (New Braunfels, TX), 36
Hapsburg Empire, 14, 24, 27
Hardy, Nat, 127
Harpers Ferry, 43
Harris County, 190–91
Harrison, Hubert, 136
Harvey, William, 94
Haynes, Sr., A., 115, 117
Hays County, Texas, 58
Haywood, William "Big Bill," 114, 120, 137, 140, 142–45, 210
health care, 121, 128, 152
Hearst, William Randolph, 149
Hernández, F. A., 150, 160, 167, 172–73
Hernández, José Ángel, 146–47, 168–69, 172–73
Herron, George, 109
Hickey, Clara, 132, 140, 175, 182, 184, 246n69
Hickey, Thomas A., 107, 120, 126–27, 132–34, 140–42, 157, 159–60, 177, 194, 215, 246n69; arrest of, 182–84; death, 210; and Haywood, 144; and Irish republicanism, 129–30, 139, 175; and Mexican Revolution, 137, 139, 167; and NPL, 178–80, 185–86; and single-tax, 161–62; and SLP, 126
Hicks, Joshua L., 115–16, 123, 130–31
Hicks, W. P., 116
Hillquit, Morris, 142–43, 174
Hobby, William P., 189, 192–95
Hogg, James S., 81–84, 88–90, 103, 111–13, 138
Holmgren, Jens Engelbrecht, 16
Holy Roman Empire, 14
Homestead strike, 126
Hoover, Herbert, 212
House, Edward, 81
Houston, Sam, 41–43, 139, 213
Houston, Texas, 33, 49, 64, 146–47, 151–52, 161, 188, 196, 213; and 1920 famer-labor alliance, 190–91; and FU, 122; and KKK, 198; and NAACP, 202; and NPL, 188; and People's Party, 100; and SLP, 108; and SP, 120, 150
Houston Chronicle (newspaper), 191
Houston County (Texas), 76
Houston Informer (newspaper), 202
Houston Labor and Trade Council, 190
Houston Labor Journal, 191
Houston Post (newspaper), 113, 191
Houston Ship Channel, 147, 153
Huerta, Victoriano, 145, 239n38
Hughes, Charles Evan, 176
Hughes, Charles V., 187
Human Party, 70
Hungate, A. P., 61–62

Huntsville, Texas, 114

Idaho, 93, 188
Illinois, 29, 48, 163, 207, 225n9; and GLP, 66; and Southwest Railroad Strike (1886), 69; and Farmers' Mutual Benefit Association, 80; and Populism, 98, 100; and SP, 123, 174
immigration, 113, 118. *See also* Asian immigration; French Immigrants; German Texans; Mexicans; Polish immigration
imperialism, 152, 168, 174, 184, 207, 215–16
income tax, 88, 90, 96, 216
Independent Citizen's Ticket, 195
Independent Labor Party, 111
Independent Springs, Texas, 200
Indiana, 30, 91, 101, 141, 146
Indianapolis, 37, 141, 147, 168
Indian Territory, 76
industrial courts, 198, 204
industrialization: in Germany, 15–18, 25; in Mexico, 137; in US, 36, 54, 73, 82
industrial unionism, 108, 141–42, 152, 160, 212
Industrial Workers of the World (IWW), 137, 145–46, 159–60, 168, 177, 182, 211, 236n77
International Labor Defense (ILD), 10, 210
International Longshoremen's Association, 193
International Typographical Union, 151
International Workingmen's Association (First International), 40, 224n89
Interstate Commerce Commission, 71
Iraq War (2003–2011), 218
Ireland, 126, 129–30, 139, 175, 194
Ireland, John, 67, 69–70, 171
Irish National Land League, 160
Irish Socialist Republican Party, 130
Irons, Martin, 70, 108

Jefferson, Thomas, 29
Jeffersonian ideology, 35–36, 52, 70, 85–86, 192, 201, 203–4
Jews, 141; in Germany 19; in Texas, 160. *See also* Arbeiter Ring
Jim Crow, 6–7, 9, 102–3, 107, 114, 118–19, 155, 168, 216
Jones, Evan, 79, 84
Jones, George Washington, 66–67
Jones, Jesse H., 147
Jones, Mary (Mother Jones), 120, 142
Jones, Samuel "Golden Rule," 108

Kalckreuth family, 15
Kaneko, Kiichi, 124

Kansas, 69, 80, 98, 165, 180, 183
Kansas City, Missouri, 163
Kansas-Nebraska Act, 42
Karsner, Rose, 210
Katz, Friedrich, 149
Kearby, Jerome, 69–70, 102–3
Keep, Jean, 142
King Ranch, 168
Kiołbassa, Peter, 35, 225n9
Kiołbassa, Stanisław, 35
Kirby, John Henry, 81, 136–37, 147, 154
Kirk, J. W., 87
Kirkpatrick, George, 174
Knights of Labor, 2, 62, 68–72, 78–80, 82, 85, 89, 102, 107–8, 209
Know Nothings, 40–42. *See also* nativism
Knutson, Alfred, 209–10
Kuechler, Jacob, 65
Ku Klux Klan, 6, 9–10, 51, 105, 198, 200–202, 207, 214

Laborer (newspaper), 121
Laborers, Farmers, and Stockraisers convention, 78–79
labor party: Arkansas Labor Party, 209; attempt to form in US, 9, 13, 111, 205–8, 211; Texas Labor Party, 209–10
La Follette, Robert, 3, 9, 194, 206–8, 211–12
La Grange, Texas, 35, 39, 50–51, 56–59, 72, 80, 95
Lake City, Florida, 210, 213–14
Lamb, William, 71, 79–80, 82, 84–85
Lampasas County (Texas), 61, 110
Land League of America, 160, 165–66, 169, 172, 179, 184
Landlord and Tenant Act, 55, 58–59
Lane, R., 173
Lang, William W., 60–61
Laredo, Texas, 138, 173
Lause, Mark, 5, 30
Lavaca County, Texas, 42, 65, 76, 116, 129, 157, 161, 182, 213; African Americans, 42, 86, 88, 96–97, 112, 117, 173; and American Party, 193, 196; and Democratic Party, 78, 80, 82, 87; and Farmers' Alliance, 77–79, 83–85, 91; and FLUA, 200; and FU, 115–16; and Germans, 34, 94; and Populism, 85–91, 94, 105, 112, 193; and socialism, 113–19, 151, 173, 193; and White Man's primary, 112–13, 117
League of Nations, 204
Leavenworth prison, 183, 186
Ledbetter, Hamilton, 58–59
Ledbetter, William Hamilton, 58–59

Left Opposition, 10, 210
Lemke, William, 178, 199, 208, 211–13
Lenin, Vladimir I., 10, 191, 204, 207
lesser-evil (voting), 101, 176, 218
LeSueur, Arthur, 165, 174, 177–78, 180
Liberador, El (newspaper), 150
liberalism, 4, 14, 36, 58, 111, 138, 162, 205, 211; of 1848 Revolution, 17–18, 20, 24–25; and Farmers' Alliance, 71–72; free market, 203; neoliberalism, 217; New Deal, 10, 213
libertarianism, 204
liberty bonds, 182, 184
Liberty Party, 31, 218
Liebknecht, Wilhelm, 162
Liegnitz, Prussia, 23, 27; Democratic Club of, 4, 13, 25, 35, 46; Meitzens in 4, 16, 22, 25–26, 33, 35; socialism in, 22
Lincoln, Abraham, 45, 88, 218
Lindbergh, Charles (son), 246n75
Lindbergh, Charles A. (father), 188, 246n75
Linden, W. C., 146–47
Literary Digest, 149
Live Oak, Florida, 210
Lloyd, Henry Demarest, 95, 98–99, 101
Looking Backward: (2000–1887), 109, 121
Los Angeles Times bombing, 147, 163, 240n44
Louisiana, 9, 75–76, 136–37, 180, 197
Louisiana Farmers Union, 75
Louisville Convention and Platform (1854), 36–38
Lowe, Caroline, 133
Loyal Union League. *See* Union Loyal League
Lucha de Clases (newspaper), 169
Ludlow Massacre, 163
Lueders, Texas, 177
lumber industry, 16, 81, 126, 136–37, 147, 154, 182, 186, 191
Lusitania, 173
Lutheran Church, 77–78
lynching, 41, 43, 49, 88, 103, 105, 168

Macune, Charles, 72, 75, 79–80, 82
Madero, Francisco, 145, 239n38
Maetze, Ernst Gustav, 34
Maine, 100
Maley, Anna, 174
Martin, Marion, 79–80, 87, 92–93
Marx, Karl, 4, 19–21, 30–32, 36, 109–10, 121, 126, 128, 221n28, 237n87
Marxism, 4, 19–21, 40, 104, 109, 129, 162, 203, 213, 215
Massachusetts, 26, 144
Matthäi, Ewald, 19, 21

Matthäi, Ludwig, 19, 21
Matthäi, Rudolph, 21–22, 25, 221n29
Mayfield, Earle, 201
McAdoo, William Gibbs, 199, 206, 211
McBride, John, 92
McCormick, Cyrus, 138
McCutchan, W. R., 117
McDonald, Duncan, 207–8
McDonald, William "Gooseneck Bill," 102
McFadden, Alice, 125
McGregor, T. H., 194–96
McKinley, William, 100–103
McMath, Robert, Jr., 54
McMinn, Theodore, 105–6
Meagher, Thomas, 139
Medicaid, 217
Medicare, 217
Meitzen, Albert Charles (E. O. and Johanna's son), 65, 77, 107, 109, 118, 130, 155; and SP, 65, 113, 183–84
Meitzen, Edward Otto, 1, 3, 53, 107, 194, 200, 203, 213, 215–18, 233n130; birth, 34; children of, 77–78; as county judge, 113, 116–18, 234n27; and Democratic Party, 78–79, 82, 84–85, 213, 217; and Farmers' Alliance, 68, 75–76, 79–80, 83–85, 87, 89, 91; and FU, 114–16, 122, 218; and Grange, 67, 72; and GLP, 64–65; influence of 1848 Revolution, 35, 50; and KOL, 68, 89; and Marxism, 21, 109; and NPL, 7–8, 178, 180, 182; and Populism, 75, 86–90, 92–97, 99, 101–5, 112; and religion, 77–78, 118; and Renters' Union, 135, 137, 149; shot, 156–57; and socialism, 109–10, 113; and SP, 109, 113, 120, 123, 128–31, 140, 174–75, 177, 185; as teacher, 65, 68, 76; and Walsh Commission, 165–66; and White Man's primary, 113, 117; and UFEL, 210
Meitzen, Ernest August (E. O.'s brother), 34, 76, 86
Meitzen, Ernest Richard (E. R.), 1, 3, 65, 77, 107, 118, 128, 194, 208, 215–18, 246n69, 249n17; children of, 210; and Democratic Party, 186–87, 211–14, 217; and FLP, 10, 206–7, 210; in Florida, 6, 10, 210–14; and FLUA, 9, 197, 203, 207–8; and FU, 115, 122, 151 ; and ILD 10; and Marxism, 109; and NPL, 7–8, 178–80, 182, 185–88, 190–91, 199, 206; and Plan de San Diego, 168; and race, 107, 155, 173; and religion, 215; and Renters' Union, 148; and single-tax, 161–62; and socialism, 110, 179–80; and SP, 65, 120–21, 123, 125, 130, 140–45, 150–51, 154–56, 158–59, 173–75, 177,

191; and Texas Program, 127; and UFEL, 10, 210; and Walsh Commission, 165; women and socialism, 133–34; and Workers Party, 205
Meitzen, Herman (E. O.'s brother), 34, 86
Meitzen, Ida (Otto and Jennie's daughter), 34
Meitzen, Jennie Holmgren, 3, 13, 16–17, 33, 49, 64
Meitzen, Johanna Kettner (E. O.'s wife), 64–65, 76, 133, 180, 213; children of, 77–78
Meitzen, Julia (Otto and Jennie's daughter), 34
Meitzen, Lillie Carson McCullough (E. R.'s wife), 210, 215
Meitzen, Marie Gentner/Cunerth (Otto's sister), 25, 33, 35, 46, 50, 53
Meitzen, Otto, 1, 3, 13–17, 22–23, 25, 28, 33–34, 49–51, 64–65
Meitzen, William (E. R.'s and Lillie's son), 214
Meitzen, William (Otto's brother), 15–16, 33–34, 49–51
Memking, Otto, 196
Memphis, Tennessee, 104
Mendell, G. W., 233n130
Mercedes, Texas, 149
Methodist, 72, 110, 153, 187, 215
Metropolitan, 149
Mexican Americans, 7, 40–42, 136, 140, 146–47, 155, 159, 167, 172–73, 224n94; and Populism, 88–89, 197; and Renters' Union, 137, 140, 149–50, 155; and SP, 140, 150, 155, 159–60, 172–73, 184, 197. *See also* Mexican Protective Association; Tejanos
Mexican American War, 30, 168
Mexican Protective Association, 165, 167
Mexican Revolution, 137, 171; and Catholic Church, 238–39n20; transnational influence of, 3, 6–7, 135, 138–40, 143, 145, 147–49, 159, 164, 167, 169, 176, 216
Mexicans, 105, 113, 140, 159, 164, 171–72, 224n88, 243n2; and immigration, 3, 40, 137, 140, 160, 167, 243n2
Mexico, 105, 138–40, 143, 145–46, 148, 152, 159, 173, 224n94; border with Texas, 120, 139, 167–68, 172; foreign economic exploitation of, 81, 137–38, 149, 172; Texas land grants, 34; and Texas Revolution, 57; and Texas slave revolts, 41–43; and US Civil War, 49, 65
middle-of-the-road Populists, 95, 97, 100–102, 104–5, 232n87
Milam County, Texas, 136
Miller, Gary, 114

Index

Mills, Walter Thomas, 180
Mills, Word H., 120
Milwaukee, 123, 142
Milwaukee Leader (newspaper), 139, 159
Mineola, Texas, 187–88
mining, 5, 17, 94, 114, 127, 159, 163, 182, 207
Minnesota, 7, 178, 188, 199, 206–7
Minnesota State Federation of Labor, 188
Mississippi, 9, 68, 76, 102, 114, 197
Missouri, 66, 68, 76, 133, 138, 163, 174
monopoly. *See* trusts
Montana, 93, 126, 188, 190, 212
Moravians, 34, 223n68
Morgan, J. P., 138
Moscow, Russia, 14, 204, 210
Moyer, Charles, 114
Murphy, Charles, 190–91
mutual aid, 60, 160

Nagle, Patrick, 157, 165
Napoleon, Bonaparte, 14
National Agricultural Wheel of Arkansas, 76
National Association for the Advancement of Colored People, 202
National Farmers' Alliance and Industrial Union, 85, 88; Ocala convention, 82–85; and St. Louis platform, 80–81, 83, 87
National Guard, 91, 171; Texas National Guard, 194–95, 201
National Reform Association, 30–31, 36
National Reform Press Association, 95, 103–4
National Rip-Saw (newspaper), 116
Native Americans, 1, 30, 32, 42, 167. *See also* Comanche
nativism, 38, 40
Navarro County, Texas, 102
Nazis, 14, 215
Nebraska, 126, 188, 207, 246n75
Neff, Pat, 195, 200–201
Neue Rheinische Zeitung, 24, 28, 222n49
Neutrality Act (US), 147
New Braunfels, Texas, 32–33, 36, 160
New Deal, 2, 10, 203, 211–14, 216
New Harmony, Indiana. *See* Owen, Robert
New Jersey, 144
New Mexico, 81, 138, 150, 167; and socialism, 150
New Orleans, Louisiana, 147
New York, 29–30, 36, 52, 81, 134, 142, 144, 163, 174, 193
Nicaragua, 98
Nineteenth Amendment, 189

Noble, J. L., 151
Noble, W. S., 142, 151–52, 156, 158, 165, 175
Noeggerath, Julius, 52–53, 55, 57
Nonpartisan Leader (newspaper), 179–80, 185, 187
Nonpartisan League (NPL), 1–2, 7–9, 177–82, 184, 186, 188, 193–94, 199, 204–5, 208–9; and former Socialists, 180; and Germans, 180, 187; and organized labor, 188, 190–91; in Nebraska, 246n75; in Oklahoma, 180, 185; in Texas, 178–80, 184–88, 190–91
Nonpartisan Political Conference, 199, 201
Nordheim, Texas, 150
North Carolina, 76, 80
North Dakota, 93, 209; and NPL, 7, 177, 179–80, 182, 185–86, 188, 191, 211; and socialism, 165, 174, 177
Norton, S. F., 101
Nueces Massacre, 49–50, 65
Nugent, Clarence (son of Thomas), 175
Nugent, Thomas L., 87, 89–90, 92, 94, 175

Obama, Barack, 7, 217
Occupy Wall Street, 217
Offut, M. M., 187
O'Hare, Frank, 120
O'Hare, Kate Richards, 120, 133, 158, 174, 186
Ohio, 29, 42, 92, 108, 126, 144, 186
oil, 81, 147, 154. *See also* Spindletop; Standard Oil; Texas Oil Company
Oklahoma, 9, 208; and NPL, 180, 185. *See also* Socialist Party (Oklahoma)
Olmsted, Frederick Law, 40
Olney, Texas, 183
Open Port law (1922), 194–95
open shop, 190, 192, 195–96, 198, 247n108
Oregon, 161, 236n70
Ortiz, Antonio, 173
Otis, Harrison Gray, 149
Owen, Robert (father), 30, 36
Owen, Robert Dale (son), 30

Paine, Tom, 5, 29–30, 38, 216
Panama Canal, 147, 168
Panic of 1907, 122
Park, Milton, 95–96, 103–4, 108
Parker, Jo. A., 111
Partido Liberal Mexicano (PLM), 138, 140, 145–47, 149, 159, 168–69
Pastoriza, J. J., 161–62, 165, 190
Patterson New Jersey silk strike, 163
Paulus, David Augustus, 113, 161

Payne, Laura, 123–25, 132, 236n77
Pennsylvania, 62, 126, 134, 144, 227n69
People's College (Kansas), 165
People's Party, 1, 21, 58, 83, 104–5, 108, 111, 129, 175, 197, 216; and 1894 election, 94–95; and African Americans, 6, 84, 86–88, 92, 94, 96–97, 102–3, 107, 233n130; Cincinnati convention, 84; creation in Texas, 83–85, 87–91; encampments, 89, 120; and fusion, 94–95, 97–103, 107; and German Texans, 92–94, 96; and Mexican Americans, 88–89; and labor, 84, 87, 89, 92, 98–99, 102; and Omaha platform (1892), 85, 88, 95, 97, 99–100, 103–4; and reform press, 91, 95–97, 104–5; and religion, 96; and St. Louis convention (1896), 97, 99–101, 104; and women, 88–89
People's Party (1873), 5, 56–59, 73, 226n44
Pepper, Claude, 214
Philippine Islands, 207
Phoenix, Arizona, 127
Pinkerton detectives, 69–70
Plan de San Diego, 167–69
police brutality, 63, 218
Polish immigration (Texas), 34–35, 47–48, 225n9
Polish Revolution (1830), 19
Polk, Leonidas L., 80, 88
poll tax, 6, 66, 112, 117–18, 121, 128, 152, 154, 159, 167, 190, 199, 214
Populism, 2, 4, 13, 21, 39, 45, 73, 135, 171, 215; and "bloody shirt," 87–88; and communists, 206; defined, 6; ideological divisions within, 98–99, 107–8; and FLUA, 197; and FU, 114–15; in Ohio, 92; in North Dakota, 178; and race, 119; return to Democratic Party, 112, 121, 200; transition to socialism, 95, 98, 104, 105–6, 108–11, 116, 129, 151, 197, 233n130. *See also* People's Party
Portland (Oregon) Central Labor Council, 161
Powderly, Terence, 69
producerism, 2, 8, 54, 70, 76, 109–10, 200, 203–4
Progress and Poverty, 160
prohibition, 36, 56, 92–93, 116, 121, 148, 152–55, 161, 176, 189, 196, 201, 204
Prohibition Party, 79, 93
Prussian (Berlin) Assembly, 24–25, 27, 34
Public Ownership Party, 111
Puerto Rico, 207
Pullman strike, 91–92, 98

railroad brotherhoods, 189, 199, 201, 206, 209
railroads, 22, 54–58, 117, 147, 152, 154, 156, 168, 191; and Democratic Party, 64, 66–67, 81, 84; and Farmers' Alliance, 75, 80, 111; and GLP, 65; and Grange, 60; nationalization of, 73, 80, 87–88, 92, 98, 104, 121; railroad commission, 81–83, 90, 121, 125, 201; Railroad Labor Board, 198; strikes, 62, 68–71, 91, 102, 105, 108, 163, 201; and Union Labor Party, 79; US Railroad Administration, 199
Rains County, Texas, 114
Rangel, Jesús M., 145–46, 239n41
Rayner, John B., 96–97, 101
Rebel (newspaper), 146, 153–54, 162, 166, 174, 178–80, 182–84, 208, 216, 245n53; and birth control, 133–34; and Christian socialism, 109–10; and FLPA, 176; founding of, 130; and Mexican Americans, 136, 149–50, 160, 169, 172; and Mexican Revolution, 140, 148–50, 159, 169, 236n20; and race, 135–36, 160; and suffrage, 133, 174
Reconstruction, 6, 39, 45, 50–51, 55, 61, 64, 65, 73, 90, 112–13
Red Cross, 187
Red Scare (1917–1921), 172, 182, 185–86, 216–17
Red Scare (1947–1957), 215–17
Reed, John, 149
Reform Press Association (Texas), 96–97, 104. *See also* National Reform Press Association
Regeneración (newspaper), 138, 140, 167, 238–39n20
religion, 29, 31, 37–39, 72, 110, 116, 139, 192, 245n49. *See also* Baptist; Catholic; Christian socialism; Christianity; evangelism; Jews; Lutheran Church; Methodist
Renters Union (Socialist Party), 6, 135–37, 140, 148–51, 155, 160
repression, 45, 53, 69, 79, 91–92, 103, 108, 172, 191, 201, 203; of Galveston dockworkers strike (1922), 193–95; in Germany, 18; German Counter-Revolution, 4, 27–28; of FLPA, 182–84; of German Texans, 40, 48–49, 187; of Mexican Americans, 146–47, 150, 168–69, 172, 184; of Mexican Revolution, 138, 168; of NPL, 187–88, 199; of Occupy Wall Street, 217; of Populist movement, 7, 90, 105, 107; of SP, 7, 166–67, 171, 182–84, 186, 208. *See also* African Americans, disenfranchisement; Bureau of Investigation; Espionage Act; lynching; Red Scare
Republican Party, 2, 31, 43, 90–91, 108, 115, 130, 159, 176, 182; and African Americans, 6, 9, 51, 52, 58, 64–65, 88, 90, 102, 112, 195, 227n69; Black and Tans, 10, 195–96, 202; and foreign policy, 215–16; and Forty-Eighters, 40, 50; and free silver, 93–95, 97; and German Texans, 50–51, 56–58, 65, 67,

112; and GLP, 65–67; Lily Whites, 10, 195–96, 202; national convention (1924), 208; and NPL, 178, 188; and Populism, 100–102; progressives, 211; Radical Republicans, 52, 55, 61, 65; and slavery, 41, 218; and Union Labor Party, 79; and women, 37.
Rhodes, Jacob, 108, 120, 123, 125, 128
Rhodes, Lee, 108, 115, 120–21, 196–97, 208, 210
Richardson, Clifton F., 202
Roberts, Oran, 61
Rockefellers, 138
Rockwell County, Texas, 156
Rogers, Fred S., 199–201
Roosevelt, Franklin D., 211–13
Roosevelt, Theodore, 144, 216
Rose, A. J., 68
Rosenthal, A. J., 90
Rotan, Texas, 177, 182
Ruby, George T., 52
Rusk County, Texas, 173
Russell, Charles Frances, 142
Russian Empire, 171
Rustic Alliance (*Rustikalverein*), 4, 13, 26, 28, 35

San Antonio, 46, 82, 138, 146, 151, 167, 169, 196, 198; and African Americans, 58; and German Texans, 41, 46, 50, 56, 96; and nativism, 41; and Populism, 88–89, 96; *Sängerfest* (1854), 38; and SLP, 108; and socialism, 159, 173; and Tejanos, 50, 88. *See also* San Antonio Convention and Platform (1854)
San Antonio Convention and Platform (1854), 38–40, 73
San Antonio Express (newspaper), 60–61
San Antonio Zeitung (newspaper), 38, 40, 42
Sanders, Bernie, 6
Sanger, Margaret, 9, 133–34
San Marcos, Texas, 146–48
Santa Anna, Antonio López de, 57
scabs, 69, 136, 193
secession, 40, 42–43, 45–46, 50–51, 61
Sealy, Texas, 196
secret (Australian) ballot, 87, 216
Secret Service, 183
Seguin, Texas, 160
Seidel, Emil, 142
Sewall, Arthur, 100, 103
sewer socialism, 108, 144
sharecropping, 5, 54, 105, 121, 128, 137, 134, 148, 153, 212
Siemering, August, 36, 38, 56
Silesia: during 1848 Revolution, 4, 13, 22, 25–28; class formation, 16, 18–20; textile industry, 15; industrialization, 17; influence on Texas radicalism, 22, 51; peasant revolts, 15–18; rule of, 14; Silesian immigration to Texas, 34–35, 130
Silesian Weaver's Revolt (1844), 4, 18, 20–21
Simmons, William, 198
Simpson, W. J., 189
single tax, 111, 148, 160–62, 165, 190
Sixteenth Amendment, 21
Skidmore, Thomas, 5, 29–30
Slater, George, 198–99
slave revolts, 41–43
slavery, 31, 35, 37, 39, 41, 218; African slave trade, 41–43, 73
Smith, Adam, 203
Smith, Alfred, 211
Smith, M. A., 110, 120–21, 125, 128, 208, 210
Snyder, Texas, 183
Social Democratic Party, 108
Social Democratic Society (La Grange, Texas), 41
socialism, 83, 129, 134, 159, 162, 177, 179–80, 193, 216, 218; and FU, 114–17; and German Texans, 39; and New Mexico, 150; and Populism, 95–96, 98, 104, 106, 108, 111; and race, 117–19; true socialism, 221n29; and women, 39. *See also* Christian socialism; Debs, Eugene; Marxism; sewer socialism; utopian socialism
Socialist Labor Party, 40, 62, 98, 108, 126–27, 142
Socialist Party, 1–2, 6–7, 13, 35, 110–11, 121–28, 205–6, 216, 218, 219n7; ethno-language federations, 150, 174; and Haywood expulsion, 144; and Mexican Revolution, 138–40, 143, 159; national convention (1912), 141–42, 177; and National Women's Committee, 124–25, 133; and NEC, 124, 142–44, 174, 179–80; and NPL, 178–81; and race, 136; and single-tax, 161; split in party, 7, 127, 140–41, 143, 145, 174. *See also* Arizona, and SP; repression, of SP; Socialist Party (Oklahoma); Socialist Party (Texas)
Socialist Party (Oklahoma), 125, 158, 165, 180, 241n104
Socialist Party (Texas), 117–31, 147–48, 152–55, 159–62, 164–65, 174–76, 196, 208, 214, 241n104; and African Americans, 117–19, 136–37, 155, 173, 176; encampments, 120, 150, 158; and farmer-labor bloc, 108; and FLPA, 176–77, 183; and FU, 114–16; and German Texans, 35, 109, 130–32, 150, 160, 237n98; in Hallettsville, 114–15; and Mexican Americans, 137, 149–50, 160, 172–73, 184;

Socialist Party (Texas) (*continued*): and Mexican Revolution, 138–40, 145, 148–49, 159, 167–69; and NPL, 179, 187; and race, 118–19, 135–37; and Texas Program, 127, 134, 141, 151; and women, 124–25, 132–33, 174, 236n77. See also *Rebel* (newspaper), Renters Union; repression, of SP
Socialist Printing Company, 130
Socialist Trade and Labor Alliance, 126
Socialist Woman (newspaper), 124–25, 236n77
Socialist Workers Party, 216–17
Sorge, Friedrich, 40
South Dakota, 80, 93, 123, 188, 207
Southern Farmers Co-operative Marketing Association, 208
Southern Mercury (newspaper), 72, 79, 81–82, 91, 95, 97–98, 103, 108–9, 111, 114–15
Southland Farmer (newspaper), 188
Southwest Railroad Strike (1886), 69–71, 84, 91, 102, 105, 108
Soviet Union, 10, 203–4, 206–7
Spargo, John, 174
speculation, 36, 38, 54, 75, 81, 105, 128–29, 148, 210, 217
Spindletop, 81
Stalinism, 10, 204, 210
Stallard, H. H., 180
Standard Oil, 81, 87, 115
Starks, George, 200
States Rights Democrat (newspaper), 46, 51
Stephenville, Texas, 87
Stevens, W. J., 96–97
Stewart, Levi and Beulah, 165
Stonewall County, Texas, 130
St. Paul, Minnesota, 188, 206–8, 210
Stuttgart International Socialist Congress (1907), 124
subtreasury plan, 80–85
suffrage (woman), 9, 72, 79, 88, 121, 176, 189, 192, 197, 204; and SP, 124–25, 128, 132–33, 152, 174

Taft, William Howard, 139, 144, 163
Tarkington, Ed, 105
Taubeneck, Herman, 93–95, 97, 99–100
Tea Party, 204
Tea Pot Dome scandal, 206
Teichmueller, Hans, 95
Tejanos, 7, 40, 50, 88, 140, 150, 155, 160, 167–68, 173, 224n88
Telluride Miners Union, 114
temperance. *See* prohibition

Temple, Texas, 153
tenant farming, 1, 5, 19, 54, 90, 150, 153–55, 173; and birth control, 133; and bonus system, 238n1; and Farmers' Alliance, 82; and James Ferguson, 164, 166, 189; and FLP, 207; and FLPA, 176, 183; and Land League, 160; and Liegnitz Democratic Club, 25; and Otto Meitzen, 50, 53, 64; and Mexican Revolution, 137, 145, 147, 216; and New Deal, 212; numbers in Texas, 105, 107, 154; and Populism, 98–99; in Rains County, Texas, 114; and SP, 123–25, 128, 134, 147, 151, 158–59; and UFEL, 210; and Walsh Commission, 165–67. *See also* Landlord and Tenant Act; Renters Union
Tennessee, 30, 48, 114
Terrell, Ben, 89
Terrell Election Laws, 155, 202
Texarkana, Texas, 9, 208
Texas Advance (newspaper), 92
Texas Oil Company (Texaco), 81, 138
Texas Rangers, 69–70, 146–47, 168, 172, 182–83, 201
Texas Revolution, 31, 57, 139
Texas State Federation of Labor, 84, 121, 148, 161–62, 189, 195, 198–200, 203, 209
Texas Vorwärts (newspaper), 93
Third International, 207–8
Thirteenth Amendment, 55
Thomas, Frank W., 102
Thompson, Carl, 123
Thompson, J. C., 209
Thompson, Victor, 51
Thurman, W. L., 165
Tillotson, Leonard, 196
Toiler (newspaper), 210
Toledo, Ohio, 108
Townley, Arthur, 178–80, 184–85, 199
transnationalism, 3, 7, 11, 135, 139, 171, 216
Travis County, Texas, 46, 48, 233n130
Treaty of Detroit (1950), 212
Trenckmann, William, 112–13
Trotsky, Leon, 191
Trump, Donald, 6–7, 218
trusts, 62, 69, 87, 111, 121, 175, 192
Turnvereine, 40
Tyler, Texas, 121, 187

Union Democrats, 42–43, 51–52
Union Labor Party, 79
Union Loyal League, 40, 48, 52
United Confederate Veterans, 198

United Farmer (newspaper), 209
United Farmers Educational League, 10, 209–10, 213
United Fruit Company, 147
United Labor Party, 62, 194
United Mine Workers, 92; of Illinois, 207
University of Texas, 189
U'Ren, William S., 161
utopian socialism, 21, 30, 32, 109, 121

vagrancy laws, 147, 152, 167, 169
Val Verde County, Texas, 120
Vandervoot, Paul, 103
Van Lear, Thomas, 188
Van Zandt County, Texas, 108, 120
Victoria, Texas, 156
Victoria Advocate (newspaper), 56
Victoria County, Texas, 42
Villa, Pancho, 145, 148–49, 159
Virginia, 48, 88
Von Bismarck, Otto, 53
Von Westphalen, Edgar, 32, 36
Von Wurden, Burghard, 16
Vörwärts (newspaper), 20

Waco, Texas, 59, 65–66, 75, 78, 92, 94, 105, 115, 135, 160, 188
Wagner, Josef Georg, 34
Walker, Jack, 57
Waller County, Texas, 191
Wall Street, 149, 183, 217
Walsh, Frank, 163
Walsh Commission. *See* Commission on Industrial Relations
Washington (state), 93; and NPL, 188, 190; and SP, 126, 180
Washington, Booker T., 96
Washington County, Texas, 34, 49, 51, 196
Watson, Tom, 3, 98–102
Wayland, Julius A., 98
Weaver, James, 88, 93, 97, 100
Weitling, Wilhelm, 36
West Virginia, 5, 37, 62
Wharton County, Texas, 88
Wheeler, Burton, 212
Whig Party, 41–42

White Man's primary, 112–13, 117
White Man's Union, 94, 117
White Primary Law (1923), 8–10, 202, 204
white supremacy, 6, 80, 94, 113, 117, 140, 119, 197, 201–3, 214–15; and Democratic Party, 10, 59, 105, 111, 192; and farmer-labor bloc, 107
Whiteside, William, 97
Whitman, Walt, 43
Williams, Frieda Meitzen (E. O.'s and Johanna's daughter), 49, 77, 157, 213
Williamson County, Texas, 125
Wilson, Woodrow, 138, 144, 163, 166, 175–76, 183, 196, 216, 218; administration of, 181, 186, 204; Wilsonian Democrats, 189, 192
Wisconsin, 123, 144, 181, 206, 208
Wochenblatt, Das (newspaper), 113
Wolf, Karl, 132
Wolff, Wilhelm, 19–21, 24, 28, 221n28, 222n49
women's rights, 9, 30, 124, 190, 192, 199, 202, 212; and Populism, 72, 117, 197; and socialism, 37, 39, 133, 197; Women's Equal Rights Amendment, 207. *See also* suffrage (woman)
Wood, Francis B., 178
Woodward, C. Vann, 98
Work, John, 174
Workers Party (communist), 10, 205, 207–10, 249n17
World War I, 13, 140, 152, 154, 171–77, 181, 189, 203
World War II, 215
Wright, Frances, 30
Wrocław, Poland. *See* Breslau, Prussia
Wüstrich, Otto, 23
Wurzbach, Harry, 196
Wyoming, 93

Yoakum, Texas, 89, 119, 215
Yoakum Times (newspaper), 215
Yorktown, Texas, 150–51
Yucatan, Mexico, 169, 180

Zapata, Emiliano, 145, 149, 159
Zetkin, Clara, 124

THOMAS ALTER II is an assistant professor in the department of history at Texas State University.

The Working Class in American History

Worker City, Company Town: Iron and Cotton-Worker Protest in Troy and Cohoes, New York, 1855–84   *Daniel J. Walkowitz*

Life, Work, and Rebellion in the Coal Fields: The Southern West Virginia Miners, 1880–1922   *David Alan Corbin*

Women and American Socialism, 1870–1920   *Mari Jo Buhle*

Lives of Their Own: Blacks, Italians, and Poles in Pittsburgh, 1900–1960   *John Bodnar, Roger Simon, and Michael P. Weber*

Working-Class America: Essays on Labor, Community, and American Society   *Edited by Michael H. Frisch and Daniel J. Walkowitz*

Eugene V. Debs: Citizen and Socialist   *Nick Salvatore*

American Labor and Immigration History, 1877–1920s: Recent European Research   *Edited by Dirk Hoerder*

Workingmen's Democracy: The Knights of Labor and American Politics   *Leon Fink*

The Electrical Workers: A History of Labor at General Electric and Westinghouse, 1923–60   *Ronald W. Schatz*

The Mechanics of Baltimore: Workers and Politics in the Age of Revolution, 1763–1812   *Charles G. Steffen*

The Practice of Solidarity: American Hat Finishers in the Nineteenth Century   *David Bensman*

The Labor History Reader   *Edited by Daniel J. Leab*

Solidarity and Fragmentation: Working People and Class Consciousness in Detroit, 1875–1900   *Richard Oestreicher*

Counter Cultures: Saleswomen, Managers, and Customers in American Department Stores, 1890–1940   *Susan Porter Benson*

The New England Working Class and the New Labor History   *Edited by Herbert G. Gutman and Donald H. Bell*

Labor Leaders in America   *Edited by Melvyn Dubofsky and Warren Van Tine*

Barons of Labor: The San Francisco Building Trades and Union Power in the Progressive Era   *Michael Kazin*

Gender at Work: The Dynamics of Job Segregation by Sex during World War II   *Ruth Milkman*

Once a Cigar Maker: Men, Women, and Work Culture in American Cigar Factories, 1900–1919   *Patricia A. Cooper*

A Generation of Boomers: The Pattern of Railroad Labor Conflict in Nineteenth-Century America   *Shelton Stromquist*

Work and Community in the Jungle: Chicago's Packinghouse Workers, 1894–1922   *James R. Barrett*

Workers, Managers, and Welfare Capitalism: The Shoeworkers and Tanners of Endicott Johnson, 1890–1950   *Gerald Zahavi*

Men, Women, and Work: Class, Gender, and Protest in the New England Shoe Industry, 1780–1910   *Mary Blewett*

Workers on the Waterfront: Seamen, Longshoremen, and Unionism in the
    1930s   *Bruce Nelson*
German Workers in Chicago: A Documentary History of Working-Class Culture
    from 1850 to World War I   *Edited by Hartmut Keil and John B. Jentz*
On the Line: Essays in the History of Auto Work   *Edited by Nelson Lichtenstein
    and Stephen Meyer III*
Labor's Flaming Youth: Telephone Operators and Worker Militancy, 1878–1923
    Stephen H. Norwood
Another Civil War: Labor, Capital, and the State in the Anthracite Regions of
    Pennsylvania, 1840–68   *Grace Palladino*
Coal, Class, and Color: Blacks in Southern West Virginia, 1915–32
    Joe William Trotter Jr.
For Democracy, Workers, and God: Labor Song-Poems and Labor Protest, 1865–95
    Clark D. Halker
Dishing It Out: Waitresses and Their Unions in the Twentieth Century
    Dorothy Sue Cobble
The Spirit of 1848: German Immigrants, Labor Conflict, and the Coming of the Civil
    War   *Bruce Levine*
Working Women of Collar City: Gender, Class, and Community in Troy, New York,
    1864–86   *Carole Turbin*
Southern Labor and Black Civil Rights: Organizing Memphis Workers
    Michael K. Honey
Radicals of the Worst Sort: Laboring Women in Lawrence, Massachusetts, 1860–1912
    Ardis Cameron
Producers, Proletarians, and Politicians: Workers and Party Politics in Evansville and
    New Albany, Indiana, 1850–87   *Lawrence M. Lipin*
The New Left and Labor in the 1960s   *Peter B. Levy*
The Making of Western Labor Radicalism: Denver's Organized Workers, 1878–1905
    David Brundage
In Search of the Working Class: Essays in American Labor History and Political
    Culture   *Leon Fink*
Lawyers against Labor: From Individual Rights to Corporate Liberalism
    Daniel R. Ernst
"We Are All Leaders": The Alternative Unionism of the Early 1930s
    Edited by Staughton Lynd
The Female Economy: The Millinery and Dressmaking Trades, 1860–1930
    Wendy Gamber
"Negro and White, Unite and Fight!": A Social History of Industrial Unionism in
    Meatpacking, 1930–90   *Roger Horowitz*
Power at Odds: The 1922 National Railroad Shopmen's Strike   *Colin J. Davis*
The Common Ground of Womanhood: Class, Gender, and Working Girls' Clubs,
    1884–1928   *Priscilla Murolo*
Marching Together: Women of the Brotherhood of Sleeping Car Porters
    Melinda Chateauvert

Down on the Killing Floor: Black and White Workers in Chicago's Packinghouses,
    1904–54   *Rick Halpern*
Labor and Urban Politics: Class Conflict and the Origins of Modern Liberalism in
    Chicago, 1864–97   *Richard Schneirov*
All That Glitters: Class, Conflict, and Community in Cripple Creek
    Elizabeth Jameson
Waterfront Workers: New Perspectives on Race and Class
    Edited by Calvin Winslow
Labor Histories: Class, Politics, and the Working-Class Experience
    Edited by Eric Arnesen, Julie Greene, and Bruce Laurie
The Pullman Strike and the Crisis of the 1890s: Essays on Labor and Politics
    Edited by Richard Schneirov, Shelton Stromquist, and Nick Salvatore
AlabamaNorth: African-American Migrants, Community, and Working-Class
    Activism in Cleveland, 1914–45   *Kimberley L. Phillips*
Imagining Internationalism in American and British Labor, 1939–49
    Victor Silverman
William Z. Foster and the Tragedy of American Radicalism   *James R. Barrett*
Colliers across the Sea: A Comparative Study of Class Formation in Scotland and the
    American Midwest, 1830–1924   *John H. M. Laslett*
"Rights, Not Roses": Unions and the Rise of Working-Class Feminism, 1945–80
    Dennis A. Deslippe
Testing the New Deal: The General Textile Strike of 1934 in the American
    South   *Janet Irons*
Hard Work: The Making of Labor History   *Melvyn Dubofsky*
Southern Workers and the Search for Community: Spartanburg County,
    South Carolina   *G. C. Waldrep III*
We Shall Be All: A History of the Industrial Workers of the World (abridged
    edition)   *Melvyn Dubofsky, ed. Joseph A. McCartin*
Race, Class, and Power in the Alabama Coalfields, 1908–21   *Brian Kelly*
Duquesne and the Rise of Steel Unionism   *James D. Rose*
Anaconda: Labor, Community, and Culture in Montana's Smelter City
    Laurie Mercier
Bridgeport's Socialist New Deal, 1915–36   *Cecelia Bucki*
Indispensable Outcasts: Hobo Workers and Community in the American Midwest,
    1880–1930   *Frank Tobias Higbie*
After the Strike: A Century of Labor Struggle at Pullman   *Susan Eleanor Hirsch*
Corruption and Reform in the Teamsters Union   *David Witwer*
Waterfront Revolts: New York and London Dockworkers, 1946–61   *Colin J. Davis*
Black Workers' Struggle for Equality in Birmingham   *Horace Huntley
    and David Montgomery*
The Tribe of Black Ulysses: African American Men in the Industrial South
    William P. Jones
City of Clerks: Office and Sales Workers in Philadelphia, 1870–1920
    Jerome P. Bjelopera

Reinventing "The People": The Progressive Movement, the Class Problem, and the
    Origins of Modern Liberalism   *Shelton Stromquist*
Radical Unionism in the Midwest, 1900–1950   *Rosemary Feurer*
Gendering Labor History   *Alice Kessler-Harris*
James P. Cannon and the Origins of the American Revolutionary Left, 1890–1928
    Bryan D. Palmer
Glass Towns: Industry, Labor, and Political Economy in Appalachia, 1890–1930s
    Ken Fones-Wolf
Workers and the Wild: Conservation, Consumerism, and Labor in Oregon, 1910–30
    Lawrence M. Lipin
Wobblies on the Waterfront: Interracial Unionism in Progressive-Era
    Philadelphia   *Peter Cole*
Red Chicago: American Communism at Its Grassroots, 1928–35   *Randi Storch*
Labor's Cold War: Local Politics in a Global Context   *Edited by Shelton Stromquist*
Bessie Abramowitz Hillman and the Making of the Amalgamated Clothing Workers
    of America   *Karen Pastorello*
The Great Strikes of 1877   *Edited by David O. Stowell*
Union-Free America: Workers and Antiunion Culture   *Lawrence Richards*
Race against Liberalism: Black Workers and the UAW in Detroit
    David M. Lewis-Colman
Teachers and Reform: Chicago Public Education, 1929–70   *John F. Lyons*
Upheaval in the Quiet Zone: 1199/SEIU and the Politics of Healthcare
    Unionism   *Leon Fink and Brian Greenberg*
Shadow of the Racketeer: Scandal in Organized Labor   *David Witwer*
Sweet Tyranny: Migrant Labor, Industrial Agriculture, and Imperial
    Politics   *Kathleen Mapes*
Staley: The Fight for a New American Labor Movement   *Steven K. Ashby*
    and C. J. Hawking
On the Ground: Labor Struggles in the American Airline Industry
    Liesl Miller Orenic
NAFTA and Labor in North America   *Norman Caulfield*
Making Capitalism Safe: Work Safety and Health Regulation in America, 1880–1940
    Donald W. Rogers
Good, Reliable, White Men: Railroad Brotherhoods, 1877–1917   *Paul Michel Taillon*
Spirit of Rebellion: Labor and Religion in the New Cotton South   *Jarod Roll*
The Labor Question in America: Economic Democracy in the Gilded Age
    Rosanne Currarino
Banded Together: Economic Democratization in the Brass Valley   *Jeremy Brecher*
The Gospel of the Working Class: Labor's Southern Prophets in New Deal
    America   *Erik Gellman and Jarod Roll*
Guest Workers and Resistance to U.S. Corporate Despotism   *Immanuel Ness*
Gleanings of Freedom: Free and Slave Labor along the Mason-Dixon Line, 1790–1860
    Max Grivno

Chicago in the Age of Capital: Class, Politics, and Democracy during the Civil War and Reconstruction   *John B. Jentz and Richard Schneirov*
Child Care in Black and White: Working Parents and the History of Orphanages   *Jessie B. Ramey*
The Haymarket Conspiracy: Transatlantic Anarchist Networks   *Timothy Messer-Kruse*
Detroit's Cold War: The Origins of Postwar Conservatism   *Colleen Doody*
A Renegade Union: Interracial Organizing and Labor Radicalism   *Lisa Phillips*
Palomino: Clinton Jencks and Mexican-American Unionism in the American Southwest   *James J. Lorence*
Latin American Migrations to the U.S. Heartland: Changing Cultural Landscapes in Middle America   *Edited by Linda Allegro and Andrew Grant Wood*
Man of Fire: Selected Writings   *Ernesto Galarza, ed. Armando Ibarra and Rodolfo D. Torres*
A Contest of Ideas: Capital, Politics, and Labor   *Nelson Lichtenstein*
Making the World Safe for Workers: Labor, the Left, and Wilsonian Internationalism   *Elizabeth McKillen*
The Rise of the Chicago Police Department: Class and Conflict, 1850–1894   *Sam Mitrani*
Workers in Hard Times: A Long View of Economic Crises   *Edited by Leon Fink, Joseph A. McCartin, and Joan Sangster*
Redeeming Time: Protestantism and Chicago's Eight-Hour Movement, 1866–1912   *William A. Mirola*
Struggle for the Soul of the Postwar South: White Evangelical Protestants and Operation Dixie   *Elizabeth Fones-Wolf and Ken Fones-Wolf*
Free Labor: The Civil War and the Making of an American Working Class   *Mark A. Lause*
Death and Dying in the Working Class, 1865–1920   *Michael K. Rosenow*
Immigrants against the State: Yiddish and Italian Anarchism in America   *Kenyon Zimmer*
Fighting for Total Person Unionism: Harold Gibbons, Ernest Calloway, and Working-Class Citizenship   *Robert Bussel*
Smokestacks in the Hills: Rural-Industrial Workers in West Virginia   *Louis Martin*
Disaster Citizenship: Survivors, Solidarity, and Power in the Progressive Era   *Jacob A. C. Remes*
The Pew and the Picket Line: Christianity and the American Working Class   *Edited by Christopher D. Cantwell, Heath W. Carter, and Janine Giordano Drake*
Conservative Counterrevolution: Challenging Liberalism in 1950s Milwaukee   *Tula A. Connell*
Manhood on the Line: Working-Class Masculinities in the American Heartland   *Steve Meyer*
On Gender, Labor, and Inequality   *Ruth Milkman*
The Making of Working-Class Religion   *Matthew Pehl*

Civic Labors: Scholar Activism and Working-Class Studies
    Edited by Dennis Deslippe, Eric Fure-Slocum, and John W. McKerley
Victor Arnautoff and the Politics of Art   *Robert W. Cherny*
Against Labor: How U.S. Employers Organized to Defeat Union Activism
    Edited by Rosemary Feurer and Chad Pearson
Teacher Strike! Public Education and the Making of a New American Political
    Order   *Jon Shelton*
Hillbilly Hellraisers: Federal Power and Populist Defiance in the Ozarks
    J. Blake Perkins
Sewing the Fabric of Statehood: Garment Unions, American Labor, and the
    Establishment of the State of Israel   *Adam Howard*
Labor and Justice across the America   *Edited by Leon Fink and Juan Manuel Palacio*
Frontiers of Labor: Comparative Histories of the United States and Australia
    Edited by Greg Patmore and Shelton Stromquist
Women Have Always Worked: A Concise History, Second Edition
    Alice Kessler-Harris
Remembering Lattimer: Labor, Migration, and Race in Pennsylvania Anthracite
    Country   *Paul A. Shackel*
Disruption in Detroit: Autoworkers and the Elusive Postwar Boom   *Daniel J. Clark*
To Live Here, You Have to Fight: How Women Led Appalachian Movements for
    Social Justice   *Jessica Wilkerson*
Dockworker Power: Race and Activism in Durban and the San Francisco
    Bay Area   *Peter Cole*
Labor's Mind: A History of Working-Class Intellectual Life   *Tobias Higbie*
The World in a City: Multiethnic Radicalism in Early Twentieth-Century
    Los Angeles   *David M. Struthers*
Death to Fascism: Louis Adamic's Fight for Democracy   *John P. Enyeart*
Upon the Altar of Work: Child Labor and the Rise of a New American
    Sectionalism   *Betsy Wood*
Workers against the City: The Fight for Free Speech in *Hague v. CIO*
    Donald W. Rogers
Union Renegades: Miners, Capitalism, and Organizing in the Gilded Age
    Dana M. Caldemeyer
The Labor Board Crew: Remaking Worker-Employer Relations from Pearl Harbor to
    the Reagan Era   *Ronald W. Schatz*
Grand Army of Labor: Workers, Veterans, and the Meaning of the Civil
    War   *Matthew E. Stanley*
A Matter of Moral Justice: Black Women Laundry Workers and the Fight for
    Justice   *Jenny Carson*
Labor's End: How the Promise of Automation Degraded Work   *Jason Resnikoff*
Toward a Cooperative Commonwealth: The Transplanted Roots of Farmer-Labor
    Radicalism in Texas   *Thomas Alter II*

The University of Illinois Press
is a founding member of the
Association of University Presses.

Composed in 10.5/13 Minion Pro
by Lisa Connery
at the University of Illinois Press

University of Illinois Press
1325 South Oak Street
Champaign, IL 61820-6903
www.press.uillinois.edu